POLITICS IN CAPTIVITY

just ideas

transformative ideals of justice in ethical and political thought

series editors
Drucilla Cornell
Roger Berkowitz

POLITICS IN CAPTIVITY

PLANTATIONS, PRISONS,
AND WORLD-BUILDING

Lena Zuckerwise

FORDHAM UNIVERSITY PRESS

NEW YORK   2024

Copyright © 2024 Fordham University Press

All rights reserved. No part of this publication may be reproduced, stored in a retrieval system, or transmitted in any form or by any means—electronic, mechanical, photocopy, recording, or any other—except for brief quotations in printed reviews, without the prior permission of the publisher.

Fordham University Press has no responsibility for the persistence or accuracy of URLs for external or third-party Internet websites referred to in this publication and does not guarantee that any content on such websites is, or will remain, accurate or appropriate.

Fordham University Press also publishes its books in a variety of electronic formats. Some content that appears in print may not be available in electronic books.

Visit us online at www.fordhampress.com.

Library of Congress Cataloging-in-Publication Data available online at https://catalog.loc.gov.

Printed in the United States of America

26 25 24   5 4 3 2 1

First edition

for PLL—and because of it

Contents

A Note on Terminology and Method   xi

Introduction: Politics in Motion   1

1. From Plantations to Prisons   25
2. Black Carceral Political Thought   44
3. Historical and Theoretical Erasures of Slave Resistance   64
4. The Racial Limits of Liberalism   83
5. The Concept of World   110
6. Politics in Captivity   135
7. Beyond Democracy: The Attica Prison Uprising   164

Epilogue   185

Acknowledgments   189
Notes   195
Bibliography   251
Index   277

A Note on Terminology and Method

Naming terms in a book on Black politics is as important as (and sometimes synonymous with) defining them. "Prisoners" or "incarcerated people" appear throughout the book, although I do not use the term "inmate" in my own voice, but only in direct quotations or when referencing carceral rationalities. Relatedly, the word "slave" is linguistically fraught, turning people into chattel and befitting the ideology of white supremacists for whom the reduction of enslaved people to slaves is desirable and convenient. I do not refer to people with this term, yet I do use the word slave in descriptive contexts. For example, "slave society" and "slave rebellion/slave uprising" also appear occasionally because the descriptor acknowledges the pervasive authority of the institution and squarely situates it at the center of social, political, and economic life from the colonial through antebellum periods. The inevitable tension between avoiding the reductive effects of the word "slave" and the subsequent harm the use of the word could cause *and* rejecting white tendencies to euphemize and otherwise overlook historical conditions and legacies of anti-Black racism, including slavery, remains very much alive in this book. Refusing the term "slaves," as a direct reference to people, but drawing on it as a descriptor partially reconciles this. "Enslaver" or "planter" appear as alternatives to "slaveholder" or "slave master," both of which are too closely associated with the logic and preferences of enslavers themselves. Although these authorial decisions about which terminology to adopt and omit are decisive, fully settling the crucial questions that underlie them are not my intentions here.

The terms "rebellion" and "resistance" appear relatively interchangeably over the following chapters. "Revolt" and "uprising" also describe armed, organized, and/or large-scale rebellion. I avoid the word "riot," not to disavow the chaotic and discordant qualities of politics in captivity, but because the term tends to sever the event from the conditions under which it took place. The phrase "race riot," for example, paints a picture of angry, disaffected Black Americans rising up in a common rage, inviting readers to disavow the myriad forces of exclusion, domination, violence, discrimination, and erasure that produced the riotous moment. I prefer resistance and rebellion because they directly confront their objects. The intelligibility of the terms hinges on the power and force that they challenge and contest. Both are, by definition, *against something*. Proper analysis of Black challenges to white domination means keeping the latter visible within the terminology itself.

The temporality of riot versus resistance and rebellion is also of consequence here. Riots typically signal sudden, explosive events that are often swiftly subdued by the state. Of course, this also describes politics in captivity, although riot discourse does not capture its substance and sustainability. Resistance does not have a clear beginning or end but is rather productively indeterminate: a condition reflecting the ongoing castigation of white supremacy at the center of Black captivity, before and after their culminating moments. Approaching the Attica prison uprising as a "riot" narrows critical focus to the occupation and retaking of the prison, while leaving aside the enduring dimensions of resistance in its aftermath, including its global ripple effects. While rebellion is often conceptualized as an event, its adjectival form "rebellious" transcends episodic singularity, and suggests a posture, persuasion, or spirit. Rebellion is a more expansive, decisively political category than riot, for its effects reverberate long past the moment of eruption.

Framing the actions of enslaved and incarcerated people in terms of resistance and rebellion is both a politicizing move, underscoring the sophisticated and meaningful politics that bondpeople and Black prisoners have forged, and one of intellectual accountability and accuracy. If the research that I conducted for *Politics in Captivity* has yielded any one conclusive "finding," it is that resistance and rebellion are the discourses through which captives understand their own political lives. Archival research is the leading method of *Politics in Captivity*, drawing mostly on material from the Library of Congress, the Schomburg Center for Research in Black Culture, the Tamiment Library and Robert F. Wagner Labor Archives at New York University, and the Freedom Archives in Oakland. Prison writings and bondpeople's narratives comprise the vast majority of the collections that I used, including materials such as prison newspapers, pamphlets, prison radio transcripts, and correspondence. I did make use of the WPA (Works Progress Administration) interviews, while acknowledging the many problems associated with the collection.[1] The resounding message of this documentary history is that resistance is the heart of politics in captivity.

POLITICS IN CAPTIVITY

Introduction

Politics in Motion

"The prison has not changed. It is my mind that has changed."
—TIYO ATTALAH SALAH-EL[1]

I had not known what to expect on the icy day in February when I arrived at the medium security men's prison south of Boston, where I was slated to teach introduction to political theory to twenty-seven incarcerated men.[2] That morning, I had naively readied myself as I always had in collegiate settings: by copying syllabi and updating my lecture notes. Despite my airtight recall of the four dialogues in *The Trial and Death of Socrates*, I was woefully unprepared for what lay ahead. I had been to the prison several weeks earlier for "orientation." The new faculty who would teach in the education program were corralled in a small, windowless conference room and lectured to for an hour on the moral depravity of "inmates." Their penchants for manipulating well-meaning liberal professors into doing them illegal favors were described in detail, as well as the dangers of giving them anything, from candy to drugs to personal information.

I listened to this with all the skepticism of a critic of the carceral state, took a few notes, and realized upon my return on the first day of classes that I had virtually no information of practical use for even getting through the door of the receiving area (aptly named "the trap"). And this was due to the likelihood that the orientation facilitators had not had it to give, for, as I would learn, regulations changed constantly. Yet, somehow on that winter morning, it seemed that I was in violation of all of them. My briefcase was wrong (all bags must be transparent plastic). Its contents were wrong (paper cannot be distributed until it is "flora-scooped," as apparently some drugs can be invisibly concealed and smoked on blank paper). My bra was wrong (underwire, a potential weapon, sets off metal detectors). My scarf was wrong (no accessories or jewelry are permissible except, tellingly, wedding rings). The corrections officer (CO) eyed the staples binding my syllabi with exaggerated, performative incredulity. Almost everything that I had with and on me that day, from cough drops to earrings, was prohibited and had to be stowed in coin-op lockers. Of course, I did not have any quarters.

Once my outlaw bra and syllabi were secured in a lockbox and no longer deemed threatening to anyone, I was authorized to enter the facility. It became clear from that moment that if my first encounters with prison bureaucracy offered a glimpse into a carceral vortex of arbitrary, restrictive, and ever-fluctuating rules, the regulations to which my students were compelled to adhere might have been copied verbatim from an encyclopedia entry on bio-power.[3] They determined when and to whom prisoners could speak; the time of day they would dress and what they could wear; how much food they would eat during meal times; when they used the toilet; what shows were available to them on television and books they could read. One of the first things that caught my attention on that initial day, and the ones that followed, from the offhanded comments of the students in my course, as well as my own observations, was the intensity of control applied to their physical movements. From what I could discern, this is the most strictly managed aspect of their lives. The times at which they could traverse the grounds; the speed of their pace; whether they were permitted to stop while in transit; and where they may go within certain buildings are all tightly monitored by COs, down to the minutiae of ambulation. Two hours into our first session, one student apologetically pointed out that if I did not give them a "movement break" at that moment, they would be required to wait another hour before they could leave their seats again. Nearly every time I was escorted from the trap to the education building, COs could be seen disciplining prisoners for a variety of related infractions: for walking too quickly or dragging their feet; for pausing too long or traveling unauthorized between the floors of a building.

Strictures imposed on the movements of prisoners are not particular to this single New England state prison. Indeed, they are not even specific to this physical form of movement. If the bodily shifts, maneuvers, and traversals of incarcerated people are tightly controlled, political movements are even more surveilled (and sabotaged, and disbanded) by prison agents. Decades of retributive punishment aimed at political prisoners and their activities are well documented: rank and file members of the Black Panther Party and the Black Liberation Army, both heavily incarcerated in the late 1960s and 1970s, were disproportionately beaten and harassed by prison guards and placed in solitary confinement. The same is true of movements born behind bars, such as George Jackson, George "Big Jake" Lewis, and W.L. Nolen's Black Guerilla Family, founded during their incarceration at Soledad State Prison in 1966.[4] Spurious claims that these political prisoners perpetrated violence were often used to rationalize such treatment. In reality, revenge, retaliation, and preemption of new member recruitment were, more often than not, the actual reasons for their physical abuse and isolation.

I do not intend this linguistic shift from physical to political movement as an artful segue into a discussion of prison-based organizing, for Dylan Rodriguez in *Forced Passages* has already brilliantly taken up this subject, as well as Dan Berger in *Captive Nation*.[5] Instead, I want to pause for a moment on "movement," a word with multiple meanings, the most widely used of which is, of course, physical: the act of motion, a change in posture or position, and passage from one place to another. Its distinction from the political form of the term, an organization of people working toward common objectives, is generally taken for granted. Etymologically, there is a 419-year gap between the emergences of the two in English. The first documented use of movement in a political register can be traced to a weekly London newspaper in July 1812, in which the word appears in an article on a report delivered by a special committee of the House of Commons, detailing a series of riots in several English counties. The rebels "assembled at nighttime with their faces blackened, armed with the implements of their trades, and other offensive instruments, with which they destroyed the property of those who were obnoxious to them."[6] Described as an "organized system of lawless violence," the riots lasted over three months and resulted in a great deal of vandalism, arson, and other forms of property destruction. Although the committee was quite disturbed by the scale and intensity of the riot, the fact that they could find evidence of neither a plot nor outside instigators was far more disconcerting:

> And this is the circumstance that will most puzzle the ministry. They can find no agitators. It is a *movement of the people's own*, as far as it goes, and, if the ministry say, that it does not arise from the dearness of provisions and from other causes of distress; if it does not arise from that source, it follows, that it must arise from some dislike of what the government itself is doing or has done; it follows that the people are displeased with something in their rulers; and this is what is called disaffection.[7]

Two points can be gleaned from this: first, the term "political movement" was born in riot, chaos, and discord. Second, the "movement of the people's own" is physical in nature: bodies colliding with one another; setting fire to buildings; dismantling and destroying property. Thus, movement, in a political vein, retains in its origins the physicality of its predecessor: the act of motion, a change in posture or position, passage from one place to another. Perhaps the conditions of carceral domination invite readers to consider the convergence, or more fittingly *collision*, of these two meanings.

In prison, both compliant and insurgent physical movements are uniquely political, for intense surveillance and policing renders them sites of control *and* resistance. The aspiration of total domination that is definitive of carceral power centers on the bodies of prisoners, their whereabouts, activities, behavior, and movement through space. Most prevailing discourses would suggest that such strictures are the neutral, incidental consequences of incarceration, marking the division between confinement versus "freedom": nonincarcerated people may move as they choose, while the movements of prisoners are tightly managed. But this misses the crucial point that Michel Foucault understood well: in carceral settings, movement is a site of ongoing command, regulation, and surveillance.[8] It is misleading to read the earlier anecdote as mere suppression. Movements are invoked as much as they are restricted, for carceral power works not only upon the incarcerated body but also *through* it. The prisoner waiting in line for commissary items; reporting to work; standing at attention for routine inspections; exercising in the yard for a single hour of a twenty-four-hour period, otherwise spent in solitary confinement, is producing and enacting the power to which he is also submitting.[9]

Further, resistance to the prison regime in the form of large-scale, organized rebellion begins *physically:* a glance, hand signal, punch, scrawl, gesture, or handshake incites a chain of events with unforeseeable consequences and challenges the authority of the carceral regime. Thus, in prison, all motion is political, and political resistance begins in motion. While such discourses of movement are generally separable from one another in ordinary language and public life, they converge in scenes of captivity. Much like the riot that inaugurated the entrance of "political movement" into the English vernacular in 1812, prison rebellion surfaces in uniquely embodied forms of revolt: the refusal to fall in line, eat, or report to work; to destroy state and federal property; to throw feces and other bodily fluids through a tray slot in solitary confinement; to enter prohibited areas within prison grounds; to take command of the space—all lead, in some way, with the body.[10] This is never clearer than when carceral agents tamp down prison uprisings by physically policing protestors. Both punishment for their participation and preemption of future resistance inevitably center on bodily movements of rebellious prisoners through beatings, isolation, and transfer.[11] In captivity, unlike other spheres, movement is political, and politics *moves*.

The same overlap is visible in the predecessor to the carceral state: the plantation, where the mobile bodies of enslaved people were radically politicized through fierce control and domination, and also quotidian and extraordinary resistance. Like prisoners, the physical actions, motion, and whereabouts of bondpeople were of paramount importance in a slave society and thus heavily watched and controlled by planters, overseers, traders, and slave-catchers alike.[12] The abduction and forced migration of Africans in Middle Passage; compulsory labor in the fields and homes of planters; the sexual violations of bondwomen; and the exploitations of their care work, also center on the body. Relatedly, the physical movements of enslaved people are important sites of resistance. Rebellion begins with bodies in motion: fleeing the plantation permanently (fugitivity) or temporarily (truancy); attending outlaw dances and parties; executing planters, overseers, and slave-catchers; destroying or setting fire to property; injuring or killing livestock; and deliberately breaking tools and feigning illness are insurgent practices undertaken by animated, embodied, enslaved subjects.[13] Thus, the conditions of chattel slavery, like the carceral sphere, dislodge the binary of the physical and political, offering an opportunity to consider their interconnections. In short, a political theory of movement is born out of the oppressive, but generative conditions of plantations and prisons. The convergence of the two categories of movement, and the experiences of resistance that emerge at their intersections, are unique to captivity.

This extended rumination is perhaps misleading, for *Politics in Captivity* is neither an etymological study of the word "movement," nor an intervention into social movement theory. It focuses neither on abolitionist organizing, nor the lively, dynamic essence of democratic politics. To be clear, even though the activities of bodies in flight, combat, transgression, demolition, and desire figure prominently into the following chapters, this is not why I chose the subject of movement for the earliest pages of *Politics in Captivity*. Rather, I did so with the intention of revealing the ways that politics on plantations and in prisons upend familiar concepts from their otherwise settled lodgings. Political discourses that one might take for granted lose their self-evidence in contexts of confinement and caging, enslavement and incarceration.

Politics in Captivity is about Black rebellion in captivity and the way that many of the conventional, well-worn constructs of academic political theory render its political dimensions obscure and indiscernible. While Hannah Arendt is an odd and unlikely theorist to figure prominently in any discussion of Black politics, I hold that her concepts of *world* and equally, or even more importantly, *worldlessness*, offer a unique and indispensable framework for articulating a political theory of chattel and carceral resistance. While Arendt is not alone in her formulation and mobilization of the idea of world, no other thinker has so thoroughly developed a theory of its annihilation and absence. It is in this sense that her work has genuine theoretical utility for *Politics in Captivity*.

The radical possibilities of the creation of a world in common, which I argue is entailed in captive resistance, are incommunicable without the related concept of worldlessness. Due in part to the particular forms of violence and domination prevailing in systems of slavery and incarceration, as well as the political conditions born in captivity, worldlessness is crucial to any theoretical account of the resistance of bondpeople and prisoners. Arendt conceives of it in plural and complex ways. In *The Human Condition*, worldlessness is closely associated with *animal laborans* ("the laboring animal"), whose ties to biological life and its maintenance render him more or less "oblivious to the world to the point of worldlessness."[14] Although she writes on antiquity, it is not irrelevant that slavery is closely tied to the worldless condition. The laboring classes, says Arendt, do not flee the world, but are "ejected from it," for they are "imprisoned in the privacy" of their own bodies and fully absorbed in the fulfillment of physical needs. "Slavery became the social condition of the laboring classes because it was felt that it was the natural condition of life itself."[15] If worldlessness is the effect of banishment from the world, perhaps the phenomenon maps onto plantations and prisons in the modern period, as well. In sum, a construct that articulates the utter absence of a world in common is an essential resource for a theory of political resistance meant to redress it.

To be clear, Arendt's own views of US racial politics are often misguided and sometimes explicitly prejudiced. I do not propose that her concepts of world and worldlessness are redemptive because neither diagnosis of Arendt's "true feelings" on race, nor her status as a racist, are of particular concern here. I am similarly disinterested in vindicating her as a thinker, sheltering her from accusations lobbed at her racial ideologies, or loyally adhering to her own theoretical categories. Instead, I draw out an idea that has been comparatively neglected in favor of more well-mined constructs in her oeuvre. I argue that Arendt's concept of world has genuine utility for Black radical politics. Black resistance in chattel and carceral spheres is world-building and the reverse is also true: such world-building is an act of Black resistance. I refer to both as "politics in captivity."

RACE AND BLACKNESS IN ARENDT'S WORK

Arendt's ideological positions on marginalized people have puzzled, and often troubled, her readers. Her straightforward acknowledgment that, for example, women and enslaved people absorbed the violence of the private realm in antiquity, appears in a voice more neutral than critical: "not only in Greece and the polis but throughout the whole of occidental antiquity, it would indeed have been self-evident that even the power of the tyrant was less great, less 'perfect' than the power with which the paterfamilias, the dominus, ruled over his household of slaves and family. And this was not because the power of the city's ruler was matched and checked by the combined powers of household heads, but because absolute, uncontested rule and a political realm properly speaking were mutually exclusive."[16] While, in all likelihood, Arendt does not envision a return to that bygone era, her critique of the tradition of Western political thought since Plato is entangled in the related absorption of the private and public into the realm of the "social" that gradually occurred in the intervening years between antiquity and the twentieth century. Many critics of Arendt argue that she views the modern obfuscation of the private and public divide in tragic terms, holding the phenomenon responsible for the loss of taste for political action.[17]

If Arendt's nostalgia for the pre-Socratic Greek city-state is an open, interpretive question, it is less arguable that she is extremely uneven on the subject of race. For an author who dedicated an entire book to the subject of revolution, the Haitian Revolution does not appear even once in *On Revolution* or any of her other published works.[18] Many of her views are biased, limited, and ignorant of structural forces of anti-Blackness.[19] The discrepancy between Arendt's sharp and incisive perspectives on race in the context of European antisemitism, and reductive and backward discussions of anti-Black legacies of slavery in the United States has not gone unnoticed by her readers.[20]

Even though Arendt does designate slavery a "crime against humanity" in *Origins of Totalitarianism*, it remains true that race, in general, and Blackness, in particular, are surely some of the most fraught topics in Arendt's oeuvre. Her analysis of slavery vacillates between deeply insightful and woefully inaccurate, due perhaps to her abstractions of the category from its historical locations. Slavery in antiquity does not share many likenesses with the Atlantic world, although Arendt only dimly distinguishes them. She argues in *Origins* that:

> Slavery's fundamental offense against human rights was not that it took liberty away (which can happen in many other situations), but that it excluded a certain category of people even from the possibility of fighting for freedom—a fight possible under tyranny, and even under the desperate conditions of modern terror (but not under any conditions of concentration-camp life). Slavery's crime against humanity did not begin when one people defeated and enslaved its enemies (though of course this was bad enough), but when slavery became an institution in which some men were "born" free and others slave, when it was forgotten that it was man who had deprived his fellow-men of freedom, and when the sanction for the crime was attributed to nature.[21]

Arendt observes, persuasively, that slavery's worst offenses are not only the repression of people, but also the exclusion of an entire population from the very pursuit of freedom; not the state of war in which captured people become enslaved, but the institutional arrangements that determine one's slave status as a condition of birth.

Yet, as powerful and insightful as these interpretations are, other sections of *Origins* betray genuine ignorance about the condition of Atlantic slavery: "to be a slave meant a distinctive place in society, to have one's labor exploited, etc. as opposed to the abstract nakedness of just humanity."[22] While the experience of a concentration camp is, in some ways, radically dissimilar from the plantation, the distinction she construes here is very questionable. That bondpeople *had a status* is not tantamount to "a distinctive place in society," for the domestic slave trade suspended bondpeople in perpetual motion, constantly reshuffling them through sale, treating them as foreign enemies, and preventing them from claiming any civic standing. Arendt most certainly could have grasped the state of worldlessness in which enslaved people lived, a function of the fact that they had no rights at all, despite the many economic and social functions they served. Her perspective here is likely bound up in her "need to draw distinctions" or perhaps assert a thesis of totalitarian exceptionalism.[23] Enslaved people become collateral in Arendt's aim to identify the unique dimensions of totalitarianism and its attendant discourses. The entirety of her analysis in *Origins* largely leans on her insistence that totalitarianism is incomparable to other states of coercion and captivity, for they are differently (and maybe less) totalizing and atrocious. It is likely that Arendt's totalitarian exceptionalism partially obstructs a clear view of slavery in the Atlantic world and its afterlives.

In *Origins*, Arendt's anti-Black prejudice surfaces mainly in references to Africa as "the silent wilderness of an overpopulated continent where the presence of human beings only underlined utter solitude, and where an untouched, overwhelmingly hostile nature that nobody had ever taken the trouble to change into human landscape seemed to wait in sublime patience 'for the passing away of the fantastic invasion' of man."[24] Here, she fully adopts the colonial fiction that Africa is a state of nature, an uncivilized space that has been unused and untouched by human invention.[25] The racial myths that Africans are closer to nature than Europeans and devoid of history and culture are on full display here. Similarly, she references the primal barbarism of "The Dark Continent," described as a space "in which the savages were numerous enough to constitute a world of their own, a world of folly, to which the European adventurer added the folly of the ivory hunt."[26] While Arendt insists, repeatedly, that skin color does not demarcate citizens and savages, Black Africans are the default barbarians who operate at a base level to which certain ill-mannered white people occasionally deign to stoop, including badly behaved European adventurers and the Boers of South Africa: "What made them different from other human beings was not at all the color of their skin but the fact that they behaved like a part of nature, that they treated nature as their undisputed master, that they had not created a human world, a human reality, and that therefore nature had remained, in all its majesty, the only overwhelming reality—compared to which they appeared to be phantoms, unreal and ghostlike."[27] In other words, savagery for Black Africans is a natural state, while for white Europeans, a chosen, self-conscious deviancy.

In her critical and persuasive essay, "Heart of Darkness: Africa and African Americans in the Writings of Hannah Arendt," Anne Norton observes that "Arendt's easy dismissal of Africans and African history, African literatures, African languages; her readiness to ascribe academic inferiority to black students, and squalor, crime, and ignorance to the black community, are innocent of evidence. They evince an uncharacteristic, and profound, indifference to the historical record and to the literature available on these subjects in her time."[28] Relatedly, Jimmy Casas Klausen argues that Arendt's racial discourses derive from an original "antiprimitivism" in her political thought. For her, Africans, as a population, stand outside of history, humanoid in body but not fully human, marking "the very limit of humanity."[29] Klausen says, "Ultimately, in relegating primitives to the limits of the human, Arendt exploits two senses of 'humanity': one strongly normative and effectively exclusive, one plural and inclusive. She simultaneously includes primitives within humanity qua humankind but excludes them from humanity qua historically developed faculty of culture."[30]

At other times, Arendt's voice is decidedly critical of the very same logic on which she herself seems to depend. For example, she opposes "organic naturalistic definitions of peoples," warning that these are "the first germs of later racist theories, and they have, indeed, been an outstanding characteristic of German ideologies and German historicism."[31] How Arendt can claim in one breath that Africans are of the natural world, outside of history, and lacking "specifically human character," while in another reject those very reductive "naturalistic" discourses, is a matter of ongoing confusion to many of her readers.[32] Such contradictions are all the more mystifying in the face of the genuinely astute connections that she draws between imperialism and nationalism in *Origins,* arguing that although they are contradictory, forces of racism and tribalism straddle both.[33] Her critique of racial pseudosciences showcases this well, for she states that their aim is "to prepare the destruction of societies and communities whose atomization is one of the prerequisites of imperialistic domination."[34]

One persuasive, if only partial, explanation for these contradictions, blind spots, and biases in Arendt's work is the distinction that she draws between the (abject) social and (miraculous) political realms. Her attempts to gatekeep the two categories result in a great deal of racial ignorance and inaccuracy. For example, Kathryn Gines argues in *Hannah Arendt and the Negro Question* that "Arendt is ultimately somewhat ambivalent in her characterization of slavery, whether it is a social or political question in the American context. Although she insightfully recognizes slavery as a crime in America, Arendt is somewhat dismissive of this crime in the grand scheme of the American Revolution, perhaps because slavery is also labeled a social issue."[35] Robert Bernasconi also claims that the distinction between the social and political spheres is worthy of her readers' critical attention, even if it is not wholly determinative of her prejudices. He states, "As is apparent in *On Revolution*, she gave to the distinction between the social and the political a normative status which led her to applaud the American Revolution, among other things, for ignoring the social and economic cost paid by those who did not share in the prosperity they helped to produce for others."[36] The primary function of the category of the social is depoliticization, which is to say that it names issues that should be normatively situated outside of the political realm. When Arendt mobilizes the distinction in discussions of race, the results are uniquely consequential.

First, as I intimated earlier, the divide between the two overlooks the historical connections between so-called social and political issues. There is, for example, no way to approach the subject of Jim Crow segregation laws without attending to early twentieth-century criminality and carceral captivity.[37] One cannot understand the racial exclusions of the 1949 Housing Act without its most obvious effects: impoverished neighborhoods, subpar schools, and neglected, under-resourced communities. Second, cordoning off certain matters from political consideration has the effect of emptying racial issues of their historical content and treating them as if they are problems intrinsic to Black Americans themselves.

In *On Violence*, a text Arendt completed more than a decade after the social and political distinction was most clearly established in her work, she stated: "But while boycotts, sit-ins, and demonstrations were successful in eliminating discriminatory laws and ordinances in the South, they proved utter failures and became counterproductive when they encountered the social conditions in the large urban centers—the stark needs of the black ghettos on one side, the overriding interests of white lower income groups in respect to housing and education on the other. All this mode of action could do, and indeed did, was to bring these conditions into the open, into the street, where the basic irreconcilability of interests was dangerously exposed."[38] The problem here is, of course, that "discriminatory laws and ordinances" are just as embroiled in "social conditions" as "social conditions" are in "discriminatory laws and ordinances." (And if Arendt were writing in good faith, she would have to acknowledge that her own analysis of "irrational Black rage" is likely constituted by racist narratives of Black barbarism and pseudo-scientific assertions of Black intellectual inferiority, all so-called social matters.)[39] The social/political distinction underwrites the view that crime, poverty, and educational and health inequality are specifically African American issues with no connection to laws, policies, and economies outside of Black communities.

A BRIEF EXCURSUS ON WORLD

World is a "space for politics," said Arendt in a 1962 interview with the journalist, Günter Gaus.[40] She elaborates, "I comprehend it now in a much larger sense, as the space in which things become public, as the space in which one lives and which must look presentable. In which art appears, of course. In which all kinds of things appear."[41] The instrumental character of the concept is thus established, although its relationship to politics is productively ambiguous. And that is likely due to the uncertainty of the connections between work (the human activity with which world is most closely associated), and political life. Although Arendt is clear that *homo faber* (working man) creates the world, it is located somewhat outside of the public/private framework that situates her renowned triad of labor, work, and action. Labor, usually linked to the private realm, calls to mind prepolitical, cyclical activities of biological life processes: birth, growth, decay, and death. Action, the concept that has garnered the most critical attention of the three, unmistakably occurs in the public realm. Undertaken in speech, it is the radical, transformative experience of freedom itself. Those adhering to what Patchen Markell calls the "territorial reading" of *The Human Condition* believe that politics is firmly and exclusively situated in the public sphere, surfacing only in the form of episodic action in concert with others. They are likely to miss the political qualities of world. Its position in Arendt's work is neither neat nor decisive.[42]

World is the human artifice, defined by durability, permanence, and commonality. It is shared by humans who inhabit it together, yet its existence is predicated on the fact that every one of them will have a unique view of, and relationship to, it. Homo faber creates worldly things that are built to last, a sharp contrast with the products of labor, which must be consumed almost as quickly as they are produced, and the fruits of action, ever transient miracles of human freedom.[43] Arendt is clear that worldly reality is predicated upon the varied, unique perspectives that humans bring to it.[44] To put this another way, the durability of world counterbalances the fact of plurality: it is because humans are so endlessly different from one another that the objective, stable character of the world is so essential.[45] If "we are all the same, that is, human, in such a way that nobody is ever the same as anyone else who has lived, lives, will live," it is also true that plurality could never, in itself, generate commonality, but only the subjectivity, idiosyncrasy, and quirk of original human beings.[46] Keeping people together and providing a basis for their connection are the functions of a world. Whether physical objects such as infrastructure, artwork, buildings, and furniture, or intangibles, including language, rituals, lexicons, and common sense, humans connect with, and relate to, each other through worldly things.[47]

As I will discuss later, Arendt arrived at the concept of world by working backward, via the idea of worldlessness, one of the most devastating states of human experience, left in the wake of totalitarianism.[48] The replacement of a real world with a fictitious one does away with the durability and permanence of a world in common, and largely defines totalitarian power. Perhaps the gravest casualty of worldlessness, a state in which "nobody is reliable and nothing can be relied upon," is the loss of human relationships, which are weakened or obliterated altogether in the absence of the worldly in-between.[49] The destruction of a people generally hinges on the destruction of their world.

WORLDLESSNESS AND WORLD-BUILDING IN CAPTIVITY

I hold that Arendt's concept of world is relevant here in two respects. First, worldlessness is not limited to totalitarianism, but also extends to Black captivity. One concept in *The Human Condition* to which I will return frequently is that "without a world between men and nature, there is eternal movement, but no objectivity," an insight that invites yet another perspective on the opening anecdote: rather than merely repressing the physical actions of prisoners, carceral disciplinary apparatuses keep prisoners in *constant* motion, characteristic of forced migration.[50] Transferring incarcerated people from one facility to another; rejecting their appeals before parole boards; frequently revising regulations that govern their movements; removing them from the general population to segregated housing units and solitary confinement: all create a state of flux that is inimical to worldly stability. Another forced migration, the slave trade, is also exemplary of "eternal movement but, no objectivity." Middle Passage uprooted millions of captured Africans, forcing them into lengthy voyages on slave ships to the Americas, where they had no familiarity with language, culture, or customs.[51] The constant circulation of human chattel through sale and trade fractured and destroyed familial relationships and friendships, and deprived Africans and Black Americans of vital networks of belonging and connection.[52] That captives are kept in such a state of worldlessness is not incidental to the institutions of slavery and incarceration but utterly central to both. Denying captive people a world in common is the cornerstone of chattel and carceral power, for independent relationships, common sense, physical objects, and shared, intangible meanings interrupt and undermine the aspiration of total domination. Planters understood this well and methodically implemented legal and extralegal barriers to the creation of a world, from the intense enforcement of anti-literacy laws to regulations limiting socialization between bondpeople and free Black Americans. Thus, preventing enslaved people from accessing allies and resources; receiving and transferring information beyond the reach of slave society; forming networks of support with others; and organizing and connecting with abolitionists were tantamount to keeping them from forming a world.

Furthermore, even durable objects are potentially threatening to racial regimes, for the mere fact of independence from their makers exposes the limits of captivity. Strict regulations placed on the personal property of prisoners, including the long, and often arbitrary, catalog of contraband items from which they are prohibited, reflect this. On plantations, planters and overseers closely monitored the possessions of bondpeople, allowing some favored individuals to keep gardens and raise livestock while withholding that privilege from others, and regularly searching and raiding living quarters to uncover objects that could be used as weapons, or evidence of abolitionist propaganda and plots for rebellion. The assumption that these were merely instrumental measures to preempt uprising is reductive: the worldly durability of objects is itself a problem for the total domination to which racial regimes aspire.[53]

Second, the conditions of forced worldlessness render the creation of a world an insurgent act, which can be seen in both the daily practices of captive resistance and extraordinary events such as revolt and uprising. Pilfering small items from planters' homes challenges the prohibitions on bondpeople from owning and enjoying objects of use and fancy. Enslaved women, who often used their leisure time to create colorful textiles, rejecting the cheap, dingy materials they were given for their attire, dually assert their gender identity and desire for meaningful activities, rather than forced labor.[54] Prisoners who educate themselves in US criminal law to become jailhouse lawyers are radically disclosing their capacities for substantial, nonmenial work: intellectual abilities, proficiency with legal language and judicial procedure, and the spirit of camaraderie and mutual aid. This cuts against the grain of the US polity that denies felons enfranchisement, formal political participation, and most rights.[55]

Such modes of everyday rebellion in scenes of captivity are, descriptively speaking, practices of world-building. They create relations of commonality, durable objects, meanings, and relationships, all of which assume new political significance against the institutional backdrop of chattel and carceral worldlessness. Equally worldly is large-scale rebellion, for it enables enslaved and incarcerated people to tell a vastly different story about both themselves and the structural arrangements of their captivity than dominant accounts would permit. Slave rebellions, in addition to galvanizing abolitionist action in the North and South, upended prevailing beliefs that bondpeople were naturally docile, incapable, and apolitical; that slavery was a patriarchal, benevolent institution for which enslaved people were mostly grateful; and that resistance was a rare and peripheral aspect of antebellum Southern life.[56] Relatedly, prison revolts also explode widespread views of both the carceral state and incarcerated people, including the trope of the prisoner as barbaric, irrational, and driven only by self-interest; that criminal behavior renders a person unfit for any kind of political participation; and the conventional, often unexamined, assumption that prisons are the proper and inevitable corrective to crime and institutional modality for realizing retributive justice. Organized rebellion does away with any false sense that prisons or plantations are zones of neutrality, and forever transforms the narratives of captivity on which racial regimes rely.

The political significance of captive rebellion has not garnered a great deal of critical attention in scholarly discourse.[57] Similarly, the concept of world is often passed over by Arendt scholars in favor of action, freedom, judgment, revolution, and more.[58] *Politics in Captivity* seeks to redress these twin tendencies. I develop and, to an extent, rework Arendt's concept of world so that it can be brought to bear on racial politics. Because world has received less airtime in academic political theory, a complete account of its development in her thinking is essential here. Again, I do not adhere exclusively to Arendt's terms in my usage of world, but rather alter and augment it. As a case in point, Arendtian-originalists will note that I deviate sharply from her terms in my claim that destruction, not just production, is a creative, world-building practice.[59] Its productive, worldly dimensions are not part of Arendt's analysis, beyond her discussion of instrumentality in which nature is violated for the purpose of drawing out raw materials for use by homo faber.[60] All evidence suggests that Arendt, like most, saw production and destruction dichotomously.[61] Yet the resistance of enslaved and imprisoned people suggests otherwise: violence, property damage, and arson are no less worldly than the work of a builder or artist. If captivity unsettles the otherwise self-evident distinctions between physical and political movement, I believe that it also confounds the binary of productive/destructive. Arendt holds that worldly things, in both physical and intangible forms, connect humans through finite separation.[62] Yet when the artifice in question is a white supremacist institution designed to perpetuate forced worldlessness, the destruction of its scaffolding *is* creative and generative of new conditions. At the time of writing, concerted acts of state legislatures and activists are resulting in the removal of Confederate monuments from Southern town and city squares. The built landscapes from Birmingham to Dallas, from Bentonville to Fort Myers, are forever altered, withdrawing honorable memorialization of the Confederacy from public view. Although the politics of removal, refusal, and demolition do not appear in *The Human Condition*, tearing down a statue of racial world loss makes a new world. It is no coincidence that these recent events are linked to the Confederacy, for slave resistance is the predecessor of this more recent politics of refusal. Smashing and burning of enslavers' homes; poisoning their livestock; breaking tools and otherwise ruining their property do not merely demolish but construct a world that steadfastly rejects slavery. Attending to these experiences of rebellion demands an expansive and generous concept of world that reflects the complex terrain of political life in captivity. Thus, the spirit of Arendtian worldliness endures in this book, although only provisionally.

The second aim of *Politics in Captivity* is an analysis of everyday and extraordinary rebellion. There has never been a book-length treatment of captive resistance, broadly speaking, although theorists have attended separately to the insurgent actions of bondpeople and prisoners. In *Freedom as Marronage*, Neil Roberts argues that Western theories of freedom fail to attend to flight, the liminal space between slavery and freedom.[63] In *Solitary Confinement: Social Death and its Afterlives*, Lisa Guenther discusses the creative, rebellious activities of prisoners in solitary confinement, the most extreme and totalizing form of caging that would seem, at first blush, to obliterate any possibility of resistance.[64] Most often, Black captive rebellion is not taken seriously as legitimate political praxis; nor does it figure into theories of democracy, liberation, freedom, or most other inquiries. As a result, much contemporary political theory ignores enslavement and incarceration, and, importantly, goes unaffected and unenriched by the insights, meanings, and discursive transformations that could be gleaned from politics in captivity. Even though, as a white author, I am wary of framing this book as another study of all the lessons "we" might learn from Black politics, the "sharp white background" of political theory canons is most stark when bearing witness to the many experiences of freedom and liberation it egregiously misses.[65]

Politics in captivity does not found new political institutions or propose policies. It does not involve deliberative democratic procedures or protest in a public sphere. It is not oriented toward political reform or the expansion of rights for enslaved or incarcerated people. Further still, politics in captivity is not even particularly strategic or premeditated, but makeshift and spontaneous. Importantly, while it aligns with some principles of radical democratic theory, politics in captivity is sharply distinct from it. Sheldon Wolin's renowned theory of fugitive democracy, for example, envisions an episodic emergence of the demos, consolidated around issues held in common among the people and radically opposes the status quo.[66] Once the demands of the demos are institutionalized, either in the forms of law, policy, or constitution, it recedes, marking the end of the democratic moment. Although his radical democratic theory influenced and inspired multiple generations of political thinkers, it does not map onto politics in captivity. Wolin's theory of the political draws on nostalgic discourses of the public sphere, which are generally unavailable to Black prisoners and, as Vesla Weaver and Amy Lerman's construct of "custodial citizenship" suggests, are only contingently accessible to nonincarcerated Black Americans as well.[67]

The "fugitive" in Wolin's fugitive democracy, as I will elaborate later, is purely metaphorical, for the power generated from slave rebellions rarely even resembles the demos. They were often undertaken by a small roving band of just several bondpeople and occasionally single individuals, enacting violence against whites and destroying the property of planters. Slave uprisings never overturned chattel slavery in the United States and often did not try. They were neither institutionalized nor absorbed into a constitutional form. Armed rebellions were not situated in any sort of recognizable public sphere, such as a town square or city center, and their leaders sought to avoid spectators and generally carried out their plots in secrecy. Slaughtering enslavers and their families (as did the rebels led by Kook, Quamana, Charles Deslondes, and later Nat Turner) would appear to most as merely violent and apolitical, the type of self-interested act that Wolin would associate with "groupies" rather than democratic citizens.[68] Small-scale quotidian forms of resistance including pilfering, shirking, feigning illness, and truancy were clandestine practices, relying on interdependent networks of bondpeople, but in no way resembling "the political," as Wolin conceptualized it.

The same could be said of carceral resistance, which is structurally and institutionally hidden from public view.[69] The basic principle of assembling with others is impossible in maximum security and super max settings, or in solitary confinement, thus undermining the most fundamental tenet of the demos. Rather than overturning the status quo, prison rebellion is oriented toward control of space; temporarily organizing and running operations; transforming the "general population" into a political community; attacking wardens and COs; and pushing back against the aspiration of total domination that is otherwise the prevailing condition of prison life. The "point" is not to abolish the prison or even necessarily institutionalize a coherent list of demands. Sometimes there is, in fact, no point beyond expelling anger and energy. The democratic moment, according to Wolin, forever alters political conditions and recedes when revolutionary principles are institutionalized. The form and temporality of prison resistance does not adhere to this trajectory, for it aims not to overturn the institution, but rather disrupt it. The radicalism of prison resistance lies in the *temporary suspension* of the prison regime, not the wholesale displacement of the status quo and introduction of a new order. Slavery was not abolished in New Orleans after the German Coast Slave Uprising of 1811. Neither did the 1971 Attica prison uprising permanently shut down the facility. Yet the break in the usual operations of racial captivity that each rebellion incited was transformative, forever altering the historical and political landscapes of the antebellum South and the modern carceral sphere, respectively. In sum, the conceptual utility of fugitive democracy is generally nonexistent for captive people and relatedly, the political dimensions of captive resistance are, for Wolin, unintelligible.

Beyond the blind spots of white-centric postwar democratic theory, it is also true that theorists of Black political thought regularly neglect the subject of resistance on plantations and in prisons. Although the public racial reckoning that the Movement for Black Lives incited in 2014 has meant increased scholarly attention to Black political theory over the past decade, most academics merely nod to captive rebellion, if not ignore it altogether. While Alex Zamalin, for example, has written prolifically and brilliantly on Black resistance, he only briefly mentions the Southampton Insurrection and the thwarted plot of Denmark Vesey in *The Struggle on Their Minds*.[70] This is emblematic of the tendency of theorists to sidestep politics in captivity, even as they engage deeply with Black political agency. The absence of concepts that can properly articulate its complexity and meaning is one reason it is given short shrift in academic discourse. Arendt's concept of world is a corrective to this problem, rather than the well-worn constructs of democratic theory or the conceptual repertoires of liberalism. Drawing out the theoretical utility of world and introducing it to the rich, textured terrain of politics on plantations and in prisons are the central aims of *Politics in Captivity*.

CHAPTER SUMMARY

Chapter One begins by challenging the likenesses often drawn between plantations and prisons and attending to their historical continuities. I first contest the rhetorical catchphrase common in many activist circles, "prison labor is slavery," holding instead that resistance, not labor, bridges the lived experiences of incarcerated and enslaved peoples. Imprisoned intellectuals in the 1960s and 1970s (whose work is elaborated in Chapter Two) understood this well.[71] To borrow from Dan Berger, "Blackness was a source of resistance, representing persistent confrontation with the slave state." I then trace the historical continuities between slavery and incarceration for the purposes of highlighting their nodal points; providing some context for the rallying cry and its popularity; and elaborating on the birth and growth of the prison as a racial regime.

Incarcerated authors in the 1960s and 1970s captured in their writing the living legacies of enslavement in the prison system. Focusing on a small group of theorists, including Muhammad Ahmad, Angela Davis, George Jackson, Ruchell Magee, and Assata Shakur, I name a genre of political theory "Black carceral political thought." Chapter Two explores its emergence in parallel with the rise of the Black Power Movement in the late 1960s. Here, I attend to the production of knowledge about the conditions of prison and its embeddedness in the legacies of slavery. The 1960s and 1970s saw significant shifts in these areas, when incarcerated intellectuals and activists began writing prolifically on such subjects. In *Captive Nation*, Berger discusses the myriad ways in which Black activists and scholars have mobilized slavery to articulate current forms of racial injustice or in his terms a "foundational metaphor of black intellectual life." Prisoners' use of it, is all the more provocative, "By framing their confinement as enslavement, dissident prisoners positioned themselves as the latest links in an unbroken chain of white supremacy that stretched back hundreds of years."[72] A constellation of multiple factors accounts for this turn, including legislative moves that shored up the carceral state through mandatory minimum sentences; increased criminalization of drug use and distribution; Great Society-era policies that permitted prisoners wide access to reading material, educational resources, and opportunities to publish and circulate prison newspapers; and the emergence of new Black radical organizations, including the Black Power Movement and the Black Panther Party, the membership of which were disproportionately surveilled and targeted for incarceration. The inevitable and, for the prison state, inconvenient effect of this was a highly politicized general prison population. The final section of Chapter Two considers how incarcerated Black intellectuals in the 1960s and 1970s drew on slavery to articulate and develop their strategies of resistance.

Because Black carceral political thought is so heavily rooted in traditions of slave resistance, Chapter Three looks to slave rebellion and the creative destructions of bondpeople. Everyday insurgent practices of demolition and insurgency were relatively common on plantations, including smashing tools, injuring or killing livestock, and stealing objects from planters' homes. Extraordinary acts of rebellion are similarly destructive, as high profile (though shockingly understudied) events like the German Coast Slave Uprising attest. In the Territory of Orleans in January 1811, between two hundred and five hundred enslaved men burned sugarhouses, crops, and five plantations to the ground, before marching toward the city of New Orleans, where they were overtaken by white militias.[73] With the exception of a single book, next to nothing has been written about this event. Two decades later, the Southampton Insurrection (colloquially known as Nat Turner's Rebellion) was a high-profile revolt of seventy-five enslaved men, led by Turner that resulted in the deaths of fifty-five whites. Although the subject of far more attention than the German Coast Slave Uprising, the political meaning of the Southampton Insurrection is generally passed over in favor of Turner's fanaticism and delusional testimonies.

In Chapter Three, I discuss in detail the ways that slave resistance is erased in history and, differently so, political theory. Because it was in the interest of planters to downplay the frequency and intensity of slave rebellions, the historical record is not fully accurate. Slave ship ledgers and planters' logs were occasionally falsified such that it appeared that slave resistance was a marginal and rare occurrence, although other documentation contradicts this. In addition, classic historians of the antebellum period are often pro-slavery, Lost Cause apologists whose work continued to dominate the field of American history in the twentieth century. As a political theorist, it is perhaps prudent to note that I do not intend for this chapter to offer a meticulous and thorough historical account of slave resistance. Rather, the rebellious actions of bondpeople are mobilized in service of my larger argument that their minimization or absence from academic discourses of history and political theory reflect the need for new concepts that can better speak to their power and significance.

What I call liberal myopia, in part, accounts for the failure of historians and political theorists to properly attend to plantation politics. Borrowing Chantal Mouffe's term "liberal fundamentalism," Chapter Four explores the ways in which the conceptual repertoires of liberalism conceal the political dimensions of slave resistance from the view of both liberals and their critics.[74] I argue that some of the key precepts of liberalism collapse in the domain of slave politics. Turner's Rebellion, the German Coast Slave Uprising, and certain practices of everyday resistance all showcase different limitations and deficiencies of liberalism. I first refute the common assumption that bondpeople were incapable of individual or collective action, instead proposing a view of their political work that accounts for the unique scenario of captivity: their subjection to and liberation from white power. The duality of both, their productive tensions, and interdependencies surface in scenes of captivity. Resistance is a fundamental affront to planters' aspiration toward total domination, a condition that points to both the enormity of power that bondpeople are up against, and equally, the myriad opportunities to resist it. In this way, the plantation is a site not only of violence and domination, but also unique political possibility.

Most liberal concepts exist outside the paradigm of slavery. For example, the public/private distinction, reason, individualism, the binary of self-interest versus solidarity, and more. Even critics of liberalism adopt its premises, and subsequently slave politics go unnoticed. However, to complicate matters, many formerly enslaved Afro-Modern authors, including Frederick Douglass, Olaudah Equiano, and Ottobah Cugoano, draw on liberal concepts to articulate and substantiate their anti-slavery charges. The second section of Chapter Four centers on this aspect of their work, as it considers the promises and pitfalls of their mobilizations of liberalism.

Because it is the central concept of *Politics in Captivity*, Chapter Five provides a thorough account of the concept of world in the work of both Arendt and other theorists that also mobilize the term. I briefly trace the development through Arendt's biography, in an effort to draw out its intellectual genealogy, identify its inheritances from the philosophy of Husserl and, later, Heidegger, and situate it in the broader body of her work. Beginning with Arendt's university studies, I examine the earliest origins of world, including its roots in phenomenology.[75] The version of the concept that would remain, more or less, stable in her work, emerged out of the extraordinary political conditions in which she lived. I hold that the concept is rooted in her break with Heidegger in the early 1930s and first appears in the shape of its opposite: worldlessness, which she discusses but does not define in *Origins*.[76] The concept would take further shape amid the shifts and turns in Arendt's life and work.[77]

After tracing its beginnings, much of Chapter Five is dedicated to fully explaining the concept of world as Arendt viewed it. I draw primarily from *The Human Condition*, where it is most thoroughly elaborated, as well as *Between Past and Future*, her *Lectures on Kant's Political Philosophy*, and a number of essays and interviews. In addition to Arendt's own writings, there is a modest but growing interdisciplinary literature on the category of world in an Arendtian mode, although it appears less often in the Arendt literature than her renowned theories of action, freedom, and judgment.[78] Book-length treatments of the subject include Ella Myers's *Worldly Ethics: Democratic Politics and Care for the World* and Christopher Peys's *Reconsidering Cosmopolitanism and Forgiveness: Arendt, Derrida, and Care for the World*. Frederick Dolan, Roger Berkowitz, John McGowan, Lawrence Biskowski, Emily Zakin, and others have also engaged with Arendtian worldliness in their work.[79]

After a thorough discussion of world, as Arendt and others conceptualize it, Chapter Six largely breaks with Arendt's terms, altering and augmenting the concept so that it can be brought to bear on racial politics. I first develop the idea of worldlessness, which Arendt initially laid out in *The Origins of Totalitarianism,* in preparation for the ways this will link up with the loss of world associated with captivity. While Arendt was averse to metaphoric mobilizations of totalitarianism, the term does provide a useful framework for better comprehending the political stakes of captivity. Intense relations of domination and subordination that prevail on plantations and in prisons, above all, generate the conditions of forced worldlessness. Under these circumstances, the creation of a world becomes a uniquely political act. Second, as I intimated earlier, Arendt does not consider the radical, worldly potential of destruction, demolition, erasure, or refusal, as *Politics in Captivity* does. Here I challenge the vocabulary of contemporary political theory by considering the ways world confounds the conventional binary of productive/destructive.

Chapter Six concludes with a discussion of the worldly effects of large-scale, organized rebellion and spontaneous, everyday resistance in captivity. Even the most microlevel acts of creation are insurgent events of world-building: Guenther describes a prisoner in solitary confinement who made pralines by saving nuts and packets of sugar from his meal trays and fashioning a makeshift oven out of tinfoil.[80] Although not a practice that would otherwise garner political recognition, I hold that this small act is one of many instances of rebellious world creation. When near total domination stamps out every effort to claim any sort of power, even the smallest creation, movement, or practice is insurgent, challenging institutions of captivity.

Like daily carceral resistance, large, organized prison uprisings, although perhaps more politically legible, are vastly understudied. Spotlighting their political and worldly dimensions is the central aim of Chapter Seven. The Attica prison uprising of 1971 is one of the few prison revolts that has secured a prominent position in public discourse. It has been the subject of documentary films, music, novels, spoken word performance pieces, as well as a foundational book by Heather Ann Thompson *Blood in the Water*.[81] The immense attention that Attica has received, compared to the hundreds of prison rebellions that have occurred since, is likely due to the political landscape of the early 1970s. Black radical movements, both in and outside of prison, articulated the connections between the carceral state and the Black American experience. At the time the Attica prison uprising took place, it was politicized in a way that other rebellions had not been, due to the energy and expertise of Black activists. Chapter Seven attends to that crucial political moment, drawing on prison newspapers, pamphlets, and other source materials to consider its world-building effects.

1

From Plantations to Prisons

"PRISON LABOR IS SLAVERY?"

The rallying cry "prison labor is slavery" echoes in and outside of prison walls. The call is not new. In September 1971, for example, the leaders of the Attica prison uprising made the termination of "slave labor" the second item on their list of demands. It is both a mantra with broad rhetorical appeal and a critical take on the historical continuities of racial captivity. Leftists favor it because it captures the exploitative effects of carceral labor on both prisoners and nonincarcerated workers and conservatives use it in defense of the so-called dignity and value of work and its imagined rehabilitative functions. The view that the oppression of prisoners is a problem of labor exploitation, captured in the resounding declaration that extreme, low-wage carceral labor is merely slavery under a different name, spans the moderate deliberation of prison reformers and radical imagination of abolitionists.

This phenomenon surfaces in academic and nonacademic circles alike. Writing on trends in convict rehabilitation schemes, the historian Vijay

Prashad notes the mid-century shift in focus from the "troubled minds" of prisoners to the healing power of work, resulting in the "emerging system of penal slavery."[1] Howard Winant states that "prison-based quasi enslaved labor" is fully operational today, lest one believe that draconian practices of punishment are outdated or archaic.[2] On these points, practitioners are like-minded: Angela Hanks from the Center for Law and Social Policy, a nonprofit, low-income advocacy organization, states, "Forced labor for low or no wages—we have a term for that. We call it slavery."[3] Jaron Browne, an organizer with the Oakland-based group POWER, argues that redressing the injustice of prison servitude is the principle demand of "the slavery abolition movement of the 21st century."[4] Even the Right-leaning commentator Chandra Bozelko nods to the subject in a conservative critique of "prison slavery" that appeared in a 2017 issue of the *National Review*.[5] Indeed, it is more than evident that the use of slavery as a critical descriptor of carceral labor cuts across the political spectrum, as well as the conventional lines of academic disciplinarity.

Echoes of this critique continue to reverberate from inside prisons today: the organization of incarcerated workers, Jailhouse Lawyers Speak, along with the Incarcerated Workers' Organizing Committee made exploitative carceral labor the centerpiece of a recent national prison work strike. State minimum wage was the second item on their list of demands, which called for "an immediate end to prison slavery. All persons imprisoned in any place of detention under the United States jurisdiction must be paid the prevailing wage in their state or territory for their labor."[6] Kevin Rashid Johnson, an incarcerated artist and author, equates prison labor and slavery in a manifesto that he published in *The Guardian* in September 2018: "I'll be supporting my fellow inmates here and across the nation who will be refusing to work in what amounts to a modern form of slavery . . . I see prison labor as slave labor that still exists in the United States in 2018. In fact, slavery never ended in this country."[7]

The tendency to collapse prison and slave labor together is embedded in a decades-long critical tradition that takes aim at carceral servitude and other inheritances of racial slavery. Its origins can be traced to the aftermath of two events: the aforementioned Attica prison uprising, undoubtedly the most renowned and well-mined prison rebellion in US history, and the lesser known revolt at the McAlester State Penitentiary in 1973, during which prisoners engaged in concerted acts of property destruction and set fire to the solitary confinement unit, known as "the Rock."[8] In the years following both events, criminologists and corrections administrators proposed increased convict labor in effort to maintain order in the general prison population and preempt further resistance. Incarcerated people understood well the dual purposes of this move: it allowed the state to tighten control over their movements and actions, and simultaneously avail itself of a cheap, captive labor pool.

In an article titled "Slave Labor in American Prisons," an anonymous incarcerated author takes a critical, postcolonial, global perspective on this phenomenon: "with growing liberation struggles overseas making foreign exploitation more difficult, the industrialists and corporate businessmen are also beginning to find that the US prison system is another target to exploit. While they can't yet move large factories into the prisons, they are more and more using slave labor which exists in prisons around the country. For the factory owner, the best possible situation is one where workers are supervised and controlled as tightly as possible on and off the job, where workers are paid as little as possible—and prisons are perfect."[9] In the same year, a special issue of *The Black Scholar*, dedicated to Black prisoners, included an essay by Muhammad Ahmad, who lists underpayment for labor among the key ways that Black prisoners, "captured captives in a captive nation," endure worse suffering than other Black people in the United States. The rise of such labor-centric discourse in the early 1970s aligns with discursive shifts in favor of carceral work ethic, expansions to programs of prison labor, and radical critiques of both.

PRISON LABOR IS NOT SLAVERY

"Prison labor is slavery," as an idea and catchphrase, is undoubtedly persuasive and rhetorically powerful, with genuine utility for scholarly and activist attempts to call attention to the enduring facets of racial captivity. While on the one hand, the equation of chattel and carceral servitude is understandable and even intuitive, for both are unequivocally racialized, highly exploitative, and historically linked. On the other hand, it is ultimately misguided. By this, I mean neither to issue a conservative vindication of prison labor by indicating that it is less inhumane or coercive than slavery, nor suggest it is a just punishment for crime or rehabilitative technique of instilling values of personal responsibility in the psyches of the morally depraved. Instead, I hold that the inaccuracies of equating the two are not matters of mere academic hairsplitting, but consequential and ultimately productive of a view that misunderstands the historical, political, and economic realities of both.

First, the economic import of prison labor pales in comparison to slavery. In 2016, only about 8.5 percent of 1.5 million prisoners in the United States were incarcerated in private prisons, where labor for private companies is most heavily undertaken. Even in publicly funded state and federal prisons, about 25 percent of the incarcerated labor force works for UNICOR (Federal Prison Industries), which sells prisoner-made products and services to private companies. Prison maintenance jobs, by comparison, comprise 75 percent of prison labor. This is further reflected in UNICOR's own statement. In response to complaints from the private sector, that the corporation possesses unfair competitive advantage due to its unique access to a captive and cheap labor force, UNICOR counters that it has little economic effect on the private sector and its true purpose is to provide functional life skills training to "inmates." Statistically, this statement is largely accurate: a very small percentage of incarcerated people do work that actually contributes to the economy.

Pairing prison labor with slavery inadvertently produces a minimalist picture of the latter, for it erroneously suggests economic parity between them. Historically and otherwise, this is deeply misleading: prisoners have jobs, but bondpeople were, fundamentally, workers. Acknowledgment of this fact is crucial to a genuine understanding of the power to which captives are subjected, as well as the foundational quality of slavery to the US economy. The historian Edward Baptist attests to this: "Both South and North depended on slavery's expansion. The products generated from the possibilities of co-exploitation explain much of the nation's astonishing rise to power in the nineteenth century. Through the booms and the crashes emerged a financial system that continuously catalyzed the development of US capitalism. By the 1840s, the United States had grown into both an empire and a world economic power—the second greatest industrial economy, in fact, in the world—all built on the back of cotton."[10] He holds that chattel slavery transformed the United States from a small-scale agrarian economy to a global economic superpower. By contrast, the economic impact of prison labor is comparatively minuscule: its primary function is to cut operations costs to the prison. Abolishing carceral labor would have little effect on the world outside the prison, while the legal termination of slavery in 1865 necessitated a complete reconstruction of the postbellum Southern economy. For these reasons, synonymizing carceral and chattel labor misleadingly downplays the economic significance of slavery in modern US history.

Second, despite deep interconnections between them, the historical status of race differs considerably between the two forms of captivity: race was introduced to solve a labor problem in the seventeenth century, while prisons were trotted out to solve a race problem in the nineteenth. After the economies of formerly depressed European countries improved in the 1670s, far fewer white Europeans emigrated to the colonies to work as indentured servants for American landowners. Colonial elites, thus, looked to other sources of cost-effective labor, the result of which was large increases in transatlantic importation of Africans to the Americas.

Until this era, African workers and European indentured servants lived and worked side-by-side and shared similar civic standing: they were legally bound to landowners, and enjoyed some limited rights, including property, possession of arms, interracial marriage, the vote, and the ability to run for local political offices. This changed when the concept of race was introduced to preempt class rebellion by disbanding relations of solidarity between poor white and Black workers.[11] A series of laws were swiftly passed, first in the Virginia General Assembly, and later other legislatures, that marked differences in standing solely on the basis of race. These new measures established, to borrow a term from the political theorist, Joel Olson, a fabricated and fictional "cross-class alliance" between whites in the early American colonies.[12] It was intended to produce an illusory sense of racial privilege in the collective psyche of poor whites, a discourse at the center of a counterintuitive social order that ultimately advantaged white elites. For example, prior to physically punishing a white servant, a landowner would have to acquire a court order, while it was permissible to beat a Black servant at will. It was during this period that slavery, limited exclusively to Black Americans, was first legally recognized as a hereditary, lifelong condition, rather than a time-limited period of servitude.[13] This marked its early transformation from a mere form of labor to a massive human economy. It is no exaggeration to say that slavery is foundational to the United States, given the economic need that it met, the social relations that it consolidated, and the white polity that it founded (the survival of which would later require carceral safeguards).

From another angle, the equation of prison labor and slavery obscures the very specific *racial history* of the carceral state. Prisons were, at their core, intended to sustain the racial status quo after Emancipation, rather than simply serve the instrumental purpose of providing nonwage labor to states or private businesses. To be clear, the investment in the preservation of Black servitude and white domination after 1865 *was* driven in large part by the economic devastation of the South caused by the Civil War. Yet noncarceral solutions were available for this, such as sharecropping, tenant farming, and other forms of debt peonage. White anxiety about the postwar Southern economy was largely indistinguishable from the newfound precarity of white supremacy provoked by the liberation of 3.9 million African Americans. Tremendous increases in Black prisoners after 1865 reflect the fact that the penal system stepped in to maintain Southern racial hierarchies. In Georgia, for example, between 1864 and 1868, the prisoner population increased by 157 percent. That number would later triple after 1875, following the passage of laws that mandated lengthy sentences for criminalized behavior associated with newly emancipated people, such as loitering and pilfering livestock. Black men ages eighteen to twenty-two accounted (primarily) for this meteoric rise in prison populations: by the early decades of the twentieth century, Southern prisons were 80 to 90 percent Black.

WHY IT MATTERS

While I elaborate on the history of the US prison system later, the point here is that, although they are both grounded in, and generative of, white domination, chattel and carceral labor are rooted in fundamentally different conditions. This distinction matters, both theoretically and politically, particularly in the present moment. At the time of writing, the Movement for Black Lives is leading the United States through a moment of racial reckoning. Reignited demands for justice following the public execution of George Floyd, a Black American man who suffocated under the knee of a white policeman in May of 2020, showcase radical shifts in public sentiment from the earlier, decidedly carceral aim of indicting and convicting "killer cops" and toward a more imaginative and ambitious future of defunding police and introducing reparations for African Americans. As genuine anti-racist policies and programs are floated in mainstream political debates, an accurate account of the magnitude of slavery's role in the birth and growth of the US economy and polity is vital. How should government agencies approach the calculation of payments for losses? Why single out African Americans for compensation? What is the justification for disbanding police departments and reimagining the way that public safety is administered? All these important political questions require critical attention to the ways in which slavery figured into the American founding; the transformative impact of slavery on the economy, society, and geopolitical status of the United States; and the slave-catching origins of the contemporary police force. At stake in these questions is the heretofore unprecedented opportunity to redress centuries of racial injury. Synonymizing chattel and carceral labor muddies the historical precision needed to answer them.

Even prior to the most recent resurgence of collective action for racial justice, mass incarceration, for more than a decade, has been on the receiving end of new sociopolitical scrutiny. The racial origins of the postbellum penal system provide evidentiary support for arguments against it. The widespread perception that the prison system is the guarantor of public safety is unsettled by a clear view of its anti-Black foundations, the backbone of both reformist and abolitionist opposition to the carceral state. Now that decarceration proposals and strategies are no longer limited to Leftists and radicals, a historical and political perspective on how the birth of modern prisons was imbricated in the maintenance of the white-dominated social order challenges public sentiment inflected with color-blind myths; law-and-order beliefs that prison is the proper institutional response to crime control; and racially coded narratives conjoining the identities, "Black" and "criminal" in the public imaginary. To be fair, the tendency to liken prison labor to slavery is often provoked by a critique of these very constructs. Yet, despite best intentions, the conflation does a disservice to incarcerated people by reducing their experiences of abuse and exploitation to labor alone. The social, political, moral, and economic wrongs of prisons far exceed it.

The theoretical implications are equally consequential. Political imagination, to which abolitionist thinkers appeal to envision a world without prisons, is short-circuited by the tendency to conflate chattel and carceral labor.[14] Davis asks, "What, then, would it mean to imagine a system in which punishment is not allowed to become a source of corporate profit? How can we imagine a society in which race and class are not primary determinants of punishment? Or one in which punishment itself is no longer the central concern in the making of justice? An abolitionist approach that seeks to answer questions such as these would require us to imagine a constellation of alternative strategies and institutions, with the ultimate aim of removing the prison from the social and ideological landscapes of our society."[15] Echoing the idea that prison dominates the political and cultural landscape of the United States, Kim Gilmore argues that it is precisely when the carceral system seems hopelessly impenetrable that the abolitionist imagination is most crucial: "In this moment, it may seem more difficult than ever to envision a state that supports humanity rather than eviscerates the possibility of freedom and health for so many of its people. Yet it is precisely now, when prisons crowd the physical and psychic landscape, that imagining abolition is most critical."[16] If prison abolition requires such exercises in imagination, synonymizing chattel and carceral labor implies that abolition of prisons would cause a seismic upheaval akin to Emancipation. It would not.

Such a view is not only materially inaccurate but hampers the capacity to conceive of a society without prisons. That full abolition appears daunting or impossible because of the presumed entanglements of carceral labor in the US economy is a fiction that its marriage to slavery propagates. Also relevant to the abolitionist imagination is the way in which the refrain "prison labor is slavery" overlooks the more economically impactful force of the carceral state: namely, the tremendous capital that is currently invested in punishment. While the effect of prison labor on the economy is relatively minimal, the prison *business* is a booming billion-dollar industry, generating profits from the monopoly contracts of telephone companies, bail bond businesses, price-gouging commissary vendors, and of course, private corporations that manage and operate prison facilities.[17] "What has been enabled in the US and the proliferation of prison facilities and prison populations; the rapid degree to which capital has moved into the punishment industry in such a way that it is no longer a small niche, but rather a major component of the US economy—all this has global implications."[18] Thus, the preoccupation with prison labor is a missed opportunity to imagine an anti-capitalist alternative to prison; critique its neoliberal structure (what Davis calls the "prison industrial complex"); and conceive of creative abolitionist strategies that combat the reduction of human lives to profit motive. Changes in law or administrative policy that would compensate incarcerated workers at the level of state minimum wage, for example, might redress exploited labor, but would also leave intact the immense corporate stakeholdings in punishment.

In sum, collapsing together prison labor and slavery reproduces a discourse that misunderstands the philosophical underpinnings of both: chattel slavery is a system of racial labor, while prison is a system of racial control. Extracting maximum profit from the uncompensated work of bondpeople was, prior to 1865, an end in itself, and race was invented in service of this purpose. The inverse is true of prisoners, where it is *labor* that is instrumentalized for the purposes of racial domination.

The conflation narrative of prison labor and slavery weakens the ability of historians and political thinkers to both distinguish between them and identify their commonalities. In *Politics in Captivity*, I examine one nodal point that has been conspicuously missed by theorists of protest, radical democracy, and the African American political tradition: captive rebellion. To date, there are few political theories that foreground the resistance of enslaved or imprisoned people, and none that conceive of the two together in a theory of politics in captivity. I suspect this is not unrelated to the discursive ubiquity of the claim "prison labor is slavery." It is likely also due to the common academic tendency to ignore the political actions and theories of prisoners. Just as Old South apologists and their critics undermine or dismiss the political capabilities of enslaved people, the erasure of prisoners' political work is likely traceable to predictable liberal assumptions that criminal behavior is expressive of an irrationalism that renders one unfit for democratic participation. Or more sympathetically, that the repressive, abject character of the prison institution makes it an unlikely site of political engagement, despite the intellectual or political acuity of its inhabitants. Regardless of the reasons, it remains true that academic political theorists so often ignore or merely footnote carceral politics. In reality, they are untapped reserves with the potential to shape and rearrange theories of action, freedom, liberation, and more. Prison politics are rich and fraught, evolved and sophisticated, embedded in history, and both rooted in and generative of theory. They are marked by a rebellious praxis.

Borrowing from the insights of incarcerated intellectuals and activists from the Black Power era, I argue that *resistance*, not labor, conjoins the political lives of prisoners and bondpeople. I first outline academic critiques of the prison system by drawing on the historical backdrop of chattel slavery and then carceral captivity.[19] The inaccurate conflation of the two forms of labor is symptomatic of disproportionate attention to the later history of prisons in the last two decades of the twentieth century, at the expense of the earlier years (including the Progressive Era) when the contemporary penal system was established.[20] In particular, the rise of neoliberalism in the 1970s and the subsequent emergence of private prisons, have received the lion's share of airtime in many academic and activist circles.[21] This chapter provides a corrective to this by looking to its growth from the postbellum period through the 1970s in order to explain the development of what Rodriguez calls the "prison regime." In his words:

The prison regime encompasses the material arrangements of institutional power that create informal (and often nominally illegal) routines and protocols of militarized physiological domination over human beings held captive by the state. This domination privileges a historical anti-Black state violence that is particularly traceable to the latter stages of continental racial chattel slavery and its immediate epochal aftermath in "post-emancipation" white supremacy and juridical racial segregation / apartheid—a privileging that is directly reflected in the actual demography of the imprisoned population, composed of a Black majority.[22]

The prison regime is, among other things, an extension of the knowledge and practices born in slavery. That the status of labor differs considerably between the two should not cloud their historical continuities, on which I elaborate here.

"A NEW SLAVERY AND A NEW SLAVE TRADE"

Beyond rhetorical assertions about exploited labor, there is no shortage of writing that details the connections between plantations and prisons, and for good reason: that the carceral state is an inheritance of chattel slavery is well documented. In her bestselling 2011 book, *The New Jim Crow*, Michelle Alexander popularizes the view that slavery was never abolished, but merely repurposed into sharecropping, tenant farming, convict leasing, Jim Crow segregation, the War on Drugs, and finally, mass incarceration.[23] Following Alexander, Ava Duvernay's 2016 hit documentary, *13th*, catapulted the contemporary racial carceral state into popular political discourse, locating its origins in the postbellum penal system.[24] Both Duvernay and Alexander's perspectives are situated in lengthy academic and activist traditions that view the exploitation of prisoners as one of many historically embedded strategies of racial control, traceable to the year 1619, when the first Africans arrived in the American colonies. This section aims to identify and analyze the continuities of slavery and criminal punishment from the postbellum period to the 1970s for the purpose of establishing the foundations for the genre of Black carceral political thought in Chapter Two.

The popular view that bondage ended with Emancipation is confounded by the counterargument that, following the passage of the 13th Amendment in 1865, slavery was merely repackaged to circumvent racial equality promised in the Reconstruction period. The 13th Amendment codifies a loophole, stating that involuntary servitude remains legal when its function is punishment for crime. Its undergirding strategies are both logistical and political. First, because mandatory nonwage labor was already a common carceral practice in the postbellum United States, its eradication would have been politically unpopular and economically inconvenient.[25] Second, the perpetuation of bondage established in the 13th Amendment left operations of white supremacy firmly intact, neatly transferring the legal ownership of human chattel from the planter to the state, and enslaving humans through criminalization, courts, and imprisonment, instead of abduction, auction blocks, and selective breeding.

As early as 1913, in an article titled "Prison Labor and Social Justice," the prison reformer F. Emory Lyon states the following:

> History records the perpetuation of many injustices to portions of humankind through custom, through prejudice and self-interest and through limited notions of universal justice. A striking example of this is found in the long continuance of slavery into a civilized and Christian era. We now boast that chattel slavery, at least, has been abolished. But our quickened consciences remind us that certain forms of wage-slavery may contain essential elements of the ancient evil.[26]

Shortly after, in 1931, Howard P. Gill, the superintendent of the State Prison Colony in Norfolk, Massachusetts made a similar argument: "to relieve a prisoner of all responsibility for the support of himself and his family is to create an unsocial attitude, which the prison is intended to correct . . . Hence both social and economic considerations support the payment of wages to prisoners."[27] Of course the "wage-slavery" to which Lyons objects is likely sharecropping and tenant farming, both Southern inventions of debt peonage designed for the economic benefit of landowners at the expense of Black workers. Sharecroppers lived on the lands they tilled, paying rent with a portion of the crops they harvested and collecting the meager remainder for themselves as payment. Tenant farmers, like sharecroppers, did the same, although they enjoyed slightly more authority, including possession of their own tools and livestock for personal use. Yet in both cases, exploitation of Black workers was rampant, for landowners often used their wages as personal slush funds, underestimating the day's harvest for the purpose of underpaying their workers.[28]

Also common at the time that Lyons wrote was convict leasing, a system of nonwage labor undertaken by prisoners for the benefit of individual estates and businesses. In return, responsibility for feeding, clothing, and housing convicts was outsourced to lessees, who thus absorbed the expenses of incarceration and profited off the captive workforce. Because they were farmed out to perform nonwage labor, convict leasing more closely resembles chattel slavery than other practices of postbellum debt peonage. Writing on the criminal punishment of Black women, the historian, Sarah Haley, considers the "gendered continuities" between plantation labor and convict leasing, which she states "are critical to understanding the southern carceral regime as a form of neoslavery with 'gender neutrality,' the employment of black women in hard labor alongside men, being one of its critical features."[29] James Manos takes note of both the economic and social dimensions of this form of carceral punishment, which extends beyond the categories of production and profit:

> After the abolition of slavery and the corresponding development of convict leasing as a new mode of punishment, incarceration would no longer serve the modes of production alone. Instead, it would begin to shape the organization of society. I would like to suggest that we cannot fully understand the implications of separating crime from punishment, or even the relationship between economy and prisons, until we have accounted for the transformation of slavery into a form of punishment and its after-effects.[30]

Critical scholarship linking the abuse and exploitation of convict lessees with the legacy of slavery abounds in historical literature. David Oshinsky's *Worse Than Slavery: Parchman Farm and the Ordeal of Jim Crow Justice* details the horrendous conditions of convict labor and the transformation of criminal punishment from a marginal practice in antebellum Mississippi to a massive system of racial control after Emancipation.[31] In the renowned *Slavery by Another Name*, the journalist Douglas Blackmon performs a kind of autopsy on US corporations, revealing their dependence on Black convict labor after the Civil War.[32]

This was not lost on W.E.B. Du Bois, who observed the following in his 1906 essay "Die Negerfrage in den Vereinigten Staaten ("The Negro Question in the United States"):

> Thus the criminals in the South seemed suddenly, at a single stroke, to increase acutely; so large was the increase that the state could not reduce or control it, even if it had wished; and the state did not wish. In the

entire South laws were immediately passed according to which the officials had the right to hire out convict labor to the highest bidder. The bidder assumed the care for the prisoners and let them work according to his own discretion under nominal control of the state. Thus a new slavery and a new slave trade was introduced.[33]

Prison studies scholars note that the conditions of convict labor were often more brutal than slavery because leasers, unlike enslavers, were not incentivized to provide any protection or care for their charges whatsoever.[34] They regularly worked them to death, knowing that a fresh supply of convicts could easily replace them, and because prisoners did not enjoy the modicums of autonomy over their time and whereabouts that bondpeople did, leasers did not provide them even the most modest comforts or pleasures for fear of rebellion. "If slave owners arguably had an economic interest in preserving the health of their slaves for their laboring power (much in the way a farmer would have an interest in maintaining his or her horses or team of oxen), the industrialist who leased convicts to work in a mine or to cut lumber had no such incentive. This led to widespread abuse."[35] This system generated major profits and its economic benefits are well documented. For example, by the end of the nineteenth century, 73 percent of Alabama's state revenue was generated from convict labor.

NEW FORMS OF PUNISHMENT

Although convict leasing originated in the North and had been in use since the 1820s, the introduction of the Black Codes was responsible for its tremendous expansion in the postbellum period. As revised versions of the Slave Codes, these were a series of state laws, most of which passed in the wake of Emancipation in 1865 and 1867, that placed severe legal restrictions on the rights of newly "freed" Black Americans. Economic devastation wrought by the Civil War and white racial anxiety in the South necessitated cheap or free labor that servitude provided and, relatedly, formal assurance that white domination over the social order would overcome the legal discontinuation of slavery. The Black Codes limited, and in some cases, outlawed free people's ability to buy and own property, conduct business, and simply occupy and traverse public spaces. Miscegenation remained illegal and the Mississippi Black Codes decreed that interracial marriage was a felony, punishable by life in prison.[36]

Vagrancy statutes, outlined in the Black Codes, resulted in the criminal punishment of African Americans for even the most benign "offenses," such as arguing, wandering, or even daydreaming in public. In Saidiya Hartman's words:

> In the south, vagrancy laws became a surrogate for slavery. In the north, vagrancy statutes were intended to compel the labor of the idle, and, more importantly, to control the propertyless, by denying them the right to subsist and elude the contract. Those without proof of employment were considered likely to commit or be involved in vice and crime. Vagrancy statutes provided the legal means to take ownership of free people after Emancipation. The origins of the workhouse and the house of correction can be traced to these efforts to force the recalcitrant to labor, to manage and regulate the ex-serf and ex-slave when lordship and bondage assumed a more indirect form.[37]

This new legal category was not only largely responsible for the repopulation of prisons with Black convicts, but also the postbellum racial order, replete with new forms of white supremacy that surfaced once white Southerners could no longer rely on the "peculiar institution."

In this sense, vagrancy illuminates the irreducibility of servitude to chattel slavery, and abolition to Emancipation. It exposes the continuities among forms of racial captivity and confinement, and the impossibility of using discrete binaries to differentiate formal states of subjection from freedom. In Hartman's words:

> While the legal transformation from slavery to freedom is most often narrated as the shift from status to race, from property to subject, from slave to Negro, vagrancy statutes make apparent the continuities and entanglements between a diverse range of unfree states—from slave to servant, from servant to vagrant, from domestic to prisoner, from idler to convict and felon. Involuntary servitude wasn't one condition—chattel slavery—nor was it fixed in time and place; rather, it was an ever-changing mode of exploitation, domination, accumulation (the severing of will, the theft of capacity, the appropriation of life), and confinement.[38]

Vagrancy troubles both linear narratives of "progress" that are so often inaccurately (and strategically) projected onto the history of race in the United States, and the ostensible separability of enslavement from imprisonment.

As Hartman notes, it de-exceptionalizes chattel and reveals its enduring effects in the aftermath of Emancipation.

As a vague legal category by design, vagrancy endowed law enforcement with expansive interpretive authority, working hand-in-hand with Jim Crow laws to simultaneously criminalize a host of social conditions and prevent African Americans from escaping them. The designation of unemployment as a criminal status created a state of Black dependency on low-wage work, while Jim Crow segregation barred them from pursuing more lucrative careers that would mean greater financial stability. Thus, African Americans were only eligible for a limited range of (low paying) jobs *and* subjected to severe punishment for failure to attain wage work. The Black Codes simultaneously produced and penalized joblessness, laying a linear path to incarceration. In addition, the statutes penalized African Americans for wholly fabricated crimes. Black women were routinely arrested and imprisoned for racialized infractions like profanity and suspicion of prostitution, with little or no evidence to support the allegations. Black men were regularly beaten and sentenced to prison time for baseless accusations of theft and intoxication.

Police routinely used the vagrancy charge in retaliation for even the most minor acts of insubordination, as well as refusal to submit to sexual and physical abuse. In sum, vagrancy was less a formal category of illegal acts than a criminal signifier used to exert control over Black lives and bodies. Hartman calls it "status criminality," defined, not by deviant, harmful deeds or behavior, but rather the racial category to which the accused belongs. This was enough to supply police with the interpretive lens through which to view criminal threats. Blackness, in this case, is the primary indicator of criminality. The idle Black body is loitering, not leisurely; the Black worker at rest is lazy, not seeking respite; Black assembly is a societal threat, not a social group. What is innocent, amusing, dismissible, justifiable, reasonable, or neutral for whites is deviant, dangerous, threatening, illegitimate, suspicious, and criminal in Black people. Hartman writes, "Antiblack racism fundamentally shaped the development of 'status criminality.' In turn, status criminality was tethered ineradicably to blackness."[39]

Vagrancy laws remained active until 1971, although convict leasing was steadily banned throughout the early decades of the twentieth century and terminated in all fifty states by 1939. The practice was swiftly replaced with "Chain Gangs" that ensured that the state, if not private companies, would continue to benefit from the free labor of prisoners. Haley's rich discussion of this history exposes how racial and gendered punishment in the South during the postbellum and "Progressive" eras had the dual effects of both resuscitating conditions of racial servitude after Emancipation and consolidating twentieth-century Jim Crow segregation. In 1908 the Georgia General Assembly ruled against convict leasing but passed legislation that essentially replaced the practice with chain gangs, a "reform" particularly consequential for Black women. Judges were given discretion to sentence convicts either to the chain gang or Milledgeville Georgia State Farm Prison to serve their sentences. Though race was not named explicitly, this legal move created a system of carceral racial segregation in which Black women were almost exclusively assigned to backbreaking chain gang labor, while white women completed their (often abbreviated and softer) sentences in confinement at Milledgeville.[40]

Also included in the laws was the advent of a new parole system that further fortified the apparatuses of captivity: while claiming to do away with the private punishment of convict leasing, parole essentially maintained the practice under different terminology. Once convicts were eligible for parole, white women were often permitted to rejoin their families and communities, while Black women were required to perform domestic service for white sponsors who compensated their charges at their own discretion. To borrow a term from C. Riley Snorton, "gender fungibility," to which Black women were subjected in slavery, neatly translated to criminal punishment. They benefited from none of the protective, conventional gender discourses of feminine fragility and vulnerability afforded to white women.[41] The malleability of Black women's gender identity exploited them across multiple domains: state refusal to recognize their womanhood required them to work alongside men in the chain gang, undergoing the grueling carceral labor from which white women were spared.[42] On the other hand, through contingent acknowledgment of their womanhood, they were subjected to forced domestic labor in white households. In *No Mercy Here: Gender, Punishment, and the Making of Jim Crow Modernity*, Haley calls this the "unbearable flexibility of nonbeing," meaning that the incoherent and contradictory gender identity foisted onto Black women enabled the state to extract maximum labor from them by alternately disavowing or affirming their womanhood.[43] Black women were thus positioned as ever-available for any type of labor, drawing on and reproducing discourses of their physical strength and hardened, noninnocent spirits.[44]

Just as vagrancy extended the terms of slavery beyond chattel, chain gang punishment, according to Haley, did the same. It drew on practices of slavery to lay the groundwork for both Jim Crow segregation and even modern ideologies of gender difference that endure in the present.[45] If slavery is definitive of the nineteenth century racial polity, and segregation the twentieth, criminal punishment of Black women in the early 1900s bridges the two: first, by forcing them into chain gang labor and domestic service parole, Black women were resituated in conditions closely resembling those of the field and "house slave," respectively; second, by making racial distinctions between Black and white women in sentencing, through the relegation of Black women to harsh punishment and white women to milder, rehabilitative corrections, the carceral system established the foundations for Jim Crow segregation that would prevail until 1965.[46]

By the early twentieth century, it became fairly clear that incarceration was no longer a marginal response to predominantly white crime, but rather a large-scale "solution" to the so-called modern "race question." Whether white supremacist (read: "what practices and institutions will ensure the continuation of white domination?") or race liberal ("how can Black Americans assimilate to the norms, traditions, and institutions of a nation previously bent on the denial of their rights?"), incarceration is the answer that cuts both ways. While perhaps predictable for anti-Black racists, it seems counterintuitive for race liberals: how could a carceral system that cages African Americans, curtails their freedom, and bars them from the most basic benefits of citizenship, square with the commitments of whites to their equal rights? Naomi Murakawa sheds light on this in her extraordinary book, *The First Civil Right: How Liberals Built Prison America*, detailing how the current prison system was constructed in parallel with the civil rights movement at its origins. In what Micol Seigel calls "a searing polemic against postwar American liberalism," Murakawa claims that the differentiation between respectable Black citizens, deserving of a full pallet of constitutional rights and privileges, and degenerate Black criminals entitled to none, was an organizing principle for white supporters of civil rights.[47] Such a reductive juxtaposition was the condition for both racial equality and rational, law-and-order responses to a so-called crime epidemic. Murakawa argues against popular narratives that desegregation and rising urban poverty resulted in an uptick in Black lawbreaking in the twentieth century, necessitating tough-on-crime policies and greater incarceration: "The United States did not face a crime problem that was racialized; it faced a race problem that was criminalized."[48]

It is not a matter of insignificance that expansions to the carceral state unfolded in parallel with the civil rights movement that was steadily increasing in momentum throughout the mid-twentieth century. Despite the use of nonviolent direct action, activists were regularly jailed for so-called crimes of disturbing the peace and insubordination. Between 1940 and 1960, the historical crescendo of civil rights activism, the prison population expanded nationwide by 36 percent.[49] Southern states, the epicenter of civil rights activity, showed far greater rates of increase than even the national average. In Virginia, the number of incarcerated people in state and federal prisons increased by 175 percent, and in North Carolina and South Carolina, by 175 percent and 258 percent respectively, during the same period.

Following the passage of the Civil Rights Act, the formal end of legal segregation, and the Voting Rights Act, landmark legislation abolishing poll taxes, literacy tests, and many other strategies of Black disenfranchisement and voter suppression, the preservation of the racial status quo relied, all the more strongly, on the carceral state. Increased underground state surveillance of Black individuals and groups, as well as new law-and-order legislation were the other sides of the coin of Black progress. Although Martin Luther King Jr. had been surveilled by the FBI since the 1956 Montgomery Bus Boycott, the Bureau stepped up its efforts in 1967 by turning the attentions of the Counterintelligence Program (COINTELPRO) to King's Southern Christian Leadership Conference, the Student Nonviolent Coordinating Committee (SNCC), and Black Power groups. Originally an FBI Cold War program, launched in 1956, COINTELPRO targeted, infiltrated, and internally disrupted organizations suspected of communist ties (later including the Black Liberation Army, of which Assata Shakur was affiliated, and Muhammad Ahmad's Revolutionary Action Movement).

Simultaneously, a new wave of mass incarceration was ushered in under the banners of "safe streets" and "crime control." Originating during the Johnson administration as a result of a confluence of factors, including desegregation, increased migration to cities, rising urban crime rates, and escalating political dissent from a growing anti-war movement, law-and-order legislation funded the militarization of police departments across the United States and rolled out new discretionary power for police. Title I of Johnson's 1968 Omnibus Crime Control and Safe Streets Act established LEAA (Law Enforcement Assistance Administration) to distribute federal money to state planning agencies in an effort to crack down on crime. The relationship of reciprocity between police and prisons mirrors the Black Codes and convict leasing: the more empowered the police, the higher the rates of incarceration. Nixon would later transform tough-on-crime discourse into a program of full-blown racial control, beginning with his infamous "southern strategy." This scheme to court Southern votes by playing to the racial anxieties of working-class whites mobilized the narrative of "the Black criminal." Racializing crime was both a means of reconstituting the white polity after the gains of civil rights and a cynical, opportunistic Republican ploy to wrest power from Southern Democrats.

2

Black Carceral Political Thought

"Believe me, my friend, with the time and incentive these brothers have to read, study, and think, you will find no class or category more aware, more embittered, desperate, or dedicated to the ultimate remedy—revolution. The most dedicated, the best of our kind—you'll find them in the Folsoms, San Quentins, the Soledads. They live like there is no tomorrow, and for most of them, there isn't."

—GEORGE JACKSON[1]

The historical connections between plantations and prisons are best known to Black incarcerated authors themselves and appear regularly in their writings, for resistance is their political inheritance. Drawing on Berger's work, which focuses on Black prison activism in the 1970s, and Afro-Modern political theory, named as such by Robert Gooding-Williams, here I look to the archive of prisoner writings during the rise of the Black Power Movement, focusing in particular on Muhammed Ahmad, Angela Davis, George Jackson, Ruchell Magee, and Assata Shakur.[2] Their work comprises a broader genre of political theory that I term "Black carceral political thought," which lives in widely-circulated autobiographies, unpublished pamphlets, fugitive prison newspapers, collections of poetry, underground hand-drawn fliers and more. The category is defined by explicit acknowledgment and analysis of the relations between the plantation and prison and, of course, resistance to both.

These authors conceive of their own political activities and convictions by appealing to discourses of "flight" and "fugitivity"; referring to themselves and their comrades as "rebellious slaves"; and shifting seamlessly between the terms "plantations" and "prisons." Thus, I do not pretend to advance a *new* argument here, but rather amplify one that is at least partially concealed behind the walls of its birthplace. Prisons are extensions of slavery, but resistance, not labor, best describes the continuities between them.

THE EMERGENCE OF BLACK CARCERAL POLITICAL THOUGHT

The origins of Black carceral political thought can only be properly understood in context of the rise of the Black Power Movement in the late 1960s, for thousands of its members were incarcerated at any given time. It is uncoincidental that every one of the aforementioned authors spotlighted in this chapter is, in some way, connected to the Movement, from Assata Shakur's leadership in the Black Liberation Army to Muhammed Ahmad's ties to the Revolutionary Action Movement (RAM). Black Power emerged in the wake of the passage of the Civil Rights and Voting Rights Acts, the ever-growing student anti-war movement, and deepening divides between the more radical and moderate wings of the long civil rights movement. Though named by Kwame Ture (formerly Stokely Carmichael) in a June 1966 speech, Black Power is a vast and diffuse movement associated with a wide network of groups and organizations.[3] Their members were regularly imprisoned for subversive or illegal activities and, in turn, prisoners without prior political convictions strongly identified with the movement and awakened to politics while incarcerated.[4]

The increased captivity of Black Power activists and subsequently greater radicalism within the general prison population contributed to the birth of Black carceral political thought. Also key were President Johnson's Great Society initiatives that allocated generous federal funding for prison education and provoked an explosion of carceral print culture. Prisoners wrote prolifically and created their own newspapers, periodicals, and anthologies of prose and poetry, which were widely circulated both inside and outside prison walls. They sharpen the political sensibilities of their readers; give rise to acts of resistance; animate prison memoir as a literary form; and awaken the public to the grim realities of captivity.

Consolidating the writings of this period into a genre is useful, for prison writing like any other literary form, according to Simon Rolston, adheres to certain literary conventions and common tropes. For example, the "badman," whose crimes are motivated by broad systemic critiques of capitalism and racism surfaces in Malcolm X, George Jackson, and Eldridge Cleaver's autobiographies.[5] H. Bruce Franklin observes that, due to the institutionalized opacity and secrecy of prison, literature produced by its inhabitants is "intrinsically subversive, revealing what is supposed to be concealed and what is often unimaginable."[6] The content of Black carceral political thought is rich and diverse, spanning subjects from Black leadership and decolonization, to anti-imperialist critiques of the Vietnam War. Here, I attend primarily to the authors' mobilization of chattel slavery and slave rebellion, which are definitive of the genre and supportive of my earlier claim that enslaved and imprisoned people have in common resistance rather than labor.

In Davis's words:

> Nat Turner and John Brown were political prisoners in their time. The acts for which they were charged and subsequently hanged, were the practical extensions of their profound commitment to the abolition of slavery. They fearlessly bore the responsibility for their actions. The significance of their executions and the accompanying widespread repression did not lie so much in the fact that they were being punished for specific crimes, nor even in the effort to use their punishment as an implicit threat to deter others from similar armed acts of resistance. These executions and the surrounding repression of slaves were intended to terrorize the anti-slavery movement in general; to discourage and diminish both legal and illegal forms of abolitionist activity. As usual, the effect of repression was miscalculated and, in both instances, anti-slavery activity was accelerated and intensified as a result.[7]

Indeed, identifying affinities between insurgent acts of bondpeople and prisoners, as Davis does here, is the hallmark of Black carceral political thought, distinguishing it from the larger field of African American political theory. Berger echoes this as well: "The 1970s witnessed a new historiography of slave politics that emphasized slave agency on the plantation and began a fuller accounting of slave resistance."[8] Knitting together past and present forms of captivity situates prison rebellion in a centuries-long freedom struggle, upending narratives that carceral resistance is criminal and self-interested.

The idea that the modern penal system is meant to replicate conditions of bondage following the formal termination of chattel slavery is a material, historical fact, reflected clearly in the writings of prisoners. They recognize that slavery and incarceration are forced migrations; institutions of coercion, captivity, and confinement; and systems aspiring to total domination. They share the view that "the prison coexisted with the plantation and incorporated a certain plantation logic in becoming a site of racial discipline."[9] If slavery is, as Berger suggests, "a foundational metaphor for black intellectual life," its consistent invocation in prison writing underscores the centrality of Blackness to carceral captivity.[10] Describing both institutions as long-standing regimes of racial domination disrupts assumptions that prisons are race neutral, lawful systems of crime control, and reorients readers to view them as extensions of plantations.

While most moderates and race liberals conceded the evils of slavery by the mid-twentieth century, prisons grew steadily during the same period and were rarely questioned in mainstream public life. Black carceral political thought aims to address this dissonance, for its authors' accounts of the linkages between chattel and carceral captivity are interventions into pervasive popular discourses that utter, in the same breath, the wrongs of slavery and the necessity of prisons. "Challenging the apathy that, according to these dissident prisoners, allowed chattel and carceral slavery to continue" motivates this effort.[11] Thus at work in this half-buried genre is a simultaneity of intellectual insight and political strategy: prison authors showcase the sophistication and radicalism of their perspectives on captivity; the global terms through which they view their struggle; and their interest in unsettling prevailing assumptions about criminal "justice."

The authorship of Black carceral political theory is vast and includes far more authors than I discuss here, many of whom wrote anonymously for fear of reprisal. It should go without saying that the genre is in no way reducible to the authors on which I focus in this chapter. Indeed, there are likely hundreds more, some renowned—such as Eldridge Cleaver, Ericka Huggins, Etheridge Knight, and Huey P. Newton—and many known only to their communities. I look to the work of Muhammed Ahmad, Angela Davis, George Jackson, Ruchell Magee, and Assata Shakur because they are all contemporaries in the Black Power Movement whose work best exemplifies the features differentiating Black carceral political thought from related theoretical traditions.

The authors are diverse in their backgrounds and perspectives, and marked by some clear divides—intellectual, political, and demographic. Their experiences of incarceration vary considerably, as some, such as Jackson and Magee, lived their entire adult lives in prison, whereas Davis and Ahmad endured only short stints. Some had personal relationships with one another: Davis and Jackson, for example, had a known, long-distance love affair, detailed in their correspondence. Some, like Shakur and Davis, reflected in writing on the carceral system most extensively only after leaving prison, while others, like Jackson, wrote prolifically while incarcerated. Their mobilization of chattel slavery, in general, and slave rebellion, in particular, is one of the key common threads among them. Slavery is far more than metaphorical for these authors: it is a historical window into their own captivity. Blurring the lines between the two different institutions, as they regularly do, is one of the more common rhetorical moves of authors in this genre, an intentional slippage that urges readers to grasp their continuities.

BLACK CARCERAL POLITICAL THEORISTS ON SLAVERY

It was learning for the first time about slave resistance that initially awakened Assata Shakur's interest in politics. After enrolling at Manhattan Community College, she joined the Black student organization, the Golden Drums, where she became versed in Black politics and culture beyond the lessons of white-washed, depoliticized high school curricula. That she had never heard of Nat Turner, or really any form of slave rebellion beyond the Underground Railroad, was initially shocking to her.[12] Shakur's newfound knowledge of this subject was pivotal and transformative for her political sensibilities. That her true education began with slave resistance and sparked her deep commitment to liberation perhaps foreshadowed her future as an activist and author:

> The subject of one of the many lectures scheduled by the Drums was about a slave who had plotted and planned and fought for his freedom. Right here in amerika. Until then, my only knowledge of the history of Africans in amerika was about George Washington Carver making experiments with peanuts and about the Underground Railroad. Harriet Tubman had always been my heroine, and she had symbolized everything that was Black resistance to me. But it had never occurred to me that hundreds of Black people had got together to fight for their freedom. The day I found out about Nat Turner, I was affected so strongly it was physical. I was so souped up on adrenalin i could barely contain myself. I tore through every book my mother had. Nowhere could i find the name Nat

Turner. I had grown up believing slaves hadn't fought back. I remember feeling ashamed when they talked about slavery in school. The teachers made it seem that Black people had nothing to do with the official "emancipation" from slavery. White people had freed us."[13]

Shakur's activism began during these early years of her college life. She first joined the Black Panther Party, working at its Oakland headquarters, before eventually returning to New York to lead its Harlem chapter. Soon after, she became an active member of the Black Liberation Army (BLA), a loose affiliate of the Panthers that engaged in open, armed struggle against the US government through strategies such as robbing banks and killing police officers. Shakur was charged with numerous crimes between 1971 and 1973, some of which she perpetrated and others the result of erroneous accusations. She was eventually arrested in connection with the murder of the state trooper Werner Foerster during a confrontation on the New Jersey Turnpike in 1973 and subsequently sentenced to life in prison. Shakur was held in solitary confinement for lengthy periods and transferred multiple times to different prisons before she was moved to the Clinton Correctional Facility for Women in New Jersey. With the help of BLA operatives, she escaped prison on November 2, 1979. Shakur fled to Cuba, where she continues to live today, despite continued calls for her extradition to the United States.

Her identification with slavery and slave resistance has been consistent throughout her life and work. While these subjects initially incited her to action as a young student, Shakur continues to frame her own and other Black political experiences, in relation to slavery. Even after her exile in Cuba, a society that is *not* organized around systemic, anti-Black racism, she remains sharply aware of the conditions of Black Americans and their enduring captivity. In her words, "Every day out in the street now, i remind myself that Black people in amerika are oppressed. It's necessary that I do that. People get used to anything. The less you think about your oppression, the more your tolerance for it grows. After a while, people just think oppression is the normal state of things. But to become free, you have to be acutely aware of being a slave."[14] Such themes echo elsewhere in her writings, as well. In 1987, Shakur published a poem about slave resistance, aptly titled "Tradition." The poem plays on location, both physical and temporal, beginning in chattel slavery and ending in prison. Throughout the entirety of the piece, slave resistance is the central motif of political action, for Shakur holds that rebellion is constitutive of the Black tradition itself:

> We hid in the bush
> when the slavemasters came holding spears.
> And when the moment was ripe,
> leaped out and lanced the lifeblood
> of would-be masters.
> We carried it on.
>
> On slave ships,
> hurling ourselves into oceans.
> Slitting the throats of our captors.
> We took their whips.
> And their ships.
> Blood flowed in the Atlantic—
> and it wasn't all ours.
>
> We carried it on.
>
> Fed Missy arsenic apple pies
> Stole axes from the shed.
> Went and chopped off master's head.
>
> We ran. We fought.
> We organized a railroad.
> An underground.
>
> We carried it on.
>
> In newspapers. In meetings.
> In arguments and streetfights.
> We carried it on.
>
> In tales told to children.
> In chants and cantatas.
> In poems and blues songs
> and saxophone screams,
> We carried it on.
>
> In classrooms. In churches.
> In courtrooms. In prisons.
> We carried it on.[15]

That captive rebellion so pervasive throughout her prose is reflective of its significance to Black liberation. The interplay between Shakur's own subjecthood and broader racial conditions is not only visible in her writings, but also in the genre of Black carceral political thought in general. The same flexible movement between self and society surfaces in Jackson's letters and Davis's autobiography as well. Following her successful prison break, Shakur drew on discourses of marronage and fugitivity to describe her condition: "My name is Assata Shakur, and I am a 20th century escaped slave. Because of government persecution, I was left with no other choice than to flee from the political repression, racism and violence that dominate the U.S. government's policy towards people of color." Framing her struggle in terms of slave fugitivity lends legitimacy to her illegal flight, enabling her readers to situate her actions in a lengthy tradition of Black resistance to captivity.[16]

Similarly overt references to slave fugitivity surface in Angela Davis's work. In August 1970, she fled the state of California following a warrant for her arrest in connection with the storming of the Marin County Courthouse. Jonathan Jackson, the brother of George Jackson, occupied the building at gunpoint, along with three accomplices, including Ruchell Magee. They took several hostages, the judge and two jurors, and demanded the immediate release of the Soledad Brothers (George Jackson, Fleeta Drumgo, and John Cluchette) from prison. The gun that was used in the assault was allegedly purchased in Davis's name, thereby resulting in charges of first-degree murder under the California Penal Code. She successfully evaded capture for two months, hiding in the homes of different friends until she was found in New York and subsequently incarcerated at the Marin County jail in San Rafael, California for eighteen months.[17] Her story inspired a massive, global campaign for her release, occurring in June 1972, when she was acquitted on all charges.

Davis did not write very much during this period, with the exception of one article, "The Black Woman's Role in the Community of Slaves," which would later be published in the *Massachusetts Review*.[18] There she acknowledges that resistance was at the center of Black women's experiences of slavery: "If resistance was an organic ingredient of slave life, it had to be directly nurtured by the social organization which the slaves themselves improvised. The consciousness of their oppression, the conscious thrust toward its abolition could not have been sustained without impetus from the community they pulled together through the sheer force of their own strength."[19] It is no coincidence that both slavery and slave rebellion are the subjects of her only substantive prison writing. Months after the incident at the Marin County Courthouse, she gave a telling interview with Malcolm X's publication, *Muhammed Speaks*. When her interviewer intimated that her flight from California could be easily interpreted as incriminating evidence of her guilt, she responded as follows: "Let me ask this question. When a slave, who managed to escape from the whips and wheels of the white slave master, fled to another state, was this evidence of his guilt?"[20] Like Shakur, Davis's own experience of imprisonment is indelibly tied to chattel captivity, perhaps inspiring her later abolitionist political thought and activism. Full dismantlement of the prison industrial complex is, today, the centerpiece of Davis's oeuvre. It is in this spirit that she draws on discourses of slavery. The likenesses between plantations and prisons expose the ways in which the carceral state makes use of its historical predecessor, thereby establishing the case for its abolition.

In Davis's words, "one might say that the institution of slavery served as a receptacle for those forms of punishment considered to be too uncivilized to be inflicted on white citizens within a democratic society. With the abolition of slavery this clearly racialized form of punishment became deracialized and persists today under the guise of colorblind justice."[21] Of concern to Davis is how the legacies of slavery produce subjects uniquely vulnerable to incarceration. She pushes back against the tempting narrative that if Black people are more heavily incarcerated than whites, it is simply an extension of the fact that they committed more crimes. Of course, this assumption is complicated by the causal relation between individual choices and deficits in resources, which is to say that people from underserved communities without access to quality public education, services, and employment are significantly more likely to tend toward criminal behavior. In addition, taking a long view of the exclusion of Black Americans from opportunity structures under Jim Crow, such as education, lucrative careers, and FHA-backed mortgages in the mid-twentieth century, reveals the relation between such racial discrimination and the prison boom. She holds that "there is a direct connection (of prisons) with slavery: when slavery was abolished, black people were set free but they lacked access to the material resources that would enable them to fashion new, free lives. Prisons have thrived over the last century precisely because of the absence of those resources and the persistence of some of the deep structures of slavery."[22]

Of all the authors discussed here, Davis has been the most prolific and the only one with a career in academia, although she also remains an organizer and activist. That she is the most renowned author within the genre of Black carceral political thought is attributable to her prolific scholarship. Davis's areas of expertise are vast and diverse, mostly oriented toward themes of race and gender and also including the interconnections between the Black and Palestinian liberation struggles; abolition feminism; critiques of capitalism; and, especially, the prison industrial complex. Davis, along with other activists and academics, founded the prison abolitionist organization Critical Resistance in 1997, following a conference on alternatives to incarceration. Centering on the lived experiences of currently and formerly incarcerated people, Critical Resistance works at the intersection of activism and academia to disempower and dismantle the prison system. Davis's scholarship is aligned with this mission, especially her books *Are Prisons Obsolete? Abolition Democracy*, the title of which is drawn from W.E.B. Du Bois's *Black Reconstruction,* and most recently her co-authored text, *Abolition. Feminism. Now.*[23]

Intersectional analysis has been the guiding approach in her work, even years before the term "intersectionality" was coined. Davis explored the racial exclusions of early women's rights movements and the socioeconomic elitism of white feminism in her seminal text, *Women, Race, and Class.*[24] Although an active member of the Communist Party, she does not equivocate about her most salient identities. When asked by her interviewer from *Muhammed Speaks* why she is a communist, she answered: "Before anything else, I am a Black woman. I dedicated my life to the struggle for the liberation of Black people—my enslaved, imprisoned people."[25]

It is worth noting that Davis is personally and politically connected, with varying degrees of depth, to most of the authors of Black carceral political thought noted here. She was involved in multiple campaigns dedicated to Shakur's release from prison and wrote the foreword to her autobiography. Due to their mutual involvement in the Marin County Courthouse ambush, Davis also corresponded with Ruchell Magee, whose writings she included in her edited volume *If They Come in the Morning*.[26] Finally, as I indicated earlier, her intimate relationship with George Jackson, well documented in *Soledad Brother*, is partly responsible for his influence and wide readership.[27] In the opening remarks of her aforementioned essay on Black women in slavery, Davis wrote:

> I would like to dedicate these reflections to one of the most admirable black leaders to emerge from the ranks of our liberation movement—to George Jackson, whom I loved and respected in every way. As I came to

know and love him, I saw him developing an acute sensitivity to the real problems facing black women and thus refining his ability to distinguish these from their mythical transpositions. George was uniquely aware of the need to extricate himself and other black men from the remnants of divisive and destructive myths purporting to represent the black woman.[28]

Davis's devotion to Jackson was evident across her writings, including both her letters to him and reflections on his death. She mourns her loss: "For me, George's death has meant the loss of a comrade and revolutionary leader, but also the loss of an irretrievable love. This love is so agonizingly personal as to be indescribable. I can only say that in continuing to love him, I will try my best to express that love in the way he would have wanted—by reaffirming my determination to fight for the cause George died defending. With his example before me, my tears and grief are rage at the system responsible for his murder."[29]

To say that the life and death of George Jackson were equally significant for Black carceral political thought presupposes a dichotomy between life and death that Jackson notes is blurred in carceral settings. Orlando Patterson's category of "social death" is perhaps a term better befitting the conditions of carceral captivity. Thematically speaking, death is a consistent, although incoherent, motif in his work: its conceptual ambiguity in captivity is incomparable to noncarceral conditions. At times, Jackson seems to be awaiting and embracing death, while at other moments, disavowing it. Such fluctuations seem contradictory only if life and death exist in a settled binary, which Jackson invites his readers to reconsider. The liminal space, which is, strictly speaking, neither life nor death but somewhere in between, characterizes the experience of "doing time." Prisoners, Jackson suggests, await either state execution, expiration of life or sentence, or state execution on death row. He does not only anticipate his own death, but also the power that he will continue to claim following it: "Hurl me into the next existence, the descent into hell won't turn me. I'll crawl back to dog his trail forever. They won't defeat my revenge, never, never. I'm part of a righteous people who anger slowly, but rage undamned. We'll gather at his door in such a number that the rumbling of our feet will make the earth tremble."[30] These are prescient statements, for, if anything, Jackson's death only further consolidated his power and authority, directly inciting the Attica prison uprising and a global explosion of prison activism and organizing.

Jackson was killed on August 21, 1971, by a guard at San Quentin in an alleged standoff, although the details of this remain hotly contested. He was immortalized as a fallen leader, his death galvanizing Black activists, imprisoned and nonincarcerated alike over the following decades. Prison newspapers, popular periodicals, and the Black Panther Intercommunal News Service paid tribute to Jackson by dedicating entire issues to his life and work. Speculation about the questionable circumstances of his death; praise for his selfless leadership, intellectual acumen, and political ferocity; and excerpts from his prose were all featured in these publications. Erik Che Young, an incarcerated author, claimed in 1971 that the Soledad Brothers were doomed by their radicalism, for they "were branded as militant agitators. In other words, they had refused to compromise and conform to the submission of prison slavery."[31] In response to a question about the circumstances of Jackson's death, James Baldwin tellingly replied that "no black person will ever believe George Jackson died the way they say he did." When pressed on whether he believed the murder was ordered by an officer or agent within San Quentin, he responded as follows: "It was dictated by a system. It was a system that made his death inevitable. He was a bad nigger. A bad example to other slaves."[32]

Jackson spent the majority of his life, from 1941 to 1971, behind bars for crimes ranging from petty theft and assault to the murder of a prison guard at Soledad State Prison. Originally given the indeterminate sentence of one year to life in prison, the parole board never ruled in his favor. Jackson understood that captivity is the modus operandi of US racial polity and, despite this (or perhaps because of it), his lengthy prison sentence did not hinder his activism. Along with his friend, W.L. Nolen, later killed by a watchtower guard, Jackson founded the Black Guerilla Family, a revolutionary group committed to overthrowing capitalism, as well as the US government. He read avidly and became well educated in American history and the political thought of Marx, Engels, Lenin, Trotsky, and Mao. A posthumous search of his cell recovered ninety-nine books, mostly works of revolutionary theory. His political radicalism, refusal to capitulate to the disciplinary norms of prison, and intellectual acuity made him an easy target for the draconian punishments of corrections officers. Predictably, Jackson was deemed a threat to the general prison population and spent long periods of his sentences in solitary confinement.

Throughout his short adult life, Jackson wrote prolifically on subjects including Black politics; police brutality and violence; structural racism in society; racial stratifications within prison; and incarcerated activists in the Black Power Movement. In his renowned book, *Blood in My Eye*, which he completed less than a week before his murder, Jackson's stature as a brilliant revolutionary theorist, with a global view of imperialism, fascism, and class war, was secured. Similar to Frantz Fanon's *Wretched of the Earth*, the book maps Jackson's theory of revolution, the only possible response to global racism, capitalism, and colonialism.[33] Unlike Jackson's first book, *Soledad Brother*, a compilation of letters, *Blood in My Eye* is a genre-bending hybrid of manifesto, memoir, letters, and essays that weave in and out of Jackson's personal story, including the death of his brother, Jonathan, and a sharp political and social critique of racial capitalism.[34]

Like other authors associated with the genre of Black carceral political thought, such as Shakur, Jackson's writing is peppered with intentional slippage between slavery and incarceration. "Blacks are still doing the work of the greatest slave state in history. The terms of our servitude are all that have been altered."[35] For Jackson, slavery is a historical fact, no less relevant to the present than the antebellum period. Just as scholars of racial politics today take note of the lineage of prisons in slavery, the same is observable in Jackson's writing. In a letter to his father, Jackson says, "Robert, can you see how absurd you sound to me when you speak on 'the good life,' or something about being a free adult? I know you have never been free. I know that few blacks over here have ever been free. The forms of slavery merely changed at the signing of the Emancipation Proclamation from chattel slavery to economic slavery. If you could see and talk to some of the blacks I meet in here you would immediately understand what I mean, and see I'm right."[36] Here and elsewhere, Jackson attempts to enlighten his father to his own subjugation by drawing on the capitalist underpinnings of both chattel slavery and Black poverty in the twentieth century.

Captivity is, for Jackson, both metaphor and material reality, the hallmark of Black life in the United States. He maintains that African Americans are born into a symbolic cage and thus, it is only a matter of time before they enter the formal confinement of prison. As Davis puts it, "His book reveals the indivisible nature of the struggle on the outside of the prison system with the one inside."[37] An ongoing shift between resignation and anguish is visible throughout his discussions of the inevitability of incarceration. On the one hand, Jackson holds that the US racial polity has primed him for prison since birth. On the other hand, nothing could have prepared him for the psychic torture of carceral captivity.

In a letter that Jackson penned to the editor of *Soledad Brother*, he claims that it is a foregone conclusion that Black men will become entangled in the prison system: "Blackmen born in the US and fortunate enough to live past the age of eighteen are conditioned to accept the inevitability of prison."[38] That adjustment to near total domination is, for Black men, a relatively seamless transition, speaks to their prior experiences of nonincarcerated captivity and the myriad ways in which the state readies them for life behind bars. This is the centerpiece of Jackson's critique of the United States. In his words, "being born a slave in a captive society and never experiencing any objective basis for expectation had the effect of preparing me for the progressively traumatic misfortunes that lead so many blackmen to the prison gate. I was prepared for prison. It required only minor psychic adjustments."[39] Elsewhere, Jackson's view of acclimation to prison shifts considerably, as he describes the shock and psychological horrors of his initial days "on the inside": "The very first time, it was like dying. Just to exist at all in the cage calls for some heavy psychic readjustments. Being captured was the first of my fears. It may have been inborn. It may have been an acquired characteristic built up over the centuries of black bondage."[40] The fluctuations between flat resignation and genuine anguish parallel the similarly ambiguous, allegorical position of slavery in Jackson's work. Both the chattel and carceral spheres are, at once, daily ways of life and exceptional nightmares. This duality that cuts across the temporal divide of plantations and prisons is at the center of Jackson's analysis and is perhaps uniquely definitive of captivity. The simultaneity of horror and resignation observable in his work, is an affective performance of his critique: the cavalier tone that Jackson takes toward Black confinement matches the timeless embeddedness of captivity in the racial landscape of the United States, while his suffering is part of a broader politics of refusal to accept it.

If Jackson foregrounds in his work Black captivity in general, Ruchell Magee, more so than the aforementioned authors of Black carceral political thought, is most explicit on the synonymy of the chattel and carceral spheres. In a letter to Davis, shortly after the courthouse ambush and his subsequent life sentence, Magee, who narrowly survived the shoot-out, states the following: "I can and I will prove that I had a right (a human right) to rebel against slavery after receiving 7 years of flagrant racist courts, insults, and denials. I can and will prove the conspiracy that exists from the US Supreme Court, President Nixon (on down) to the prison guards in this case."[41] Here and elsewhere, flight from and resistance to slavery are principle themes in

Magee's work. His polemics exemplify the view that it is rebellion, not labor, which brings together the lived experiences of bondpeople and prisoners.[42]

Magee wrote regularly about the ambush, his style and content matching his political convictions: "Ruchell, having no other recourse, rebelled slavery attempting to reach the people to expose his flagrant racist slave case."[43] In June 1971, when he stood trial for his role in the attack, he demanded a court hearing on the "illegal slavery" to which he had been subjected in prison. He favors the use of the third person, a stylistic move that generalizes his experience to other incarcerated Black men: "In truth, Ruchell Magee represents the average black man who has been the victim of one racist assault after another upon his person, his manhood, his legal and human rights. Ruchell is a symbol of revolt against a decadent society that systematically incarcerates poor, oppressed, non-white peoples in the 'slave camps' of America."[44]

While certainly a lesser-known figure than the aforementioned three, Magee's political and intellectual contributions are rich and significant. Unique to his work is his challenge to the temporality of slavery, and the narrative that it is a bounded, time-limited institution. For Magee, slavery is neither a mere metaphor to be mobilized, nor the foundation of the carceral state. Much like Shakur, he not only situates his own resistance in the historical tradition of slave uprising, but also the relationship he draws between incarcerated Black men and enslaved bondmen is literal, not allegorical. This is a notable departure, even from other authors who take note of the continuities between the two institutions: it is not that prison is an inheritance of slavery, or that prison bears likeness to slavery, but rather the prison *is* slavery. He advances this view by self-identifying as a "rebel slave," even taking the name "Cinque" as an homage to the West African leader of a slave revolt aboard the Spanish ship *La Amistad*.[45] Conflating slavery and incarceration is, for Magee, an intellectual argument, a political conviction, and a legal strategy. Together they amount to his life's work of revealing the inherent racism of chattel and carceral captivity. In Magee's words, "My fight is to expose the entire system, judicial and prison system, as a system of slavery . . . This will cause benefit not just to myself but to all those who at this time are being criminally oppressed or enslaved by this system." His perspective echoes Berger's view that Black prison organizers thought of themselves as "rebellious slaves" and viewed prison as an "extension of slavery." They were committed to the abolition of prison as an "institution and an idea."[46] Magee's writing repeatedly attests to this: "slavery 400 years ago or slavery today—it's the same, but with a new name."

Although often buried in incriminating media narratives and lost in the shadows of more renowned thinkers, Magee's writing showcases historically nuanced and politically astute critiques of incarceration. In an essay he coauthored with a fellow prisoner Meharibi Muntu titled "The Barbarian Conspirators—Judges Contz, Christian, and Colvin," Magee identifies the ways in which chattel conditions were repurposed to accommodate both white supremacy and the legal demands of the post-Emancipation era and beyond, or what Hartman terms the "afterlives" of slavery. Here Magee identifies, point-to-point, the parallels between practices of explicit violence and domination, and their concealment and codification in sanitized legalese:

> White skin was the paragon; black skin the disgrace. To inculcate this disgrace to both blacks and whites, the sanctimonious demagogues declared that blacks were the chattel of whites and had no rights. After a series of slave revolts, the great farce entitled the Emancipation Proclamation was presented and/or acclaimed to free Blacks, but was actually an exchange of chattel slavery for economical slavery. However, these so-called former slave masters, enacted some laws called "The Black Codes," which merely represented the reduction to legal phraseology the atrocities of the institution of slavery. A slave had no standing in the courts. He could not be a party to a suit at law; he could not offer testimony except against another slave; he could make no contact . . . The courts are the toll of the political structure. The physical hang-to-a-tree lynch has been replaced by legal lynching, to the gas chamber. The prohibition of a slave to offer testimony against the slave master is the modern day gag rule. And the slave's proscription against striking white folks is the contemporary ban on filing civil suits against them. The killing of a slave, no matter how atrocious, if committed by a member of the neo-slavemaster Ku Klux Clan clique, goes unpunished and as in the case of Ruchell is shrouded around legal niceties under the veil of justice.[47]

Like Hartman's analysis of vagrancy, Magee subverts the distinctions between these forms of captivity. Against the deceptive narrative that there are meaningful differences between the violence of lynch mobs and the parody of justice meted out by kangaroo courts, Magee collapses them together to articulate a coherent account of anti-Black racism. Like the arguments of Muhammed Ahmad (formerly Maxwell Stanford) to which this discussion will soon turn, Magee holds that Black captives owe absolutely nothing to state: "Slaves have every right to revolt in any and every conceivable manner—and as always in the history of this country, slaves have revolted against intolerable conditions that time has come to show the rest of us that we have a vested interest in the conclusions of each and every one of these insurrections that are vented against the oppressors, the warmongers, profiteers, and the overseers of finance and capital, and should out of necessity cement our desire and commitment to the struggle of freedom for all of us against this enemy that is common to us all . . ."[48] Magee's radicalism is on display here. Not only does slavery persist after so-called Emancipation, but revolting against conditions of domination and oppression is the right and responsibility of all bondpeople in the present.

Just as Magee holds that Black Americans have never received any of the benefits of citizenship and, thus, should harbor no particular allegiance to the United States, Muhammed Ahmad also argues that the original moral crime of the transatlantic slave trade nullifies any claim that Africans in the United States are politically obligated to the state and its laws. Although lines of critique surface across the works of authors of Black carceral political thought, they are particularly apparent in his work.[49] Ahmad, a Black nationalist militant and academic, has been engaged in radical politics since his college years in the early 1960s, and worked closely with such prominent revolutionary leaders as Malcolm X (of whom he was a protégé), Jesse Gray, Imamu Amiri Baraka, Kwame Ture, Rap Brown, and Robert Williams. Ahmad experienced mere brushes with the carceral system, compared to other authors discussed here. Yet he was imprisoned several times; in 1967 he served a ten-month sentence without a trial, and experienced repeated assault and harassment by corrections officers: "As a result of defending himself as a man, another charge was added on to the Swiss cheese charges of conspiracy to commit anarchy for which he was originally arrested in the world-famous 1967 'RAM assassination plot.'" Several years later, Ahmad was briefly imprisoned after an arrest in San Diego during a conference of the African People's Congress in September 1972.

In 1963, he founded the Revolutionary Action Movement (RAM), which brought together philosophies of Black nationalism, Marxism-Leninism, and Third World internationalism. The mission of RAM drew largely from Maoist principles, preceding other Black nationalist organizations such as the Black Panther Party and the League of Revolutionary Black Workers that would later do the same.[50] RAM was one of the first Black radical organizations to succumb to the sabotaging schemes of the FBI's COINTELPRO, for it folded in 1968 and has been largely forgotten. Yet Ahmad remains politically active; he is an ardent and vociferous advocate of reparations, linking them with Black Power principles of self-determination.[51] He also organized the third Black Power conference in 1968, even as RAM was crumbling; supported the Black Liberation Army under Assata Shakur; assisted in the creation of the African Liberation Support Committee, a Pan-African organization; and founded the nationalist African People's Party in the early 1970s.

While he flies under the radar of mainstream, academic political theory, Ahmad is a prolific author and theorist of anti-capitalist resistance and Pan-Africanism, both of which are consistent themes in his writing and political work: "The main characteristics of Pan-African parties is their goal: to replace capitalism with communalism. Pan-Africanists are in the forefront of African people's struggle for power because they believe that for revolutionary change of capitalist society, African people must seize political power and establish a democratic centralized government controlled by us."[52] Ahmad also writes extensively on student activism, underscoring the importance of education to the Black freedom struggle, once suggesting that schools should become the sites of Black nationalist training centers.[53]

Of the small group of authors addressed here, Ahmad's castigation of anti-Black racism in the United States is most suffused with broad internationalist critiques of colonialism: "The system of racism has produced a phenomenon never before seen in the world's history. This is particularly true of the African held captive within America. The African captive was torn from his homeland, loved ones, family, and thru the process of colonialism had his heritage, language, and religion stripped of him. So racism and colonialism is not just an economic and political system but also a psychological and cultural system."[54] Even though prison operates in Ahmad's writing as more of an allegory than material reality, he nonetheless maintains a harsh critique of the carceral state, claiming that the purpose of prisons is to "contain and break the will of rebellious African captives."[55] Like Jackson, whose work confounds the binaries of slavery and emancipation, life and deaths, and prison and freedom, Ahmad also believes that the reach of imprisonment extends well beyond the physical walls of the prison. Black Americans, says Ahmad, are born into confinement through the original forced migration of Middle Passage and currently held against their wills, through inferior civic standing.

Ahmad states, "The black prisoner is the captured captive within the captive nation and is treated as the worst of a class of people in the whole

Amerikan empire."⁵⁶ His intentional blurring of the categories of physical incarceration and nonincarceration surface in a 1972 essay, aptly titled "We are All Prisoners of War," where he argues that captivity is shared in common among every Black person in America: "After the signing of the Emancipation Proclamation, which supposedly made us freedmen, a vote was never taken to see whether we wanted to be citizens of the kidnapper government, return to our motherland or whether we wanted land right here. So, the so-called citizenship that we are supposed to have, but don't enjoy, is a forced citizenship and is therefore ill-legal, making our status colonial subjects held in captivity. Every African person in America is therefore in prison."⁵⁷

Both bondage and a strange form of freedom characterize the resulting condition: on the one hand, the very presence of Black Americans in the United States is the result of abduction and human trafficking, rather than consent and natural rights. On the other hand, as prisoners of war, they decidedly exist outside of the social contract and should not harbor a sense of duty to adhere to it: "We are forced to abide by the responsibilities of citizenship but are denied the equal rights of citizens. So, our status has changed from chattel slavery to citizen slavery."⁵⁸ Here and elsewhere, the connections that Ahmad draws between chattel and carceral captivity center on the hypocritical expectations that Black Americans abide by the law, even as they are denied its privileges and protections. It follows that their formal prison sentences are also invalid, thus opening up possibilities for resistance. If Magee synonymizes the rebellious acts of bondpeople and prisoners, Ahmad picks up on this with his claim that Africans in the United States are captives with no formal or informal allegiance to the state. The revolutionary potential of this cannot be overstated.

CONCLUDING THOUGHTS

In November 1970, an anonymous Black prisoner, living in solitary confinement, published a short article titled "Life in 4A—The Hole." He describes his desire to participate in the "pronounced insurrection" reverberating across the California penal system, despite the structural impossibility of doing so: "It is no longer possible to accept the role suggested we play. Which was in essence to do nothing."⁵⁹ The author's rebellious spirit is the reason for his forced segregation from the general population. Solitary confinement is an additional punishment, specifically for those who will not comply with the regulations of incarceration: "the isolation and segregation which equals adjustment centers have always been used as a repressive condition for those would rebel." In their essay, "Take a Look Around," Herbie Scott X and Deane Akil, both incarcerated authors, write, "As we look around, we see that the Brothers and Sisters who have been abducted and confined to such slave plantations / neo-concentration camps as Auburn, Attica, Clinton, Green Haven, San Quentin, Folsom, Soledad, Jolliet, Marion, Westfields, Rahway, Walpole, etc. are assiduously working, studying, and communicating their findings."[60]

Both of these pieces, written by incarcerated authors without the name recognition of the others, reflect the depth of the spirit of rebellion throughout Black carceral political thought. From the most widely circulated letters of George Jackson to a brief reflection of an anonymous prison author buried in an archive, resistance is the definitive feature of this literature. The invocation of slavery reflects, either through explicit arguments or subtle slippage, the insights of incarcerated people into their own captivity. Such views are similarly characteristic of the genre. As Berger puts it, "by challenging prisons as slavery, nationalist prisoners upheld racial solidarity as an ideological counterpoint to the prison of racism."[61] If the mobilization of slavery and theorization of resistance are the cornerstones of Black carceral theory, prison rebellion is its praxis.

Because Black carceral authors drew so heavily from traditions of rebellion on plantations, the next chapter attends to these origins. Slave resistance, in the forms of both extraordinary uprisings and daily practices, matters to contemporary Black carceral politics beyond rhetoric alone. If the prison system is grounded in and derived from slavery, the insurgent acts of enslaved people are how the resistance of prisoners becomes politically intelligible. It is to this legacy that Chapter Three turns.

Historical and Theoretical Erasures of Slave Resistance

"The Negroes brought into the New World situation and presently reduced to perpetual servitude became very rapidly accommodated to the environment and status. The explanation of the comparative ease with which this was brought about doubtless lies in the peculiar racial traits of the Negro people themselves. They are strong and robust in physique and so everywhere sought after as laborers. In disposition they are cheerful, kindly and sociable: in character they are characteristically extrovert, so readily obedient and easily contented. More than most other social groups they are patiently tolerant under abuse and oppression and little inclined to struggle against difficulties. These facts of racial temperament and disposition make the Negroes more amenable to the condition of slavery than perhaps any other racial group."

—EDWARD BYRON REUTER[1]

"Arise! Arise! Shake off your chains!
Your cause is just, so Heaven ordains;
To you shall freedom be proclaimed!
Raise up your arms and bare your breasts,
Almighty God will do the rest
Blow the clarion's warlike blast;
Call every negro from his task;
Wrest the scrouge from Buckra's hand,
And drive each tyrant from the land!"

—UNKNOWN, "The Hymn of Freedom"[2]

EXTRAORDINARY REBELLION

In 1790, a Virginia bondman named Gabriel Prosser organized a massive rebellion for which he anticipated the support of over 1,100 free and enslaved people. Leading accounts of the plot suggest that the rebels planned to assemble, march to Richmond in the night, and seize control of the penitentiary and powder house as a home base and arsenal before invading the city and killing as many whites as possible. So testifies an observer, "It was the central force, armed with muskets, cutlasses, knives, and pikes, upon which the chief responsibility rested: these men were to enter the town at both ends simultaneously and begin a general carnage, none being excepted save the French inhabitants, who were supposed for some reason to be friendly to the negroes."[3] Prosser's efforts were never realized, as one insider revealed his plans to local authorities and Gabriel was summarily executed, along with twenty-seven conspirators.[4] The disclosure of his plot resulted in a general rise in public panic about slave insurrection; strict amendments to existing laws governing the activities of bondpeople; and rollbacks to the kinds of privileges that Gabriel and other enslaved urban men like him had previously enjoyed, including the ability to hire out their own services and move relatively freely in public. It is no coincidence that the freedom dreams of Gabriel flourished in Jeffersonian Virginia, where the influence of natural rights and republican ideologies associated with the American Revolution were most strong.[5]

Two decades later, inspired by the Haitian Revolution of 1791, the largest act of armed resistance against US slavery took place outside of New Orleans in January of 1811. The historical record of the German Coast Slave Uprising is shockingly thin compared to other, even much smaller, rebellions. Perhaps Louisiana, a recently acquired frontier territory, was perceived as a more likely place for a bloody revolt than a so-called civilized Confederate state, such as the Carolinas or Virginia. Despite its scale and sophistication, the uprising has not received the airtime in historical literature that it warrants.[6] It was led by several enslaved men, including the slave-driver-turned-rebel, Charles Deslondes, and two field bondmen known as Kook and Quamana, Akan people from the Asante Kingdom in the former Gold Coast. Although historical records on them are inconclusive, they were likely born around 1790, kidnapped, forced into Middle Passage, and later sold to planters on the German Coast. The two were part of an influx of about twenty thousand West Africans into New Orleans between the periods of 1790 to 1810, 10 percent of whom were from the same West African region.[7] The Gold Coast (what is today Ghana) was in the midst of a period of political unrest at the beginning of the nineteenth century. Intertribal conflict was frequent and culminated in a war between the two largest Akan confederacies, the Asante and Fante, from 1806 to 1807. Because prisoners of war that were not held in bondage within the region were often sold to European slave traders, a sizable percentage of Akan people arrived in the Americas with significant military training and were well versed in local guerilla tactics. Kook and Quamana were likely among them.[8]

The temporal proximity of the Haitian Revolution strongly influenced the rebels' plans, as did the heavy Creole influences in the region, and the migration of thousands of Haitians to New Orleans in the early nineteenth century.[9] The demographics of the Orleans territory, which included the German Coast, were similar to those of Haiti on the eve of revolution. In both cases, enslaved people comprised an overwhelming percentage of the population, whereas planters were fewer and often lived remotely from their plantations.[10] Anti-white sentiment was also a shared value. C.L.R. James notes in *The Black Jacobins* that this was "no infringement on liberty and equality," but rather, "the soundest revolutionary policy."[11] Conditions were thus fertile for resistance. While the exact number of participants is contested, the revolt was by far the largest in American history, involving between two and five hundred men. They killed only two whites, but their destruction of private property is notable: the rebels burned down five plantations, three sugar houses, and a multitude of crops. The uprising ended in a standoff between bondmen and a planter militia, where the rebels were eventually overtaken, captured, and executed. Their heads were mounted on pikes to impart a grisly warning to other enslaved people who might be tempted to resist captivity.

A little more than a decade later, the former bondman Denmark Vesey was convicted and hanged following the revelation of a plot for a large-scale slave rebellion (known as "The Rising") that he ostensibly masterminded, along with five other rebels. The insurrection, also inspired by the success of the Haitian Revolution, would have taken place on Bastille Day in 1822 as an homage to the liberation of Saint-Domingue following the French Revolution.[12] Like the German Coast revolt, The Rising was well-organized, involving a vast network of over nine thousand bondpeople who would be stationed along the Carolina coast, for the purpose of easily massacring enslavers, emancipating bondpeople, and then fleeing the United States for Haiti. Vesey was a free Black man with a successful business, who regularly socialized with enslaved locals.[13] The exposure of his plan for revolt provoked stricter laws governing the proximity of bondpeople to manumitted and free African Americans; specifically forbade the latter from entering South Carolina; and outlawed the purchase of bondpeople from the West Indies, Mexico, South America, Europe, and any state north of Maryland, in an effort to preempt "revolt contagion."[14]

In the most renowned slave rebellion, Nat Turner led an armed uprising of about seventy-five enslaved men (known today as the Southampton Insurrection) in Virginia, in 1831. Believing himself a messianic prophet called upon to carry out a divine obligation, Turner stated in his confession: "And on the 12th of May, 1828, I heard a loud noise in the heavens, and the spirit instantly appeared to me and said the Serpent was loosened, and Christ had laid down the yoke he had borne for the sins of men, and that I should take it in and fight against the Serpent, for the time was fast approaching when the first should be the last and the last should be the first."[15] The revolt led to the murder of fifty-one white people and the subsequent execution of Turner and other leading rebels.

While most analyses tend to emphasize his zealotry and downplay the background conditions of unrest in Southampton, the social and political impact of Turner's rebellion was enormous. It galvanized abolitionists, who declared it evidence that slavery must be immediately terminated, while planters and political elites used the uprising as an occasion to railroad draconian slave laws through the Virginia General Assembly. Of course, Turner's rebellion dramatically increased public panic, leading directly to the surveillance and murder of innocent African Americans. Black preachers and congregations fell under greater scrutiny, while evangelizing white ministers ramped up their efforts to encourage bondpeople to internalize Christian principles of obedience, responsibility, and servility, core values of a slave society.[16] Perhaps due to the brutality of the rebels' methods; the fact that Turner was known to have a close and congenial relationship with his enslaver, Joseph Travis; or the location of the uprising in the heart of the Confederacy, the insurrection rocked the social order of Jeffersonian Virginia. As the historian Scot French notes, Turner's story remains alive in historical memory and his name is often invoked as shorthand for slave rebellion itself.

EVERYDAY RESISTANCE

High-profile, large-scale rebellions are only a part of the story of slave resistance, though they do tend to receive the lion's share of attention in the canon of US history. The ingenuity and creativity of bondpeople are never more evident than when considering the myriad, quotidian ways in which they refuse the terms of their captivity. What James C. Scott calls "weapons of the weak" are most apparent in the "everyday resistance" of enslaved people: "Here I have in mind the ordinary weapons of relatively powerless groups: foot-dragging, dissimulation, false compliance, pilfering, feigned ignorance, slander, arson, and sabotage, and so forth."[17] The enslaved grandmother of the former bondman Lorenzo Ivy regularly fled the woods to escape the abuse of her enslaver.[18] Ivy recalls the way that his mother clandestinely snuck food and other provisions to her, enabling his grandmother to stay away from the brutal planter for lengthy periods of time. Truancy of this kind was extremely common on plantations, especially among women, and an ongoing source of tension between planters and bondpeople. Another bondwoman named Mariah, enraged at her overseer, A.R. McCall, for moving her daughter Mary to his home with the intention of training her to be a "house slave," protested the decision by taking temporary leave of the plantation.[19] The bondman Henry Bibb regularly left the slave quarters after dark to visit friends and lovers on neighboring properties, thereby carving out time for a pleasurable social life amid grueling daily responsibilities.[20]

One enslaved woman in Virginia, Nancy Williams, spent a good number of her precious free hours collecting berries for fabric dye. She fashioned clothes for herself out of drab, cheap, standard issue fabric given to bondpeople and wore them to outlaw dances on neighboring farms and plantations. Another bondwoman known as "Aunt" Adelaide was also skilled in producing artistic textiles. Here, she recounts a dress that she claimed she would remember "as long as I live. It was a hickory stripe dress they made for me with brass buttons at the wrist bands." She recalls that she "felt so dressed up in it. I just strutted."[21] Such strategies of everyday resistance posed direct challenges to the regime of slavery. Others included shirking responsibility for tasks, pilfering small items from planters' homes, breaking equipment, and stealing and destroying livestock.

The sociologists Raymond and Alice Bauer confirmed, in their 1942 analysis, that such behavior was not mere disobedience, but affective positions that should be read as modes of daily resistance to their conditions. Feigning illness, refusal to work, and deliberate clumsiness were practices so prevalent on plantations that they were pathologized into diagnosable conditions—such as the pseudoscientific "dysaesthesia aethiopica," also known as "rascality," a so-called mental illness that causes laziness in enslaved people.[22] Plantation logs consistently indicate that bondpeople seldom reported illness on Sundays, traditionally their one weekly day off, while the greatest rates of sickness occurred on Saturday, likely in attempt to extend the weekend.[23] The calendric and seasonal impacts on such "illnesses" were also significant, as greater rates were recorded during times during the planting year when field labor would be most arduous.

What political and theoretical lessons might one glean from these forms of resistance, both extraordinary and everyday? Slave rebellions were both exceptional events and daily practices. They mocked planters' aspirations of total domination, although they occurred under conditions of force, violence, coercion, and control. This chapter does not intend to provide an exhaustive historical account of slave resistance, but it will mobilize the rebellious activities of bondpeople for two purposes: first, to refute several oft-repeated assumptions about their political subjecthood, and second, to propose an alternative view of slave politics that is dually defined by their *subjection to* and *liberation from* white power. I argue that both the consensus among many twentieth-century historians that enslaved people were voiceless *and* the related tendency of political theorists to overlook their politics are rooted not only in academic structures of white domination but also a dearth of concepts. Thus, scholars often do not properly see slave resistance for what it is: an insurgent politics vital to antebellum US history and Western traditions of freedom and liberation, with enduring effects on the present.

ERASING SLAVE RESISTANCE IN HISTORY

While historian William Dusinberre observes that "the slaves' strongest bulwark against dehumanization—stronger even than their Afro-Christianity—was their nearly universal spirit of dissidence," the prevailing view of many leading historians that enslaved people lacked agency is the provocation for much of my discussion here.[24] The precedent for this view is very apparent in the words of antebellum pro-slavery scholars and actors. For example, in 1833, Thomas R. Dew said, "We cannot fail to derive the greatest consolation from the fact that although slavery has existed in our country for the last two hundred years, there have been but three attempts at an insurrection—one in Virginia, one in South Carolina, and we believe, one in Louisiana—and the loss of lives from this cause has not amounted to one hundred persons in all."[25] Likewise, the attorney and planter James Henry Hammond, along with a cohort of South Carolina political and business elites, maintained that "his slaves" were "too civilized" to rise.[26] A narrative, popular among slavery apologists, also disavowing the prevalence of slave revolt, is the conviction that it is generally incited by external agitators, particularly Northern abolitionists, as a way of discrediting the idea that bondpeople were displeased with their conditions. Stephen Howard Browne claims, "If it is at all possible to generalize, we can with certainty note one unshakable assumption among slavery apologists: rebellions were prompted by forces outside the slave system; they were aberrations, the origins of which were owing not to slavery itself but to alien agents who stood in a perverse or eccentric relation to the status quo. Slavery did not produce slave rebellions—its enemies did."[27]

Twentieth-century historians, including those critical of the institution, often drew considerably from pro-slavery discourse. Such accounts vary considerably but tend to share the perspective that bondpeople were without political capacities and convictions. These impoverished views of the enslaved were certainly not limited to Old South Confederacy apologists but cut across the political spectrum. Three interrelated tendencies are generally associated with the position and animate my inquiry: ignoring firsthand accounts of bondpeople's experiences in captivity; insisting on their political ignorance; and minimizing the prevalence and power of slave resistance through history.

The renowned American historian Stanley Elkins states in his seminal text *Slavery: A Problem in American Institutional and Intellectual Life* that slave narratives are "of little value" to scholars.[28] While he regularly cites the eyewitness testimonies of white people, Elkins is suspicious about the veracity of bondpeople's accounts of their own experiences in captivity. Even though Kenneth Stampp did make limited use of several slave narratives to advance his claim that bondpeople were unable to create a social world of their own, he also argues in *The Peculiar Institution: Slavery in the Ante-Bellum South* that the material from the WPA interviews, from which most slave narratives are drawn, is useless for academics. He believes readers can only gauge the perspectives of enslaved people from their behavior, enslavers' accounts, and the "logic of their situation."[29] In a similar vein, the historian Ulrich Bonnell Phillips, a slavery apologist, whose scholarship has essentially defined the field of antebellum Southern history, states that slave narratives, in general, are not trustworthy resources for historical inquiry because they are shot through with abolitionist rhetoric and revisionism.[30] That Phillips claims bondpeople were generally happy and content with their situation aligns with his disavowal of their firsthand voices, for these tarnish the rosy view of slavery that he espouses.[31]

The inclination of certain historians to minimize the prevalence and intensity of slave uprisings is perhaps derived from the planter tradition of downplaying the frequency of resistance in order to both present slavery in a favorable light and preempt rebellion-contagion among bondpeople. Perhaps because of these holes in the historical record, such historians are comparatively less attentive to slave resistance (the only political recourse available to bondpeople) than other aspects of slavery, such as fugitivity, labor, family structure, religious practices, and cultural production. The falsehood that resistance was uncommon, then and now, serves to strengthen the institution of slavery, both practically and discursively: in the antebellum period, by using manufactured compliance narratives to render slavery ethically justifiable; in the present, by drawing on an incomplete archive to legitimize its widespread acceptability. The Marxist historian Albert Thrasher, who compiled the lone documentary history of the German Coast Slave Uprising, notes that "it was the stated policy of the slave owners and their intellectual scribes to deliberately omit mention of slave revolts in the normal documentary sources they created (i.e. court records, newspapers, even personal letters). According to their own statements, this was done to preempt the spread of revolts and prevent the enslaved Africans from knowing their strength."[32] Indeed, underreporting slave resistance was part of a broader politics of disavowal that sedimented harmonious images of passive Black bondpeople and benevolent white planters, backed by an orderly, congenial, patriarchal system of labor.

For all of these pro-slavery authors, the "fact" that bondpeople either did not resist slavery with any significant frequency or were manipulated by the ulterior motives of outside agents is clear evidence of its virtue. Of course, this perspective contrasts sharply with a contradictory counternarrative: ongoing public hysteria over the *threat* of slave uprising that endured from the earliest arrival of Africans in the colonies to the American Civil War.[33] Law, policy, and public sentiment in the antebellum South was suffused with white anxiety about the possibility of rebellion. The renowned historian

Eugene Genovese states that insurrection panic was exacerbated everywhere in white society by daily gossip of planter families and the political messaging of party elites, in the hope of silencing their opponents.[34] For example, the following was reported in 1857 by the Texas newspaper, *Galveston News*: "Never has there been a time in our recollection when so many insurrections or attempts at insurrection, have transpired in rapid succession as during the past six months. The evidence in regard to some of these has indeed proved very unsatisfactory, showing nothing but that the negroes had got hold of some indistinct and vague ideas about their freedom."[35] Shortly after twenty-five enslaved people fled from Texas to Mexico in January of 1845, the Congress of the Republic of Texas passed a law that anyone who kills or maims a bondman will be punished as much as they would if the victim were a white man, except in the case of insurrection, in which such violence was entirely permissible. Public unrest regarding slave conspiracies reflects the state of white society more so than the sentiments and activities of bondpeople themselves: when planters believe that their control over bondpeople is in jeopardy, rumors of insurrection plots proliferate.[36] A strange doubletalk is apparent here: slave rebellion was simultaneously downplayed and exaggerated, both in service of upholding the "peculiar institution" and tightening the reins of white domination.

IMPOVERISHED VIEWS OF RESISTANCE

Many twentieth-century historians, slavery critics, and apologists alike are aligned with planters when underestimating occurrences of resistance. While Herbert Aptheker holds that rebellious bondpeople formed a distinct revolutionary tradition in the United States, Genovese refutes this, arguing that revolts were rare in the United States and dwindled to nonexistent in the nineteenth century.[37] This of course relies on a thin, ungenerous concept of resistance, one that is generally dismissive of rebellions that did not "successfully" abolish slavery altogether.[38] Genovese states, "the slaves of the United States always faced helpless odds. A slave revolt anywhere in the Americas, at any time, had poor prospects and required organizers with extraordinary daring and resourcefulness."[39]

His account is hotly contested by more recent historians, including Stephanie Smallwood and Marcus Rediker, both of whom have written extensively on rebellion in Middle Passage.[40] Ship ledgers reveal that resistance was common in the form of hunger strikes, refusal of medicine, suicide, and armed insurrection. Public records attest to this as well, including a hearing on the slave trade in the House of Commons in 1790–1791: "Mr. Towne says, that inquiring of the slaves into the cause of their insurrections, he has been asked what business he had to carry them from their own country. They had wives and children whom they wanted to be with."[41] Such testimony reveals that rebellion was frequent enough to be considered relevant in a debate on the abolition of the slave trade in Britain. Also indicating this is the introduction of a special form of insurance during this period, to recoup losses resulting from insurrections aboard ships.[42] John David Smith and Carter G. Woodson, note that the pro-slavery historian Phillips ignored slave rebelliousness, often cherry-picking evidence that best suited his favorable portrayal of slavery: "Phillips never considered that what he interpreted as examples of the crudity of Black labor might have been expressions of slave resistance."[43] In sum, whether a slavery apologist, holding that resistance was rare due to bondpeople's general contentment with the institution, or a critic upholding an abject narrative of enslaved people, the discourse of compliant slaves prevailed in much twentieth-century historical scholarship.[44] In the words of Bauer and Bauer, "both sides presented the Negro as a docile creature; one side because it wished to prove he was contented; the other because it wished to prove that he was grossly mistreated. Both conceptions have persisted to the present time."[45]

Relatedly and exemplified by Genovese, many leading twentieth-century historians of the plantation South do not often describe slave resistance in "political terms." Like the tendency to downplay the frequency of rebellion, they undermine its political significance, viewing revolts as "disorganized outbursts which counted for little or nothing."[46] Genovese holds that most bondpeople adopted practices of "accommodation," which is to say that they complied with the many regulations to which they were subjected in order to live with as much dignity and as little brutality as possible. This, asserts Genovese, seriously curbed inclinations toward rebellion. Further still, he rejects all political interpretations of everyday resistance, claiming that these are merely accommodationist in character. Against the grain of his contemporaries such as Bauer and Bauer and Oakes, Genovese claims that only armed uprising should be read as political resistance:

> Stark physical resistance did not represent a sharp break with the process of accommodation except in its most extreme forms—running away to freedom and insurrection. Strictly speaking, only insurrection "counted

as" political action, which some choose to define as the only genuine resistance since it alone directly challenged the power of the regime. From that point of view, those activities which others call "day-to-day resistance to slavery"—stealing, lying, dissembling, shirking, murder, infanticide, suicide, arson—qualify at best as prepolitical and at worse as apolitical.[47]

Here, Genovese draws some troubling lines in the sand: cordoning off insurrection as the only genuine form of political resistance depoliticizes a wide array of rebellious strategies of which bondpeople made frequent use. To say that only armed uprising genuinely confronted the regime of racial slavery, exclusively laying claim to the political, is as reductive as the idea that voting is the lone form of participation in a democracy. Ordinary acts of resistance originated in interdependent relations of trust and reciprocity among bondpeople, and far from accommodating slavery, chipped away at its authority.

Genovese's limited concept of resistance also propagates the myth that Black women did not resist enslavement, since the conditions of gendered labor in slave communities prevented them from both participating in armed revolt and (often) permanently fleeing plantations. Implicit in his argument that only fugitivity and insurrection pose "direct challenges" to the regime of slavery is the misguided belief that bondwomen were largely compliant. A number of factors prevented women from escaping slavery altogether, including familial obligations, social stigma, and enforced sexual divisions of labor.[48] Enslaved women were almost never issued passes to leave the property for errands or leased out to work on neighboring plantations (as men regularly were), thus they were unfamiliar with the geography and terrain outside the boundaries of the plantation where they lived. Heightened surveillance thwarted their attempts to escape, for a Black woman in transit, for example, would automatically attract suspicion in the slave South, increasing chances that she would be apprehended midflight. Yet, these structural barriers to organized revolt and permanent fugitivity should not be mistaken for compliance. Enslaved women rebelled in other ways, including shirking tasks, pilfering goods, stealing time, taking temporary leave of plantations, and making their own clothes with stolen materials—methods and strategies falsely dismissed by Genovese.[49]

Genovese does not only miss the fact that *all* slave resistance is political, but that the political actions of bondpeople are resistive, by definition. These have often gone unnoticed. Many historians underestimate the degree to which bondpeople were influenced by the Haitian Revolution, as were the aforementioned rebels of the German Coast Slave Uprising, and of course, the American Revolution.[50] Despite the fact that slavery was the law of the land at the time of the founding, Constitutional doctrine, that all men are created equal, was also destabilizing to the racial caste system. Enslaved people both encouraged and exploited this.

A bondman, Quillo, from Granville, North Carolina was accused of plotting an uprising in 1794. His unorthodox methods are noteworthy: Quillo assembled a group of enslaved people in Granville, served them cider and brandy, and planned an "election." He proposed that bondmen would vote for burgesses, justices of the peace, and sheriffs "in order to have equal justice distributed so that a weak person might collect his debts, as well as a Strong one."[51] Under other circumstances, this would be considered a fairly straightforward, noncontroversial political event undertaken by a figure well-versed in the rudiments of representative government, although the fact that Quillo was an enslaved man claiming some de facto citizenship and assuming a leadership role provokes a double take. While Genovese is correct that the impact of a single bondman, who momentarily attempted to seize political authority without any civic standing, is limited at best, he underestimates the political significance of Quillo's act. "Something unsettling to whites was happening when slaves could speak of 'equal justice' and contemplate the democratic election of a shadow government. The contagion of liberty that had been released by the American Revolution was spreading to the 'wrong' people."[52]

The assumption that enslaved people were incapable of politics is an extension of historical discourses that diminish the frequency, impact, and legacy of slave rebellion. It solidifies convictions that bondpeople are mentally and intellectually inferior, justifying their captivity and exclusion from even the most modest forms of citizenship. Relatedly, racist, apolitical tropes of "African culture" and "slave personality" ostensibly explain, if not defend, the endurance of the system of slavery over centuries. Roper and Brockington state, "The other compelling reason for black slavery sprang from more attributes of African culture and physiology. Simply put, African men and women adapted themselves better than did Indians to European-directed agriculture and to European people."[53] For opponents of slavery, the conviction that bondpeople had no political lives bespeaks a broader critique of the institution, for what better evidence of its inhumanity is there than the fact that enslaved people were forbidden from any participation in government?

Whether the image of the passive slave serves to defend or critique slavery, it is not amenable to the counterclaim that bondpeople *did* exercise political agency.

The historians Steven Hahn and Manisha Sinha echo the earlier claims of Aptheker that enslaved people in fact forged robust traditions of resistance, refuting historically inaccurate apolitical narratives. Arguing against the leading account of abolitionism as a movement of white men, Sinha credits enslaved Black Americans with its success.[54] Focusing on the decades following the American Civil War, Hahn also argues against the assumption that African Americans are a downtrodden people without political convictions of their own.

> They (southern enslavers) could scarcely acknowledge, let alone dignify, the disruptive or communal behaviors of their slaves as worthy of the name "political," for by doing so they undermine their own claims of absolute power. And yet slaves did express and act according to their individual wills, fashion collective norms and aspirations, contest the authority of their owners on many fronts, build institutions to mobilize their resources and sensibilities, produce leaders who wielded significant influence, and, in ways we have still to appreciate fully, press on the official arenas of politics at the local, state, and national levels.[55]

Here, Hahn's claims are reminiscent of Du Bois in *Black Reconstruction*, when he argues that enslaved Black workers organized a general strike that ended the American Civil War, thereby refuting the oft-repeated narrative that the Union army embarked on a moral crusade against slavery.[56] Both Sinha and Hahn take aim at historians that either minimize, or ignore altogether, the crucial political work of bondpeople in the antebellum period and postbellum, free Black actors.

ERASING SLAVE RESISTANCE II: POLITICAL THEORY

If historians such as Genovese and Phillips are forthcoming about the peripheral status of slave resistance, the blind spots of political theorists are apparent in subjects left untouched. They regularly overlook the way that slave politics transform and upend classic political constructs such as freedom, equality, rights, liberty, choice, democracy, individualism, republicanism, and more. This is not only to say that the fact of slavery contradicts so-called universal theories (i.e., the Lockean myth of natural rights), but also that politics undertaken by enslaved people radically alter and reshape them.⁵⁷ Like the oversights of historians, the erasures of theorists take two forms: scholarship on democracy, freedom, and justice that simply does not attend to legacies of racial slavery; and work that does engage with slavery, but elides analyses of captive resistance.

As the national spotlight shone on racial violence following recent high-profile police murders of Black men, with the organizing and activism in Ferguson, Missouri, and the emergence of the #BlackLivesMatter movement, more academic political theorists than ever before have turned to the politics of anti-Black racism in the United States.⁵⁸ Over the past decades, theorists have considered the impact of Black political thought on US democracy; the ways that racial domination prohibits the full realization of democratic ideals; lessons from Black theoretical traditions that can address broad political questions; how race confounds well-worn theoretical constructs; and the anti-Black racist roots of the US polity.

Given that these works are comparatively attentive to legacies of African American struggle, it is noteworthy that few of them explicitly address slave rebellion. While Alex Zamalin's *The Struggle on Their Minds* is an exceptional book that centers on Black political resistance, slave revolt makes no more than a brief appearance in the text.⁵⁹ Zamalin gestures at the Southampton Insurrection and Denmark Vesey's thwarted plot, but the majority of his chapter on the antebellum period engages David Walker and Frederick Douglass.⁶⁰ Walker's *Appeal* is a radical, abolitionist jeremiad, although the author was neither enslaved nor involved in any slave uprising.⁶¹ Frederick Douglass, a former bondman who did resist by physically overpowering the slave-breaker Edward Covey, escaped from Baltimore to New York at age twenty and spent the majority of his life as an outspoken, free abolitionist and public intellectual. The writings of rebellious bondpeople such as Harriet Jacobs, Lucy Delaney, and Solomon Northup, among others, do not appear in Zamalin's book. Neither do extended discussions of large- or small-scale slave resistance, nor the differences between these insurgent practices.⁶² Similarly, Nick Bromell briefly attends to slave resistance in the context of Douglass, but does not engage with exceptional or quotidian rebellions of bondpeople, in depth.⁶³ A mere paragraph of Eddie S. Glaude Jr.'s *Democracy in Black* alludes to slave politics.⁶⁴ Nikhil Pal Singh does not discuss it in *Black is a Country*, neither does the subject appear in Jack Turner's *Awakening to Race*.⁶⁵ Given that Turner's work considers ways that critical attention to race productively reworks the tradition of American individualism, politics in captivity, perhaps, would have enriched his discussion.[66] Many rebellious activities could be read as insurgent practices of individualism, as I will discuss later, although Turner did not discuss it as such. In sum, the above authors, all of whom take up the subjects of Black politics and American democracy, remain firmly entrenched in an academic discourse that sidesteps slave politics, even as they delve into Black political agency. Despite their smart, insightful, and rich contributions to the field of contemporary political theory, their accounts of slave resistance (generally) do not extend significantly beyond Frederick Douglass.

WHERE THEORIES OF FREEDOM FAIL

Many white twentieth-century political theorists of freedom and liberation make little or no mention of white domination or Black resistance, as if neither holds particular relevance. The consequence is not only the creation and reproduction of inaccurate and incomplete theories, but also the political work of bondpeople goes ignored. The renowned theorist Isaiah Berlin states, "I am normally said to be free to the degree to which no man or body of men interferes with my activity."[67] His highly influential concept of negative freedom is based on the premise that a subject is free as long as there is no individual agent or group impeding their freedom. Rebellious acts of enslaved people, and the kind of freedom they exercised and pursued, is derived directly *from* the power of white enslavers, against which they exert resistance. In this way, the "interference" of whites is the condition of the possibility that enslaved people can, and did, claim agency.

The holes in Berlin's idea of liberty are revealed anew in Harriet Jacobs's narrative autobiography. Using the pseudonym Linda Brent, she describes her escape from the plantation of Dr. Flint and eventual flight to Philadelphia. Hers is a paradoxical concept of freedom, unique to slavery, which defies the rationality of Berlin's positive and negative binary. After enduring years of abuse from Flint, Jacobs began her escape from slavery, taking cover in a garret in her grandmother's attic, located on Flint's property, where she remained hidden for seven years before escaping north. Most importantly for this discussion, her experience of freedom in the garret blurs lines between liberty and captivity that, for Berlin, are discrete and separable. Unlike the categories of freedom and unfreedom for whites, the proximity of the two states is far closer for enslaved people, perhaps especially women.

The feminist geographer Katherine McKittrick says, "Importantly, she (Brent) claims that in the garret she is not enslaved and that her loophole of retreat is a retreat of emancipation. For Brent to declare that her emancipation begins in the garret—which she also repeatedly refers to as her dismal cell, her prison, and this dark hole—is evidence of how she uses the existing landscape and architecture to name the complicated geographies of black womanhood in/and slavery."[68] It is only under conditions of captivity that one could perceive a "disabling, oppressive, dark, and cramped" hole or prison as a legible site of freedom. In this way the simultaneity of her experiences of freedom and entrapment upends Berlin's divide. McKittrick states, "Linda Brent's experiences in her grandmother's garret exact, geographically, what she describes as the shape of mystery: Brent must suffer to avoid self and familial sufferings. The question of geographic freedom is wrapped up in the racial, sexual, and bodily constraints before and during her retreat to the attic."[69] In other words, Brent's enslavement is not incidental, but central to her experience of liberation in the garret.

Berlin draws on the linguistic categories of slavery and other forms of coercion as mere devices meant to substantiate the concept of freedom through juxtaposition. For example, his use of the term "economic slavery" highlights the practical similarities between the absence of a right and the inability to exercise it.[70] This term attests to the functions that slavery performs for his theory of freedom, rather than any serious attention to the interconnections between *actual slavery* and freedom. Jacobs's story is a distinct counterpoint to Berlin's theory: captivity and freedom, for her, are parallel and simultaneous, two sides of the same coin. Slavery is not a theoretical tool meant to more effectively illuminate liberal theories of freedom, but rather the very condition from which freedom is pursued. The garret is, at once, the site of her liberation and intrinsically, physically, and metaphorically, tethered to her enslavement. Further troubling the myth of a clear analytical, geographical separation between the states of freedom and unfreedom is that the literal location of her hiding place (her loophole, refuge, and escape) is on Flint's plantation.[71] This unique geography, charted by Jacobs, only exists in the shadow of the dominant one.[72]

What is true of Jacobs's account of freedom in the garret can also extend to the temporary and unstable freedom that enslaved women seized through truancy. When bondwomen took to the swamp or woods for limited periods of time, knowing that they would eventually return to the plantation, they enacted a unique kind of liberation that also confounds

Berlin's sharp divide between freedom and unfreedom. Drawing on, but deviating slightly from, Neil Roberts's *Freedom as Marronage*, I hold that ephemeral encounters with freedom in the form of truancy extend the liminal experience of flight and, as in Jacobs's narrative, are constituted simultaneously by liberation and captivity.[73] When women temporarily fled plantations, freedom was bound up in their captivity in two respects: first and most obviously, flight would be emancipatory but for their bondage, and second, they remain captive even as they dwell in a space of limited, highly contingent liberation.

Borrowing a term from Edward Said, Stephanie Camp repurposes the concept "rival geography" to explain "alternative ways of knowing and using plantation and southern space that conflicted with planters' ideals and demands."[74] In a similar vein, Saidiya Hartman describes truancy or "stealing away" as a means of claiming time for oneself against the grain of white domination: "Stealing away defied and subversively appropriated slave owners' designs for mastery or control—primarily the captive body as the extension of the master's power and the spatial organization of domination."[75] The spatial organization of domination to which Hartman refers is disrupted by enslaved women's use of rival geography. The practice of truancy encapsulates this well. The power that bondwomen exercised over captive spaces bespeaks a resistive orientation to their conditions associated with fugitivity, rather than the wholesale abandonment of them. This is a politics that cannot be contained by conventional dichotomies of freedom/unfreedom.

In her renowned essay "What is Freedom?" Hannah Arendt famously states that "to be free and to act are the same." At the center of all political action is, for her, speech. The question of who a person truly is can only be answered through speaking in public and among peers.[76] Yet this theory either presumes that speech is possible to begin with, or limits it to demographics of people who are, in a sense, already free. Conditions of enslavement do not just forbid bondpeople from speaking, they withhold from them the very techniques and spaces necessary for the materialization of such speech acts. For example, learning literacy skills is unlikely in the face of laws prohibiting it, and even physically appearing in public is impossible when barred from entering places in which they could ever be heard. It is hardly surprising that Arendt, like so many of her contemporaries, is dismissive of captive resistance, for she states, offhandedly, in *The Human Condition* that slave rebellion is rare and barely elaborates on its historical significance.[77] Again, Arendt writes the political agency of enslaved people out of her work altogether. As a consequence, her concept of freedom is irredeemably incomplete.

Some political thinkers have critically taken note of such erasure of slave resistance from contemporary political thought. In *Intimate Justice: The Black Female Body and the Body Politic*, Shatema Threadcraft discusses ways that Black women's rebellion against slavery is marginalized in favor of masculinist discourses. Reproduction, sexuality, and care, all associated with women, are often sidelined in favor of individual control over one's own body and environment, normatively male principles.[78] Roberts argues against the common tendency of political theorists to overlook slave agency, arguing that doing so has consequences for political theory at large. He observes that the fugitive actions of bondpeople associated with escape or marronage are altogether different forms of freedom than those thinkers writing from within the Western tradition acknowledge—from classic liberal to radical democratic. Roberts refutes the oft-repeated assumption that freedom is a fixed state, attending instead to the liminal spaces outside the familiar dichotomy of freedom and captivity: "Experience teaches us lessons about flight and the dialectics of human and all-too-subhuman conditions. Political theorists, therefore, must pay more attention to the experience of the process by which people emerge from slavery to freedom."[79] The consequences of the omission of flight from political theory are thus not limited to the marginalization of Black history and political thought, but also to the outsized presence of inaccurate and incomplete theories of freedom within the canon.

Similarly, the disavowal of slave resistance has two troubling effects on academic political theory: First, the discipline remains complicit with white supremacist academic traditions by ignoring Black agency prior to 1865 and, subsequently, the political work of enslaved people. Second, prevailing theories of politics, action, freedom, liberty, and more fail to account for the fundamental ways in which the rebellious actions of bondpeople disrupt their terms and assumptions. While white domination undoubtedly persists in academia, it is reductive to attribute the disavowal of slave resistance to racism alone. Instead, I hold that the absence of theoretical constructs, as well as the prevalence of dichotomies that are grounded in falsehoods of universal freedom and liberty, perpetuates the invisibility and unintelligibility of the political work of bondpeople.

To be clear, this is neither to suggest that the exclusion of slave politics is an innocent academic misstep nor that the unavailability of concepts to address it is unrelated to racism in the academy. Instead, I am attempting to further elaborate on academic traditions of racial domination by exposing its less visible contours. A photographer looks through a viewfinder to focus and frame her photograph. My suspicion is that liberalism, which so dominates political vocabularies in the West, performs this function for theorists, even those who are critical of it. The framing work of liberalism, what I refer to here as "liberal myopia," prevents thinkers from perceiving and comprehending actions outside of conventional liberal discourses, including (and especially) politics in captivity. Slave resistance is often irrational and defies conventional reason; enslaved actors do not aim for inclusion in a system of rights; both organized uprisings and everyday rebellion contradict the personal interests of bondpeople, as most of the time, insurrections resulted in execution and ordinary resistance, in punishment; rebellious bondpeople are not oriented toward reform of the institution of slavery or even necessarily incremental improvements to their own conditions. In all of these ways, slave rebellions are political actions, illegible in liberal terms and thus often overlooked.

Attending to the limits of liberalism is only part of the story here. The following chapters will also identify and develop an alternative political vocabulary meant to give voice and visibility to captive resistance. Relinquishing some of the well-worn constructs of liberalism and democratic theory in favor of Arendt's concept of "world," which is constitutively indifferent, if not directly opposed to liberalism, casts light on slave politics otherwise underrepresented or ignored. I first offer an account of liberalism, focusing on constructs most relevant to the themes of *Politics in Captivity*, before turning briefly to usages of liberal theory by enslaved intellectuals. I hold that liberal terms, ultimately, do not map onto slave resistance, which I demonstrate by explaining their irrelevance to both armed uprisings and small-scale resistive practices. Drawing on the concept of world, I argue that US chattel slavery is an institution of forced worldlessness, against which enslaved people rebelled through concerted acts of world-building.

4

The Racial Limits of Liberalism

Because slave politics are forged outside of conventional discourses including rights, choice, law, and equality, they cannot be comprehended through the lenses of liberalism. Nonetheless, they dominate the theoretical landscape of US politics, amounting to what I call "liberal myopia"—the primary concern of this chapter. Referring to the singular deployment of liberal assumptions and constructs by both proponents and critics of liberalism, liberal myopia largely accounts for the erasures of slave resistance in political theory. While the racial tensions within liberal political thought are widely acknowledged, less treated is the way that critics, too, become so enmeshed in its terms that politics outside of the liberal purview are concealed from view.[1] The purpose of this chapter is neither to provide an account of classical liberalism, nor even a critique of its racial deficits. Rather, the focus here is on the dimensions of liberalism which I believe are most responsible for the tendency to overlook the political significance of politics in captivity.

A BRIEF EXCURSUS ON LIBERALISM

Neatly summarizing liberalism is an impossible task, for, to borrow from Duncan Bell, it has become "the meta-category of Western political discourse."[2] Echoing Judith Shklar's charge that liberalism is an "all-purpose word,"[3] Bell notes that it has become a catch-all concept upon which many disparate ideas and positions are projected. Thus, liberalism is less a coherent political philosophy than a loose concatenation of interconnected constructs that are hotly contested, even among liberals themselves. According to the philosopher Carol Hay, there are certain values upon which liberals do tend to agree, including liberty, individualism, choice, and checks on the authority and power of government. In her words:

> Liberals, most obviously, agree that *liberty* is the most important political value. They agree that the best possible state is one that secures the greatest amount of liberty for each individual that is compatible with like liberty for all. They agree that this politically important liberty should give individuals freedoms such as freedom from the unwanted interferences of others, freedom to live the life of one's choosing, and freedom to choose one's own conception of the good. They agree that the rights and interests of the individual, not those of the larger social group, are both the justification of and the limiting condition on the power and authority of the state.[4]

Despite her clear account, Hay is quick to note that liberals diverge sharply from one another on many key issues. Deep fractures and debates over the concept of liberty; the morality of the social contract; the role of the state in securing and protecting rights; and the status of the welfare state pervade the liberal canon. One of the most central points of conflict is the normative position of private property. Classical liberals, in the mode of John Locke, have consistently argued that liberty and private property are inseparable from one another, differing only on the question of whether property is an expression of, or synonymous with, individual liberty. In *The Second Treatise on Civil Government*, Locke states that life and liberty *are themselves* forms of property, suggesting that the latter is the natural right from which the others spring.[5] Classical liberals draw on his intellectual legacy, arguing that property is fundamental to a liberal polity (although occasionally disagreeing on the terms of this), and that capitalism, the tried and true economic system of private property, is best aligned with principles of individual liberty. Later, this hyperextended conflation of individualism and property morphed into Cold War ideology, as liberty became associated with capitalism and collectivism with communism.

A contrasting iteration of liberalism, grounded in the welfare state and social justice more broadly, emerged near the end of the nineteenth century in the work of thinkers including Karl Polyani, John Maynard Keynes, and John Dewey. Departing from the premises of classical liberalism, these thinkers question the so-called intrinsic relation between liberty and property and, particularly, economic systems based on accumulation of the latter. Polyani defends the idea that (typically) markets have been subjected to varying forms of state control and should not be considered self-regulating entities. Keynes solidifies the idea that government can do for the rights and well-being of citizens what the market cannot: that is, ensure social and economic stability and freedom for citizens.[6] This shift in liberal thinking is likely due to a confluence of several historical factors: the democratization of Western nation-states in the early twentieth century, which inspired greater faith in the capabilities of representative government and democracy; and the growing conviction, provoked in part by catastrophic events such as the Great Depression and two imperial wars, that private property is limited in its capacity to produce prosperity and stability for the majority of citizens.[7] In philosophy, the emergence of pragmatism at the turn of the twentieth century also presented a challenge to classical liberalism, even as it abides by some of its precepts. The forefather of pragmatism, John Dewey, argued in 1930 that the core values of classical liberalism, particularly its emphasis on individualism and negative freedom, would have to be reworked if liberalism is to deliver on its promises of liberty for all.[8]

If the allegiances between liberalism and pragmatism include the high status of reason for both, perhaps one break between them is the position of the individual, which has been unequivocally central for liberals and an object of critique for pragmatists. The two are interrelated, for the capacity to reason is a (maybe *the*) defining feature of the individual and justification for the rights that he enjoys, whereas the loss or absence of reason is characteristic of the barbarian. Kenneth Minogue states the following:

> The reason with which we are concerned is by definition an agency or power in the mind, one which asks and answers questions like: What do I want? By which kind of behavior can I attain the greatest number

of my ends? How can I attain them most efficiently, that is, with least danger to other ends which I also pursue? Reason explores the logic of policies, and supplies knowledge derived from experience relevant to attaining the ends desired. Rational behavior excludes habitual action, impulsive action, or acts done in slavish imitation of ossified traditions. Rational individualism assumes that all behavior can be explained in terms of desiring policies, and that we are in a position to discover and rationalize the ends which arise in our striving.[9]

Reason is thus bound up in individual self-interest, rational political calculations, and behavior intended to optimize desired outcomes. Thomas A. Spragens notes the implicit praise embedded in the designation "reasonable," which casts certain people, policies, conventions, and more as "fitting and proper." Clearly inspired by the work of Rawls, to whom I will turn presently, Spragens claims that "political actions, doctrines, and principles should be considered reasonable when they are what someone would do, believe, or accept were he or she to presume that human beings are properly treated as free and equal, that the right takes priority over the good, and that social inequalities are almost wholly the result of contingencies for which people cannot properly be held accountable."[10]

In addition to the priority of reason for these thinkers, individual liberty remains undisputed in both classical and newer liberal theories. While various matters are widely debated, such as the normative position of the market or proper functions of government, orbiting them is the question of what best safeguards the individual. The political theorist Nadia Urbinati describes the concept in normative, even romantic terms: "Society and its political institutions should be so directed that they promote individual and social dispositions, the value of which transcends the actual social and cultural conventions and is measured by common perspective of limitation and of belonging to humanity. The individual is a unique and irreplaceable infinity, and this applies to all human beings."[11] Readers are called on to embrace a universal myth and ignore the ways that the category of "individual" has been historically weaponized against enslaved and colonized people. The constructs of individual and private property grew up alongside each other as the transatlantic slave trade expanded. The discourse of property is entirely inseparable from the institution of slavery. Since the ownership of private property demarcates the individual as a rights-bearing subject and given that enslaved people were considered high-value private property, it follows that they would never be able to draw on the privileges that the status of individual confers.

Race liberals believe that the solution to this problem is to expose the hypocrisy of slavery and extend the benefits of individualism to African Americans.[12] Ostensibly, this move should do away with both the ethical justification for slavery and racial inequality altogether. Of course, it is evident that such progress has not occurred, but rather, following Charles Mills's argument in *The Racial Contract*, the absorption of Black Americans into liberal values and practices has merely reshuffled the terms of racial domination. As Mills puts it, "Whereas before it was denied that nonwhites were equal persons, it is now pretended that nonwhites are equal abstract persons who can be fully included in the polity merely by extending the scope of the moral operator, without any fundamental change in the arrangements that have resulted from the previous system of explicit de jure racial privilege."[13] The false assertion that the individual is a universal category introduces a new, insidious form of inequality in which racial differences are maintained, and even deepened, through their apparent disappearance. Liberals claim to "render (racial differences) inoperative" in the domain of law-making and enforcement, in short, asserting false ideals of state "colorblindness."[14] The problem with this is that it overlooks the fact that race remains an organizing principle for arms of state power, including the police, public housing, welfare, public schools, criminal justice, and family court. The liberal disavowal of racial difference offers a conveniently neutral cover under which explicitly racist policies operate. As Julie Novkov observes, "The unreliability of abstract liberal principles like equality, individual choice, liberty, and fairness to ground progressive racial change. Perhaps no abstract theory could provide a permanent grounding for racial remediation, as US state—and the US states'—involvement in the process of generating and supporting racial hierarchies has been so varied throughout history."[15]

Building on the erasure of difference and the accompanying practices of racial exclusion that emerge from it, there is likely no one more influential than the twentieth-century philosopher John Rawls, whose writings laid the groundwork for contemporary liberalism.[16] Picking up on the claim of his liberal predecessor, John Stuart Mill, that the relation between economic and personal liberty is ambiguous, Rawls argues that the ostensible conflict between freedom and equality is false, thereby upending the terms of well-worn debates between generations of thinkers. By way of a concept of justice as fairness, Rawls unites freedom and equality in a single construct, instead of repeating the tendencies of past liberals to subordinate one value to the other.

Not only has Rawls's seminal work, *A Theory of Justice*, and the philosophical questions that it poses occupied the interests of a broad range of thinkers since its 1971 publication, it is also responsible for the turn in liberal thought to the realization of social justice.[17] The enduring connection between liberalism and justice is Rawls's fundamental contribution to contemporary political theory. Relatedly, it is where his work has most powerfully influenced his readers. Urbinati, for example, reveals the effect of Rawls's philosophy on her work: "Democratic liberalism is both a culture and ideology and a theory of the institutional techniques required to limit political power and enable the organs of the state to deliver impartial justice."[18] The philosopher Richard Rorty, also a contemporary of Rawls, emphasizes the potential of liberalism to increase empathy and solidarity in social relations for the purposes of social justice.[19] Similarly, Michael Sandel's *Liberalism and the Limits of Justice* makes use of a concept of liberalism "in which notions of justice, fairness, and individual rights play a central role."[20] While Thomas Pogge both defends and critiques *A Theory of Justice* in his book, *Realizing Rawls*, its centrality to his work is not in question.[21]

Given the profound influence of Rawls's work to the fields of twentieth-century philosophy and political theory, it would be redundant to say that *A Theory of Justice* is a canonical text of contemporary liberal political thought. It is, thus, not of small significance that Rawls is essentially silent on race, the central social and political force of injustice in the United States since its founding. Rawls completed the writing of *A Theory of Justice* during the peak of the civil rights movement in the mid-1960s and published it at the height of the Black Power Movement in 1971.[22] On this, Mills claims, "we face a paradox: Rawls, the celebrated American philosopher of justice, had next to nothing to say in his work about what has arguably historically been the most blatant American variety of injustice, racial oppression. The postwar struggle for racial justice in practice and in theory and the Rawlsian corpus on justice are almost completely separate and nonintersecting universes."[23] Despite the fact that Rawls himself attributes the success of *A Theory of Justice* to the prevailing civil rights and anti-war movements, both of which had the political spotlight at the time of its publication, the book both builds on and enacts new liberal erasures of race.[24] Although the absence of race in Rawls's work fits squarely into the status quo of postwar white intellectuals, its omission from discussion is perhaps more consequential than that of his contemporaries, due to his enormous influence in philosophy and political theory, and more importantly, the fact that his primary intellectual contribution lies in the liberal turn to social justice. By ignoring race in his seminal work, Rawls, in effect, created a permission structure for his readers to do the same. Subsequent generations of Rawlsians wrote prolifically on justice without attending to slavery and its anti-Black legacies, or indeed any other form of racial inequality.

Evidence that race generally goes unacknowledged in contemporary liberal discourses is abundant in the literature, although the mode of erasure varies among thinkers. Some, like Minogue, simply overlook racist events and practices and appear to pretend that domination and subordination are not structural relations of power, but subjective matters of personal choice. He argues, "Individuals in a free society may be described as independent. This means, for one thing, that they will organize themselves, and resist attempts by other people to dominate them. But that is only possible if such people dislike not only domination by others, but also submission by others. Independent individuals have no desire to crush the independence of others, for independence is not simply a social relationship, but a characteristic which only exists by rejecting both domination and submission."[25] To follow the apolitical, ahistorical logic of Minogue, one would think that unencumbered individuals simply awaken each morning and issue a sovereign decision about whether to dominate another person that day, entirely missing the tacit, systemic realities of how power operates. Indeed, it is difficult to square his characterization of "independent individuals" with Southern planters, whose "independence" did nothing to counteract their aspiration of total domination over enslaved people. By jettisoning all discussions of institutional power in favor of personal preferences, Minogue invites his readers to ignore entire societies of independent individuals that owned fellow humans, even as many of them openly expressed their "dislike" of slavery. Minogue is far from alone in such moves. Clearly placing choice at the center of politics, Jeffrey Raiman states the following:

> The right to liberty is a right of people to act on their choices. It is a moral right, because its claim on us derives from its inherent rightness, rather than from being part of people's actual moral beliefs, or of some actual legal code. I call it a natural right, because it does not require any act of consent or authorization by others to exist, nor is it derived from some more basic right. It's a negative right because it is a right to

noninterference with one's ability to act as one sees fit, a right against unwanted coercion by others, rather than to some particular performance on the part of others. It's a right against unwanted coercion, because it is not a right against all coercion; it allows coercion that is necessary to protect against the violations of liberty, and it allows coercion that people consent to.[26]

Slave societies are predicated upon the unattainability of this discourse of liberty for a large stratum of the population. Simply sidestepping the fact that slavery existed at all, or that it was of even minimal relevance to the polity, as Raiman does, is a technique of liberal erasure. The moral philosopher David Conway echoes it here: "At bottom what distinguishes from all others that form of societal order which classical liberals maintain is best for all human beings is the magnitude of the measure of liberty which it accords its sane adult members. This form of polity uniquely grants them the liberty to do whatever they want, provided no one but, at most, themselves is harmed by their doing it."[27] While sane and adult, bondpeople were not "members," a fact that seems not to particularly trouble Conway. Further, he adopts a position that is often used to render the relations between liberalism and race indeterminate and absent, namely the cynical view that the ideals of liberalism are aspirational, but never fully realizable.

Such a move simultaneously begs the question of which groups become collateral in liberal "imperfections," and evades criticism by authorizing them: "No classical liberal is so starry-eyed as to suggest that a utopia is or will ever be possible in which all human problems have been solved and complete happiness and virtue attained by every member. However, on behalf of their preferred form of societal order, a no less important, if somewhat less extravagant claim has been defended in this work. This is that this form of order enables its members to attain greater well-being or happiness than does any other societal form."[28] The elision of race is thus enacted through the twin forms of loose acknowledgment and strategic minimization: contrived recognition of liberalism's inherent failures and the reduction of deep, systemic, racial inequality to them. In this light, slavery does not appear as an institution that is foundational to society and the economy. In fact, slavery is never named at all, but subsumed in a vague reference to liberalism's inevitable and ultimately forgivable flaws. Racial injustice, anti-Blackness, and white domination thus disappear from the discussion before they ever needed to appear.

Those even dimly versed in the historical development of liberalism are aware of the likelihood that the silence of contemporary liberals on the subject of race is an effect of the explicitly white supremacist investments of their predecessors. Locke, and later Mill, both benefited from racial regimes of slavery and colonialism, respectively, a fact inseparable from the intellectual content of their work. Locke was an investor in the Royal Africa Company and Bahama Adventurers, both in the business of the transatlantic slave trade.[29] Even though he never actually visited the Americas himself, Locke was responsible, albeit remotely, for the implementation of chattel slavery in the colonies. He drafted the fundamental constitution of the Carolinas, which authorized the use of slave labor in 1669.[30] In that document, Locke made many provisions for the rights of Native Americans, claiming that they could coexist peacefully with whites, successfully assimilate to US norms, and eventually enter the polity. African slaves were notably distinguished from this group, for Locke determined they were wholly inferior on the basis of Blackness. In Barbara Arneil's words:

> It should be noted that the "just" treatment of the aboriginal people encompassed by Carolina's borders was, as in other English settlements, partially based on an ontological distinction drawn between the Amerindian as "natural" pre-Christian man who, with the fullness of time, would be transformed from his natural state into civil Christian men, and the African black who was somehow less than human. In other words, the latter could be enslaved while the former could not, and consequently, Locke and his patron could simultaneously hold shares in the African slave trade and author explicit instructions against slavery as quoted above. [31]

Given Locke's own financial interests in the Atlantic slave trade, the distinction he draws between Native Americans and Africans is very purposeful. By claiming that Black Africans cannot be civilized and assimilated into the polity, Locke is able to provide an ethical rationale for slavery, which he describes in *The Second Treatise* as an extension of the state of war. According to his logic, it is not that slavery is a justifiable institution as much as the enslavement of Black Africans (specifically) is reasonable and legitimate, due to their "backward and barbaric" natures.

Mill was a high-ranking official of the East India Company, an arm of British colonial power that maintained a presence in India from 1600 to 1874.[32] His considerable stakes in economic and political systems of racial domination are quite apparent throughout many of his written works. In *Representative Government*, for example, Mill does not equivocate on the point that rule over "barbaric people" is necessary for their own good. Colonialism is, thus, entirely justifiable as long as it improves the situation of the colonized: "The ruling country ought to be able to do for its subjects all that could be done by a succession of absolute monarchs, guaranteed by irresistible force against the precariousness of tenure attendant on barbarous despotisms, and qualified by their genius to anticipate all that experience has taught to the more advanced nation. Such is the ideal rule of a free people over a barbarous or semi-barbarous one."[33] Mill and Locke are not merely complicit with racial domination, but philosophers of it.[34]

THE LIBERAL MYOPIA OF DEMOCRATIC THEORY

While sidestepping racial domination and captivity serves fairly straightforward functions for liberals, less clear is the grip of liberal myopia on its critics, including democratic theorists that question or contest liberalism. While Chapter Seven will explore the limits of their capacity to address prison rebellion, the liberal myopia of democratic theorists is bound up in the tendency to avoid or ignore slave resistance. One form of liberalism's power lies in its ability to circumscribe political terms, even for those who do not abide by its philosophical principles. It accomplishes this through insidiously expansive and falsely universalistic claims of normativity. For example, humans should be able to live as they so choose; they should exercise personal liberty to the extent that it does not interfere with the freedom of another; and they should pursue their natural rights to life, liberty, and property.

While many critics of liberalism balk at the sanctity of private property, other liberal precepts make tacit appearances in their work, including the primacy of the individual, the imbrications of liberalism and capitalism, principles of reason, and more. Bell claims that "we" are all "conscripts of liberalism," even when disagreeing strongly with it. He states that it "has expanded to encompass the vast majority of political positions regarded as legitimate."[35] In her discussion of neoliberal feminism, Michaele Ferguson identifies a rationality that she terms the "honey trap" that maps onto liberal political thought, as well. To argue against personal choice or individual liberty often hurls the speaker into the unsavory company of authoritarian or autocratic individuals and regimes, intent on curbing or eliminating freedom altogether. The critic of liberalism finds herself stuck in the honey trap: personal choice and individual liberty become conflated with freedom, and opposition to them collapses into oppression.[36] If she is not arguing on behalf of individual liberty, she might appear on the side of individual domination. Perhaps this honey trap squelches, not only critical discussion, but also critical *vision*, creating slippage between the nonliberal and the illiberal, while concealing the former from view.

Judith Shklar, a democratic constitutionalist, and Sheldon Wolin, a radical democratic theorist, are critics of liberalism who nonetheless rely on certain liberal precepts. Both are productive examples of how liberal myopia guides the views even of those who sharply diverge from it. On Shklar and Wolin, Chad Levin observes, "They both read its (liberalism's) rise not as a radical assertion of a new political ethos, but rather as a thoroughly defensive attempt to stave off the social and political disorder resulting from the limitations on human reason and the collapse of religious consensus. In absence of uncontested metaphysical foundations, the individual rights and merit-based distributions corresponding to an ontology of a bounded, discrete, and rational subject promised a sense of social order and temporary relief from unpredictability and groundlessness."[37] To borrow a framework from Bonnie Honig's *Political Theory and the Displacement of Politics*, Shklar and Wolin argue that the appeal of liberalism, a "virtue" theory, is its ability to anesthetize its followers to the agonistic, discordant, and unpredictable effects of politics.

Wolin is one of many thinkers who is simultaneously critical of liberalism and whose work leaves intact multiple liberal tropes upon which his argument rests. The demos forms on the basis of issues held in common among its members. These must concern all citizens, such as environmental matters, gun control, the military industrial complex, etc.[38] While Wolin is a radical democrat, he, not the demos, adjudicates which matters are and are not appropriately "common." But this, of course, begs the question of how such issues are determined as fit for democratic concern? Wolin is known to be critical of what he considers "small group" or "special interest" issues that are not of common concern, such as feminism and multiculturalism. To paraphrase from Barbara Cruikshank's polemical reading of Wolin, why does such a committed democratic thinker chastise those who seek to set the terms of their own citizenship?[39] If liberal discourses of reason and rationalism do not drive this process of establishing what constitutes the common good, Wolin is wholly unclear about what does, thus suggesting that he, too, cannot escape the discursive terrain of liberalism. Partly responsible for this is the ambiguous relationship between the liberal and radical democratic traditions, which are simultaneously opposed and aligned—which repel one another and travel together.

Even within the field of contemporary political theory, there is little consensus among thinkers on the relation between the two. Jason Frank and Jack Turner, for example, differ sharply on their allegiances and ruptures. Turner argues that liberalism and radical democracy are reciprocal and that liberal principles provide conceptual and political anchors for radical Democrats whose aims and commitments might otherwise devolve into a nebulous and disoriented no-man's-land. Turner is far from alone in this charge. Peeter Selg similarly argues for stronger linkages between (Rawlsian) liberalism and radical democracy: "The rationale for initiating a dialogue between political liberalism and radical democracy stems from the fact that it is often argued that the institutional proposals of the latter are vague at best or nonexistent at worst despite their constant underlining of the need to build institutions that would promote the radical democratic form of politics."[40] Frank counters that the tradition of radical democracy is autonomous from liberalism and sharply disagrees that it should be subjected to liberal norms.

Both authors believe that there are complex historical entanglements between the two theories, the result of which is that liberalism's colonization of the terrain of radical democratic thought is inevitable. The distinction that Wolin draws between politics and the political parallels Turner's rejoinder to Frank. In the mode of constitutional liberalism, Turner attempts to subject radical democracy to the regulatory schema of liberal principles. Similarly, Wolin deploys a liberal rationality when he demarcates the boundaries of the political. "The citizen, unlike the groupie, has to acquire a perspective of commonality, to think integrally and comprehensively rather than exclusively. The groupie never gets beyond politics, the stage of unreflective self-interest."[41] The noble work of "the political" says Wolin, should never be confused with the petty self-interest of politics.

Wolin, again, mobilizes this distinction when he conflates what he calls "interest groups" with corporate power. He bemoans current political conditions, which are:

> All politics all of the time but a politics largely untempered by the political. Party squabbles are occasionally on public display, and there

is a frantic and continuous politics among factions of the party, interest groups, competing corporate powers, and rival media concerns. And there is, of course, the culminating moment of national elections when the attention of the nation is required to make a choice of personalities rather than a choice between alternatives. What is absent is the political, the commitment to finding where the common good lies amidst the welter of well-financed, highly organized, single-minded interests rabidly seeking governmental favors and overwhelming the practices of representative government public administration by a sea of cash.[42]

Wolin borrows extensively from liberal tropes in this passage, most notably in his insistence on a distinction between abject politics and the worthy political realm (which calls to mind recent liberal indictments of identity politics), as well as his use of the "common good."[43] Although this concept has a long history, beginning with Aristotle, the phrase itself first appears in Jean-Jacques Rousseau's *The Social Contract* and has since been both a problem for, and principle of, liberalism.[44] Even though liberals nurse worries that the "common good" could run into the problem of prescribing certain ways of life, rather than leaving them up to individual choices, a simple reformulation of the common good could easily align it with the core tenets of liberalism.[45] Thus, even as Wolin is critical of classical and contemporary liberal discourses, he nonetheless draws on them, a paradox attesting to the pull of liberalism in, and outside of, his work.

Wolin was a prolific scholar, whose book *Tocqueville Between Two Worlds* does address slavery by contrast with his more recent writings on "inverted totalitarianism," although the specific content of this work concerns me less than the tacit liberal debts he accrues.[46] Despite the fact that slave resistance is, by definition, fugitive, Wolin never mentions it. This is less a careless omission than the elision of an insurgent politics that defies norms of liberty, reason, and the common good. By contrast, large-scale, armed slave rebellions were often fanatical, irrational, and sometimes self-interested, and the everyday resistance of bondpeople was certainly not extraordinary and episodic. Their interests would never have been characterized as part of the common good. At the same time, other political theorists read Wolin as a distinctively anti-racist thinker whose views grew from the most radical lessons of the civil rights movement.[47]

LIBERALISM AND ABOLITIONISM

Liberal concepts and dichotomies that frame common assumptions about political life are confounded by the lived experiences of bondpeople, and, in particular, their resistance. To put this differently, slavery exposes the limits of those liberal and democratic constructs that are often viewed as self-evident discourses of political life in the United States. The ideals of universal rights and liberty, promises of early liberal theorists of the seventeenth century, are lies exposed by the mere existence of bondage. Locke's philosophy of so-called natural rights to life, liberty, and private property are irrelevant to the political subjecthood of enslaved people, for they enjoy no such rights in the enduring state of war that they occupy.[48] Rather, as a population with no civic standing, they are owned as property. Freedom for Locke is the state into which men are born, while freedom for bondpeople is stolen. Liberty for Locke means that men are subject to no superior earthly power, while for Harriet Jacobs, it meant subjecting oneself to extraordinarily repressive conditions. And finally, the central claim in *The Second Treatise on Civil Government*, that every man has property in his own person is, of course, the fundamental right to which enslaved people are denied altogether.[49]

At the same time, liberal and democratic tropes carried great meaning for many enslaved intellectuals. For example, in his renowned address, "What to the Slave is the Fourth of July?" the abolitionist Frederick Douglass draws on the liberal tradition that so inspired the founders of the United States to deliver a fiery and impassioned diatribe. "Would you have me argue that man is entitled to liberty? That he is the rightful owner of his own body? You have already declared it. Must I argue the wrongfulness of slavery? Is that a question for Republicans? Is it to be settled by the rules of logic and argumentation, as a matter beset with great difficulty, involving a doubtful application of the principle of justice, hard to be understood? How should I look to-day, in the presence of Americans, dividing, and subdividing a discourse, to show that men have a natural right to freedom? Speaking of it relatively, and positively, negatively, and affirmatively."[50] Here Douglass uses the concepts of natural rights and liberty as rhetorical devices meant to shed light on the contrast between the realities of Black and white Americans and the gross hypocrisy of slavery. Some, including the political theorist Peter C. Myers, argue that the appearance of such constructs in Douglass's work is not merely rhetorical, but that the reinvention of liberalism in accordance with principles of racial equality is Douglass's central contribution to American political thought.⁵¹ Liberalism, states Myers, is the moral core of Douglass's work, substantiating the ideal that "all men are created equal." Nick Bromell echoes this, arguing that Douglass expresses a broad-minded openness to ideas and others, which is itself a key liberal tenet.⁵²

In his autobiography, the former bondman, author, and abolitionist, Olaudah Equiano, positively links abolitionism with both liberalism and capitalism, a move that is all the more strategic and prescient, given that he wrote and published the book in Britain in 1789, in the early decades of the Industrial Revolution.⁵³ His appeals to the liberal and capitalist sensibilities of his readers should not downplay the fact that Equiano was also well-versed in aggressive forms of slave resistance. After he was kidnapped as a young boy from his village, in what is now Nigeria, Equiano refused food aboard the ship that first brought him to Barbados and then England. That small rebellious act likely saved him from sale in Barbados, a country notorious for its most brutal treatment of enslaved people, for when Equiano was taken to the slave market there, he appeared a skinny, sickly, undesirable commodity.

His autobiography was wildly successful upon publication, likely due to its affirmation of predominantly liberal values, as well as its riveting firsthand account of the Middle Passage. Rather than describing slavery's violations of liberal ideals, Equiano focuses on the ways in which abolition would only serve them. He states, "Population, the bowels, and surface of Africa, abound in valuable and useful returns; the hidden treasures of centuries will be brought to light and into circulation. Industry, enterprise, and mining will have their full scope, proportionably as they civilize. In a word, it lays open an endless field of commerce to the British manufacturers and merchant adventurers. The manufacturing interests and the general interests are synonymous. The abolition of slavery would be in reality a universal good."⁵⁴ Here Equiano appeals to the enterprising spirit of capitalists, drawing on liberal sensibilities like "the general good" to build a case for the discontinuation of the slave trade. In so doing, he refutes popular logic that slave labor is economically efficacious and necessary for a plantation economy. The complexity of Equiano's political thought should be acknowledged in accordance with the plurality of his subject positions. Elizabeth Bohls notes that "Equiano, the anti-slavery polemicist, skillfully uses Abolitionist geography to advance his political ends. Equiano, the traveler and travel writer, I conclude, finally departs from that spatial schema, with its rhetorical separation of colony and metropole. The two are systemically connected: Equiano, the discrepant cosmopolitan, tacitly affirms this fact by living it."[55]

Quobna Ottobah Cugoano turns Locke's equation of life and liberty with property on its head when he claims that those who take children, loved ones, and freedom from another are far more inhuman than those who steal only property. He states:

> If they determine it so (that those who steal only property are less harmful than those who steal lives), as reason must tell every man, that himself is of more value than his property; then the executors of the laws of civilization ought to tremble at the inconsistency of passing judgment upon those whose crimes, in many cases, are less than what the whole legislature must be guilty of, when those of a far greater is encouraged and supported by it wherever slavery is tolerated by law, and, consequently, that slavery can no where be tolerated with any consistency to civilization and the laws of justice among men; but if it can maintain its ground, to have any place at all, it must be among a society of barbarians and thieves, and where the laws of their society is, for every one to catch what he can.[56]

Unlike most abolitionists of the time, who fought for the discontinuation of the slave trade, rather than elimination of the entire institution altogether, Cugoano was a radical emancipationist, calling for the immediate end of all slave labor. Also, unlike Equiano's gentler autobiographical narrative, Cugoano's is an uncompromising jeremiad. He refuses to capitulate to any enslavers or slavery apologists, although, like Douglass and Equiano, he uses liberalism as a bulwark against all defenses of slavery. Through what Adam Dahl calls the "creolization of natural liberty," Cugoano exposes the hypocrisy inherent in the slave trade for simultaneously expanding the property economy and also violating property rights.[57] In so doing, he reconstitutes a dehydrated construct of natural liberty. Just as Equiano opposes the prevailing view that chattel slavery is economically beneficial by claiming that abolition would generate far greater prosperity, Cugoano refutes the assumption that slave societies are civilized, asserting instead that they are thieving and barbaric. In this way, both authors disrupt dominant discourses that slavery is a necessary, just, and economically sound institution.

While their intellectual and political commitments differ, Douglass, Equiano, and Cugoano make use of liberal ideas in their abolitionist thought. There are many strategic reasons for this, namely framing their discussions in terms of reason, rationalism, and individualism likely appealed to the sensibilities of white Americans and Europeans with great investments in these discourses. It is also true that liberal ideals held genuine promise and possibility for the three authors and for good reason: liberalism was swiftly becoming the dominant political ideology in the time that all three were writing. Outside of the United States, one of the central provocations of the Haitian Revolution, for example, was the recent French Revolution and accompanying Enlightenment principles of universal rights and liberty.[58] This is to say that, given the myriad ways in which slavery violates both, it is easy to see the political and intellectual utility of liberalism for abolitionist thought.

It is understandable that Douglass, Equiano, and Cugoano would make use of liberal discourse in their work. However, the practical utility of these constructs, I argue, hits a dead end in the domain of slavery. This is not to chastise the three authors for their recourse to liberalism nor hold that it is entirely without genuine potential for abolitionists. Still, attending to slave resistance reveals the ways that reason, the public/private sphere, and the binary of self-interest versus solidarity fail to articulate the political meaning of slave politics. Even though these are only a few of many liberal discourses, their limitations are fully apparent.

TURNER'S REBELLION AND THE LIMITS OF REASON

The Southampton Insurrection can neither be described as reasonable, nor its leader, Nat Turner, a man of "reason." Spragens states in *Reasonableness and Liberal Political Theory* that "persons are 'reasonable' when they behave and respond in ways that seem suitable to the situation at hand and to the powers, rights, and responsibility which they bear."[59] Turner, according to that definition, was decidedly unreasonable. He was a fire-and-brimstone preacher, who claimed to be chosen by God for a spiritual mission. He smashed the head of a young baby during the rebellion; believed in signs, including a solar eclipse ostensibly signaling readiness for the attack; and claimed to hear divine voices. "Fanatic" is a far better descriptor of Turner than "rational actor":

> And immediately on the sign appearing in the heavens, the seal was removed from my lips, and I communicated the great work laid out for me to do, to four in whom I had the greatest confidence (Henry,

Hark, Nelson, and Sam)—It was intended by us to have begun the work of death on the 4th July last—Many were the plans formed and rejected by us, and it affected my mind to such a degree, that I fell sick, and the time passed without our coming to any determination how to commence—Still forming new schemes and rejecting them, when the sign appeared again, which determined me not to wait longer.[60]

Elsewhere in his lengthy confession, Turner described his own delusions, including fields of corn dotted in blood; a white man who developed a pox in which blood oozed from his pores immediately after hearing the same divine signs that Turner was receiving; and heavenly forms appearing in the leaves of trees.

His rebellion was not an effort to secure rights for enslaved people or issue coherent political demands to the Virginia General Assembly. Turner never even mentions slavery in his confession, throwing into doubt the question of whether his act can rightly be called "abolitionist." Regardless of Turner's intentions, which are not easily gauged from one, slim, first-person testimonial, the political significance of the revolt is clear. The cavalry of rebels paraded silently through the street, some on horseback, methodically carrying out "a general destruction of property." It was undertaken collectively and with order and organization. Unsurprisingly, local newspapers merely vilified Turner and his comrades: "He is a complete fanatic, or plays his part most admirably. On other subjects he possesses an uncommon share of intelligence, with a mind capable of attaining anything; but warped and perverted by the influence of early impressions."[61] The fanatical narrative is used to discredit the political legitimacy of the event. Other commentary is no less biting: "Thus, has a spirit of fanaticism among a set of ignorant blacks, for a time spread consternation over a wide extent of the country and robbed fifty-five innocents of their lives."[62] If this reaction is more or less expected from Turner's contemporaries, it is perhaps less self-evident why so few scholars, past and present, consider the politics of Turner's rebellion. For example, Stephen Howard Browne's analysis of *The Confessions of Nat Turner* addresses secular and sacred readings, the first of which considers the insurrection an act of human depravity, while the second suggests that Turner was acting in accordance with forces beyond his control. While Browne gestures briefly at the legal impact of the revolt, the interpretation that he outlines explores neither the political drives of Turner and his followers, nor the impact of the revolt on Jeffersonian Virginia and the rest of the Confederacy.

Much of the secondary literature on the insurrection is exclusively concerned with its aftermath, including the usages and appropriations of Turner and his contested status in historical memory. Scott French's *The Rebellious Slave: Nat Turner in American Memory* examines the ways in which Turner is mobilized to reconcile the "troubled past" of the United States.[63] True to its name, Mary Kemp Davis's *Nat Turner Before the Bar of Judgment: Fictional Treatments of the Southampton Slave Insurrection* explores literary mobilizations of the rebellion, arguing that Turner has remained on trial long after his execution.[64] Moral questions of slavery are worked out through interpretive treatments of the rebellious bondman. While these studies attend to the retrospective accounts of Turner, including the importance of the uprising to the historical imaginary of slavery, none of them approach Turner as a political actor. His messianic proclivities easily dismiss him as an irrational zealot, for liberal reason dominates popular political discourse, policing the boundaries of what "counts" as serious versus nonserious political practice; civil disobedience versus bad behavior; negotiation and compromise versus fanaticism and zealotry (or what Olson calls the "pejorative tradition").[65]

The dictates of liberal reason frame success and failure in binaristic terms, indicating that slave rebellions were fated to fail. Plots were often uncovered before uprisings were executed. For example, the aforementioned Gabriel's rebellion and Vesey's "Rising." On a handful of occasions, bondpeople on slave ships were able to overpower the crew and return to Africa, including captives aboard the *Clare* in 1729, and the extraordinary revolt on *La Amistad* in 1839.[66] Torture, execution, and tighter legal strictures further regulating the whereabouts and activities of enslaved and free African Americans were far more common than these exceptional moments of "success." That it is objectively counter to the personal interest of an enslaved person to resist captivity, given the likely repercussions, attests less to the futility of rebellion than futility of reason to explain it. The drive to rebel against enslavement cannot be understood through the rational calculus of self-interest. The default liberal assumption that reason universally prevails across political contexts conceals from view the actions and events that occur outside of those frames.

THE PUBLIC/PRIVATE DISTINCTION, MAROONS, AND THE GERMAN COAST SLAVE UPRISING

Although the public/private distinction predates liberalism, the construct nonetheless invites reflection on the ways that dominant liberal discourses fall apart in politics in captivity. As early as 431 BCE, there is some evidence that philosophers were at least thinking in terms of separate spheres.[67] Clear lines between the public and private realms are drawn in other premodern contexts as well. According to Morton Horowitz, the codification of the distinction can first be seen in late medieval English law, specifically in attempts to delineate different forms of monarchical land ownership. The lands held by the king as feudal lord were his to use as he wished, but another category called "crown lands" were essentially an early version of public property that the king was not permitted to alienate.[68]

Traces of the idea of separate spheres are also observable in antiquity and the Middle Ages, and they fully emerged with the rise of liberalism in the seventeenth century. The public/private distinction underwrites the conceptual categories of early liberal thinkers, most notably Locke's concept of private property, which he elevates to the status of life and liberty, as well as the raison d'être of government itself. For Hannah Arendt, the private sphere in the pre-Socratic, Greek city state is where men handle the messy but necessary business of domination (of their own bodies and those of their dependent charges: women, children, and enslaved people) for the purpose of then entering the public realm to speak and act. By contrast, for Locke the core purpose of government and politics is to safeguard the private property of its citizens. His perspective on the two spheres is, thus, a loose inverse of Arendt's account of ancient Athens: the public exists for the sake of the private.

Much contemporary criticism of the public/private distinction fixes on its *consequences*, not the pertinence of the construct itself.[69] Today, theorists tend to focus on the injustices generated by the separate spheres, rather than the contextual irrelevance of the division altogether for a people who had access to neither public nor private realms. These overwhelmingly white discourses reify the public/private distinction through critique, failing to identify the institutions and social and political domains for which it has *never* existed, such as US chattel slavery and, arguably, African American political life since its legal termination. It is hardly a coincidence that there are virtually no Black feminist critiques of the public/private distinction, for it is only worth engaging if there is some content and integrity to the individual categories themselves. Enslaved people had access to neither the private realm of the household nor the public realm of society and polity. The private lives of bondpeople were regularly disrupted; they were forbidden from participating, formally or informally, in public life; they were rarely permitted to occupy public spaces of any kind; and, of course, they were forbidden from availing themselves of public facilities and resources such as public libraries or schools.

In the former Confederacy, both bondpeople and free Black men and women were generally treated as foreign enemies and strict laws governed their movements, behavior, and whereabouts. Slave patrols, particularly after the passage of the Fugitive Slave Law of 1850, terrorized bondpeople, cracking down on truancy, illicit social activities, and, of course, fugitivity. Strict laws and local ordinances regulated the proximity of free African Americans to enslaved ones. The historian James Oakes puts it well here: "Formal separation of slavery from the polity was simply the institutional context for relations between politics and society in the Old South."[70] The banishment of bondpeople from both the public and private realms, mirrors this. If a (white) woman's rightful place was in the home during this time, an enslaved person's rightful place was nowhere. They neither benefited from the privileges afforded by the separation between spheres, nor were they disadvantaged by its consequences. Thus, the pervasiveness of the public/private in academic political theory marks, not only another instance in which the lived, political experiences of enslaved people are ignored and forgotten, but also how concealed from view are social and political contexts upon which the distinction does not map.

Slave rebellion confounds the public/private dichotomy in several key ways. First, the rebellious activities of bondpeople, while unmistakably political, are neither public nor private in character. Second, the condition of slavery, in general, is unthinkable on the axis of the public and private spheres. It is not that bondpeople were oppressed in the private sphere but included in public; or excluded from public life but enjoyed even a modicum of equality in the private realm; or further still, that they were dominated and abused in both the public and private spheres. Rather, the public and private realms conceptually cease to exist altogether on plantations. These spaces straddle the lines between personal, economic, social, and political, and thus cannot be described as a public or private realm, properly understood. The plantation was the basic economic site of production and profit in the Confederate South, *and* home to individual planters, servants, and bondpeople; plantations were often owned by elite men who exercised a great deal of political influence in the states where they resided, and they were the sites of their livelihood, class position, and family heritage. The lines between work, home, politics, and economy were obscure and generally indecipherable on plantations.

Also inviting readers to appreciate the irrelevance of the public/private distinction are the rebellious practices of maroon communities, existing in the shadows of plantations. Maroons included both fugitive bondpeople and free African Americans who formed shadow societies in swamps and backwoods of the slave South. Neither private nor public, the mere existence of maroons, by definition, confounds the distinction between the two spheres. They, too, showcase Stephanie Camp's revised concept of "rival geography," for they were known, but not visible; they were hidden, by necessity, from public view; their location in rural outposts exposed them to vulnerabilities of natural elements as well as the constant threat of invasion from white militia. They certainly did not enjoy any of the conventional protections of a private realm.

Historical records suggest that there were about fifty known maroon communities in the United States between 1672 and 1864 in South Carolina, North Carolina, Virginia, Louisiana, Florida, Georgia, Mississippi, and Alabama.[71] Some were settled, complete with stable homes and workplaces; others were more makeshift and itinerant, located in swamplands and forests. Maroons stole livestock and other provisions from nearby plantations and traded with poor whites who lived near their borders. They offered safe havens for truant and fugitive bondpeople and provided base camps for uprisings.

Despite a 1672 law that rewarded those who captured and killed maroons, these societies continued to thrive through the antebellum period and American Civil War. Aptheker stated, "These (maroons) were seriously annoying, for they were sources of insubordination."[72] They absorbed a good deal of white anxiety about slave rebellion, particularly since slave fugitivity was reportedly higher in maroon regions. For Aptheker, maroon communities were a constant reminder of the fallacy of common, white supremacist narratives that slavery was a benevolent institution and enslaved people were grateful for their own bondage. In his words, "The story of American maroons is of interest not only because it forms a fairly important part of the history of the South and of the Negro, but also because of the evidence it affords to show that the conventional picture of slavery as a more or less delightful, patriarchal system is fallacious."[73] Maroons explode this view of slavery and other dominant ones, including the idea that bondpeople were docile, amiable, and rarely resistant to their captivity;

that there were no real paths of escape from bondage; and that slavery was an inevitable condition.

Like maroon resistance, the German Coast Slave Uprising also illuminates the irrelevance of the categories, public and private. First, slave quarters, while certainly not private in any discernible sense, were crucial sites of political organizing. Kook, Quamana, and Charles Deslondes were able to congregate and plot the rebellion without attracting unwanted attention from planters. Even though they and other bondpeople could enjoy greater discretion in slave quarters, it would be a misnomer to think of them as a "private sphere," for they neither belonged to their residents, nor did they have any expectation of genuine security within them. The quarters were surveilled, policed, and regularly raided by enslavers and slave patrols. In the early nineteenth-century Orleans territory, slave patrols were particularly vigilant about monitoring the leisure time of bondpeople, given the success of the recent Haitian Revolution, the presence of so many Haitians in the region at the time, heavy Creole influences, and the demographic similarities between Haiti and Orleans.[74]

Second, the uprising, while unquestionably political, was not carried out in public, but on the private property of plantations. A small collective of enslaved men, including Kook, Quamana, Deslondes, and Harry Kenner, began the revolt by attacking the residences of planters in the late-night hours of January 8, 1811.[75] The rebels first targeted the plantation of Alexandre Labranche, before moving on to those of James Brown and Francois Trepagnier. While Brown fled, taking to the swamp for protection, Trepagnier, a brutal racist who was said to have kept a Black boy as a house pet, stood his ground. Kook hacked him to death. The band of rebels swiftly moved through the area plantations, recruiting more bondmen as they did. When they arrived at the Meuilion plantation, about thirteen more enslaved men joined the revolt. As Rasmussen states, "the rebels then laid waste to Meuilion's grand home, pillaging and destroying much of the wealth the planter had accumulated."[76] By the second day of the attack, the cavalry, now between two hundred and five hundred strong, traveled twenty-one miles in the direction of New Orleans where they faced off with a militia formed by local planters. Because the enslaved men carried mostly makeshift weapons, they quickly succumbed to their attackers. Most were summarily executed, their heads mounted on pikes.

The German Coast Slave Uprising, like other similar revolts, took place on the bodies and property of planters in their living spaces, not city centers,

106   *The Racial Limits of Liberalism*

public squares, or even battlegrounds. There is no clearly recognizable political narrative for the property destruction and carnage associated with it. Slave rebellion cannot be characterized as "action in public," for its lone method was violence and included neither political speech nor recognizable public spheres. If the revolt defies the logic of the public and private distinction, the institution of slavery itself does, as well. It contains both public and private elements, such as class status, civil standing, and citizenship (public), as well as wealth, private property, family structures, sexuality, labor, and embodiment. It is thus fitting that politics in captivity dissolves the imaginary line between the public and private, taking physical aim at the bodies and lives of enslavers as well as the material conditions of domination.

SELF-INTEREST AND DAILY RESISTANCE

Other common liberal or liberal-adjacent binaries, such as individual versus collective action, and relatedly self-interest versus solidarity, are largely undone by both the extraordinary and everyday realities of slave resistance. William Dusinberre references the story of an enslaved girl, Fannie Berry, who accidentally set a barn on fire and allowed others to take the blame for her actions to argue that "enslavement could sometimes breed individualistic pursuit of self-interest, rather than honorable solidarity."[77] The same is true, claims Dusinberre, of those bondpeople who sought approval and material benefits from planters (what Genovese calls "accomodationism.") Dusinberre cites the testimony of a formerly enslaved man, who recounted a play scheme from his childhood in which he cast himself in the role of overseer. He sat on the doorsill shouting out orders and whipping his playmates to enforce them. On this, Dusinberre states that the child "observing that black people were bullied by white people, the bullied child transformed himself into a bully of other black people. This may have protected the little bully's self-esteem, but it was scarcely training in solidarity, and it did nothing for the other enslaved children."[78] In both cases, Dusinberre erroneously projects the dichotomy of self-interest/solidarity onto the plantation, chastising Berry for failing to take responsibility for her actions and allowing her fellow bondpeople to wrongfully suffer, and the boy for imagining himself into privileged positions in the racial hierarchy of the slave South.

That Dusinberre makes enslaved children the standard bearers of moral judgment is itself odd and problematic, but regardless, this way of characterizing the behavior and practices of any bondperson warrants critical scrutiny.

I argue that the utility of the self-interest / solidarity dichotomy breaks down altogether under conditions of slavery and proves useless as a metric for judgment. When one is prohibited from the exercise of both self-interest and autonomy, the ethical distinction between "honorable solidarity" and "individualistic pursuit of self-interest" breaks down. Under conditions that specifically deny humans the very construct of a self, acts that might otherwise appear selfish are uniquely productive and even political. The pursuit of self-interest becomes potentially transformative, a radical assertion of an insurgent self, or what Saidiya Hartman calls "an appropriation of the self," which transgresses the law of property.[79] Acts of self-interest undertaken by white people with civic standing and Black bondpeople without it occur in different theoretical paradigms. When Fannie Berry acts in her own interest, she is upending property relations that affix her to an enslaver. Categorizing her actions within a binary of deplorable self-interest versus honorable solidarity fundamentally misunderstands the circumstances under which enslaved people do both.

The practice of fugitivity, probably the most studied and well-documented form of slave resistance, also confounds the dichotomy of self-interest versus solidarity. The bondman Moses Roper, who was three-quarters white, was sold several times during his early childhood, eventually to a vicious, tyrannical owner named John Gooch, who regularly and mercilessly beat and humiliated him. Despite enduring torturous punishment after attempting to run away, Roper relentlessly and repeatedly fled the plantation, on one occasion chained to a fellow bondwoman:

> On the Monday, he chained me to the same female slave as before. As he had to go out that day, he did not give me the punishment which he intended to give me every day, but at night when he came home, he made us walk round his estate, and by all the houses of the slaves, for them to taunt us; when we came home he told us we must be up very early in the morning, and go to the field before the other slaves. We were up at day-break, but we could not get on fast, on account of the heavy irons on my feet. It may be necessary to state that these irons were first made red hot and bent in a circle, so as just to allow of my feet going through; it having been cooled, and my leg with the iron on lifted up to an anvil, it was made secure round my ancles. When I walked with these irons on, I used to hold them up with my hands by means of a cord. We walked *about a mile in two hours,* but knowing the punishment he was

going to inflict on us, we made up our minds to escape into the woods, and secrete ourselves.[80]

The act can neither be described as self-interest nor solidarity but obscures the line between them. On the one hand, fugitivity was often tantamount to abandonment, for runaways were forced to sever ties with family and loved ones, or at least risk losing those connections. (The associated stigma of leaving behind one's children, partially accounts for why women were comparatively less likely than men to attempt to permanently flee plantations, for maternal responsibilities for children and other kin often overcame the pursuit of freedom.) Although individual desire (to escape abuse, seek permanent freedom, or carve out a few days or weeks for themselves) likely motivated flight, characterizing it as mere self-interest overlooks the interdependencies among bondpeople and vast networks of social relations and practices of care that made these illicit activities possible. Roper, for example, was literally tethered to an enslaved woman with whom he agreed to forge escape, all the while knowing that harsh punishment awaited them. In so doing, he acted on behalf of himself as well as her. Numerous slave narratives describe the unique role of friends and kin in aiding and abetting the rebellious activities of one another by leaving food and other provisions so they could survive for temporary periods in the wilderness, as well as offering shelter and providing clandestine information. Even though it is tempting to consider fugitivity and truancy purely individualistic pursuits, they entail support and mutual assistance that radically subverts individual sovereignty. An interview with the former bondman, Harry Jarvis, reveals the impossibility of viewing fugitivity in such simplistic and reductive terms:

> Well, tell us how you escaped.
>
> Dat war de fus yeah' ob de war, madam. It war bad enough before, but arter de war come, it war wus nor eber. Fin'ly, he shot at me one day, 'n I reckoned I'd stood it 'bout's long's I could, so I tuk to der woods. I lay out dere for three weeks.
>
> Three weeks in the woods! How did you live? How did you help being taken?
>
> Couldn't get out no sooner, ye see, fur he had his spies out a watchin' fur me. He hunted me wid dogs fust, but I'd crost a branch, an dey los' de scent, and didn't fin' it, an' den he sot his slaves all up an' down de sho,' waitin' fur me to come out.

Would they have taken you?

Dey wouldn't a durs' not to, ef I had come out, but I had frien's who kep' me informed how t'ings war gwine on, an' brought me food.[81]

The daily resistance of enslaved women also unravels prevailing constructs of self-interest. Bondwomen spent a good deal of their meager spare time making their own clothes, such as hoop dresses that were fashionable among wealthy white women, and accessorizing with found objects and items pilfered from planters' homes. Their creations did not merely mimic the trends of white society, but often incorporated a distinct style that hybridized West African, Creole, and American aesthetics and made use of materials that were readily available.[82] Head scarves, shells, bones, and other decorative pieces adorned their apparel. They wore these in secret when escaping plantations for outlaw parties and other illicit events. While sewing clothes and fashioning makeshift accessories are commonly considered hobbies and apolitical pastimes, good for little more than self-interest, it is my contention that they are of equal political significance as large-scale rebellion.[83] Because, for example, it was conventional for bondwomen to wear the identical garments and undertake field labor for the same number of hours as enslaved men, sewing and crafting enabled them to form an improvisational, feminized gender identity that resisted the strictures of white enslavers as well as the embedded narrative that only white female bodies were worthy of delight and pampering.

Simultaneously, the care labor of female "house slaves" was called upon to raise planters' children, tend to the elderly, and assume the domestic burdens that would otherwise fall to white wives. Sarah Haley refers to the malleability of Black female labor as *the* "unbearable flexibility of nonbeing." Also mapping onto this is C. Riley Snorton's concept of gender fungibility.[84] Whatever privileges could be derived from sexual divisions of labor among whites were unsurprisingly withheld from enslaved women, who were simultaneously cast as hardened, tough, and masculine in effort to justify the harsh conditions to which they were subjected, *and* sexually voracious, promiscuous, and noninnocent, which made them readily available for sexual assault. Their resistance to this double exploitation does not take the form of grand, armed revolts like the Southampton Insurrection or the German Coast Slave Uprising, but nonetheless, are rebellious, political testaments to their agency and creativity.

5

The Concept of World

"Work provides an 'artificial' world of things, distinctly different from all natural surroundings. Within its borders each individual life is housed, while this world itself is meant to outlast and transcend them all."

—HANNAH ARENDT[1]

RACE, BLACKNESS, AND THE SOCIAL/POLITICAL DISTINCTION

In a letter dated June 12, 1968, sent to reader Donald Barclay, Hannah Arendt stated the following:

> You see that I too would think that "the root cause" of all riots, protests, and demonstrations is political in nature. Except that the general loss of authority and the growing disorder also, though accidentally, opens the doors to a great number of nonpolitical grievances which then may turn out to be more violent in nature than the political grievances that caused them to appear. As "the loss of political expression" as I see it, very briefly and schematically, this is what happens. The civil rights movement taught the students how to act, how to achieve results by action, and how to enjoy themselves while doing so. Everything went fine so long as they were primarily confronted with the clearly unconstitutional laws and ordinances in the Southern states. The moment the movement had achieved what it could achieve there and came North, they were

confronted with the social questions of poverty, uneducation, criminality, slums, etc. Nothing of this can be changed by political power and the attempt to do so could only end in frustration.[2]

While her sharp distinction between the social and political has always been a lightning rod for her critics, there are, as the letter to Barclay attests, no better moments to bear witness to its genuine futility than when Arendt tries to wrest Black politics into its cages. In so doing, she sidesteps the interconnections between ostensibly "social questions" and political ones, including the ways that "poverty, uneducation, criminality, and slums" are direct descendants of the same "clearly unconstitutional" laws and ordinances that, for her, hold proper political status. Even though it is downright bizarre that a thinker as astute and politically savvy as Arendt could speak about Southern segregationist laws and poverty in the North as if they are not thoroughly intertwined, such moves are well-worn patterns in her work. The glib, conjectural "everything went fine" is an undoubtedly odd choice of words, given that the desperate attempts of white supremacists to cling to the vestiges of racial hierarchy in the Jim Crow South took shape in ongoing terror, sexual assault, and murder of civil rights activists in the 1950s and 1960s.[3] But then, Arendt is an undoubtedly odd choice of theorist for a book on Black political resistance. Despite her biased and uneven views of race and, as this letter makes plain, ungenerous take on "riots," further analysis yields some important conclusions about her anti-Blackness and also, counterintuitively, the theoretical utility of worldliness for African American resistance.

On the one hand, many of Arendt's writings on European racism are rich and insightful, particularly its imperialist drives and origins in the nation-state. On the other hand, her personal correspondence and much of her later work (notably the essays "Reflections on Little Rock" and "On Violence") reveal glaringly anti-Black biases and genuine, perhaps willful, ignorance of the structural conditions of white domination in the United States. The contradictions between these two facets of her thinking are worth critical attention, for her analysis of race and racism in *Origins* can speak more presciently to contemporary racial issues than some of her staunchest critics would likely concede. Yet, the coexistence of her insightful theories of race and distinct anti-Blackness invite readers to consider, among other things, the specificity of Blackness that cannot be collapsed into "race," broadly speaking.

Following Robert Bernasconi, I argue that Arendt's gatekeeping tendency to cordon off the social from the political is perhaps the preservative, if not the origin, of her anti-Black prejudice. Michael Hanchard holds that Arendt misinterpreted, particularly in her essay "Reflections on Little Rock," the attempts of Black activists to transform the US polity. A proper understanding of this would require her to "first acknowledge the shifting analytical distinction between the political and the social." Taking this a step further, I argue that Arendt's infamous binary collapses (spectacularly) in the domain of US racial politics.[4] Structural anti-Black racism blurs the lines between the political and social to the point of unrecognizability.[5] For example, vagrancy statutes (political) declared unemployment a criminal status, while Jim Crow-era employment discrimination meant that precious few jobs outside of low-wage domestic and agricultural work were actually available to Black Americans. Prison and poverty (social) naturally resulted. Redlining is a government policy (political) that ghettoizes and segregates Black communities, deepening inequalities in education, health, and housing (social). The legal termination of racial segregation in the passage of the Civil Rights Act of 1964 (political) resulted in the shuttering of public facilities, like community pools and green spaces, throughout the South, for local white leaders preferred to close, rather than integrate them.[6] As a result, wealthy whites joined private country clubs, excluding African Americans from membership (social). There are dozens, if not hundreds, of other identical phenomena, signaling the mutual reciprocity of so-called social and political issues in US racial politics. Every one of them is, contrary to Arendt's aforementioned statements to Barclay, transformable through the exercise of political power. None can be neatly (or even messily) divided into one of two camps, for the concepts are never autonomous.[7] Attempts to situate them in separable categories are doomed from the outset, for this overlooks the basic fact that structural forces of racism are, by definition, fusions of the social and political with both public and private consequences. The distinction obscures this condition.[8] While her most ignorant and problematic treatments of race and slavery orbit the division between the social and political, Arendt's most successful and useful engagements with these subjects are unmoored from it. This is particularly clear in *Origins of Totalitarianism* when she had not yet established the autonomy of the categories social and political, and where, uncoincidentally, her most rich and robust treatments of race and slavery live.

This chapter attends to Arendt's theory of world, which is free of the conceptual pressures associated with many other ideas in her political thought. That her concept of world is bound to neither the public/private nor the social/political bespeaks its theoretical utility for politics in captivity, for it is largely immune from the territorial impulses of both Arendt and her readers.[9] In parallel with Patchen Markell's critique of the "territorial reading" of *The Human Condition*, the common tendency to read Arendt's renowned triad of labor, work, and action as if these categories are fully separable, discrete, and sacrosanct, I hold that world is *already* outside of the well-mined dichotomies in her work. While Markell argues against interpreting the trifold capacities of the human condition as "disjunctive categories into which individual instances of human activity can be sorted," I add that world is conveniently untethered from the conceptual forces that produce temptations for the "territorial reading."[10] It is possible that, by contrast with other ideas in her oeuvre, world is less fully conceptualized, or perhaps its relationship to the public and private realms is simply indeterminate and ambiguous.

I first discuss the full meaning of world by exploring its mobilization across various works of Arendt and her followers, focusing in particular on *The Human Condition*, where it appears in its most evolved form. The interplay between world and other concepts in her political thought, including labor, work, action, plurality, authority, and freedom, prominently appears in this inquiry. Because world is the conceptual anchor of this book, a full elaboration of its meaning and relation to the rest of her political thought is essential.[11] Arendt's own lived experiences, including her coming of age during the end of the Weimar Republic, and flight from the Third Reich, are undoubtedly crucial to the origins of the concept as well, although they are not fully elaborated here.[12] The same is true of her early encounters with phenomenology as a university student; an intense, on-again-off-again love affair with Martin Heidegger; and a dissertation on St. Augustine and early philosophical commitments—all of which are also undoubtedly formative.[13]

THE CONCEPT OF WORLD

In a posthumously published essay, "Introduction Into Politics," Arendt writes: "For at the center of politics lies concern for the world, not for man—a concern, in fact, for a world, however constituted, without which those who are both concerned and political would not find life worth living."[14]

World is the condition of political life and also its raison d'être, for it makes politics possible and, reciprocally, service to the world is the very centerpiece of political life. Contrary to its popular meaning in everyday language, world is not a universal descriptor of nature and the Earth, but the contingently permanent ground of human commonality. It is comprised of physical use objects (for example, tools, furniture, art, buildings, machines), and intangible things (language, convention, social norms, figures of speech, ritual), both of which make humans intelligible and recognizable to each other.[15] Far from the ultrasubjective experiences of love and pain, which are private and fundamentally incommunicable, despite the best efforts of poets and artists, world is precisely the opposite.[16] Standing independently outside of humans, rather than buried deep within them, world provides commonality among those who inhabit it. Without a shared language, there would be no basis for making oneself understood to another. Without a table or some other means of finite separation, how would otherwise disparate people connect? Anyone who has ever struggled to find a common topic of conversation in a social setting; participated in a marriage, birth, or mourning ritual; or observed children becoming acquainted through a familiar playground game, has in some way encountered the need for a worldly in-between.[17]

World is both given and constructed, fabricated by homo faber (working man) and reified by its "thing quality" in the form of both physical objects and intangible constructs.[18] These are vital to the human landscape, lending themselves to life in common with others. World is simultaneously a reality, a contingency, and a possibility. It is the ground on which humans stand, as well as the ground they laid; the conditions into which they have been born and the conditions that they create; the conventions, norms, and discourses that they inherited and those which they invent and alter; the substance of all that is "second nature," and the inevitability of its transformation. It was fabricated through the human activity of work, owing its existence to those who made it and the events that shape it. World is, in a sense, always unfinished, for it requires regular attention and care.[19] Relinquishing responsibility for its maintenance has historically resulted in disaster, for a world can be destroyed as readily as it was created.

World is not the biological condition for survival or mere life, as is labor, or solely the effect of spontaneous action. World and Earth, like power and violence, travel together, but are radically dissimilar. Even though Earth is the terrestrial home of world, it should not be confused with it. To obfuscate the distinction between the two is to risk the future of both, for falsely synonymizing Earth and world misses the crucial point that each requires vastly different human care. Namely, world relies on the work of its inhabitants to survive, a process which always entails the violation of nature. The Earth will only endure to the extent that humans leave enough of it intact.[20] The consequence of the dangerous assumption that world is purely a given, is the abdication of responsibility for its maintenance. Just as Jerome Kohn notes that "it would be an error to infer that Arendt simply assumes freedom as an inherent and essential property of human nature," one could say the same of world.[21] It did not exist prior to the evolutionary arrival of human life, nor will it far outlast its extinction. There is no natural origin of world because the cyclical fluctuations of nature cannot, in themselves, offer organic commonality or objectivity. Thus, the need for an artificial construction of world is all the more essential. And of course, as I noted earlier, what is created by humans can also be destroyed by them. The loss of world has taken a variety of forms in the modern age, including colonialism, genocide, Stalinism, Nazism, fascism, capitalism, and of course, those that receive the lion's share of attention in this book—US slavery and incarceration.

World does not refer to one particular culture, location, or individual, but depends upon genuine human diversity. Arendt holds that "only where things can be seen by many in a variety of aspects without changing their identity, so that those who are gathered around them know they see sameness in utter diversity, can worldly reality truly and reliably appear."[22] The terms "my world" or "your world" are thus utterly paradoxical, as the possessive forms imply either impossible sovereignty or the total subjectivity of a single individual. Recall the playful remark in *Alice and Wonderland*: "If I had a world of my own, everything would be nonsense. Nothing would be what it is, because everything would be what it isn't." Incomparable intellectual goals notwithstanding, Arendt and the lyrical mistress of Wonderland are in fairly literal agreement here.[23] A world driven by the will of one would offer nothing beyond the idiosyncrasies and quirks of a single person.

Furthermore, world renders singularity a theoretical impossibility: "We know from experience that no one can adequately grasp the world in its full reality all on his own, because the world always shows and reveals itself to him from only one perspective, which corresponds to his standpoint in the world and is determined by it."[24] The interplay of objectivity and subjectivity is noteworthy here, for the world requires widely variant perspectives *and* independence from them. On the one hand, it is a bounded totality of shared things and meanings, and on the other hand, a realm of limitless plurality, for no two people will have identical relations to it. Both sides of this duality are equally essential: "If someone wants to see and experience the world as it 'really' is, he can do so only by understanding it as something that is shared by many people, lies between them, separates and links them, showing itself differently to each and comprehensible only to the extent that many people can talk about it and exchange their opinions and perspectives with one another, over and against one another."[25] Thus, world is a trifold combination of intermingling durability, commonality, and plurality, providing its residents with a stability derived from the fact that it is shared by many, rather than ruled by one.

THE INTERPLAY OF PLURALITY AND COMMONALITY

It is because of the "plurality" of the human condition that commonality is so essential. For Arendt, plurality is the incontrovertible fact that every individual born into the world is different from every other: "we are all the same, that is, human, in such a way that nobody is ever the same as anyone else who has lived, lives, will live."[26] While the queer theorist Eve Sedgwick marvels at the relative absence of theories that prepare their readers to genuinely comprehend and act in accordance with this principle, perhaps Arendt offers one here.[27] By positioning objective things against the subjectivity of its human inhabitants, world generates commonality in the face of boundless human plurality. "Men, their ever changing nature notwithstanding, can retrieve their sameness, that is, their identity, by being related to the same chair and the same table."[28] While deeply suspicious of any theory of "human nature," which she finds inherently contradictory, Arendt concedes that unifying principles are drawn from worldly commonality. At the same time, the objectivity of the world is not at all tantamount to universality. Worldliness may present humans with impartial matters, but nonetheless, as Kimberley Curtis claims, "makes no claim to 'correspond' transparently to its object."[29] While worldly commonality presupposes mutual adherence to certain facts—that the item upon which one fixes his gaze is a vase or kitchen sink, that the sky is blue or gray—Arendt does not expect that any two people will identically negotiate or respond to worldly affairs in accordance with the uniform objectivity of fact.

The differentiation between the objectivity of the world and the subjectivity of living in it, is helpfully captured in Lisa Jane Disch's distinction between commonality and "essential identity." The diversity and differences of human experiences are unequivocal and, like the world itself, hold no natural opportunity for commonality, which is precisely why its artificial fabrication is so important. Curtis puts it well: "By 'objective standards of the world' Arendt refers to a certain impartiality we can have with respect to the world we share in common, an impartiality that transcends subjective perception . . ."[30] The objectivity of world provides a foundation for such understanding, precisely because it stands outside of, and apart from, the subjective inner lives of individuals, and sits firmly between them. Although the possible conversation topics, tasks, or play that one initiates while seated at a table are endless, the metaphorical and literal objectivity of the table provides a necessary sameness in the face of such complete difference. The card game played at the table has rules that must be followed, despite the varying talent, strategy, and luck of the players. Language, idioms, and grammar create a similar experience of worldly commonality that functions in much the same way as a physical thing. Despite unique temperaments, personality, lives, and capabilities, the stability of grammatical conventions, and the meanings of words and figures of speech, stand up to them. From cities to linguistic lexicons, worldly things situate otherwise disparate people in common contexts and experiences to which they can mutually relate. In a related vein, Margaret Canovan argues that (perhaps counterintuitively) the common world does not so much provide a check on plurality, but rather an opportunity for its full realization. She states, "without the world, it is very hard for human beings to be plural individuals rather than interchangeable members of a species. Only the human world can provide the stable setting within which human beings can reliably appear as distinct individuals: only the world which they share can hold human beings together by keeping them distinct."[31] Plurality, on its own without a world, is an unstable basis for human life; Canovan argues that without a world, plurality would not reliably exist at all.

While common matters are, to an extent, fixed, human relationships to them are not. A painting may hang on a gallery wall, but the elements that draw the eye, its aesthetic value, the meaning or significance of the work, and even the perception of the content depend on the subjective positions of its viewers. Disch states, "According to this model, the possibility for commonality is not in the essential identities of the persons in conversation but in the fact that they exist in the same world. But even though the sameness of that world is a given, the commonality is not. This distinction between sameness and commonality follows from plurality: that any situation is constituted by plurality of perspectives means that people can be in a 'same' situation without having a common experience."[32]

A WORLD BUILT TO LAST

Much like commonality, worldly durability is the work of humans, whether they are craftspeople constructing tools, structures, or other utility items; artists imagining and then creating original artwork; or intellectuals writing books, introducing new meanings, and resurrecting old ones, worldly things outlast the ultimately finite lifetime of their makers. The grand, stately beauty of the United States Capitol, and its functionality as a building, are surely not tethered to the individual enslaved people who built it; nor does Herman Melville's 1851 death detract from the brilliance and tremendous readership of *Moby Dick*. Such physical and intangible durability provides otherwise unique humans with connection through the intelligibility of shared things. Relations among people form out of the finite distance that worldly things both open and close.

Without durable objects such as furniture, buildings, bridges, homes, streets, and infrastructure, humans would be suspended in disorganized space. In a different sense, this is also true in the absence of nonphysical matter, including language, rituals, figures of speech, grammatical conventions, social norms, political procedures, events, and their tangible records of collective memory: books, poetry, statues, artwork, and more. "Human life without world would be akin, politically speaking, to vehicles in motion without roads or traffic signals." In short, disordered life without a human landscape.[33] The commonality, durability, and (contingent) permanence of the world live in a variety of forms, but I limit this discussion to three: authority, common sense, and judgment, all of which are political categories of substantial interest to Arendt. As sources of reality, they serve epistemological purposes in similar ways that sturdy-use objects do topographic. The physical things of the world are orienting. One makes their way through familiar areas via visual landmarks that so strongly provide a sense of place, navigation of them is almost second nature. The three aforementioned concepts function comparably. Common sense and authority, in different ways, translate shared knowledge into self-evident terms. When these values are in jeopardy, the pending loss of common sense and authority is resisted with judgment, the practice of determining what does and does not belong in a common world.[34] For example, opposition to the fascistic Trump presidency was often rhetorically captured in the telling refrain "this is not normal," simultaneously a criticism of the assault on the rule of law, ethical norms, and democratic institutions, and an effort to restore the status quo of "normal."

In a lecture delivered to the American Political Science Association in 1960 on the subject of political action and the pursuit of happiness, Arendt spoke of Thomas Jefferson's criticisms of Plato by stating: "Jefferson could write as indignantly as he pleased about the 'nonsense of Plato,' the truth is that Plato's 'foggy mind' has predetermined the categories of political thought to such an extent and has enacted a conceptual framework of such stability that Jefferson was no more, and perhaps even less, capable of escaping hidden Platonic notions than any avowed admirer of *The Republic*."[35] In other words, the durability of Platonic categories renders even his most hostile critics incapable of fully evading them. "Categories of political thought," for example, do not assert themselves or fall away at the behest of the individual. To say that Jefferson, whose own intellectual and political commitments are inheritances of the Western philosophical tradition, held political ideas that entirely abandoned Plato, is as ridiculous as the belief that Jefferson could walk through cement walls. The point here is that despite his criticisms, Jefferson cannot sidestep the fact that Platonic philosophy forms the basis of the political and philosophical discourse that shapes his own vocabulary. The inescapability of these categories highlights their worldliness: for better or worse, they are both durable and common, outlasting their authors and laying the intellectual terrain for their descendants. Arendt argues this neither to chastise the US founders nor to demonstrate the near-universal influence of Plato. Rather, Jefferson's inability to abandon Platonic ideas showcases the simultaneously constructed and given dimensions of world, a duality that is particularly salient to the features at issue here: authority, common sense, and judgment.

AUTHORITY, COMMON SENSE, AND THE REALIZATION OF REALITY

While not part of the built landscape, authority is unmistakably worldly. The intelligibility and stability that it produces do not have to be regularly reinvented but endure across locations and generations. Like a table, authority outlives the life spans of individuals. Such lasting foundations that are both external and legible to humans offer insights into authority's distinct worldliness. Authority, writes Arendt, "gave the world the permanence and durability which human beings need precisely because they are mortals—the most unstable and futile beings we know of. Its loss is tantamount to the loss of the groundwork of the world."[36] She distinguishes authority from coercion and force, and from persuasion and manipulation, arguing that the appearances of these are only indicative of its failure. Rather, one observes the worldliness of authority in the tacit recognizability of its hierarchical shape, which produces order and organization. In a lecture that she delivered in 1953 at NYU titled "The Breakdown of Authority," Arendt considers its legal forms, stating that authority establishes a "common sphere" that invites members of a polity to adhere to it. Regardless of whether laws are followed or broken, they are fixed and certainly "more permanent than our own lives," establishing the boundaries of permissible civic activity. She states, "The authority of the law has established a 'common sphere' outside of which not even those who challenge this authority can act."[37]

Beyond the law, authority also lives in discourse. A student/teacher relation, for example, is maintained by a series of traditions and conventions, district regulations, local ordinances, institutional arrangements, embedded customs, communicative norms, cultural practices, and daily rituals. A student navigates the physical space of a classroom altogether differently than a teacher. His behavior and comportment, from where he sits to when he speaks, are largely determined by the authority that governs the relationship and its associations with the disciplinary structures of the K-12 and postsecondary educational systems. Typical students do not need to be constantly reminded that they will likely face consequences for failure to follow the explicit and unstated regulations of a classroom, for their general adherence to its rules and norms reflects the powerful presence of authority. Arendt says, "The authoritarian relation between the one who commands and the one who obeys rests neither on common reason nor on the power of the one who commands; *what they have in common is the hierarchy itself,* whose rightness and legitimacy both recognize and where both have their predetermined stable place."[38] The relevant factor is neither the will of the stronger, nor the docile subject, but the mutually acknowledged hierarchy of authority that establishes relations between the two.

For Arendt, the legitimacy of authority is rooted in the past and grounded in tradition. The Romans, whom Arendt describes as the most political people in history, understood this better than anyone else. The trinity of authority, including the church, the people, and the republic, as well as their steadfast reverence for the foundations of the past endowed the Roman republic with unique durability. However, the worldly costs of authority's decline are apparent in the fall of the Roman Empire. "The breakdown of the Roman trinity threatens to carry with it our sense for the past and our capacity to ask ultimate questions for which religion provided answers and our sense for a common world protected by law and more permanent than our own lives. This is the modern danger which grew out of the modern age and came into full light only in the modern world in which we now live."[39] The collapse of authority is a profound threat to the world, exposing it to myriad dangers and opportunities for co-optation. If one of the "services" that authority provides citizens of a polity is, as Arendt puts it above, "our sense for a common world," the loss of authority is tantamount to the loss of common sense altogether.

The vital political importance of common sense, which Arendt describes as "the one sense that fits into reality as a whole our five strictly individual senses," is not to be undermined.[40] Because common sense is so foundational to the world, it is often the target of fascist and totalitarian subversion and appropriation. Such regimes often appeal to "common sense logic" to influence mass sentiments and spread propaganda. Shortly after the publication of *The Origins of Totalitarianism*, Arendt delivered a lecture titled "The Difficulties in Understanding," in which she stated: "The chief political distinction between common sense and logic is that common sense presupposes a world common to us all into which we fit and where we can live together because we possess one sense which controls and adjusts all strictly particular sense data to those of all others, whereas logic and all self-evidence from which logical reasoning proceeds can claim a reliability altogether independent from the world and the existence of other people."[41] The "logic" deployed within totalitarian and fascist states defers to destiny, nature, blood, and other volk attachments external to human affairs. If common sense is the conduit between people and reality, it follows that totalitarian regimes would deliberately target it for dissolution. As Arendt puts it, "the revolt of the masses against 'realism,' common sense, and all 'the plausibilities of the world' [Burke] was the result of their atomization, of their loss of social status along with which they lost the whole sector of communal relationships in whose framework common sense makes sense."[42]

Unlike thought, which generally entails some withdrawal from the world, common sense (properly understood) anchors its inhabitants to it.[43] If order, organization, and political legitimacy are the hallmarks of authority, orientation to reality is the central feature of common sense. Like authority, it serves a similar purpose as a worldly object. Common sense stands between the inhabitants of the world, connecting them through the shared knowledge that it imparts and breaking with the subjectivity of plurality. Common sense saves its subjects from an upside down nonworld in which nothing is certain, and anything is possible. That the Earth is round, that pigs do not fly, that the sun rises in the east have a grounding, stabilizing effect on otherwise disparate humans. Common sense is, thus, an antidote to the uncertainties, diversity, and spontaneity of human existence, although it is neither singular nor universal. Changing over time and across cultural location, judgment contests, buttresses, revises, and augments its terms.

JUDGMENT: WHAT BELONGS IN A COMMON WORLD?

Judgment is a practice of world-making, for it determines, as Linda Zerilli puts it, what should and should not be included in a world in common.[44] Relatedly, as Disch explains, to lose one's place in the world is to relinquish their capacity for political judgment: "to be an outsider is not to enjoy a privileged critical vision but on the contrary, to be altogether incapable of political judgment."[45] The failure or abdication of judgment both reflects and generates a state of worldlessness. The ability to judge is predicated on the existence of a robust world, and the onset of totalitarianism is very often a consequence of the failure of collective judgment. From the 1930s onward, Arendt was unabashedly hostile toward those (especially German intellectuals) who withheld judgment from the fascist regime unfolding before their eyes. In a later work she criticizes relativistic justifications for this: "Who am I to judge? Actually means we're all alike, equally bad and those who try or pretend that they try, to remain halfway decent are either saints or hypocrites, and in either case should leave us alone."[46]

Even though Arendt died (literally) while writing *Judging*, the final volume of her three-part work *Life of the Mind*, much of her account of judgment can be pieced together from her writings on Kant's third critique, focusing, in particular, on his theory that aesthetic judgment eschews recourse to transcendent truth-claims in favor of intersubjective consensus, established by groups and communities. Kantian judgment entails collective negotiation that sets specific and varying terms for different populations.[47] Considering Arendt's view that most Western philosophy does away with particulars in favor of generalizations, the influence of Kant on her thinking is evident. Perhaps her Kant lectures are a break from her concept of action and return to normative philosophical commitments, also evident in *Life of the Mind*.[48] Or it is possible that her earlier work contains the seedlings of her future Kantian engagements, which are consistent with (and even supportive of) her arguments in *The Human Condition*. I argue that her use of Kant enables Arendt to articulate the unique relationship between the private and public that gives the concept of judgment substance and meaning: "Private maxims must be subjected to an examination by which I find out whether I can declare them publicly. Morality here is the coincidence of the private and public. To insist on the privacy of the maxim is to be evil. To be evil therefore is characterized by withdrawal from the public realm."[49]

Here, Arendt suggests that judgment originates in the subjective and individual process of thinking, but ultimately projects outward toward the public, political realm. In that sense, both judgment and the commonality that it generates straddle the line between the public and private. Arendt argues, "when everybody is swept away unthinkingly by what everybody else does and believes in, those who think are drawn out of hiding because their refusal to join in is conspicuous and thereby becomes a kind of action. In such emergencies, it turns out that the purging component of thinking ... is political by implication. For this destruction has a liberating effect on another faculty, the faculty of judgment, which one might call with some reason the most political of man's mental abilities."[50] For Arendt, judgment is one of the defining capabilities of humans and also the mental activity that most politicizes thinking. When the majority appears to be of the same mind (thinking the same thing or not thinking at all), judgment radically counters the status quo. In the popular children's fable, "The Emperor's New Clothes," the foolish leader is duped by a profit-driven con artist into parading naked before his subjects in the public square, while believing that he is, in fact, beautifully dressed. As the result of some cocktail of groupthink, peer pressure, and royalism, his subjects perform awe and amazement over the beauty of his nonexistent clothing.[51] Only a child, unmoored from the customary courtesies and doctrines of absolutism that undermined the good sense of the adults, states the obvious and, to borrow from Sedgwick, enters the realm of the transformative: "the Emperor is not wearing any clothes."[52] This factually accurate judgment (in the full Arendtian sense of the word) incites a chain of events that, through laughter, strips authority from the publicly shamed ruler.[53] While the trite liberal moral of the story is "think for yourself," the Arendtian message is—when in the presence of mass thoughtlessness, judge.

Beyond the children's parable, many of Arendt's readers have explored the subject of political judgment as well.[54] Lawrence Biskowski argues that judging "is the capacity to insert oneself into the world, to appear in one's unique identity, to say what is or what appears from one's own perspective, to begin new processes, and to take one's share of responsibility for the world."[55] For him, judging is an exercise of plurality, a way of expressing one's own unique view and reshaping the world. Zerilli echoes this saying, "If the world is the space in which things become public, then judging is a practice that alters what will count as such."[56] It simultaneously reflects and establishes worldly commonality, meaning that its practice (judging) makes use of already-existing standards, values, and common sense, while the object of judgment offers an altered and reconfigured construct of commonality. Thus, judgment is evidence that a world, one that is flexible and capable of transformation, has already inserted itself between people. Authority, common sense, and judgment, which expose the imbrications of durability and commonality, are crucial for fully comprehending the concept of world.

LABOR, WORK, ACTION, AND WORLD

Although worldlessness appears in *Origins*, *The Human Condition* is where the concept of world is first fully developed. Much of the account that I offer here is drawn from that text, although other writings, during and after the 1950s, also animate this inquiry. World, in both its physical and intangible forms, can only be understood in association with other concepts in Arendt's oeuvre, particularly the triad of labor, work, and action. Unlike labor, which is endless and cyclical, work, the world-making activity, is governed by instrumentality, with clear beginnings and ends. In Arendt's words, work is "the reification of writing something down, painting an image, composing a piece of music, etc. which actually makes the thought a reality."[57] Homo faber fabricates worldly things, which subsequently become independent of their makers. "It is this *durability* which gives the things of the world their relative independence from men who produced and use them, their '*objectivity*' which makes them withstand, 'stand against' and endure, at least for a time, the voracious needs and wants of their living makers and users."[58]

The sharp distinction between labor and work, which Arendt fiercely criticizes Marx for obscuring, illuminates each of the two categories and the relation between them.[59] In the notes of a 1967 lecture, Arendt holds that because of its close connection with the biological life of humans, labor is the "least worldly and, at the same time, most natural and most necessary of all things."[60] It closely corresponds with life processes. For example, at certain hours of the day, in accordance with metabolic rhythms, one becomes hungry (nature) and prepares food (labor). One satisfies one's hunger (consumption) in the short-term, although one's appetite will eventually return (nature), and in response, one will cook a meal (labor) and eat (consumption). Thus, the fruits of labor are, from inception, bound for consumption or decomposition. If one makes a meal, it must be eaten fairly swiftly before the natural process of decay sets in. Chairs or tables are built for the purpose of use, not consumption. While they will eventually succumb to the degenerating forces of time, such an inevitability is incidental, not central, to the products of work.[61] Laundered clothing, however, has no function other than being worn and dirtied again, thereby fed back into the process of laundering. (There is no more appropriate term for what takes place inside a washing machine than "cycle"). As Arendt puts it, "end is not their [use objects'] destiny in the same way as destruction is the inherent end of all things for consumption."[62] In sum, the relation between labor and work is highly clarifying. The instrumental rationality of work contrasts sharply with the cyclical logic of labor, as does the brief temporality of the products of labor against the long-lasting endurance of worldly things. Labor is responsive to the rhythms of nature while work disrupts them.

Action is the most human of the three categories, for it appears nowhere in nature. It is political by definition, always involving spontaneous speech that is undertaken in the public sphere among peers. By virtue of its unpredictability, action entails some risk. Its consequences are never foreseeable by the actor and cannot be determined in advance of the moment it is undertaken. Action is the full realization of human freedom, the sole opportunity for an individual to reveal who, as opposed to what, they truly are. "To be free and to act are the same," Arendt famously emphasizes in her essay "What is Freedom?"[63] Its measure is immortality, remembered long after the moment has passed and made manifest through work, including artistic representations, poetry, and historical documentation. Work, as the activity that creates the world, and action, its raison d'être, thus share a unique reciprocity that does not map onto labor. In Arendt's words, "Acting and speaking men need the help of homo faber in his highest capacity, that is the help of the artist, of poets and historiographers, of monument-builders or writers, because without them the only product of their activity, the story they will enact and tell, would not survive at all."[64] It is therefore workers, including historians, storytellers, artists, and poets, that reify the meaning of action and guarantee it an enduring place in the world. Without work, action is ephemeral and forgettable, its greatness receding almost as quickly as it appeared. In turn, without action (and its spectators), work would have little significance.[65] Arendt says:

> In order to become worldly things, that is, deeds and facts and events and patterns of thoughts or ideas, they must first be seen, heard, and remembered and then transformed, reified as it were, into things—into sayings of poetry, the written page or the printed book, into paintings or sculpture, into all sorts of records, documents, and monuments. The whole factual world of human affairs depends for its reality and its continued existence, first, upon the presence of others who have seen and heard and will remember, and second, on the transformation of the intangible into the tangibility of things.[66]

The interdependence of action and work is also a subject of interest to Arendt's readers. Canovan states, "Although work is not in itself a public activity, it has a strong affinity with the public realm because the things it produces exist in the world in front of everyone."[67] World is not only instrumental for politics, but also a site of its enactment and an object of transformation. George Kateb posits, "Freedom exists only when men engage in political action. Political action can take place only where there is a common commitment to the reality, beauty, and sufficiency of the world— of the world 'out there.'"[68] Care for the world and political action are, for Kateb, intertwined. It is not only that world serves the instrumental purpose of providing a space for action, but also that its very emergence depends on commitments to care for it. The radical self-disclosure entailed in freedom rests entirely on "a worldly place, sustained by a common commitment to worldliness, in which men are expected to act—and do act, by word and deed"[69] Without such a "worldly place" action would be as impossible as self-disclosure without speech.

If Kateb argues that political action requires an orientation to the world, Arendt underscores the inverse: that the world must be a place where action can occur. "In order to be what the world is always meant to be, a home for men during their life on earth, the human artifice must be a fit place for action and speech, for activities not only entirely useless for the necessities of life but of an entirely different nature from the manifold activities of fabrication by which the world itself and all things in it are produced."[70] The unequivocal connection between the concepts of work and action is apparent here: one does not exist without the other.

The world depends as much on action as action does on a world.[71] Because it is not only a fact of the human condition, but also the most miraculous promise of natality, every birth brings an altogether new beginning and the possibility to remake and change the world. It is because of action, and the plurality it discloses, that one expects the unexpected from fellow humans; that miracles happen; that change is inevitable; and that greatness is possible. On the other hand, the obliteration of action and the world go together, to which Arendt alludes in her acceptance speech for the Lessing Prize in 1959, stating that it is not conflict between "men" that threatens human affairs, but the uniformity of uniting "in a single opinion, so that out of many opinions only one would emerge, as though not men in their infinite plurality but man in the singular, one species and its exemplars, were to inhabit the Earth. Should that happen, the world, which can form only in the interspaces between men in all their variety, would vanish altogether."[72]

Scientific developments that fundamentally transform the precepts of the human condition, including genetic engineering, the colonization of outer space, cloning, atomic weapons, and artificial intelligence could spell the end of action and world. Arendt's early reference to the launch of Sputnik in the opening pages of *The Human Condition*, suggests that technology is ahead of the human ability "to think what we are doing."[73] She speaks further to this in an essay on Karl Jaspers, published shortly before *The Human Condition*. Sharing his critical perspective on the nuclear age and the rise of technology, which she claims attack human differences on both individual and national levels, replacing them with uniformity and universalism, she said: "Its [the destructiveness wrought by the age of technology] result would be a shallowness that would transform man, as we have known him in five thousand years of recorded history, beyond recognition."[74] The age of technology, as she hints at here and in the conclusion of *The Human Condition*, subjects all action, political and otherwise, to scientific imperatives. Arendt's suspicious views of such "progress" are attributable to the destructive effects of such developments.[75]

If technology expedites the end of the world and the eradication of human plurality, her critique of the modern age speaks to the ways in which the Western tradition of political thought has chipped away at the conditions that sustain both. This is not to say that action itself has been destroyed, for as long as humans are born into the world its potential will endure in some form. She criticizes the political vocabulary of the modern age for replacing spontaneity and unpredictability with behavior and management, freedom with sovereignty, and power with rule. In liberalism, concepts of politics and freedom are distant from one another: not only has the political ceased to be the site of freedom, but flight from the political altogether became freedom's objective. All of this is backward thinking, because the revelation of plurality is the promise of politics, not a problem in need of correction. Although plurality is an unequivocal fact of birth, despite the best efforts of the modern age, the capacities to express it are dependent upon the ever-changing tides of politics. Even if the modern age does not bring an end to the human condition (notwithstanding how dangerously close technology comes to doing just that), it has profoundly subverted its terms to near-unrecognizability.

LIFEWORLD AND THE LIFE OF WORLD

The conceptual life of world both precedes and exceeds Arendt's political thought. While he was primarily concerned with otherworldly matters, Augustine's *City of God* powerfully influenced Arendt's later concept of world, even though she deviated considerably from it. Augustine claims that God is the fixed ontological center of human existence. All that follows him is essentially derivative of and subject to his will. "This then is the original evil: man regards himself as his own light and turns away from that light which would make man himself a light if we would set his heart on it."[76] The zealous and misguided sense of self, which characterizes most humans, distracts them from embracing God. Augustine thus instrumentalizes the human world on their behalf. Arendt comments on this, saying, "Just as man is for the sake of God, the world is for the sake of man. The relation of man to a thing, that is, to everything that exists, is determined by love as desire. Thus, love of the world, guided by an ultimate transmundane purpose, is essentially secondary and derivative. Striving for the 'highest good' which is not of this world, the world in its independent 'objectivity' has fallen into oblivion, even though the lover himself still belongs to it."[77] Augustine believes that the human world is valuable only in its indirect service to the realm of God and never the object of any prior "for the sake of." This crucial point is best illuminated in his early distinctions between the sensible and intelligible realms, another construct that shaped Arendt's concept of world.

For Augustine, the sensible is associated with the earthly, individual, and temporal, while the intelligible is transcendent, collective, and eternal. The sensible is transitory, while the intelligible is permanent; the sensible fluctuates while the intelligible is fixed; the intelligible checks the unpredictability and inconsistency of the sensible. Most importantly, God is at the center of the intelligible, while the Earth houses the sensible. Thus, the relationship between humans and the earthly world is nonreciprocal. The world is not an object of human loyalty and care but should exist to serve the purpose of readying humans for full commitment to the otherworldly spiritual matters of the intelligible. In this sense, the world is for humans, but humans are not for the world:

> It is indeed most probable, that we shall then see the physical bodies of the new heaven and the new earth in such a fashion as to observe God in utter clarity and distinctness, seeing him present everywhere and governing the whole material scheme of things by means of the bodies we shall then inhabit and the bodies we shall see wherever we turn our eyes. It will not be as it is now, when the invisible realities of God are apprehended and observed through the material things of his creation, and are partially apprehended by means of a puzzling reflection in a mirror. Rather in that new age the faith, by which we believe, will have greater reality for us than the appearance of material things which we see with our bodily eyes.[78]

Augustine believes that the world (or the sensible realm) is inextricably bound to human life, meaning that it does not possess a primary objective importance or permanence unto but is always subordinate to the "highest good."

Love of the world attests to the sinful drives of humans, or at least their confusion. They are either greedily preoccupied with material matters of the flesh, or at best mistakenly committed to the creation (world) rather than the creator (God). In either case, "amor mundi," to borrow from Arendt, compromises the primacy of God, the one, true a priori, and reverses the spiritual hierarchy. "In covetousness he turns to this world and desires it, and in loving the world for its own sake, he loves the creation rather than the Creator. Through inquiring back and seeking his own perpetuity, covetous man meets the world, and over the world's priority he forgets the absolute priority of God."[79] Living in accordance with God is essentially an escape from the world, for it is a counterproductive distraction from the realization of heavenly destiny.

The world, in this sense, is the incidental, terrestrial medium in which humans live. Arendt writes, "By the explicit acceptance of divine grace we accept ourselves as creatures and realize our pre-existing dependence on the Being that has made our existence what it is. Since this existence is lived in the world, it is still determined by what is wholly outside and before the world. However, divine grace takes man out of the world; it is the choice out of the world. Man comprehends himself as belonging not to the world, but to God through this choice." As he states in *Confessions*, Augustine does not call upon humans to reject the sensible world for the intelligible, but rather warns them of the moral dangers of exclusive attunement to it, including the worship of false idols and misrecognition of God's power. Luckily, humans are capable of comprehending that the intelligible is of a higher order. Following Augustine's logic, political matters, firmly the province of the sensible, are of minimal importance. Action is valuable only insofar as it works in service of heavenly contemplation, a point which highlights one of the fundamental tensions between Augustine's philosophy and Arendt's later work.

"No matter how 'worldly' the church became, it was always essentially an other-worldly concern which kept the community of believers together."[80] Arendt argued that the political goal of early Christian philosophers was to locate a common bond between people that was pervasive enough to replace a common world of politics. The way in which Augustine foregrounds charitable relations, rather than the web of human relationships, is a case in point, for the latter is the very nerve center of the public sphere. This is an inherently anti-worldly exercise because it attempts to fashion human commonality, not out of politics and plurality, but such completely personal and incommunicable emotions as love, pity, and pain—experiences that are by definition private and can never endure translation into a public realm. As Richard Wolin (under)states, "the later Arendt is known primarily as a philosopher of 'worldliness,' such concerns are hard to reconcile with an orientation as manifestly otherworldly as Augustine's."[81]

Despite its appearances in Augustine's philosophy, the origins of world are phenomenological. It was first defined by Arendt's teacher, Edmund Husserl, in his 1936 work, *The Crisis of European Sciences and Transcendental Phenomenology*. Similar to his student Heidegger, who would later adopt the construct of "life-world," Husserl's was (largely) defined by its objectivity, the "obviously existing" fact of world:

> If we have made this clear to ourselves, then obviously an explicit elucidation of the objective validity and of the whole task of science requires that we first inquire back into the pregiven world. It is pregiven to us all quite naturally, as persons within the horizon of our fellow men, i.e., in every actual connection with others, as "the" world common to us all. Thus it is, as we have explained in detail, the constant ground of validity, an ever available source of what is taken for granted, to which we, whether as practical men or as scientists, lay claim as a matter of course . . . Now if this pregiven world is to become a subject of investigation in its own right, so that we can arrive, of course, at scientifically defensible assertions, this requires special care in preparatory reflections. It is not easy to achieve clarity about what kind of peculiar scientific and hence universal tasks are to be posed under the title "life-world" and about whether something philosophically significant will arise here. Even the first attempt to understand the peculiar ontic sense of the life-world, which can be taken now as a narrower, now as a broader one, causes difficulties.[82]

Husserl's theory of world centers on commonality and givenness, qualities that both Heidegger and Arendt would later engage in at length. That world is created, nurtured, and ultimately subjected to change by the humans inhabiting it, does not figure prominently in his work. Heidegger would later conceptualize world in very similar terms, emphasizing objectivity and like Husserl, givenness. That Arendt both drew on but deviated from both is a well-mined subject in academic political theory. Seyla Benhabib notes that Heidegger's claim in the early sections of *Being and Time* that "being-in-the-world" differentiates human from nonhuman beings is foundational to Arendt's arguments in *The Human Condition* and *Between Past and Future*.[83] In those texts, world is a specifically human artifact, unavailable to any other life form. Arendt decidedly breaks from Heidegger in her unwillingness to subject the concept of world to the ontological question of being, as he does in *Being and Time*.

While Arendt repurposes the interconnection that Heidegger draws between humans and world, she rejects the idea that world is solely a realm of givenness, upon which humans are thrown. She would sharply disagree with the political theorist Frederick Dolan when he asserts that "loving the world means embracing it as something that comes and goes and waxes and wanes, ephemeral, intangible, and irreducibly particular."[84] This account of amor mundi is almost meteorological, as if the world is no more than a series of external forces outside of human hands. Instead, loving the world means caring for it, with full knowledge of the contingency and precarity of its permanence. The world does not "come and go." It is built and destroyed by humans. To misunderstand this is to deny the agential fact of world-building and disavow human responsibility for its care.

For some Arendt scholars, this is the most important intellectual difference between Heidegger and Arendt. Richard Bernstein, for example, characterizes Arendt's political thought as a "trenchant critical response to Heidegger—one that highlights Heidegger's failure to grasp the significance of what Arendt calls 'the human condition of plurality.'"[85] Dana Villa claims that subjecting the matter of human freedom to Heidegger's ontological approach is a paradigm shift, laying the groundwork for Arendt to conceptualize freedom as a tangible political possibility and not a state of mind or matter of will.[86] By considering human existence in terms of being, an approach that Heidegger believed canonical Western philosophers egregiously neglected, he established the terms that Arendt would later use when situating action within the human world. Arendt's essay "What is Freedom?" supports this interpretation: "The decisive difference between the 'infinite improbabilities' on which the reality of our earthly life rests and the miraculous character inherent in those events which establish historical reality is that, in the realm of human affairs, we know the author of 'the miracles.' It is men who perform them—men who because they have received the twofold gift of freedom and action can establish a reality of their own."[87] Echoing Villa, it is fairly conclusive, here and elsewhere, that Arendt conceives of freedom in the realm of human (and not otherworldly) existence.

Heidegger theorizes freedom in existential and ontological terms, rejecting the idea that it resides in philosophical contemplation (Plato), or the interior realm of the will (early Christians): "Being-human is determined by the relation to beings as such and as a whole. The human essence shows itself here as the relation that first opens up Being to humanity. Being-human, as the urgency of apprehending and gathering, is the urging into the freedom of taking over technē, the knowing setting-to-work of Being."[88] Here Heidegger links the human form of being to the freedom of apprehending technē, defined earlier in the text as "a kind of knowledge" of "generating, building, as a knowing pro-ducing."[89] That Heidegger associates not just human being but freedom with the activities of creation and production marks clear resonances between Arendt's work and his: namely, the way in which he existentially embeds freedom in fundamental ontology, and her claim that freedom is a solely human experience. In sum, Heidegger's initial argument that freedom is, ontologically speaking, the province of humans, then enabled Arendt to situate it in the realm of human affairs.[90]

The critical theorist, Jürgen Habermas, took up Husserl's concept of lifeworld in his renowned 1981 book, Theory of Communicative Action. Although, like Husserl, Habermas also views lifeworld as a realm of givenness, he breaks from him by grounding it in communication, not consciousness. Lifeworld is constituted by shared linguistic tropes and meanings. It is constantly at risk of appropriation (what Habermas calls "colonization") and rationalization by bureaucracies, markets, and other forces of what Arendt terms "the waste economy." When systems of instrumentality (for example, media, industry, and capitalism) invade the lifeworld, communication is deeply compromised. Habermas likens this encroachment to colonization because of the exploitation, appropriation, and assimilation that accompany both.

Most recently, in her excellent book *Worldmaking After Empire: The Rise and Fall of Self-Determination*, Adom Getachew formulates a concept of world-making in terms that radically depart from the phenomenological tradition. Pushing back against the dominant narrative that colonized nationalists merely seized and repurposed the liberal principles of colonizers to achieve national independence, she introduces world-making. Constituted by the fraught concept of self-determination, world-making is a construct that is better positioned to articulate the internationalist, anti-colonial dimensions of the political work of nationalist actors. Their vision was global, as they sought to establish international organizations and networks that would redress colonial domination. To suggest that anti-colonial actors merely co-opted the liberal tropes of colonizers for the pursuit of independence is, for Getachew, highly reductive.[91]

Why, given the panoply of theories of world, does *Politics in Captivity* make exclusive use of Arendt's? Why not go to the founder of the concept of lifeworld (Husserl) or, more intuitively, a theorist that imagines world specifically in a racial, political context (Getachew)? As I asked in the opening pages, what is the theoretical utility of Arendt's particular concept of world for Black resistance on plantations and in prisons? The answer at which I gestured is that only Arendt centers her analysis as much on worldlessness as world. In fact, as is detailed in the following pages, worldlessness preceded world in her thinking, appearing first in *Origins of Totalitarianism* and only later fully developed in *The Human Condition*. Because forced worldlessness precisely describes life on plantations and in prisons, Arendt's work is extraordinarily useful to politics in captivity. It is not possible to fully or even meagerly comprehend it without a robust account of worldlessness, for this is the actual condition that enslaved and incarcerated people are resisting. And again, as Chapters Three and Four discuss, without theoretical constructs that can properly attend to slave politics, legacies of Black political rebellion are too often excluded from the canons and discourses of political thought and history. Theories of freedom and liberation that elide slave resistance are egregiously incomplete, for they miss the unique insights and lived experiences of enslaved people that challenge, contradict, and rearrange their conventional terms. These are some of the provocations for invoking Arendtian worldliness, and worldlessness, here.

6

Politics in Captivity

WORLDLESSNESS AND TOTALITARIANISM

While world appears peripherally in Hannah Arendt's early writings, she does not elaborate on the political importance of the concept until *The Origins of Totalitarianism*, where it shows up in the antonymic form of worldlessness. There, Arendt debunks the popular claim that the birth of totalitarianism is attributable to a long tradition of mounting antisemitism in Europe. Instead, she proposes a constellation of interrelated origins that includes the rise of the modern age, European colonialism, the nation-state system, imperialism, industrialization, and more.[1] Totalitarianism destroys the world, tolerates not even a whisper of plurality, renders humanity superfluous, and rules through terror. Its method is not absolute power, but total violence.

As I intimated earlier, Arendt's account of worldlessness in *Origins* is crucial to politics in captivity. Although the concept of world is vital to plantations and prisons, worldlessness offers a unique perspective on some of the background conditions from which the resistance of enslaved and incarcerated people is born. The centerpiece of this discussion is the phenomenon of *forced worldlessness* in which durability, commonality, and plurality, the three core tenets of a world, are structurally and systemically compromised, or withheld altogether from bondpeople and prisoners.[2]

The "laboratory" of totalitarianism, the concentration camp, is the physical form of such world loss, warehousing what Giorgio Agamben calls "bare life."[3] Without physical and intangible worldly things, there is no human landscape, the absence of which is strongly favored by totalitarian power and made manifest in the camps.[4] Totalitarianism works by replacing the real world with a fictitious one that constantly fluctuates according to the interests or drives of the regime. Its subjects, who have ideally lost all capacity for judgment, are thus primed to accept and believe even the most patently false and ridiculous propaganda. Seyla Benhabib states, "They [totalitarian masses] are worldless in the sense that they have lost a stable space of reference, identity, and expectation that they share with others. Not having a particular social perspective from which to view the world, they are especially open to ideological manipulation: they can believe anything and everything, for they lack the definite perspective that is tied to having a certain place in the world."[5] The reverse of Benhabib's insight is also true: the apprehension of a "definite perspective that is tied to having a certain place in the world" is a bulwark against totalitarian power and the worldlessness associated with it. Prior to the infiltration of society with propaganda, such regimes must weaken the reality of the world, grooming its inhabitants to unquestioningly accept the messages and exhortations of the totalitarian state. Common sense is replaced with logic, fact with fiction, conviction with whim, knowledge with impulse, and relationships with loyalty. Worldly stability transforms into a fluctuating imaginary, dictated by state agents, giving way to alienation and loneliness: "organized loneliness is considerably more dangerous than the unorganized impotence of all those who are ruled by the tyrannical and arbitrary will of a single man. Its danger is that it threatens to ravage the world as we know it—a world which everywhere seems to have come to an end—before a new beginning rising from this end has had time to assert itself."[6]

Even though Arendt would balk at the comparison, such "organized loneliness" is the chief point of resemblance between totalitarian states and racial regimes of captivity. Such a claim cuts against the grain of Arendt's political thought, for it is a well-known fact that she eschewed any metaphorical use of totalitarianism, including rhetorical statements and more developed analyses. For her, such comparisons are not only intellectually sloppy, but also muddy the historical and political precision necessary to fully comprehend the totalitarian condition. Such critique is linked to the "curious tendency" of social scientists to level important distinctions among disparate phenomena and concepts, such as authoritarianism, tyranny, dictatorship, and fascism; or violence, power, terror, and rage, as she noted in her renowned essays, "What is Authority?" and "On Violence."[7]

Peter Baehr offers a rich discussion of this subject in *Hannah Arendt, Totalitarianism, and the Social Sciences*, in which he describes her deep suspicion of the behavioral turn in sociology and political science.[8] Arendt claims that because they reduce human activities to calculable behavior, motivated by rational self-interest, behaviorists are utterly incapable of properly analyzing ruptures in human affairs that defy the utilitarian logic attributed to otherwise (ostensibly) predictable humans. It is perhaps due to such a critique that Arendt over-rotates, casting herself as an intellectual gatekeeper of totalitarianism by cordoning it off from other comparable political contexts.

Some of her contemporaries, on the other hand, hold more expansive views of totalitarian regimes, likening them to the US prison system and other institutions of control and domination. In his 1954 volume *Totalitarianism*, Carl Friedrich posits that the lines between totalitarian and nontotalitarian states might not be as clear and decisive as Arendt would hold.[9] Western democratic republics are not at all immune to the violent and even genocidal forces characteristic of totalitarian states. Gresham Sykes's *Society of Captives*, which he published only a few years after Arendt's *Origins*, draws on Friedrich's work (as well as the controversial social psychologist Bruno Bettelheim) when he describes the prison system in totalitarian terms.[10] Interestingly, he never references Arendt's book.[11] *Society of Captives* clearly influenced Erving Goffman's discussion of "total institutions" in his 1961 book *Asylums*, where he compares disciplinary enclosures, including psychiatric lockup facilities, boot camps, and prisons to concentration camps.[12] Given that totalitarianism was one of the most pressing political problems of the age in which Arendt, Sykes, Friedrich, and Goffman wrote, it is unsurprising that so many of them would invoke the term to lend critical heft to their accounts of the prison system.[13] Of this small group of scholars, only Arendt refuses to mobilize totalitarianism for analysis of systems of state control and coercion outside of Nazi and Stalinist arenas.[14]

Drawing on totalitarianism to describe prison is not unique to postwar white intellectuals. Many Black carceral political thinkers did the same, reclaiming the concept from Eurocentric analyses. Angela Davis's discussion of the Attica prison uprising is a case in point. For Davis, the event was not an incidental rebellion that arose circumstantially, but organized resistance to a totalitarian regime: "what unfolded inside Attica was an intensely political confrontation with the totalitarian prison hierarchy and its chiefs in government."[15] The comparisons that Davis draws between totalitarian states and carceral systems are explicit and intentional, contrasting strongly with the account that Arendt establishes in *Origins*: "by almost any standard the American prison betrays itself as a system striving toward unmitigated totalitarianism. The logic of totalitarianism defines the prison's internal processes as well as its relationship to the world without."[16]

THE FORCED WORLDLESSNESS OF CAPTIVITY

Worldlessness, both a cause and effect of totalitarianism, cuts across regimes of control and domination. The erosion of the commonality and durability of the world is already underway prior to the complete takeover of the totalitarian state. In turn, the full destruction of the world is essential, for totalitarian rule cannot tolerate even the smallest vestiges of its existence. Arendt writes in *Origins*, "The originality of totalitarianism is horrible, not because something new came into the world, but because its very actions constitute a clear break with all our traditions and have caused a tangible explosion of all our categories of political thought and all our standards for moral judgment."[17] Objectivity itself is threatening, for any fixed and stable construct exposes the limits of the regime. The mere existence of a fact as simple as "the sky is blue" is a problem for the totalitarian state because such facts command allegiance to external forces beyond it, such as sensory perception and science. If the sky is unquestionably blue, no matter what totalitarian propaganda maintains, then certain truths must be impervious to the whims and interests of the state. Speaking more materially, because the extreme terror and cruelty of the gulag and concentration camp would incite defection, it is incumbent on totalitarian regimes to keep the status of fact itself, soft and loose. Arendt states:

> The reason why the totalitarian regimes can get so far toward realizing a topsy turvy world is that the outside nontotalitarian world, which always

comprises a great part of the population of the totalitarian country itself, indulges also in wishful thinking and shirks reality in the face of real insanity just as much as the masses do in the face of the normal world. This common-sense disinclination to believe the monstrous is constantly strengthened by the totalitarian ruler himself, who makes sure that no reliable statistics, no controllable facts and figures are ever published, so that there are only subjective, uncontrollable, and unreliable reports about places of the living dead.[18]

Bringing this account of death camps into the company of the carceral system offers some telling insights into the question of why prisons, while central to the social/political imaginary, are almost always situated on the geographic margins of remote rural areas. The opacity of prison life, maintained by spatial isolation and bureaucratic unaccountability, prevents the "normal world" from contesting and resisting, maybe even believing, their inhumane realities.

Totalitarianism, as a system, does not map neatly onto plantations and prisons, but forced worldlessness is the theory and practice of captivity. Fastidious efforts to keep Black Americans suspended in a state of worldlessness, either through alienation or destruction, likely began when the first Africans were kidnapped and brought to the Americas, or perhaps when slavery was inaugurated as a lifelong hereditary status, limited exclusively to Africans and African Americans in 1662.[19] The trade, sale, and constant circulation of human chattel; disruption and breakup of the family structure; denial of basic bodily integrity; the total tyrannical rule by enslavers; forced labor; and strictures on the actions and movements of free Black Americans are only some of the many forms of worldlessness to which they have been subjected.[20] Early settlers, committed to the creation of a new world, were equally intent on offering it up to whites, exclusively.

Keeping bondpeople and prisoners from worldly commonality, durable objects, and nonphysical things and preventing them from disclosing plurality are essential for functioning systems of chattel and carceral captivity. Turning first to slavery, P. Thomas Stanford states, "The Africans enslaved on the plantations were forbidden to play the drums or to own weapons. They were even forbidden to ride horses. They were forbidden to accumulate wealth or own any object. All items made by them after their regular work, by law, belonged to their master."[21] That social and political control over the bodies and lives of bondpeople is central to slavery is fairly self-evident, but the shape and form of that domination are worth further inquiry. Of note in Stanford's account is the materiality and tangibility of the strictures imposed on enslaved people: they were specifically prohibited from availing themselves of worldly things, i.e., instruments, weapons, and of course books, and sharing in common traditions and practices, i.e., drumming, dancing, marriage and mourning traditions and religious worship.

None of this is coincidental, for the stability of a world in common poses intolerable threats to worldless regimes that rely on structural instability, says Arendt. Although racial captivity and totalitarianism in Stalinist Russia and Hitler's Germany are contextually disparate from the US racial polity, independent relationships, facts, practices, and objects do irreparable harm to all three. While the *labor* of enslaved people was indispensable to the new world, their *work* exposed its precarity. The power wielded over bondpeople is shaken when they create tools, art, instruments, and other objects; form independent relations with one another; become literate; and, especially, rebel against their conditions. This is precisely why enslavers intercepted the world-building acts of enslaved people at every turn. As William Dusinberre details, strict regimentation of most aspects of their lives; severe punishment for both truancy and fugitivity; family disruption and control over reproduction; close management of their provisions including housing, clothing, and food; and regulations on their privacy and leisure were not only inhumane, but strategically withheld the most basic conditions necessary for the creation of a world.[22]

COMMONALITY

In theoretical terms, the enduring destruction and denial of the three foundational aspects of a world—commonality, durability, and plurality—appear here. Of these categories, the obliteration of commonality is where the worldlessness of racial regimes is most apparent. Stanford states, "Now, you cannot do without the negro, because if you send him away, you will run after him. He is here to stay. The only way to deal successfully with the colored race is God's way. First, recognize that he is your guest; second, recognize that you have robbed him of his birthplace, home, family, and savings. It is these facts that are causing so much unrest on the part of whites in this country."[23] The deprivation of enslaved people from relationships with others is not incidental, but essential to the system's strength and enduring continuity. Orlando Patterson's concept of "social death" speaks to this as well when he asks, "If the slave no longer belonged to a community, if he had no social existence outside of his master, then what was he? The initial response in almost all slaveholding societies was to define the slave as a socially dead person."[24]

In *The Human Condition*, Arendt states, "without a world between men and nature, there is eternal movement, but no objectivity."[25] Forcing bondpeople into eternal movement, in both literal and symbolic ways, is tantamount to the destruction of worldly commonality. (The same is true of prisoners, to which I will turn presently.) The two operate reciprocally: worldlessness is the result of the ceaseless movement of enslaved people and vice versa—worldlessness makes such movement possible. Keeping them in constant motion maintains their distance from worldly objects, traditions, culture, language, and perhaps most importantly, relationships with others. It is most apparent in backbreaking, wageless labor, but also through circulation in Middle Passage, auction blocks, and coffle gangs.

Friendships, romantic partnerships, and familial relationships were disrupted or severed. Enslavers regularly separated families through sale and forbade "abroad" marriages (in which members of a couple resided on different plantations) in order to maintain tighter control over bondpeople, from reproduction to basic whereabouts. A planter might prevent a marriage between a strong bondwoman and a seemingly weaker bondman if he anticipated that this would compromise the market value of their children.[26] Interfering with the most personal and private human relations is not only cruel, but also reflective of the ways that enslaved people were denied the most basic ability to live in common with others. Lasting connections with others are inherently unstable in a slave society when kinships and friendships are so regularly threatened and broken.

Tight regulations over the leisure time of enslaved people invite further acknowledgment of how their proximity to the web of human relationships was strictly managed, exposing the threat that it posed to the social order. Some enslavers maintained the strictest possible chokehold over their lives, forbidding dancing, departing the plantation for any reason, practicing religion, and socializing and assembling. Others offered contained opportunities for religious observance and play by organizing church services, dances, and parties and providing food, alcohol, and other provisions.[27] This was not done out of altruism as much as self-interest: enslavers could more readily monitor and surveil bondpeople's activities and engagements when they controlled the terms of their sociality, and assuage their own anxieties about slave rebellion through such allocations of material pleasure. Planters attempted to fully determine what enslaved people ate, wore, and owned; with whom they interacted; and where they dwelled.[28] Making use of their labor while fastidiously withholding from them the capacity to form independent relations with others, the most foundational aspect of a world in common, is the modus operandi of slavery. In Arendt's words, "the realm of human affairs, strictly speaking, consists of the web of human relationships which exists wherever men live together."[29] While enslaved people "lived together" in the most technical sense, the stability on which the web of human relationships depends was compromised at every turn.

Harriet Jacobs, a former bondwoman and author of the autobiography *Incidents in the Life of a Slave Girl*, describes the dread that overtook plantations in the days leading up to the new year. "Sale Day" typically occurred shortly after January 1, igniting fear within enslaved people that their spouses, children, and other loved ones would be unexpectedly taken from them:

> O, you happy free women, contrast *your* New Year's day with that of the poor bond-woman! With you it is a pleasant season, and the light of the day is blessed. Friendly wishes meet you every where, and gifts are showered upon you. Even hearts that have been estranged from you soften at this season and lips that have been silent echo back, "I wish you a happy New Year." Children bring their little offerings, and raise their rosy lips for a caress. They are your own, and no hand but that of death can take them from you. But to the slave mother New Years day comes laden with particular sorrows. She sits on her cold cabin floor, watching the children who may be torn from her the next morning; and often does she wish that she and they might die before the day dawns. She may be an ignorant creature, degraded by the system that has brutalized her from her childhood; but she has a mother's instincts, and is capable of feeling a mother's agonies. On one of those sale days, I saw a mother lead seven children to the auction-block. She knew that some of them would be taken from her, but they took *all*. The children were sold to a slave trader, and their mother was bought by a man in her own town. Before night her children were all far away. She begged the trader to tell her where he intended to take them; this he refused to do. How could he, when he knew he would sell them, one by one, wherever he could command the highest price? I met that mother in the street and her wild, haggard face lives to-day in my mind.[30]

The precarity of the family structure that Jacobs describes here suggests that one really cannot claim that enslaved people "lived together" with any trust in the permanence of their arrangements. Given how frequently and easily social and familial bonds could be undone, any commonality that enslaved people were able to form with one another was always already under implicit threat. If the web of human relationships is the ground from which a world can arise, wiping out any traces of it or better yet, preventing its formation altogether, are strategies for safeguarding slavery.

In prisons, the breakdown of commonality appears in the carefully orchestrated sequestration of prisoners from the external world. Underwriting the loss of worldly commonality is the simultaneous invisibility and hypervisibility of prisons.[31] In one sense, they are concealed from society and in another, they are crucial to the social and political imaginary. The image of the prison as a space outside of the polity constitutes the very idea of citizenship and civic belonging. On the other hand, the laws, conventions, and norms that prevail in the public sphere do not extend to prisons, for they are largely invisible to the outside world, by design. In Arendt's words, "Just as the stability of the totalitarian regime depends on the isolation of the fictitious world of the movement from the outside world, so the experiment of total domination in the concentration camps depends on sealing off the latter against the world of all others, the world of the living in general, even against the outside world of a country under totalitarian rule."[32] Structurally speaking, prisons cordon off their occupants from communication and contact with others outside of the carceral sphere. Through high, impenetrable walls and dense security, the physical building itself restricts unregulated, spontaneous activity or human contact. Prison personnel intercept and impede relationships, interactions, and human connections for intense and arbitrary strictures on visitor protocol. Limited and irregular visiting hours; stipulations on permissible visitors; "no contact visits" in supermax settings; prohibitions on unscripted, impromptu conversation and affection; dense and time-consuming bureaucratic procedures; and the fact that prisons are often situated in places inaccessible by public transportation, seem only to serve as reminders that incarcerated people have little autonomy and limited ability to interact with others as they wish. Such pressures strain the material resources of individuals and keep prisoners outside of "the web of human relationships."

For example, the visitor handbook of MCI-Cedar Junction, a maximum security prison in Walpole, Massachusetts, includes the following regulations: "Physical contact between visitors and inmates shall be limited to a brief greeting at the start and at the completion of a visit. (e.g., one (1) embrace and one (1) closed mouthed kiss). Excessive or inappropriate physical contact may be cause for termination of the visit and loss of privileges."[33] Such policies not only aim to police and limit relationships, but also lend to profiting off of incarcerated people and their loved ones. Given that actual time with loved ones is so intensely regulated, incarcerated people must lean heavily on long-distance contact. Because state and federal prisons and county jails regularly offer monopoly contracts to phone companies with the highest rates, a fifteen-minute phone call can cost as much as twenty-four dollars, a prohibitive expense for the (disproportionately poor) population of prisoners and their families.

Such worldlessness is not lost on incarcerated people themselves. Without using Arendt's specific terminology, one anonymous author, in an essay titled "City as Prison," takes note of the way in which prisoners are alienated from human relations with others: "Genuine security is based on trust between people, pleasure in natural contact, and delight in the warmth and variety of the environment. Prisons are a paradigm of man's attempt to force other men to conform to a standard rule that bears no relationship to the human organism. Walls that are flat, dull, and heavy express the feeling of resistance to life, limits of life, enclosure of life. Fortresses and prisons are based on fear and fear breeds more fear."[34]

DURABILITY

Doing away with worldly durability is another instantiation of forced wordlessness, often taking the form of refusing captive people any real control over their own work. Enslavers not only determined bondpeople's working hours, but also which vocational skills they were permitted to pursue, sometimes punishing them brutally for practicing hobbies and requiring them to perform only low-skilled labor. Occasionally, enslaved men were given the opportunity to sell their services, raise livestock, and earn some money of their own, but this was a rare privilege and often limited to bondmen in more liberal urban areas, such as antebellum New Orleans and Richmond.[35] Following the exposure of the plot for Gabriel's rebellion in 1800, many Confederate states discontinued this practice altogether. Arendt states, "The things of the world have the function of stabilizing human life, and their objectivity lies in the fact that—in contradiction to the Heraclitean saying that the same man can never enter the same stream—men, their ever-changing nature notwithstanding, can retrieve their sameness, that is, their identity, by being related to the same chair and the same table."[36] Simply put, what are the effects of removing that chair and table altogether, along with the tools and materials with which to build them? Or from another angle, objects exist, in the most technical sense, in captivity, but bondpeople and prisoners do not have the autonomy to retrieve their sameness through their common use, either because they are required to perform constant labor or they themselves are the objects of sale and trade (in slavery), and held in solitary confinement or regularly transferred to different facilities (in prison). In other words, keeping bondpeople and prisoners from durable worldly things, through labor, market circulation, unaccountable bureaucratic decision-making, and carceral punishment, is a destabilizing mechanism of forced worldlessness.

At the most material levels of daily life, the regulation of prisoners' personal possessions, which purports to ensure security or safety within the facility, further compromises the durability of their world. "It is this durability which gives the things of the world their relative independence from men who produced and used them, their 'objectivity' which makes them withstand, 'stand against,' and endure, at least for a time, the voracious needs and wants of their living makers and users."[37] Worldly things outlast the mortal lives of their makers and sharing them in common creates an objectivity that counterbalances the subjectivity of human difference. Almost all objects external to the prison are banned, including long lists of contraband items ranging from aerosol cans to jewelry to spicy tortilla chips, and any items that could be repurposed as weapons. Prisoners are instead required to purchase their belongings from price-gouging commissaries, raising some key questions (beyond the scope of this discussion) about the junctions of racial capitalism and worldlessness.[38]

Worldly durability is withheld in less tangible forms as well, including regulations on education and access to reading material. For Arendt:

> The thinker who wants the world to know the content of his thoughts must first of all stop thinking and remember his thoughts. Remembrance in this, as in all other cases, prepares the intangible and the futile for their eventual materialization; it is the beginning of the work process, and like the craftsman's consideration of the model which will guide his work, its most immaterial stage. The work itself then always

requires some material upon which it will be performed and which through fabrication, the activity of homo faber, will be transformed into a worldly object. The specific work quality of intellectual work is no less due to the "work of our hands" than any other kind of work."[39]

Here, Arendt undoes the distinction between forms of work that produce use objects, like buildings and furniture, and intellectual ones, such as poetry and philosophy. Given that, in both cases, the worker fabricates worldly things, it seems fitting that withholding education from incarcerated people is tantamount to withholding the tools of world creation.

In 1994, the Clinton administration's Violent Crime Act rescinded Pell Grant eligibility for prisoners, and rolled back funding for programming, including prison newspapers that had been produced and circulated since the 1960s, as well as education and job training programs. The discourse of prisoner rehabilitation fully gave way to "tough on crime" ideology that prioritized punitive criminal management over readying incarcerated people for reentry into society.[40] Although there are many possible interpretations for these changes, I hold that they are an assault on worldly durability, preventing prisoners from cultural and intellectual production, as well as education.[41] Prison was thereby rendered a space of biological life without reality. Arendt observes, "For our trust in the reality of life and in the reality of the world is not the same. The latter derives primarily from the permanence and durability of the world, which is far superior to that of mortal life. If one knew that the world would come to an end with or soon after his own death, it would lose all its reality, as it did for the early Christians as long as they were convinced of the immediate fulfillment of their eschatological expectations."[42] Punishing incarcerated people by denying them the means of constructing worldly durability and permanence is a cruelty unique to captive settings, and mobilized for the express purpose of eroding prisoners' belief in, and adherence to, reality.

PLURALITY

Finally, if plurality, the fact that all humans born into the world are different from every other, can only be revealed through action, it is unsurprising that enslaved and incarcerated people are kept from all opportunities for public expression, including speech and assembly. Bondpeople and prisoners enjoy neither the franchise and any representation in government nor even informal participation in politics.⁴³ In slavery, enforced illiteracy, is an affront to plurality. Teaching bondpeople to read was a punishable offense, as was possession of printed material on their persons or within their living quarters.⁴⁴ While there are multiple reasons for this prohibition, it is likely that planters understood the connection between education and political engagement, for both are sources of voice and power. If reading and writing are gateways to enlightenment and understanding, political engagement is a path to freedom and agency. Banning both, in Arendtian terms, blocks the possibility of disclosing plurality, obviating the need for a world altogether. That all humans are born different from one another is the foundational reason for its existence. If enslavers could not stamp out plurality altogether, they did decimate the conditions for its expression.

For prisoners, plurality is the boldest target at which carceral agents take aim in an effort to expunge even traces of worldliness from prison. Cloaked in discourses of safety and security, the preemption of action, prohibition of the expression of human freedom, and the containment of the plurality of prisoners through bureaucratic, routinized practices of standardization and regulation reflect the deep threat of natality and its disclosure in the form of plurality to the carceral regime.⁴⁵ There are several interrelated reasons for this. First, the rationality of criminal punishment has no tolerance for unique humans. From the moment a person first encounters the system, whether through arrest, detention, jail, courts, or prisons, the subjectivity and specificity of their life experiences are replaced with their "cases." Their behavior and activities are surveilled when on probation; they are subject to gross invasions of privacy when on parole; their ability to post bail determines whether they may return to their home or community prior to trial or remain in detention.⁴⁶ Neither whom, nor even "what," they are have meaningful bearing on their fate in the administrative order of the criminal punishment system.

Second, and relatedly, if plurality can only be disclosed through action, as Arendt holds, its inimicality to prison life becomes all the more apparent. "To be free and to act are the same," says Arendt in the essay "What is Freedom?"⁴⁷ Squelching its expression is the theory behind the carceral apparatus within which prisoners are addressed by identification numbers instead of their names or simply the anonymous "inmate"; that requires them to adhere to arbitrary and constantly fluctuating rules; and punishes them harshly for demonstrations of individuality and spontaneity that challenge the carceral regime.⁴⁸ None of these punitive practices are intended for rehabilitative purposes, or even the security of the prison, but rather to preempt resistance by preventing its occupants from building a world in common with others, acting in concert, and exercising freedom. The disclosure of the who through action, while radical under all circumstances, is intolerable to the carceral system.

Solitary confinement nearly realizes the aspiration of total domination entailed in forced worldlessness. In *Origins*, Arendt states, "Quite apart from its origin in Roman history, authority, no matter in what form, always is meant to restrict or limit freedom, but never to abolish it. Totalitarian domination, however, aims at abolishing freedom, even at eliminating human spontaneity in general, and by no means at a restriction of freedom no matter how tyrannical."[49] The drive to terminate human freedom altogether is both the method and central purpose of solitary confinement as a form of punishment. Freedom is linked to the faculty of judgment and, relatedly, common sense, both of which curdle in extreme isolation. The capacities for both are altered and rearranged in solitary confinement when humans are faced with conditions of oppressive loneliness and subsequently, the atrophy of normative sensory perception and critical thought.

The likenesses between world alienation in Arendt's concept of totalitarianism and Lisa Guenther's discussion of solitary confinement are telling:

> The testimony of survivors of solitary confinement suggests that if one is deprived for long enough of the experience of other concrete persons in a shared or common space, it is possible for one's own personhood to diminish or even collapse, while the transcendental ego, or pure capacity for experience, remains, now unhinged from a shared world in which its perpetual flow of impressions could receive the bodily validation of others. Without the concrete experience of other embodied egos oriented toward common objects in a shared world, my own experience of the boundaries of those perceptual objects begins to waver. It becomes difficult to tell what is real and what is only my imagination playing tricks on me, and this difficulty increases with the length of solitary confinement.[50]

The constitutive elements of factual reality, including durable human constructs, the web of relationships, common spaces, and common sense, often cannot survive these conditions. Independent, sustainable relationships, structures, and objects are prohibited in such scenes of total control.[51] Thus, the similarities between Arendt and Guenther's accounts of worldlessness in totalitarian states and carceral spheres are unsurprising, for both exemplify systems fully grounded in near absolute worldlessness.

Worldlessness as Isolation

Today, extralegal policing of even the most benign behaviors of African Americans is part of the enduring legacy of world destruction, now forged on the basis of so-called racial criminality, rather than explicitly stated, de jure racial inferiority. As Vesla Weaver and Amy Lerman put it, "Being in a group of young people, being with whites in a black neighborhood, being black in a white neighborhood, being with too many other blacks, being homeless, being in poor areas / being in rich areas" are deemed threatening to the social order and thus warrant further investigation or punishment.[52] The effects of heightened surveillance and criminalization are loneliness and world alienation. The mode of this present form of Black worldlessness is what Weaver and Lerman call "custodial citizenship," the close proximity of African Americans to the criminal punishment system by contrast with whites, who can basically assume protection from the state and need not fear bodily harm at its hands. Because their relationship to the government is mutual and contractual, they may move through public and private spaces as they choose without fear of harassment, brutality, or punishment. Though of course, this privilege is not untroubled by class position, it remains true that poor white communities and individuals are not surveilled and targeted by police as are African Americans. To dwell in a world in common is not a neutral given, but a luxury conferred or withheld on the basis of race.

Deprived of common spaces and most meaningful arenas of public life, one of the participants in Weaver and Lerman's survey said this:

> I used to like hanging out in the streets but I know one thing like, now when I get up for work, I got to get up and go straight home, walk my dog. You know, just walking or watch TV, that's the best shot I have to survive. That's the best shot . . . Just stop and drink a beer, I'm asking for disaster. I can't even stop—I can't even get off and just ride with my car on the city, just enjoying the sight. I'm asking for disaster. So, my way to work with the government is to put myself in a . . . got me a big TV, I just like my house. I got to tell myself, I like my house more than I like the jail.[53]

Even though the speaker is not formally incarcerated, he is captive. Knowing that he is a target of police keeps him from entering the world, from forming relations with others, and occupying common space alongside them. Whether he remains at home, keeping a low profile, or ventures into the public realm and risks arrest, the effect of both scenarios is the loss of the world. The alienation of life spent in functional isolation, or the alienation of the cage are twin manifestations of carceral captivity. Consider this alongside George Jackson's account of prison life:

> We have a gym (inducement to throw away our energies with a ball instead of revolution). But if you walk into this gym with a cigarette burning, you're probably in trouble. There is a pig waiting to trap you. There's a sign "No smoking." If you miss the sign, trouble. If you drop the cigarette to comply, trouble. The floor is regarded as something of a fire hazard (I'm not certain what the pretext is). There are no receptacles. The pig will pounce. You'll be told in no uncertain terms to scrape the cigarette from the floor with your hands. It builds from there. You have a gym but only certain things may be done and in specified ways. Since the rules change with the pigs' mood, it is really safer for a man to stay in his cell.[54]

Although, of course, it is necessary to distinguish between what Black carceral theorists call "the minimum security" of the street and the "maximum security" of prison, world loss and alienation, inherent in both, are interconnected and mutually reinforcing.[55] The routine prohibition of Black Americans from experiencing, creating, and engaging with the world is the theory of carceral captivity from which its many practices are mobilized. What Arendt calls "this alienation—the atrophy of the space of appearance" characterizes well the survivalist imperative of isolation that both the research subject and Jackson describe.[56]

Worldlessness and Property

The continuities between the worldlessness of slavery and incarceration surface strongly in the deliberate reconstitution of a Black servile class after 1865. The formal end of slavery, following the American Civil War, saw the passage of the Black Codes (a revised version of the slave codes, which unduly punished African Americans in the postwar South for noncriminal offenses on the basis of race); disenfranchisement; the widespread epidemic of sexual assaults and lynching; and the exclusion of African Americans from institutions of higher learning, the arts, culture, public services, employment, and quality housing were postbellum "solutions" to the problem of how to maintain the state of Black worldlessness, second class citizenship, and poverty, established during slavery.[57]

Strategies of forced worldlessness in slavery as well as carceral settings were abusive and oppressive to be sure, but their impact was more complicated than even the extraordinary and quotidian trauma and injustice that they incited. Turning to Arendt's *The Human Condition*, "we saw before that property, as distinguished from wealth and appropriation, indicates the privately owned share of the common world and therefore is the most elementary political condition for man's worldliness. By the same token, expropriation and world alienation coincide, and the modern age, very much against the intentions of all the actors in the play, began by alienating certain strata of the population from the world."[58] The resonances of these sentences with actual history are profound. When enslaved, Black Americans could not own property, by definition, but were instead owned as property. Despite changes in formal status after Emancipation, they were systematically excluded from the economy of property ownership through systems of debt peonage, low-wage labor, employment discrimination, disenfranchisement, Jim Crow segregation, and incarceration. In *The Sum of Us*, the economist Heather McGhee details the ways in which the US government engineered a prosperous, homeowning middle class in the mid-twentieth century that invested generously in white families, while simultaneously shutting out Black Americans through carefully manufactured laws and policies on federal and local levels.[59] Government redlining is possibly the most cited practice, thanks to Richard Rothstein's groundbreaking book, *The Color of Law*, although anti-Black exclusion also occurred through measures taken by state legislatures, city councils, and neighborhood associations.[60]

The impact of the carceral system on Black economic inequality is profound, though understudied. Bruce Western and Becky Pettit take note of its invisible, cumulative, and intergenerational dimensions. Because congregate, institutional populations, such as prisoners and detainees, are not accounted for in most conventional studies of economics and politics, their effect on, and experience of, social inequality goes unnoticed. Given that prisoners are already disproportionately Black and poor, their inability to become class mobile while incarcerated only adds economic disadvantage to an already burdened population. Prisoners are unable to access resources for wealth building such as education, professional growth, savings, financial investment, and home ownership, the results of which are deeply felt by future generations. Exacerbating this is the fact that the majority of prisoners are in their twenties and thirties, crucial decades in which nonincarcerated people often complete their education and begin careers and families, accumulating middle-class wealth, social capital, and other assets. The prison system disrupts this normative sequence, adding additional, often impenetrable barriers to genuine economic and social equity.[61]

Depending on the state, sentence, and crime, further regulations may pose added hindrances to the ability of former prisoners to own property and build wealth. For example, despite the fact that the vast majority of sex crimes are perpetrated against victims known to the offender, Megan's Law prohibits those with such convictions from living within a certain proximity to spaces where children gather, for instance playgrounds, schools, community centers, and more. This often means that former prisoners cannot live with relatives, depending on the location of their home, and access important family and community resources. In addition, both public and private sector employers may ask job applicants to declare prior felony convictions, regularly resulting in legal employment discrimination. Finally, many states limit where parolees can travel, which again places roadblocks on their ability to pursue higher education and career opportunities. Not only do all of these measures increase rates of recidivism, but they also often prevent former prisoners from finding economic footing. Even though such structural matters are commonly viewed as mere efforts to maintain a Black servile class, the Arendtian lens offers a new perspective on "what's going on here." If property is a crucial component of human *worldliness*, hindering incarcerated people from its acquisition and ownership produces and sustains *worldlessness*.

WORLD-BUILDING AND RESISTANCE IN CAPTIVITY

If forced worldlessness is the prevailing condition of plantations and prisons, world-building is an act of resistance to it. To rebel against slavery and incarceration, either in the form of an exceptional uprising or everyday act, is to radically refuse the terms of captivity and create a world in common with others. Rebellion was a ubiquitous aspect of life in the slave South and currently, within the carceral sphere, however it is easily missed if synonymized exclusively with large-scale revolts and/or fugitivity; if theorists remain wedded to liberal interpretive lenses; and if world is limited to a narrow set of conceptual criteria. Here I aim to shed light on the worldly dimensions of plantation and prison politics by both reworking the concept of world to account for the creative force of destruction and attending to practices of resistance that fly under the radar of liberal myopia.

An analysis of captive resistance and its worldly effects demands a reinterpretation of the productive/destructive binary. For Arendt, homo faber creates durable and permanent things for the world. She never considers the subject of creative destruction or its adjacent discourses of demolition, obliteration, and refusal. Of course, rebellious bondpeople and insurgent prisoners resemble homo faber in some respects, for they are producers of use objects, infrastructure, art, and more. At the same time, common methods of large-scale revolt were arson, murder, and property damage. For enslaved people, poisoning livestock, shirking work responsibilities, spoiling crops, pilfering food and small items, breaking tools, and feigning illness are common, daily experiences resistance, much like, for prisoners, smuggling contraband, doing drugs, skipping work, studying revolutionaries, ignoring CO directions, and assembling with others. None of these actions, at face value, appear particularly worldly, for they seem neither to have "thing quality" nor recognizably contribute to the creation of a world in common. New political institutions or social movements did not emerge in their wake, and they did not fully abolish regimes of racial control. The following pages refute this view.

Sabotage, a category that Sarah Haley develops in *No Mercy Here,* troubles the binary of productive versus destructive, illuminating the radically creative possibilities left in its wake. Once the binary is upended, the full range of rebellious events and activities that countered white domination come into view. Reading sabotage into the creation of a world, in spaces of forced worldlessness, opens up opportunities to acknowledge the many shapes of resistance. Haley's subject matter is Black women's carceral resistance at the turn of the twentieth century, although the relevance of the term easily extends to other forms of captive rebellion. By considering sabotage as a generative practice, Haley calls attention to the creative elements of destruction, troubling conventional definitions of both. World-making does, of course, include constructing, building, and fabricating the artifice of things that lend durability to the world. At the same time, as I discussed earlier, destruction also has productive forces that warrant critical attention, for demolishing the objects, accessories, and institutions of racial control is part of the creative process of making something new. Sabotage enacts a politics of refusal to acquiesce to the confines of white domination, or in Haley's words, "a collective rebuke of structures of authority."[62] Setting fire to a sugarhouse, as rebels did during the German Coast Slave Uprising, does not merely damage the building but creates a world that engulfs in flame the built landscape of white supremacy. That enslaved people are responsible for this annihilation, politicizes the event and tells a new story in which they refused both the terms of their own captivity and the structures of the racial capital undergirding it. Thus, sabotage is not *merely* destructive, but also generative of a world out of compliance with the commands and conventions of chattel slavery. The same can be said of everyday resistance. Frederick Law Olmsted observed in his travel memoir, *A Journey in the Seaboard Slave States*, that bondpeople appeared to move with sluggish indifference while working: "no amount of punishment will prevent their working carelessly or indifferently. It always seems on the plantations as if they took pains to break all the tools and spoil all the cattle that they possibly can, even when they know they'll be directly punished for it."[63] Again, this daily, informal resistance is also a practice of sabotage. By working inefficiently, breaking tools, and spoiling cattle, enslaved people deliberately curtailed plantation profits and refused to accommodate the prevailing forces of their exploitation, thus creating an alternative world that counters and challenges the inevitability of their servitude.

Political practices of sabotage, and the worlds that they destroy and create, also describe the resistance of prisoners.[64] Haley considers the case of two teenage girls, who were imprisoned in 1918 after throwing a flowerpot through the window of a white woman's home in a middle-class neighborhood of Auburn, Georgia. It is unclear if this rebellious act was attributable to mere childlike mischief or more calculated political motivations.[65] It could have been a spontaneous whim or a deliberate assault on white property ownership and the aesthetic landscape of Jim Crow. Because it upholds the social hierarchy, as well as the present and future of segregation, the gendered racial order had to be aggressively asserted in law and policy, against which flower pots were smashed.[66] Regardless of the girls' intentions, "they disrupted, if temporarily, property rights in whiteness and produced significant angst about the presence of 'racial antipathy' in black girls."[67]

Property destruction has always been a practice of Black rebellion, in and out of prison, for the construct of private property itself was born out of the ownership of Black bodies. Historically, the transatlantic slave trade was the "solution" to the problem of a labor shortage in the colonies. Later, Virginia planters in the seventeenth century sought to sediment their class interests by introducing the construct of race to break up relations of class solidarity between poor Black and white Americans and preempt rebellion. The accumulation of private property, both in the form of profit and embodied labor power, is the foundation for the entire system of chattel slavery. In addition to enriching the personal wealth of planters, it transformed the United States from a small-scale agrarian economy to a booming global superpower.[68] After Emancipation, the implementation of new systems of racial labor, such as sharecropping and tenant farming, that would legally tether Black Americans to low-wage work, exposes the ways in which property underwrites racist hierarchies. Literal ruptures in this social order, no matter how small-scale, are the creative effects of sabotage—where a flowerpot meets a windowpane.

WEAPONS OF RESISTANCE

The rebellious spirit of the accused girls was undeterred in carceral captivity, for they refused, at every turn, to comply with the terms of their confinement:

> Fugitivity was immanent, freedom ingrained in their interior lives even as the external world indicated they were trapped. Depth, of both friendship and earth, was marshaled as an anticarceral resource. In prison they dug and dug and dug, deep into the terra firma in order to create a hole just big enough to loosen the stockade bars and wiggle their small bodies through. They were caught just before the escape was perfected. An escape plan carried out by girls whose trust, connection, and capacity to sabotage had been strengthened by prior political mischief: the quotidian, deviant, and gendered fugitive practice of floral theft and redistribution, the inspired collective imaginary.[69]

Although Haley does not make use of Arendt's terms, the sabotage of white supremacist, capitalist patriarchy is, I argue, a worldly act. The tools the girls fashioned for their digging and the hole itself were "anti-carceral resources" or, perhaps, worldly things created out of the raw materials of their refusal.[70]

Similarly, their friendship, while formed prior to incarceration, was deepened in captivity. Even though the sequestration from family and community was meant to keep them outside the web of human relationships, the girls rejected that principle of worldlessness as well.[71] Thus their steadfast, intangible connection with each other was also an exercise of refusal of forced worldlessness: "As fall turned into winter the girls found themselves not in their small homes in the vicinity of Standard Oil Alley, but in a Dougherty County chain gang stockade where they again refused their conscription to hard labor in the service of Jim Crow modernity. The imaginary that contested white supremacy through the shattering of a window pane and the appropriation of beauty fostered a rebellious friendship that was deep and grew more criminal with the slamming of cage doors."[72]

Forging insurgent relationships in captivity is part of a long legacy beginning in slavery, for friendship and kinship are among the most foundational ways that enslaved people rejected the extreme alienation of captivity. Not only were they strategies of survival, but also aggressive opposition to isolation. Such relations were rebellious in themselves, but also origins of new forms of resistance. Walter Johnson describes them as such:

> The formation of community in the slave trade—the creation of networks of support and sometimes resistance among individuals previously unknown to one another—began as something quite different: passing the time, engaging in conversation, offering isolated acts of friendship or succor. Indeed, the creation of a "slave community" in the slave trade was less a self-conscious project than an undesigned process by which a web of interconnection was spun out of a series of everyday interactions. There was nothing automatic about the formation of a community of slaves in the trade—the slave coffles and pens, indeed were shot through with animosity and suspicion; yet out of these contingent interactions could be fashioned connections that could sustain slaves emotionally and help them circulate important knowledge about the trade. The revolts and runaways, of course, are the most obvious examples of the subversive connections that took root in the interstices of the slave trade.[73]

These histories disclose not only the creation of communities *and* acts of small-scale rebellion, but also the insurgent character of slave communities. Friendships between enslaved women, in particular, are rich arenas for appreciating the rebellious character of human connection in bondage. Because of the precarity of marriages and romantic relationships, as the historian Deborah G. White explains, friendship between women was often far more stable and lasting.[74]

The rituals and habits of friendship among bondmen are also instructive, as the historian Sergio Lussana describes. Regimes of chattel labor in the plantation South laid the groundwork for these connections, which were nothing short of lifelines for enslaved men. Planters, particularly those with large landholdings and more than twenty or so bondpeople, generally divided their workforce into sex-segregated groupings. Drawing on plantation ledgers and slave narratives, Lussana speculates that this setup was meant to preempt romantic flirtations that could interfere with productivity, prevent bondmen from assisting women in reaching their work quotas, and protect them from physical punishment. Sex segregation affected the social landscape of the plantation beyond working hours, for the masculine camaraderie that bondmen formed extended to leisure time as well. During their free hours, they engaged in normatively masculine activities, including wrestling, gambling, and drinking.[75] In Lussana's words, "friendship offered men a vital emotional landscape through which to frame, shape, and give meaning to their homosocial relationships. These relationships raised the self-esteem of enslaved men, serving as a buffer against the dehumanizing features of enslaved life, and a source of resistance."[76] While Arendt does not write specifically on connections that form under dire conditions of captivity, friendship tethers humans to a distinct place in the world, entangling them in the web of human relationships. Claiming their places in both, despite the imperatives of forced worldlessness, is thus a rebellious practice of world-building.

REBELLION AND CULTURAL PRODUCTION

Beyond interpersonal relations, the politics of sabotage is also visible in other spheres of carceral life, including forms of cultural production that upend the neat binary of the productive/destructive. Black women's blues music, written and performed by both incarcerated and nonincarcerated artists alike, offers unique insight into this seemingly paradoxical relation. Writing on the journalist David Cohn's field research at Parchman Penitentiary, Haley posits, "women's music from Parchman—recordings and written lyrics and other cultural productions in the Cohn collection—reveal how southern black music was constructed through gendered relations not only at the prison, but in Jim Crow Mississippi more broadly."[77] For Haley, genre is a wholesale rejection of the trope that criminal punishment is a natural and inevitable mechanism of social progress, but is instead asserted as "an obstacle to (Black women's) independence, sexual, and economic freedom." These artists thus rearranged dominant, racialized terms and principles of society in accordance with their values and desires.[78] Haley argues that the insurgent resistance of incarcerated Black women, through blues music, exposes the power, paradoxes, and vulnerabilities of the gendered racial order. This is precisely the generative promise of sabotage, which is simultaneously and inseparably creative and destructive.

Similarly in slavery, the mobilization of traditional cultural forms, and invention of new ones, are indelibly linked to bondpeople's attempts to sabotage the system altogether. Cultural practice and production attest to the existence of a world in common against the backdrop of hostile social and political circumstances. Forced worldlessness is often explained away by the Eurocentric view that Africans arrived in the Americas with no worldly attachments of their own, an inheritance of colonial logic that Charles Mills elaborates on in *The Racial Contract*.[79] Both planters and colonial elites regularly denied that Black Africans "had culture." In the twentieth-century Old South, apologist historians claimed that slavery was a civilizing institution that offered bondpeople values, morals, and religious principles that would never have been available to them in backward and barbaric Africa.[80] I refute this here by considering some of the many African diasporic cultural practices that reflect the very durable, common, and permanent worlds that Africans inhabited prior to their capture, as well as those they repurposed afterward.

Bondpeople's cultural production is a well-mined subject that has garnered much critical attention in the historical literature on slavery. Writing on musical traditions and slave songs in particular, Thomas Barker takes note of their political dimensions:

> The confinement of transcendence, whether material or spiritual, to an aesthetic realm must be seen as a necessary corollary to a political reality that served the opposite purpose. One might say, therefore, that the inseparability of music, religion, and everyday life served as a means by which slaves could preserve and enact their beautiful humanity until the day when more favorable political conditions would enable them to use this humanity to overthrow their oppressors—indeed, such conditions would only ever become possible providing the slaves found a way of maintaining a space in which this sense of dignity could be preserved. However, when objective conditions conspired to loosen the death-grip of the slave owner, the radical potential of slave songs became increasingly evident, as intimation dangerously close to freedom's actualization.[81]

In addition to the creative inventions of bondpeople in captivity, the cultural traditions that they retained and invented during slavery are also salient. Writing on the Georgia Lowcountry, Karen Bell considers various factors that (partially) explain why enslaved Africans were able to retain their regional cultural identities in the United States, including the high ratio of Africans to whites, which remained consistent until the end of slavery in 1865; the steady importation of Africans to the Georgia Lowcountry even after the 1808 ban on the international slave trade; and the geography of the area in which a string of barrier islands isolated Black communities from mainland whites, thus reducing assimilation.[82] Conditions were in place for reinforcing collective cultural identities and consciousness. Their very existence challenges the well-worn racial trope that enslaved Africans had no evolved culture of their own.

CONJURATION AND CULTURALIST INTERPRETATIONS OF RESISTANCE

Conjuration, which hybridized regional African and Creole traditions, as well as distinctively American and European influences, is a cultural form that has been mobilized for slave rebellion. For the purposes of this discussion, conjure refers to, among other things, the practice of "Hudu," or folk magic that combines the beliefs and folklore associated with Native American and European with West and Central African regions, including the Congo, the Gold Coast, Senegambia, Nigeria, and Angola. Mysticism, magic, the supernatural, and the use of spells are all features of conjuration.[83] Its leading practitioners, conjurors, were often wizened community leaders, both enslaved and free, who were ostensibly capable of harnessing supernatural powers to bring about desired results. According to W.E.B. Du Bois, conjurors played a variety of roles in slave societies: they healed the sick; provided comfort in times of sorrow; interpreted earthly and unearthly forces; and avenged wrongdoing.[84] They exercised a great deal of power and influence over bondpeople, in some cases even more than planters.

Against the dominant view of Eugene Genovese and other leading historians of the antebellum period, Walter Rucker argues that conjuration was often routinely invoked for purposes of resistance and conjurors were known to incite and lead rebellions. Rucker states, "North American conjurors can be better viewed as a revolutionary vanguard inspiring and encouraging resistive behavior among their fellow slaves."[85] The deep respect that conjurors commanded placed them in a unique position of authority to influence enslaved rebels and inspire uprisings. Rucker observes that in North America, the practice of conjuration was held in very high regard by both African and American-born rebels. "They seemingly believed, without question, the ability of these spiritualists to determine the outcome of a variety of events, including resistance movements, through arcane and supernatural means."[86] Buoyed by the support of conjurors and the resources that they provided, bondpeople revolted at their direction. Because these leaders were said to have unique access to the spiritual world, they were ostensibly integral to the success of slave uprisings.

The high status of conjurors is clear in a 1712 rebellion in New York City involving twenty-eight bondpeople and the death and injury of approximately twenty-two whites. Bondmen armed themselves with swords, knives, and guns, and set a building on fire as part of an ambush to kill the whites that arrived at the scene. One of the leaders of this uprising was an African conjuror known as "Peter the Doctor," who supposedly rubbed magical powder on the clothing of the rebels to make them invincible, giving them the courage to act. African diasporic cultural practices such as these also informed rebellious activities elsewhere in the Americas.[87] For example, another slave revolt occurred in Jamaica fifty years later, led by a group of Obeah conjurors and which involved an identical usage of magic powder that, Rucker argues, attests to both the authenticity of this custom among Obeah-believers and that these rituals, administered by conjurors, emboldened rebels. Conjuration speaks to the creative inventions of enslaved people and the worldliness of slave resistance. Both the politics of conjuration and its distinct impact on rebellion are evident here, as well as the worldly materiality of African, transatlantic, and African American cultural discourses.

Of course, even though African cultural forms are part of the story of captive rebellion, the political identities of enslaved people should not be reduced to local traditions that traveled with them to the Americas. Culturalist explanations for slave rebellion are hotly contested among American historians. Perry Kyles, for example, argues that culture is far less salient to resistance than racial hierarchies, established in the Americas to enact and uphold slavery. In other words, slave resistance occurred because of white supremacy, chattel captivity, and planter brutality, not because of particularistic cultural proclivities for militant rebellion. Kyles cautions against reductive cultural interpretations, claiming that these are often both based in static, Eurocentric understandings of culture, and failure to appreciate the political roots of Black radical traditions in slavery.[88]

If Kyles claims that cultural attributions of slave rebellion tend to rely on weak or paltry evidentiary bases, the historian John Knowles counters that

African cultural factors are not at all irrelevant. For example, the military training that young Congolese men had likely undergone prior to Middle Passage could possibly have affected the physical strategies that they deployed when resisting slavery. Their heavy presence in eighteenth-century South Carolina accounted for a rash of rebellions there. Knowles draws a distinction between the militarily trained Congolese and the more provincial village folk from Bight of Benin. Yet historical records show that slave ships with large populations of women from the neighboring Bight of Biafra organized and executed more shipboard insurrections during Middle Passage than African women from other regions, suggesting that cultural factors might not be insignificant to their rebellious activities.[89] Kyles refutes this rationality, arguing that there are no historical records, ledgers from slave ships, or plantation logs that would lend support for such an account. While it is true that Central Africans were greater in number than any other enslaved African population in the Carolinas, there is little evidence that cultural practices from that region of Africa had a direct impact on their modalities of resistance. Strategies of rebellion, Kyles holds, from large-scale insurrection to smaller, indirect resistance, emerged from "the collective experience of slavery and middle passage."[90]

Instead of looking to culture, Kyles asserts that material conditions in the Americas informed strategies and practices of resistance: "These responses were highly politicized 'weapons of the weak' that marginal women and men used to either form beneficial ties with those at the top of the plantation hierarchy, destroy the plantation elites, or place themselves within a less oppressive environment. The evidence suggests that these responses bear no meaningful correlation with Afro-Carolinians' African region of origin. In fact, the responses can best be understood by examining the forces that gave rise to the rigid, racialized hierarchy of the plantation itself."[91] Kyles describes the context for the emergence of slave society in South Carolina, believing that it was largely rooted in the expansion of rice growing at the end of the seventeenth century. That there was a market for rice outside of the British Empire, the fact that rice-growing plantations required at least thirty laborers, and that there was a labor shortage in the Carolinas during this period, were the economic rationales for African slavery in the region. Just as in the rest of the Confederacy, it became essential to create and preserve a racial hierarchy to provide a theoretical rationale for the system of slavery. "The responses of Africans to the increasingly oppressive world of plantation life suggest that there is only a small correlation between the African region of origin and the strategies employed by enslaved Afro-Carolinians to alter their condition or status."[92] This claim is best understood as a political defense of African American resistance, rather than a culturalist narrative.

Despite the aforementioned skepticism of Kyles, I suggest that culture shaped a shadow, political tradition that stands outside of the pervasive discourses of liberal democracy. At the very least, the mobilization of cultural practices (such as conjuration) for resistance serves as evidence that enslaved people did share a world in common in the form of intangible ritual, custom, language, and spirituality. Keeping cultural practices alive and imparting them to children and kin is in itself a mode of worldly resistance to the moral doctrines of white supremacy. Alternatively, the idea that they are wholly determinative of slave resistance participates in a colonialist discourse that sidesteps politics and history in favor of culture and tradition.[93] Arguments against this view are often motivated by a critique of the Eurocentric tendency to misattribute political activities of Africans to culture, while reserving philosophical and political analysis for white Americans and Europeans. Critics of the culturalist view have worthy aims but end up enacting some of the same exclusions that they oppose. In an effort to present a politically evolved picture of enslaved Africans, they detach them from prior cultural contexts, and imply that their political subjecthood is wholly reactive to white domination. The spirit of their critique is strong, although perhaps acknowledgment of the political dimensions of regional African cultural forms does not disavow but only deepens analyses of Black agency. Attending to these subjects here should not be misunderstood as an appeal to culture to *explain* slave resistance, for culture does not carry prophetic or predictive power, but instead speaks to the *worldly things* of regional Africa, and the *worldly reality* that enslaved people constructed for themselves in the Americas.

CONCLUDING THOUGHTS

The concepts of worldlessness and world-building speak to the rebellious activities of enslaved people in ways which Arendt herself could not have anticipated. When she remarked, in the aforementioned interview with Günter Gaus, that world is a space for politics, she took note of one of its most crucial functions—to provide a setting for political action—while omitting another: to create a world is itself political, particularly when undertaken against the backdrop of forced worldlessness.[94] Sometimes the world is created in ways that align precisely with Arendt's conceptual vision: through the construction of objects and artwork that contribute to the world's "thing quality." In others, this world is created in unorthodox ways that are unique to the social and political arrangements of Black captivity, through refusal, demolition, and the destruction of the brutal institutions of white supremacy. Although the actions that form and shape this world span the spectrum from spectacular and exceptional to quotidian and mundane, they share the common purpose of wresting power from planters and prison personnel and relentlessly pushing against the conditions of captivity.

Such a view is less normative than descriptive, for the world-building work of captives is apparent throughout history, from the 1712 slave rebellion in New York to the insurgent digging of the imprisoned girls in 1918 Georgia to the 1971 Attica uprising.[95] From the spectacular scenes of death in Nat Turner's rebellion to a pocketed comb from the bedroom of a planter's wife; from the fire that overtook the Meuillion Plantation to the temporary flight of Lorenzo Ivy's grandmother into the woods: resistance is creative, worldly, and deeply and unequivocally political. Thomas Barker states, "In looking to the non-conceptual, slaves did not turn away from the world but sought the means to alter their world through a form of reason not weighted down by the shackles of slavery. The ability of slaves to experience freedom on the plantations was very much contingent upon their being able to think free (le conçu)."[96] Their political imagination was as robust and expansive as their appetite for dissidence. For prisoners, small-scale and spectacular events of resistance are similarly worldly. Davis observes in her 1971 essay "Lessons: From Attica to Soledad," that "human beings cannot be willed and molded into nonexistence. In reality the facts of prison life in recent years have begun to bespeak the irrationality of its goals. Even the most drastic repressive measures have not obstructed the progressive ascent of captive men and women to new heights of social consciousness. This has been especially intense among Black and Brown prisoners."[97] Despite the best efforts of the carceral sphere, prisoners will, as Davis indicates, find ways to rebel against even the most repressive forces of captivity. Such exercises of resistance are the centerpieces of the following chapter on the Attica prison uprising.

7

Beyond Democracy: The Attica Prison Uprising

"Attica is only the beginning. There will be much more of the same, and much bigger, in every prison, in every city, in every factory, in every mine, in every place where a slave confronts a master."

—STATEMENT OF THE LEWISBURG PRISONERS' SOLIDARITY COMMITTEE, 1971[1]

The Attica prison uprising of September 1971 is an iconic event in US public memory. In response to mounting tension, corruption, exploitation, and violence, 1,281 (of 2,200) prisoners temporarily seized control of the Attica Correctional Facility in Wyoming County, New York. They took hostages, produced a list of demands, and entered into negotiations with prison officials, advocates, and clergy. Several leaders of the rebellion organized their fellow prisoners, building a makeshift tent city in the prison's "D Yard" and improvising classic techniques of self-government.[2] This continued for four days until the uprising was violently subdued by order of New York Governor Nelson Rockefeller, resulting in a poorly executed, brutal bloodbath that killed prisoners and hostages alike. The abuse and torture that the incarcerated protestors endured at the hands of guards and corrections officers extended long past the retaking of the prison, as did the publicity and energy that the rebellion generated. The fact that, fifty years later, Attica appears everywhere, from hip-hop lyrics to big budget Showtime documentaries, attests to its global impact and position at the forefront of political and cultural memory.

Shortly after the event, the *New York Times* ran a highly spurious editorial titled "Massacre at Attica," describing lawless thuggery on the part of the prisoners who incited the uprising and stating that the deaths of the hostages "reflect a barbarism wholly alien to our civilized society. Prisoners slashed the throats of utterly helpless, unarmed guards."[3] (Autopsies would later reveal the fallacy of this account.) Moderates look to Attica for prison reform, arguing that the uprising catalyzed "meaningful prison legislation that addressed inmates' day-to-day experiences with physical and verbal abuse and maltreatment," thereby garnering support for a "more humane prison system."[4] Radicals counter this with the view that Attica was part of a constellation of events including Angela Davis's imprisonment, George Jackson's murder, the occupation of Alcatraz by Indigenous activists, and a revolt at Auburn Correctional Facility. Taken together, these events provoked movement toward the abolition of the prison system altogether, due to the new groundswell of support for its dismantlement.[5] Many scholars echo this view, arguing that "the organization, discipline, and rhetoric of the rebels made Attica the exemplar of prison revolutionary action."[6]

If Attica captured the attention of much of the mainstream public, the interest that it attracted among incarcerated people in the United States was nearly universal. Across regions, prisoners spoke and wrote about the event, crediting Attica rebels with their own hunger strikes, work stoppages, occupations, and more. A three-day revolt at McAlester State Prison in Oklahoma in 1973 followed in their footsteps, as well as dozens of other large- and small-scale uprisings throughout the 1970s. An anonymous, incarcerated author at McAlester wrote the following:

> Whatever occurs here will certainly effect the people of the communities, just as the rebellion of July 73 (McAlester) had its effect and just as the massacre of Attica prisoners is still having its, not only in New York, but all over the world. For this reason, it is imperative that the people of lesser oppression heed our plea for a united struggle against fascist, racist repression. Apathy is no longer desirable and it certainly is not effective . . . does anyone hear what we say? The superheroic uprising at Attica prison, New York State's maximum security dungeon, has already established itself as a milestone in the history of the revolution which is

exploding in this country, the very citadel of world imperialism and the arsenal of global reaction. The inmates overcame seemingly impossible obstacles and rose up, held out, and fought for four days around the clock, knowing that, in the end, death, immediately—or slowly—would almost certainly overtake them. That fact alone proves, beyond even a shadow of a doubt, that the conditions in the house of bondage made life unbearable. The slave drivers, smeared with blood, forced things to the breaking point.[7]

Showcased here is the author's perspective that the Attica uprising is an event of deep political significance. It was not a mere momentary episode in which prisoners expelled anger and energy, but a sophisticated and well-organized protest against the inhumane, chattel-like conditions of prison. The author's respect for the Attica rebels is on full display in this excerpt, as well as their influence on the subsequent revolt at McAlester. He is far from alone in this. Incarcerated authors in (and after) 1971 regularly described their own resistance as homages to Attica protestors. In an open letter to them several years later in 1975, the incarcerated author Malik Zir Hathim suggested that the uprising was part of the Black revolutionary struggle:

> We have received varied reports on what happened at Attica and what continues to happen. We can relate to your struggle because ours and yours are both one in the same. The struggle in the streets of the ghetto, our communities is one in the same! It is our duty and responsibility to educate the masses of our people to the many facades of repression and fascism . . . the death dealing forces that are at work against us (as a people) in this country. Brothers, we are the vanguard of the revolution, of change, let there be no mistake about that. We are not only as the bottom of the heap, but also on the front line; so what we have to offer to the masses is of first hand nature. Follow the Revolutionary Struggles throughout history and in various countries, Amerik.k.k.a included, and you will see that the main initiative—the primal thrust and ideology—came from that country's prison houses where men contemplated the ills of a sick society and rule. We must be successful!!! Our very existence as a race of people depends on our ultimate victory.[8]

The use of Attica to legitimize and politicize acts of violent resistance also shows up in defense of the political prisoner, Ruchell Magee, one of the authors associated with Black carceral political thought, discussed at length in Chapter Two. The rhetorical framing of the uprising serves, for his defense committee, a similar legitimizing function as slave insurrection. Noting likenesses between Attica and the 1970 shootout at the Marin County Courthouse, with which Magee was involved, underscores both the racial underpinnings of the carceral system and the legitimacy of resistance to it. Days into Magee's trial, his defense committee's press release stated that "as in the rebellion at Attica, the state is attempting to pin responsibility for the bloodshed and deaths of August 7 on those who rebelled rather than on prison and law enforcement officials."[9] Despite the obvious material and structural differences between the prison uprising and the courthouse insurrection, it is telling that Magee's supporters saw the benefits of linking his case to Attica. Situating both in the tradition of Black captive resistance lent Magee credibility and affirmed the widespread interpretation that Attica was a legitimate political event.

While it is hardly surprising that prison authors and actors were deeply invested in Attica, less predictable is the popular cultural interest it would provoke. "Attica became a household word and part of our popular culture; apart from many newspaper and magazine articles, it was an event remembered and analyzed in books, films, and song."[10] The rebellion has been the subject of five feature films, including a big budget documentary in honor of its fiftieth anniversary. A recent graphic novel details the life of Frank "Big Black" Smith, one of the key organizers of the revolt. Attica was the likely inspiration for Ryan Chapman's comedic novel, *Riots I Have Known*, the plot of which noncoincidentally centers on an uprising in a New York state prison.[11] The name of the Canadian band, The Attica Riots, is an explicit reference to the rebellion, although the group was founded more than forty years after it. Dozens of songs and musical compositions pay tribute to the uprising, including the avant-garde classical piece by Frederic Rzewski "Coming Home / Attica"; John Lennon's "Attica State"; and jazz musician Charles Mingus's "Remember Rockefeller at Attica." The Attica uprising's radicalism particularly resonates with hip-hop artists, where it is most conspicuously immortalized. Black Moon's 1993 album "Enta Da Stage" references Attica among other images of violence: "look out below, my flow will hit your brain / I got dough, but I still hop the train / I'm bustin' niggas open, Attica style / Yo, straight to the jugular, brother you mad foul."[12] Nas and Lauryn Hill's 1996 hit "If I Ruled the World" situates Attica among scenes of freedom and liberation: "Political prisoner set free, stress free / No work release purple M3s and jet skis / Feel the wind breeze in West Indies / I'd make

Coretta Scott-King mayor o' cities and reverse themes to Willies / It sounds foul but every girl I meet to go downtown / I'd open every cell in Attica and send 'em to Africa."[13] The Wu Tang Clan's Ghostface Killah also includes Attica in his 2001 album "Bulletproof Wallets": "Smoke the Cee Allah / Sent the kite through the Pens / Him and big Dan / Known to split wigs, with razor sharp gems / Giants from Attica riots / Halls is quiet / Co's with babies on their arms look tight."[14] Most of these were written and produced decades after the event, attesting yet again to its prominent, highly visible place in the US cultural imaginary. The event is monumental, ever appropriable by journalists, artists, and incarcerated actors alike, and a focal point of intense collective interest.

The dichotomy between public fascination with Attica and academic study of its political significance is noteworthy. By contrast with other prison uprisings, it has received the lion's share of airtime in popular culture and media; however, there is little deep analysis of its political dimensions. The top journals in both political science and political theory (including *Political Theory*, *The Journal of Politics*, *The American Political Science Review*, and *Perspectives on Politics*) have never published an article centrally featuring it. There is not one book on Attica in the field of political theory, or even a paltry entry dedicated to it in the *Encyclopedia of Political Thought*. All of this points to an unspoken consensus that Attica is not an event of import or consequence for political thinkers, a position that sharply contrasts with the world outside of the discipline.[15] The absence of constructs that can properly articulate captive resistance, the core theoretical problem *Politics in Captivity* aims to correct, might well account for this.

Here, I first look at the events and conditions that preceded (and provoked) the uprising, including the precipitative work strike at Attica and a large protest at Auburn Correctional Facility, shortly thereafter. A thorough account of the Attica revolt establishes the groundwork for the exploration of its theoretical dimensions, including the claim that most democratic theory is incapable of speaking to them. I argue in the second section of the chapter that while incarcerated activists at Attica certainly made use of the deliberative and distributive tools of democratic politics, *democratic theory* lacks the political vocabulary for rich and thorough analyses of prison resistance, in general, and this one, in particular.

As much as the discussion in this chapter centers on the Attica prison uprising, it also orbits carceral rebellion, broadly speaking. Spotlighting Attica reveals political theory's limitations: the fact that theorists have been silent in response to an event that has garnered such obvious and immense public, media, and cultural interest, suggests underlying issues in political and democratic theory that render them unequipped for deep consideration of prison politics. Constructs on which democratic theory often relies, such as the demos, public and private spheres, rights, and citizenship are (generally) irrelevant to captive rebellion, offering further evidence that the concept of world is a corrective to this. The politics that unfolded during those fateful four days in September 1971 are not exemplary of democratic action, properly understood, but rather world-building in an Arendtian register. Attica rebels worked forcefully against worldless prison conditions and, in so doing, radically constructed a world in common. Drawing on Sarah Haley's argument that sabotage and refusal are generative acts of resistance against the dehumanization and violence of captivity, I hold that carceral rebellion works through such concerted acts of creation and destruction.[16] If the narrow interpretive lenses of liberalism and democratic theory are likely to miss the unique political significance of prison resistance, perhaps this more expansive view will bring to it new voice and vision.

ATTICA IN CONTEXT

Heather Ann Thompson's Pulitzer Prize-winning *Blood in the Water* has been called "the definitive account of Attica," although not without significant contestation.[17] Through exhaustive archival research, including redacted government documents, and interviews with Attica survivors and families, Thompson chronicles not only the days of the rebellion from September 9–13, but also analyzes the events and conditions that anticipated the uprising, and of course, its aftermath. It is clear in her account that the revolt was a culminating moment, the result of a concatenation of structural conditions and individual decisions that built toward it. Chief among them were horrific, borderline illegal living conditions at Attica that betrayed the overwhelming disregard for the safety and health of its residents.

Incarcerated people were forced to work when sick, worsening their illnesses and exposing others to disease, always a heightened risk in congregate settings. There were only two doctors for the entire population of 2,200 "inmates" and they were notoriously indifferent to the pain and suffering of their patients, generally refusing to examine them and disregarding even their documented chronic conditions. Neither physician spoke Spanish, nor bothered to request interpreters. Frank "Big Black" Smith, one of the lead rebels, lost almost all of his teeth because he was denied proper dental care.[18] While they routinely withheld healthcare from their charges, Attica administrators regularly allowed prisoners to be used as human subjects for experimental medical research, a practice harkening back to slavery.[19]

The maximum capacity of the facility was almost doubly exceeded in the years prior to 1971, one of the root causes of such paltry healthcare and other services. Attica was notoriously overcrowded and understaffed as a result of both state budget cuts and rising national incarceration rates. Not only were far too many bodies warehoused in totally inadequate space, but conditions were managed by egregiously inexperienced staff. Few resources were allocated for job training. "When the new hires first reported for duty they were handed a stick, a badge, and a uniform and then put in charge of a company of forty or so prisoners."[20]

The impact of these irresponsible practices came to a head in the 1960s as a result of two paradoxical turns in prison life. First, Lyndon Johnson's Great Society initiatives significantly expanded educational opportunity for incarcerated people, including access to Pell Grants in 1965 and increases in federal funding for prison education programs. Prisoners began to enroll in college-level courses, often earning advanced degrees. Sociology was one of the most popular fields of study among Attica prisoners, and students' exposure to Mao, Marx, and other revolutionary thinkers strongly influenced their political sensibilities.[21] Second, the FBI's COINTELPRO operation, and other apparatuses of state surveillance, began to fix their sights on Black radical groups in the 1960s, criminalizing their activities and arresting and incarcerating them at high rates. President Johnson's Omnibus Crime Control and Safe Streets Act of 1968 was a landmark law that helped usher in the era of mass incarceration.

This and other laws increased not only prison populations, but also highly politicized Black prisoners.[22] Of course, Attica was no exception. Unlike earlier generations of convicts, they were unwilling to follow inmate conventions of compliance and obedience to commanding officers. "The impact of large numbers of political prisoners both on prison populations and on the mass movement has been decisive. The vast majority of political prisoners have not allowed the fact of imprisonment to curtail their educational, agitational and organizing activities, which they continue behind prison walls."[23] That more people were incarcerated for their political affiliations and activism strongly influenced the prison population at large, for the newfound exposure of formerly apolitical incarcerated men to politics, their education in the history and sociology of oppression, and the growth of Black radical movements outside of the carceral sphere ignited the spirit of activism within prisoners who had previously never taken much interest in political issues.

In Thompson's words, "Furthermore the political receptivity of prisoners—especially Black and Brown captives—has been increased and sharpened by the surge of aggressive political activity rising out of Black, Chicano and other oppressed communities. Finally, a major catalyst for intensified political action in and around prisons has emerged out of the transformation of convicts, originally found guilty of criminal offenses, into exemplary political militants. Their educational efforts in the realm of exposing the specific oppressive structures of the penal system have had a profound effect on their fellow captives."[24] The new recalcitrance of Black and brown prisoners revealed the precarity of Attica's institutional homeostasis: smooth daily operations were dependent on the assumption that inmates would follow rules and respect the directions of officers.[25] When they instead challenged authority, Attica's disciplinary structure began to erode. For the overwhelmingly white, untrained prison staff with little or no knowledge of the communities, cultures, or political movements with which Black and brown prisoners were associated, the intransigence of their charges provoked a great deal of anxiety. They responded in all the wrong ways: by doubling down on punitive restrictions and disproportionately targeting and punishing prisoners of color. These punishments ranged from petty and arbitrary indignities to brutal and abusive aggression. Of course, this treatment likely expedited, if not directly provoked a militant response.

Without reducing the Attica uprising to singular causal factors, the combined conditions of crowding and scarcity of necessary resources, the ignorance and aggression of prison personnel, and an ever-increasing population of politicized Black and brown prisoners created a perfect storm of inevitable captive resistance. In LeShawn Harris's words:

> Men were underpaid for their labor; received insufficient and inadequate amounts of clothing, food, and toiletries; were allowed to shower only once a week; were denied access to reading materials, open air, and proper medical care; and experienced stringent rules and treatment. Untrained, overworked, and unpaid prison personnel and apathetic high-ranking prison officials further complicated inmates' day-to-day experiences. Like many 1970s American penal institutions, including Folsom

and Soledad in California and New York City's Tombs, Attica was a site of violence, racial and ethnic inequality, and economic injustice. The facility sanctioned indecent treatment, operated on the margins of the law, and was a place where dignity was denied to individuals who were deemed unworthy of human rights. Inmates were considered "outside the law's imperative of protection, as well as society's normalization of human rights."[26]

Situated against this background, several specific events precipitated the September revolt: a work strike at Attica and, shortly after, a large uprising at Auburn Correctional Facility. In the early 1970s, Attica prisoners were paid between six and twenty-nine cents a day, although the prison confiscated half of these meager wages until their release. In addition, working conditions at Attica were severely racialized. Thompson writes, "Though resources were limited for all prisoners, it was obvious that some of them suffered worse hardships than others because of the highly discriminatory way that prison officials ran the institution. While everyone at Attica had to work and run various cons to supplement his basic supplies, African Americans and Puerto Ricans had to hustle a great deal more because their work usually paid much less."[27] The coveted, higher-wage jobs were primarily reserved for white prisoners and almost always began at a higher pay rate, while Black and brown workers were relegated to the much-loathed laundry and metal shop—jobs which paid significantly less per hour.

In response to both pitiful wages and the racist distribution of labor, several Black prisoners organized a work stoppage, an initially calm and discrete affair. A small delegation was appointed to negotiate with prison officials and the protestors sought to minimize attention to the event. This changed when Superintendent Vincent Mancusi cracked down on the negotiators, relegating them to "keeplock" (solitary confinement) and arranging transfer for the men that he suspected to have masterminded the protest. This iron-fisted, draconian response incited a full-scale strike in which over four hundred and fifty metal workers participated. Attica officials contacted Commissioner of Corrections Paul McGinnis in the hope that he would intervene. In a surprise move, he did not punish the protestors and instead met with their delegation, eventually agreeing to increase the metal workers' hourly wages to twenty-five cents and raise the maximum allowable pay rate to a dollar per day.[28] This Pyrrhic victory for the Attica protestors would largely inspire the next, far more significant uprising the following year.

Several months after the Attica metal shop strike in the fall of 1970, two groups of prisoners at Auburn Correctional Facility, the Black Muslims and the Black Panthers, approached their superintendent with the request to approve the celebration of Black Solidarity Day on November 2. He directed them to write to Commissioner McGinnis, who would not give a definitive answer, instead deferring to the Auburn superintendent, further delaying the decision. On November 2, when no resolution was communicated to the prisoners, Black Muslims seized a microphone in the main yard and announced that in commemoration of Black Solidarity Day, no Black men should report to work.[29] Several protestors blocked doors and prevented corrections officers from entering their space.

For much of the rest of that day, virtually all Black prisoners at Auburn celebrated by socializing with one another and listening to speeches, rather than showing up to their jobs. COs assured them, following the peaceful event, that no one would be punished for their actions. In a punitive and ill-advised move, the superintendent overrode this decision and threw the organizers of the protest into indefinite, segregated housing. In Thompson's words, "this betrayal was like flame to kindling." [30] Four hundred Auburn prisoners, of all racial groups, staged a protest, demanding the release of their fellow prisoners from solitary confinement. When administrators refused to negotiate with them, the revolt became aggressive: prisoners smashed glass and fashioned makeshift weapons out of found objects. They took over fifty hostages (whose protection was ensured by a body shield of Black Muslim prisoners) and drafted a list of modest demands for reform at Auburn. That these demands mostly included better food, sanitary conditions, and more frequent parole board reviews attests to the fact that their aims were hardly revolutionary or radical in character, but mostly simple matters of basic human rights and dignity.[31]

After a short standoff, prison administrators agreed to meet with representatives from the rebellion and guaranteed that there would be no reprisals against leaders or participants.[32] Of course, the latter promise was a lie, for rebel prisoners were subsequently abused, beaten, and confined to segregated housing units (SHU). They did not respond to this treatment with inertia or compliance: prisoners locked in the SHU communicated with lawyers who mounted legal challenges to their indefinite isolation. Auburn administrators likely did not anticipate the legal and public relations nightmare that would ensue, for the situation garnered a great deal of media attention and popular backlash.

The relatively new commissioner of the Department of Corrections, Russell Oswald, visited Auburn in the hope of reconciliation. He was not prepared for the hostility leveled at him by angry prisoners who blamed him for their months-long lockup in solitary confinement, as well as the beatings and abuse that they suffered. This enraged Oswald, who believed that the modest reforms which he had implemented at Auburn since the revolt should have earned him the gratitude and respect of the prisoners. He concluded from this contemptuous meeting that the Auburn men were irrational revolutionary militants with no legitimate grievances, a common racial narrative that both discredited prisoners' political convictions and enabled officials to sidestep their subpar carceral conditions. In short order, Oswald arranged for the transfer of the leaders and organizers of the uprising to Attica, a decision that would prove extremely consequential in the coming months.

The fear on the part of the Attica superintendent and other administrators that the Auburn transferees would radicalize the general population was misguided. Attica prisoners were fully aware of the oppressive, inhumane conditions under which they lived, and in need of no enlightenment. What ultimately incited the Attica men to action was their perception of the treatment that the former Auburn prisoners endured. Immediately upon arrival, the Auburn transferees were forced into solitary confinement, where they were threatened and abused for months. That the Auburn prisoners had been misled by promises that they would be safe from retaliatory action only further deepened distrust of Superintendent Mancusi, as well as the rest of Attica upper administration, resulting in preliminary efforts to organize against them.

THE ATTICA PRISON UPRISING

On September 8, a small quarrel erupted in the prison's D Yard, resulting in the confinement of two prisoners in segregated housing units, a bloc notorious for torture and abuse. One of the punished men was not even involved in the aforementioned scuffle, thus prompting rage and unrest throughout the Attica population. The following day, a group of prisoners retaliated, attacking the guard responsible for this incident, and thereby inciting the three-day rebellion that followed.[33] In the first hours of the revolt, nearly 1,300 incarcerated men took control of Attica's D Yard, the largest open-air section of the prison's grounds. The rebels held thirty-eight civilians and prison personnel hostage, and demanded communication with journalists, activists, and organizers. Participants would eventually include Assemblyman Arthur O. Eve, the attorney William Kunstler, and Black Panther Party cofounder Bobby Seale, with whom the prisoners discussed their grievances.

Despite media narratives of lawless chaos, the revolt, by multiple accounts, was a largely collegial and well-organized affair in which prisoners worked collaboratively and even made use of mechanisms of self-government, electing representatives and crafting a manifesto of demands, including full amnesty for the leaders of the uprising as well as more moderate reformist items, such as the termination of mail censorship and healthier food. Attica administrators and protestors remained at loggerheads over several items in the manifesto, prompting Governor Rockefeller's order that the prison should be retaken by September 13 if negotiations failed. While authorities ceded many of the demands, they refused to grant complete amnesty to the rebels leading the uprising. After multiple days of discussion, Rockefeller ordered the dispatch of hired New York State troopers to retake control of the prison, and Oswald ultimately gave the final order for them to storm the facility.[34] They opened fire on D Yard for two continuous minutes, killing thirty-three prisoners and ten hostages in a chaotic and inept operation. It is remembered as the single most violent police encounter in New York State history.

The racial dimensions of the attack were more than apparent. Black prisoners, who provided much of the uprising's organizational structure and leadership, absorbed an outsized share of the white supremacist state response. In an attempt to evade responsibility and public scrutiny, Attica authorities and state officials manufactured lies backed by racial tropes, which they fed to local and national media. They alleged that hostages were surrounded by gasoline-soaked mattresses, when in fact prisoners had supplied clean mattresses and blankets for their comfort. Others, like the aforementioned *New York Times* journalist, claimed that protestors slashed the throats of unarmed prison personnel, although autopsies would later reveal that every one of the hostages died from bullet wounds inflicted by the New York State troopers. Grisly fabrications intensified in the weeks that followed, including a claim that rebels castrated a guard and stuffed his testicles into his mouth, and another fearmongering rumor that Black militant rebels were coming to Attica to kidnap white school children.[35] All of these fantasies draw on very well established racist narratives of Black men as barbaric, bestial, irredeemable, and criminal.[36] While in reality, cross-racial solidarity prevailed during the days of the actual rebellion, the mobilization of anti-Black imagery was essential for discrediting its political meaning and manipulating white anxiety to galvanize support for the botched, incompetent state response.

The Attica uprising was a culmination of many simultaneous forces, including massive expansions to the prison system since the turn of the twentieth century; the exploitation of prisoners' extremely undercompensated labor; austerity measures that cut operational costs by withholding sufficient food, toiletries, and weather-appropriate clothing from incarcerated men; regulations denying prisoners basic dignities such as regular showers, reading material, access to open air, and healthcare; strategically stoked racial tensions between Black, Latino, and white prisoners; and gross mishandling of interpersonal conflicts. But the political meaning of Attica extends far past the oppressive conditions that provoked the revolt, for it stripped away the veil of secrecy on which the institutional arrangements of carceral power rely and, as Robert T. Chase notes, "inspired two decades of struggle by prisoners across the nation who demanded that institutions of criminal justice also act as spaces of social justice."[37]

THE LIMITS OF DEMOCRACY

The theoretical constructs of democratic theory are incapable of articulating the political significance of Attica, first and foremost because they lack an analysis of the carceral system itself. In several key respects, captivity is a state of exception, constituted by conditions that do not map onto other scenes of democratic politics. The assumption that carceral rebellion is democratic in character and best conceptualized within the terms of democratic theory is, in part, understandable. By all accounts radical democratic thinkers, unlike their liberal, statist counterparts, would seem to align well with the rationalities of prison revolt.[38] Their work centers on resistance and favors spontaneous and episodic action over pragmatic and incremental institutional change. Arguably, this too describes the protest and then standoff between the state and a cadre of highly politicized, incarcerated activists at Attica. Further still, the rebels made use of fairly conventional techniques of democratic self-government, including deliberative and distributive practices, elections of representatives, and, of course, protest.[39] They collectively negotiated community norms and rules, and abided by principles of mutual aid, ensuring that food and medical supplies were equitably distributed in accordance with need. This easily mirrors Arjun Appadurai's construct of "deep democracy" or "democracy from below."[40] While tempting as it is to call Attica an exemplar of radical democracy, this is a misnomer. Appealing mainly to the work of Wendy Brown and Sheldon Wolin, I argue that democratic theory cannot currently speak to the events at Attica, in particular, and prison politics, in general.[41]

As one of the most prolific scholars of radical democratic theory today, Brown is a focal point of this discussion. Her democratic commitments are as pronounced in her work as her critiques of liberalism and neoliberalism. These she indicts on the basis of their destructive effects on democracy: liberalism because of its tendencies toward depoliticization, and neoliberalism due to its reduction of all aspects of life to market rationalities.[42] Brown's work is influenced by, though certainly distinct from, Wolin's theory of "fugitive democracy." Unlike Wolin, much of Brown's political thought can be characterized as anti-foundationalist and avowedly Foucauldian.[43] Her resemblance with Wolin lies in their shared view that the increasing decline of democracy is the tragic casualty of unchecked and unbridled capitalism.[44] Democracy is often set up by Brown as the prized object to be saved from ruinous political and economic systems. Neoliberalism and political arrangements that accommodate it, such as the deregulation of banks and the proliferation of free trade areas, and most recently, the encroaching threat of global fascism, are prime examples of this.

Democracy is, for Brown, a self-evident universal good, although Brown is a vocal critic of the neoconservative project of "democracy promotion," reborn in post-9/11 foreign policy.[45] Wolin and Brown also share similar critiques of liberalism and its "low standards for democracy," as well as mutual doubt that the demos can compete with the pervasive forces of late capitalism. Brown has spun this conviction into multiple works on neoliberalism's assault on democracy, while Wolin's *Democracy Incorporated* similarly warns readers that the specter of "inverted totalitarianism" surfaces in the wake of boundless and unregulated corporate power.[46] I draw on Brown's writings here, not only because she is a renowned and influential thinker, but also because her work exemplifies some important tendencies of contemporary political theorists to overlook politics in captivity, and reveals the limited capacity of democratic theory to address prison resistance.

In her essay, "Democracy and Bad Dreams," Brown states the following: "The chains binding us to the state are not mere legal ones, as for Hobbes, but deeply penetrative administrative and bureaucratic ones—and it is their irregular rather than regular jerking that constitutes state power and citizen powerlessness in a regularized fashion. These dangling dependents are largely without cognizance of their chains and without significant vestiges of freedom and equality, even as they are awash in rights and privileges."[47] Like the "fugitive" in "Fugitive Democracy," the "chains" to which Brown refers here are purely metaphorical, perhaps underscoring Charles Mills's insight in *The Racial Contract* that modern conceptions of freedom and liberty rely on constructs of unfreedom and slavery, or maybe Brown's usage is meant to elicit the image of Plato's "Allegory of the Cave." In either case, the chains illustrate the power, albeit invisible and unconscious, that the state wields over its citizens.[48] Power, says Brown, should not be understood merely in formal and legal terms but also at the core of the administrative apparatus of the state. That democratic citizens are most often unaware of the state power wielded over them is the defining condition of their relationship to it, even as they enjoy the fruits and favors of liberalism, including rights, choices, and other privileges.

Prisoners exist wholly outside of this framework. While their subjection to state power also ranges from formal and legal to bureaucratic and administrative, their chains are jerked constantly and vigorously, not subtly and inconsistently. The direct, ceaseless, ubiquitous exertion of power over their bodies and minds is definitive of their carceral lives, *by design*. Complete cognizance of their chains is probably one of the few things that all prisoners share in common, for the unending reminder that they have virtually no meaningful autonomy is the beating heart of carceral punishment. Unlike nonincarcerated citizens, there is no distance between prisoners and the state, the condition that marks, perhaps, the sharpest distinction between those in and outside of prison. Further still, Brown leans heavily on the construct of "citizenship" in her articulation of radical democracy, presupposing that democratic subjects are also citizens. For prisoners, citizenship is a relatively empty category. Given that they are denied voting rights in all but two states; nonexempt from slavery under the 13th Amendment; compensated for their labor at rates significantly below state and federal minimum wage; and are denied the most basic and mundane liberties that others enjoy as a matter of course, prisoners are hardly citizens in any meaningful or recognizable sense.[49] Their legal recourse is limited when they are subjected to violations of their human and civil rights, from physical abuse to intimidation, neglect, sexual assault, and extortion. In addition, the vast majority of prisoners in detention facilities are undocumented and thus without even legal citizenship status. None of these subjects are "awash in rights and privileges" as are the citizens that Brown names (to say nothing of the likelihood that they are also white, cis-gendered, and socioeconomically advantaged).

It seems fairly evident that Brown's accounts of citizenship and state power elide the carceral sphere, although the point here is not to chastise her or others for overlooking it. Rather, it is the consequence of the omission that matters. Failing to address the unique political lives of captives not only further sequesters them from the polity, but also misses the significance and meaning of their actions altogether. The reliance of Brown's democratic theory on assumptions that citizenship is definitive of subjecthood that relations between the citizen and the state are univocal and that state power is only indirectly exerted over people not only erases prisoners but also disables her readers from analyzing both major events and everyday politics that occur outside of these narrow frames. The loss is reciprocal: politics in captivity goes unnoticed to the detriment of both prisoners, whose work is lost to history, and political thinkers, whose theories are decidedly incomplete. Brown's concept of democracy is thereby reserved exclusively for citizens, not incarcerated people, and microcosmic of the broader failure of much political theory to account for carceral resistance.

Chapter Four took up the subject of liberal dependencies on the separation between the public and private realms, arguing that this distinction had little meaning for captive people. In classical liberal discourses, the private is both a space of respite and retreat from public affairs, and a crucial site of individual rights (to accumulate and enjoy private property and live in the manner one wishes without interference from the government). As the feminist theorist Catherine Rottenberg observes, "As part of their dominant political imaginary, liberal democracies produced and maintained a discursive and normative distinction between the public and private spheres."[50] Plantations and prisons, as I elaborated earlier, are situated outside of these liberal frames, a fact which is not incidental, but fundamental to the transformation of liberalism from an experimental, Enlightenment philosophy to the (not a) dominant Western political order. Liberalism has always leaned on the nonliberal other for intelligibility. Naomi Paik observes that if the United States has made use of rights discourse to uphold its vision of capitalism and democracy, rightlessness has been no less essential: "forms of rightlessness have been crucial to US governance in the period of rights ascendant, most obviously prison, that major American institution."[51] Other examples abound as well: the rational citizen in relation to the irrational barbarian; liberty in opposition to bondage; the rule of law against criminality.⁵² In sum, liberalism relies on both a public/private divide *and* institutions of racial control for which such a distinction is devoid of any relevance, substance, and meaning.

While liberals tend not to problematize the public/private distinction, current democratic thinkers, particularly feminists, are sharply critical of the way in which it has historically served to naturalize gendered power differentials. White women have traditionally been relegated to the prepolitical, or more aptly, apolitical private sphere, ostensibly their "natural" condition. For Brown, the public/private distinction "functions to obscure the saturation of the private sphere by power and convention."⁵³ In her iconic essay "Toward an Agonistic Feminism," Bonnie Honig rearranges the terms of the public/private, repurposing the categories and opening them up to contestation and augmentation. In this new version of the distinction, she claims "not everything is political on this (amended) account; it is simply the case that nothing is ontologically protected from politicization, that nothing is necessarily or naturally or ontologically not political. The distinction between public and private is seen as the performative product of political struggle, hard won and always temporary."⁵⁴ Here, Honig calls for a public/private forever subject to debate and interrogation, although importantly, the separation between spheres is intact, if in flux. Certain matters will remain public or private, while dynamic democratic politics will continually renegotiate their terms.

The public is brought into being through assemblages of people, including political actors and spectators. Hannah Arendt's contemporary, Jürgen Habermas, a renowned theorist of the public sphere, conceives of it in a way that also makes no theoretical space for captives. The public sphere is, for Habermas, the mediating agent between society and the state.⁵⁵ It is the place where citizens come together to form and express public opinions. Importantly, conceptions of the general good that surface in the public sphere provide essential checks on state power, thus performing an indispensable service to democratic political life. Habermas, like Brown, centrally positions citizenship in his account, a move that (again) automatically writes out prisoners. In addition, the Habermasian public sphere leans heavily on a discourse of visibility that does not extend to carceral captivity.⁵⁶ Because its primary function is mediator between the state and society, the public must be prominently located and, as Habermas specifies, *open to all citizens*. Given these conditions, it is difficult to imagine how a public sphere could ever emerge in, or exist adjacent to, a carceral setting. The prison, particularly medium and maximum security, are geographically and structurally removed from public life.[57] Their occupants do not appear in public spaces, and they are forbidden from active participation, whether voting, public speaking, community organizing, assembling with others, joining civic associations, and more. The core principle of incarceration is the sequestration and isolation of prisoners *from* society while tethering them inescapably *to* the state. Their punishment is, by definition, wholesale isolation from life outside the prison. If the domain of the public sphere is the mediating space between society and the state, prisoners cannot even approach it, much less participate in the political activities and social relations within it.

Just as prisoners cannot access the public, the public cannot access prisons. The nonpublic character of prison associated with its geographic isolation is not one-sided. Just as their inhabitants cannot engage with the outside world, neither can democratic citizens in the public realm see into or meaningfully interact with the worldless carceral sphere. Prisoners cannot avail themselves of the pleasures and possibilities of political life, and, in turn, free people cannot easily access the carceral domain. As F. Bruce Franklin put it, "Secrecy is part of the essence of the prison."[58] Because they are situated far from city centers and mass transportation, prisons are physically outside of the built landscape of the public. Physically entering or exiting a medium or maximum security facility is a multi-step process in which one must first acquire approval from the department of corrections before clearing several heavily regulated security checkpoints. Information about the leadership structure, hierarchy of command, and bureaucratic regulations is kept deliberately opaque and thus is often difficult for advocates or scholars to access. Strict rules banning cameras and recording devices inhibit most documentation of prison conditions and, of course, the voices of incarcerated people from entering the public. Both carceral settings and carceral subjects are held far outside its reach.

At the same time, the compromised visibility of the prison cannot be likened to the private realm in any discernible sense, for incarcerated people are unable to enjoy even its most minimal comforts, such as basic privacy or respite. As was clearly the case at Attica, they are warehoused in often terrible living conditions with none of the personal time and space for oneself that the private normatively affords.[59] It is also worth noting that segregated housing is certainly not to be confused with privacy, but rather loneliness and surveillance in their most extreme forms.

In sum, the prison, like the plantation, is not a public or private sphere, nor is it a realm that contains both. While democratic theorists have analyzed and critiqued the public and private, as well as the distinction between them in useful and important ways, the idea that the carceral sphere exists outside of this framework altogether does not (generally) enter into their thinking. In other words, there is an unspoken consensus among democratic and feminist theorists that the public and private are ubiquitous categories of political thought, although they differ over questions of whether they are normatively distinct from one another; the ways in which both realms are constituted; and whether and how to politicize the private. These are undoubtedly important political questions, but again, they reify the public/private by presuming that it is a proper, even if contestable, framework for ordering the polity and society. By contrast, carceral settings are set apart from the geography of the two realms. Regardless of whether the line between the public and private should be preserved, redrawn, or erased, all presuppose that the separate spheres construct maps neatly onto all, or most, social and political contexts. That neither the public nor private exists in prisons fails to enter into the considerations of democratic thinkers.

Of course, this critical account is not to laud the benefits of either the public, private, or division between the two, but rather call attention to the unique forms of worldlessness generated by the nonpublic and nonprivate character of captivity. Although Arendt's treatment of the public and private realms is quite problematic, the details of which need no rehearsal here, public/private discourse orients readers to some crucial dimensions of politics and freedom, and illuminates the material and theoretical resources that incarcerated people are denied as a matter of course.[60] Put simply, just as liberal constructs could not speak to the politics of the enslaved, neither can democratic ones attend to prison rebellion.

WORLD-BUILDING BEYOND DEMOCRACY

If the conceptual repertoires of democratic theory are ill-equipped for the radical refusal, collectivity, creativity, and destruction of the Attica Uprising, world-building is far better suited for this purpose. Attica protestors transformed the prison into a genuine political community, if not a formal public sphere. Elected representatives collectively drafted a statement of demands, the "Attica Liberation Faction Manifesto of Demands and Anti-Depression Platform," modeled after Folsom State Prison inmates' 1970 manifesto. These ranged from modest reforms to radical demands, including proper healthcare, religious freedom, and basic human rights, as well as state minimum wage for their work, transportation of the lead organizers to a "non-imperialist country," and the abolition of cell confinement and disproportionately harsh discipline.[61]

Prisoners deliberated at length on each individual item; they set up stations for food and medical services; and they pilfered food items and other resources from the commissary, adding them to a community bank where they were distributed according to need. Importantly, they created a variety of inventive, worldly things, spacing speakers across D Yard so that all issues discussed at the negotiating table would be audible to everyone present.[62] Several prisoners built a "lighted wooden gazebo-like structure" over the negotiating table in order to differentiate it from others and protect it from the elements. In Thompson's words, "D Yard was being transformed from anarchy into an organized tent city with democratically elected representatives, a security force, a dining area, and a fairly well-equipped medical station."[63] For four days, mutual aid and community care, rather than discipline and racial hierarchy, were the prevailing principles at Attica: protestors ensured that all prisoners received proper medical attention, food, and clothing. They established a prisoner-led patrol to ensure collective safety in D Yard. Talking freely and forming connections with one another were their entries, albeit temporarily, into the web of human relationships. Building spaces for speech and discussion spelled the possibility for political action and imagination. Prisoners provided entertainment through music and poetry readings, creating art that is, as Arendt put it, "the most intensely worldly of all tangible things."[64] A genuine spirit of camaraderie animated the uprising, as the protestors creatively orchestrated political solutions and strategies to meet the needs of the community. In sum, Attica rebels inserted themselves into politics by taking up the processes and instruments of self-government, and radically reimagined a world in which they were not excluded from exercising political power:

> Despite the sense of foreboding, there were moments of levity and, for some, even a feeling of unexpected joy as men who hadn't felt the fresh air of night for years reveled in this strange freedom. Out in the dark, music could be heard—"drums, a guitar, vibes, flute, sax, [that] the brothers were playing." This was the lightest many of the men had felt since being processed into the maximum security facility. That night

was a deeply emotional time for all of them. Richard Clarke watched in amazement as men embraced each other, and then he saw one man break down into tears because it had been so long since he had been "allowed to get close to someone" . . . As Clarke later described this first night of the rebellion, while there was so much trepidation about what might occur next, the men in D Yard also felt wonderful because "no matter what happened later on, they couldn't take this night away from us."[65]

Recall Arendt's claim in *The Human Condition*, "Only we who have erected the objectivity of a world from what nature gives us, who have built it into the environment of nature so that we are protected from her, can look upon nature as something 'objective.'"[66] Even before the uprising, creatively imagining and constructing such objectivity took the form of everyday resistance at Attica when incarcerated men attempted to alleviate some of the discomforts of prison life. They fashioned their own electrical units known as "droppers" out of found objects and commissary items, including razor blades, paper clips, string, lamp cords, and matchsticks, putting them together so that they generated heat through electrolysis and enabled the men to make hot beverages.[67] Creating "that which they themselves are not" and living in a world of things that inserts itself between them, conditions them, and provides a space in which to act, are not merely incidental to navigating and surviving prison life, but crucial for both.

Epilogue

On September 14, 1971, four days after the bloody end of the Attica prison uprising, the Prisoners Solidarity Committee released a special edition of their regular newsletter. The eight-page document was dedicated entirely to the rebellion, including eyewitness reports from inside the prison, as well as interviews with friends and family members of the protestors. The committee wrote, "Attica, with its prisoner population 85 percent Black and Puerto Rican and the high political consciousness and clenched fist salutes displayed during the rebellion, was one more battle in the continuing war for national liberation of the Black and Brown populations in the United States. Few believe that it will be the last."[1]

They were correct. The following year, the prison periodical, *The Outlaw: Journal of the Prisoners Union,* published an issue that called upon its readers to organize for better labor conditions within prisons; brought necessary attention to abuse and exploitation within the California Institute for Women at Frontera; and publicized a scandal at Soledad in which a prison psychiatrist was framed after speaking out about the need for reform, all fairly standard topics for *The Outlaw*. Buried at the end, was a short section reserved for prisoner poetry. There, an author who identified himself as "Judy's man" wrote the following lines: "Let me hear the shouts of men / as they march ahead full bent / onward ever onward / against the Establishment / Let me hear the shouts of men who will finally win the day / Oppression gone, new life with job / Where power and love-strength will stay."[2] Although he does not identify a single uprising, revolt, or political movement, the rebellious spirit of Judy's Man appears in his writing.

In 1975, an anonymous, incarcerated author in Rhode Island wrote an article for NEPA News, the newspaper of the Northeast Prisoner Association, condemning the administrative decision to paint over a series of murals made by prisoners. This he called "symptomatic of an unhealthy impulse to deny reality and choose the mask of emptiness to the face of expression."[3] Like Arendt, he too takes note of the relationship between reality and worldly things:

> As of yet, the RI Training School has not covered up the exterior walls painted on maintenance and office buildings, but I do not trust that the murals will last. In a sense the murals are not important—what is of major significance is the right of people to shape their own environment, and transform their own environment to meet their needs. By enforcing idleness, passivity, dependency and helplessness in the prisons, the administrators act against life in a profound way. It is a person's right and ultimate need to grow. Those who would deprive living creatures of this right are doing all life an injustice. However, it is most heartening to see that men, women, and children continue to create and grow, despite the system. It is imperative that self-directed activities of all currency be fostered within the prisons, and in doing so we shall succeed in undoing that dark side of man that would build prisons.[4]

Perhaps the words of the incarcerated authors named above might call attention to the acts of writing a poem, painting a mural, or a few years prior, building a gazebo-like structure in Attica's D Yard. Under the extreme conditions of domination that prevail in carceral settings, the enduring presence of such worldly things are of crucial importance. The aspiration of total domination, and the rationality of prisons and plantations, are thwarted by these objects that possess an independent existence apart from their makers.

Their rebellious political character surfaces when one considers their worldless circumstances. Writing a verse, stealing an hour, etching a drawing into a wall, wiring a makeshift heater, or fashioning a small use object become insurgent acts of freedom. In so doing, captives not only create the world, but demand a place in it.

Acknowledgments

Attempting to finish a book during a global pandemic was every bit as fun as it sounds. Luckily for me, I was surrounded by many people who helped shepherd it into existence, directly and indirectly. I am delighted to acknowledge them here.

I first thank Tom Lay, as well as Roger Berkowitz and Drucilla Cornell, for seeing potential in this project and including it in a series as rich and intellectually exciting as Just Ideas. I appreciate Kem Crimmins and Lis Pearson, as well as everyone at Fordham University Press, for their support in the final stages of publication. Three anonymous reviewers offered generous and careful readings of the full manuscript. The recent loss of Drucilla was also a huge loss for the world. I so appreciate her support for my work.

Daniel Cervantes, who is currently incarcerated at San Quentin State Prison, allowed me to use his beautiful artwork, "Beauty Encaged," for the cover of *Politics in Captivity,* for which I am so grateful. Nicola White's logistical support was indispensable for this, as well.

My colleagues at Simmons are some of the best parts of my job there, especially my home department of political science. The presence of Abel Amado, Leanne Doherty, Greg Williams, and Kristina Pechulis lightens even the most grueling meetings. Through my years there, Carol Biewener, Ben Cole, Tatiana Cruz, Diane Grossman, Sarah Leonard, Suzanne Leonard, Bri Martino, Zinnia Mukherjee, Jess Parr, Laura Prieto, Jyoti Puri, Aaron Rosenthal, Saher Selod, Franny Sullivan, and Niloufer Sohrabji have made it a genuine pleasure to come to work each day. I am lucky to have been part of the Hazel Dick Leonard Faculty Fellowship in the spring of 2021, which provided necessary intellectual space and collaborative energy to work through some big questions in *Politics in Captivity*. Catherine Paden's quiet support, generosity, and institutional savvy gave me a professional home when it was most needed.

I am incredibly grateful for the people that I call friends and mentors in the discipline of political theory, including Ali Aslam, Lawrie Balfour, Roger Berkowitz, Angelica Bernal, Joan Cocks, Barbara Cruikshank, Tim Delaune, Laura Grattan, Bonnie Honig, Brad Mapes-Martins, Patchen Markell, Lori Marso, Lida Maxwell, Neil Roberts, Holloway Sparks, Dick Wasserstrom, Jeremy Wolf, and Nick Xenos. Laura Ephraim was a discussant on a panel where I presented an early version of a chapter and her smart, incisive comments changed the course of the discussion in very fruitful ways. The friendship, support, and solidarity of Jill Locke and Ella Myers are lifelines and I only wish geography could make our dinners and conversations more frequent.

Against the grain of raging impostor syndrome, Barbara Cruikshank helped me find the confidence to become first a graduate student capable of writing a coherent sentence and then later an academic. Her generosity, authenticity, and genuine belief in the abilities of her students are true models of great pedagogy and I am thankful to have been on the receiving end of them.

For an entirely different set of gifts, I am grateful to the most extraordinary teacher, Penny Gill, who put *The Human Condition* in my hands in January of 1999, and said, "read this," two words that became nothing short of transformative. Joan Cocks, who my Mount Holyoke friends and I used to refer to as "the brain at the front of the room," helped me find my way in political theory as an undergraduate student, and later, in graduate school, my voice as a political theorist. My intellectual debt to her work is tremendous.

I cannot begin to properly thank my students over the past seventeen years. So many of them left their marks on my life and work, either through research assistance, political debates during office hours, and thousands of class discussions. Conversations with Erin Syring and Chloe Kanas, very early on in my career, solidified my resolve to stick with academia, despite the very punishing aspects of the job market at the time. Working closely with Bryn McCarthy was a three-year reminder of everything that I love about teaching and learning alongside students. Halle Jeremie provided outstanding research assistance on Chapters One and Two of *Politics in Captivity*. I likely would not have written this book at all if Meredyth Grange had not come to my office hours at Wellesley College, in the fall of 2012, to let me know that my feminist theory syllabus was woefully incomplete. The process of making subsequent, long-overdue changes altered the course of my scholarly and political lives forever, and I am so grateful for her willingness to point out my blind spots. Finally, I thank the students in my Introduction to Political Theory course at MCI Norfolk in the spring of 2020, as well as those in my senior seminar, Prisons in Political Thought, at Simmons University in the fall of 2022.

I am grateful on a daily basis for these strong, smart women that live alongside me at the unique intersection of academia and (sometimes extreme) motherhood: Hilary Barth, Vanessa Beasley, Angelica Bernal, Lisa Bohn, Candi Carter Olson, Mary Donegan, Jen Dornan-Fish, Leigh Graham, Darci Graves, Awhina Hollis-English, Abigail Hornstein, Melissa Meadows, Katherine Moore, Kathleen Muldoon, Ardea Russo, Monica Schneider, Amy Erica Smith, Jennifer Ward, and Sarah Woulfin. Our solidarity, and the material and intangible support of one another in the unique world that we share, make life feel possible, even on the darkest days. And celebrating joyful and triumphant moments always feels, with them, like a collective win.

For friends near and far, some of whom I don't see nearly enough, I thank Jake Buckley-Fortin, Tom Chen, Caroline Christopolous, Elise DeVito, Susannah Fox, Kemi Fuentes-George, Lindsey Fuentes-George, Lauren Hibbert, Becca Hart Holder, Molly Holder, Denise Horn, Lauren McLaughlin, Katie Michael, Jen Paxton, Mike Paxton, Rachael Running, Jenny Rushlow, Kendra Sibley, Liz Simon-Higgs, Emily Smith, Elisabeth Snell, Faye Stephens, Michelle Sternthal, Molly Wallace, and Tiana Wilkinson.

I consider myself very lucky to share everyday life with Fiona Barnett, Alison Blecker, Steven Finke, Alli Franke, Jon Franke, Rainuka Gupta, Lara Holbrook, Erin Kapoor, Liz Kleinerman, Abby Klima, Constance Koesters, Sara Krakauer, Sara Lamoureux, Renande Loayza, Rachael Murray, Emily Nordone, Lucia Panichella, Andrew Paradise, Ranjani Paradise, Vince Poon, Barrett Reinhorn, Erica Remi, Sebastian Remi, Jenny Robertson, Amy Schneider, Tova Speter, Byron Stanley, Jonah Temple, Kara Temple, Sarah Threlkeld, Adele Traub, and Sarah Weintraub. A special thank you to the TND crowd, for they remind me on a weekly basis of the indispensability of friendship, community, and sharing cake together.

Many thanks to Eleonora Azenstein for countless coffees, good talks, and solidarity. Kate Carpenter Bernier is a fabulous walking partner and I have learned so much from her about the practice of friendship. Ranjani Paradise is a wonderful friend whose fabulous style and culinary talents are, for me, both aspirations and the stuff of core memories. My gratitude to Grace Bianciardi for constantly reminding me of who I am through humor, conversation, and exquisitely well-timed texts is deeper than I can say.

Jenn Pucci and James Yeagle are two of the smartest, warmest, most welcoming friends and scintillating conversationalists that I am lucky enough to know. Games, political debates, excellent meals, campfires, and great times shared with them, transformed a suburban enclave outside of Boston into a home, not just the place where I live.

I thank my family on the Mason and Zuckerwise sides, including Ann Lieberman, Harvey Lieberman, Mark Madrid, Jen Malafey, Ira Mason, Sherry Mason, and Matt Swan. Extra thanks to my nephew, Jacob Lieberman, for so many terrific discussions about politics and history at family gatherings. Harper Malafey, Hunter Malafey, Mason Lieberman, Skye Lieberman, Julia Madrid, Lionel Swan, and Toby Swan remind me what is at stake in political matters in and outside of this book.

The family we choose has been no less central to my life than the ones into which I was born, including Elias Bianciardi, Grace Bianciardi, Maria Bianciardi, Nora Bianciardi, Liane Clamen, Barbara Cruikshank, Elizabeth Glazer, Sophia Glazer, KC Haydon, Marshall Heinberg, Sophie Heinberg, Janie Herzog, Jack Lusk, Jenn Pucci, Audrey Rahm, Linda Rahm, Mary Seid, Alice Yeagle, James Yeagle, Owen Yeagle, and Xan Yeagle.

I am grateful to my parents, Babby Krents and David Zuckerwise, for their unconditional support of my (at times) questionable decision to pursue academia, as well as basically everything else I've attempted. The energy and attention they bring to their own work lives have always inspired me to do the same. When I was fifteen, in high school, my dad bought me a gift to celebrate how hard I had studied for a major biology exam—on which I scored thirty-five percent. My mom read my whole dissertation on her phone while traveling several hours to my defense. Those are the kinds of parents that they are, and their love, loyalty, and steady presence have been the solid foundation on which I have always depended. They raised me in a home where no subject was ever off limits for discussion, a value that equally informs my parenting and pedagogy.

My grandmother Irma Krents would have been immensely proud if she were alive to see the publication of *Politics in Captivity*. I know the same is true of Cristi Gadue, who departed the earthly world far too early in life, but whose political ferocity and passion for people's stories inspire this project—and me.

My sisters, Laura Zuckerwise and Randi Madrid, keep me grounded in reality and help me make sense of pretty much everything. I am grateful for the givenness of our sisterhood, our memories, their analytical minds, our shared history, their humor and support, and our daily phone calls.

My son, Harold, has an orientation to the world that is so uniquely his, that I am sometimes jealous of his freedom. He dislikes the glare of bright lights, and yet he *is* sunshine. His hilarity, imagination, original jokes, and utter delight in language are infectious and have taught me so much about the world. My daughter, Ila, is a constant asker of questions, a theorist since she started talking, and a collector of treasures. I learn new things every day from her busy brain, sardonic humor, creative spirit, and sense of justice. It is a true gift to be the mom of these two bursts of natality and I appreciate the little notes that they push under the office door, as they (mostly) uphold the rules of my work time; their comic timing; and most of all, their love.

I thank Mathew Mason, whose support for this project and for me has never waned. We have experienced the full range of joy and stress, parented together in the deep trenches, and improvised ways of making things in our life work when they seemed impossible. I am grateful for his steadiness in the face of unpredictability, the life we continue to craft, years of his uncomplaining kid-wrangling, his humor and appreciation for absurdity, his absolute faith in my abilities, his deep reserves of patience and generosity, and all of the coffees for which I did not even need to ask, deposited at my desk while I struggled to finish writing.

It is a cliché, but also truth, that my gratitude for Patchen Markell is beyond language, an ironic fact because no one has taught me more about the art of words than him. I thank him for our twenty-year-long conversation about politics, theory, and the world, in and outside of *The Human Condition*. Nothing escapes Patchen's view, from a near-invisible spider on the San Antonio Riverwalk to a word out of place on a page. *Politics in Captivity* would not have seen the light of day without him—and I am keenly aware of the luminosity of that light because of him.

Laura Grattan is the friend with whom I have talked the most about this book and without our friendship and intellectual connection, I surely would not have been able to write it. Laura's brain never takes a day off. I am in constant awe of her ability to synthesize and analyze ideas at breakneck speed, for she talks and thinks at the same pace. I have never known anyone with such serious and consistent political commitments, or who shows up to talk and listen, so completely. She read multiple chapters of this book with her signature generosity and critical brilliance.

KC Haydon, my best friend and my "person," has been there through all of the ups and downs of this project. And we have seen each other through the precarity of academia, as well as twenty-six years of shared history. Our conversations about things that matter are anchors to reality, even in the stormiest of conditions. She leaves no stone unturned in her thinking and demands the same in mine, challenging and affectionately mocking me when necessary, all against the background of a deep friendship that began over cider donuts in western Massachusetts and has since clocked thousands of miles worth of heartbreaks, laughter, deaths, births, rebirths, relationships, marriages, and even a pandemic. I cannot begin to imagine the world, or *my* world, without her.

Notes

A NOTE ON TERMINOLOGY AND METHOD

1. There is a great deal of evidence that the accuracy of the WPA "Slave Narrative Collection" is questionable. White interviewers are said to have imposed their racial biases on Black interviewees and, relatedly, that the latter felt pressure to produce a rosier narrative of their lives in slavery than they actually experienced. See John Blassingame, *Slave Community: Plantation Life in the Antebellum South* (New York: Oxford University Press, 1979); and Library of Congress, "Limitations of the Slave Narrative Collection: Problems of Memory," Washington, D.C.: Library of Congress, Accessed January 10, 2021.

INTRODUCTION: POLITICS IN MOTION

1. Tiyo Attalah Salah-El, "A Call for the Abolition of Prisons," in *The New Abolitionists: (Neo)Slave Narratives and Contemporary Prison Writings*, ed. Joy James (Albany: SUNY Press, 2005), 69.

2. DOC regulations prevent me from naming the specific facility here.

3. Biopower is a concept drawn from the work of Michel Foucault, referring to a decentralized and dispersed power operating at the level of population. The management and regulation of populations is not a repressive form of power, but a productive one. See Michel Foucault, *Security, Territory, and Population: Lectures at the Collège de France 1977–1978* (New York: Picador, 2007), and *The Birth of Biopolitics: Lectures at the Collège de France 1977–1978* (New York: Picador, 2008).

4. *Blood in My Eye* contains Jackson's early political thought in a genre-defying work of memoir, correspondence, and essay. See George Jackson, *Blood in My Eye* (Baltimore: Black Classic Press, 1990).

5. See Dan Berger, *Captive Nation: Black Prison Organizing in the Civil Rights Era* (Chapel Hill: University of North Carolina Press, 2014); and Dylan Rodriguez, *Forced Passages: Imprisoned Racial Intellectuals and the US Prison Regime* (Minneapolis: University of Minnesota Press, 2006).

6. William Cobbett, *Essential Writings, Volume 4* (Augsburg, Bavaria: Jazzybee Verlag, 2018), 132.

7. Cobbett, *Essential Writings*, 132.

8. See Michel Foucault, *Discipline & Punish: The Birth of the Prison* (New York: Vintage Books, 1995).

9. Both Huey Newton and George Jackson understood well that carceral power works through the docile body of the prisoner. This is likely why they emphasized self-mastery in their written works. See Huey Newton, *Revolutionary Suicide* (New York: Penguin, 2009), 103–9, and George Jackson, *Soledad Brother* (Chicago: Lawrence Hill Books, 1994).

10. Book three of Saidiya Hartman's *Wayward Lives, Beautiful Experiments* offers a rich discussion of prison resistance on which I heavily rely here. Her chapter on the prison uprising at the women's reformatory at Bedford Hills titled "Anarchy of Colored Girls Assembled in a Riotous Manner" is particularly helpful. See, in particular, Saidiya Hartman, *Wayward Lives, Beautiful Experiments: Intimate Histories of Riotous Black Girls, Troublesome Women, and Queer Radicals* (New York: W.W. Norton, 2019), 229–56. Although prison rebellion is not the primary subject matter of her book, Lisa Guenther discusses strategies of resistance taken up by prisoners in solitary confinement in her book, *Solitary Confinement: Social Death and its Afterlives*. Chapter seven, "Supermax Confinement and the Exhaustion of Space," is especially fruitful and very relevant to the discussion here. See Lisa Guenther, *Solitary Confinement: Social Death and Its Afterlives* (Minneapolis: University of Minnesota Press, 2013), 161–94. Also see Sarah Haley's brilliant discussion of Black feminist rebellion in *No Mercy Here: Gender, Punishment, and the Making of Jim Crow Modernity* (Chapel Hill: University of North Carolina Press, 2016), 195–249. Although she discusses strategies of resistance throughout the text, I rely heavily on her fifth chapter "Sabotage and Black Radical Feminist Refusal."

11. Of course, there are contexts technically outside of prison walls where the physical movements of nonincarcerated people—especially Black, brown, queer, trans, and disabled, and other suspect nonnormative subjects—are similarly politicized. I hold that this does not so much detract from the specificity of prison, but rather speaks to the extended reach of the carceral state. Weaver and Lerman's construct of "custodial citizenship" is very helpful here. See Vesla Weaver and Amy Lerman, *Arresting Citizenship: Democratic Consequences of American Crime Control* (Chicago: University of Chicago Press, 2014), 30–58.

Another great source on this subject is the edited volume *Captive Genders*, which combines queer, feminist, and carceral studies scholars with prisoners' writings. See Eric A. Stanley and Nat Smith, eds., *Captive Genders: Trans Embodiment and the Prison Industrial Complex* (Oakland: AK Press, 2015).

12. Ned and Constance Sublette's exhaustive history of the forced reproduction of bondpeople is a great source for understanding the embodiment of racial captivity. Part 1, "The Capitalized Womb," and Part 4, "The Star-Spangled Slave Trade," are particularly helpful. See Ned and Constance Sublette, *The American Slave Coast: A History of the Slave-Breeding Industry* (Chicago: Lawrence Hill Books, 2016), 3–65, 329–405.

13. In addition to primary sources that offer firsthand accounts of this, such as Harriet Jacobs's autobiography, several historians have taken up the subject of everyday resistance in chattel slavery. See Harriet Jacobs, *Incidents in the Life of a Slave Girl* (New York: Dover Publications, 2001); Stephanie Camp, *Enslaved Women and Everyday Resistance in the Plantation South* (Chapel Hill: University of North Carolina Press, 2004); and Haley, *No Mercy Here*.

14. Hannah Arendt, *The Human Condition* (Chicago: University of Chicago Press, 1998), 118.

15. Arendt, *The Human Condition*, 119.

16. Arendt, *The Human Condition*, 27–28.

17. See the iconic essay by Hanna Pitkin, who referred to actors in the private realm as "posturing little boys clamoring for attention." See Hanna Pitkin, "Justice: On Relating Private and Public," *Political Theory* 9, no. 3 (1981): 327–52.

18. Hannah Arendt, *On Revolution* (New York: Penguin, 1990).

19. Other thinkers have dealt extensively with Arendt's racial views. See Kathryn Gines, *Hannah Arendt and the Negro Question* (Bloomington: Indiana University Press, 2014), for a discussion of her anti-Black racism and the way that it distorts her view of the situation of Black Americans in the twentieth century. Chapter 3, "The Three Realms of Human Life: The Political, the Social, and the Private," as well as Chapter 7, "A Much Greater Threat to Our Institutions of Higher Learning Than the Student Riots," are useful. Jill Locke's excellent essay on Arendt's discussion of "social climbing" offers a very helpful account of her problematic view of Blackness. See Jill Locke, "Little Rock's Social Question: Reading Arendt on School Desegregation and Social Climbing," *Political Theory* 41, no. 4 (2013): 533–61; Anne Norton, "Heart of Darkness: Africa and African Americans in the Writings of Hannah Arendt," in *Feminist Interpretations of Hannah Arendt*, ed. Bonnie Honig (University Park: Penn State University Press, 1995), 247–61; and Chad Kautzer, "Political Violence and Race: A Critique of Hannah Arendt," *Comparative Literature and Culture* 21, no. 3 (2019): 1–12.

20. Bernasconi notes Arendt's unyielding intellectual commitment to the distinction between the social and the political, arguing that "her use of (the division) is at the heart of her failure to address adequately the 'racial issue' in the United States, a failure all the more striking given her contribution in *Origins of Totalitarianism* to the history of racial ideology." Indeed, although his social/political–centered interpretation largely accounts for some of Arendt's more troubling racial analyses, it does not do so fully. For example, *Origins of Totalitarianism,* which was published several years before she would fully formulate her concepts of the social and the political, contains both rich discussions of slavery and hollow stereotypes, mired in colonial logic. See Robert Bernasconi, "The Double Face of the Social and the Political: Hannah Arendt and America's Racial Divisions," *Research in Phenomenology* 26 (1996): 3–24: 4.

21. Hannah Arendt, *Origins of Totalitarianism* (New York: Harcourt, 2001), 297.

22. Arendt, *Origins of Totalitarianism,* 297.

23. Bernasconi, "The Double Face of the Social and the Political," 4.

24. Arendt, *Origins of Totalitarianism,* 191.

25. Charles Mills, *Racial Contract* (Ithaca: Cornell University Press, 1997).

26. Arendt, *Origins of Totalitarianism,* 191.

27. Arendt, *Origins of Totalitarianism,* 192.

28. Anne Norton, "Heart of Darkness," 248.

29. Jimmy Casas Klausen, "Hannah Arendt's Antiprimitivism," *Political Theory* 38, no. 3 (2010): 396.

30. Klausen, "Hannah Arendt's Antiprimitivism," 396.

31. Hannah Arendt, "Race Thinking before Racism," *The Review of Politics* 6, no. 1 (1944): 49.

32. Arendt, *Origins of Totalitarianism,* 192.

33. Arendt, *Origins of Totalitarianism,* 153.

34. Hannah Arendt, "The Nation," in *Essays in Understanding,* ed. Jerome Kohn (New York: Schocken Books, 1994), 208.

35. Gines, *Hannah Arendt and the Negro Question,* 75.

36. Gines, *Hannah Arendt and the Negro Question,* 15.

37. See Sarah Haley on the historical relationship between carceral captivity and Jim Crow segregation in Haley, *No Mercy Here.* She argues that the incarceration of Black women at the turn of the twentieth century laid the groundwork for Jim Crow. The sentencing disparities and divisions of labor between Black and white women, as well as the different forms of punishment to which they were subjected, produced race and gender differences that enabled Jim Crow to operate successfully in the South.

38. Hannah Arendt, *On Violence* (New York: Harvest Books, 1970), 173.

39. See Gines on Arendt's own anti-Black racism in Gines, *Hannah Arendt and the Negro Question*. Much of her analysis hinges on the distinction between the "Jewish question," which Arendt casts as "purely political" by contrast with "the Negro question," which is, for her, a "Negro problem" that is, at its core, social.

40. Hannah Arendt and Günter Gaus, "What Remains? The Language Remains," in *Essays in Understanding*, ed. Jerome Kohn (New York: Harcourt Brace, 1994), 17.

41. Arendt and Gaus, "What Remains?" 20.

42. Patchen Markell, "Arendt's Work: On the Architecture of the Human Condition," *College Literature* 38, no. 1 (2011): 15–44.

43. Arendt, *The Human Condition*, 137.

44. Hannah Arendt, "Introduction into Politics," in *The Promise of Politics*, ed. Jerome Kohn (New York: Schocken Books, 2005), 128.

45. For a more extended discussion on this, see my essay on worldliness and democratic politics. Lena Zuckerwise, "Vita Mundi," *Social Theory and Practice* 42, no. 3 (2016): 474–500.

46. Arendt, *The Human Condition*, 8.

47. Arendt's essay "What is Authority?" is one of the rare writings in which she speaks of world in nonphysical terms. See Hannah Arendt, *Between Past and Future* (New York: Penguin, 2006), 91.

48. The chapter "Totalitarianism in Power" is particularly important here. See Arendt, *Origins of Totalitarianism*, 389–459.

49. Arendt, *Origins of Totalitarianism*, 478.

50. Arendt, *The Human Condition*, 137.

51. There is a growing literature on the experience of slavery in Middle Passage. See Sowande M. Mustakeem, *Slavery at Sea: Terror, Sex, and Sickness in the Middle Passage* (Champaign: University of Illinois Press, 2016); Marcus Rediker, *The Slave Ship: A Human History* (New York: Viking, 2007); Saidiya Hartman, *Lose Your Mother: A Journey Along the Atlantic Slave Route* (New York: Farrar, Straus & Giroux, 2007); and Stephanie E. Smallwood, *Saltwater Slavery: A Middle Passage from Africa to American Diaspora* (Cambridge: Harvard University Press, 2007).

52. See Walter Johnson, *Soul by Soul: Life Inside the Antebellum Slave Market* (Cambridge: Harvard University Press, 1999); Stephanie E. Jones-Rogers, *They Were Her Property: White Women as Slave Owners in the American South* (New Haven: Yale University Press, 2020); and Alexandra J. Finley, *An Intimate Economy: Enslaved Women, Work, and America's Domestic Slave Trade* (Chapel Hill: University of North Carolina Press, 2020).

53. For an excellent discussion of enslaved people's property claims, see Dylan C. Penningroth, *The Claims of Kinfolk: African American Property and*

Community in the Nineteenth Century South (Chapel Hill: University of North Carolina Press, 2003).

54. Again, Camp's discussion of the insurgent practices of enslaved women in chapters two and three of *Closer to Freedom* are very helpful here. Also see C. Riley Snorton's rich discussion of the construct of gender fungibility, which articulates well the ways that the gender identity of Black women was treated as ever malleable by enslavers. See C. Riley Snorton, *Black on Both Sides: A Racial History of Trans Identity* (Minneapolis: University of Minnesota Press, 2017).

55. See Andrew Dilts, *Punishment and Inclusion: Race, Membership, and the Limits of American Liberalism* (New York: Fordham University Press, 2014).

56. Paul Finkelman's *Rebellions, Resistance, and Runaways* offers a helpful discussion of enslavers who downplayed the subject of uprising and Old South apologist historians who continue this legacy by minimizing the scale and impact of slave resistance in the antebellum South. See Paul Finkelman, *Rebellions, Resistance, and Runaways within the Slave South* (New York: Garland, 1989).

57. Note that I am referring here to captive rebellion. That is, the resistance of enslaved and incarcerated people as a category. I am not suggesting that the political significance of slave resistance *or* prison rebellion have gone unnoticed in academic circles, individually.

58. I have argued elsewhere (see Zuckerwise, "Vita Mundi") that much of the secondary literature on Arendt is consumed with "action-centric" readings of her work. See Jeffrey Isaac, *Arendt, Camus, and Modern Rebellion* (New Haven: Yale University Press, 1992); Dana Villa, *Public Freedom* (Princeton: Princeton University Press, 2008), 250; and Elizabeth Markovits, "Birthrights: Freedom, Responsibility, and Democratic Comportment in Aeschylus' 'Oresteia'," *The American Political Science Review* 103, no. 3 (2009): 434. Other thinkers who consider her idea of judgment, do not generally foreground world in their interpretations, despite the significant connections between world and judgment. See Maurizio Passerin d'Entreves, "Arendt's Theory of Judgment," in *Cambridge Companion to Hannah Arendt*, ed. Dana Villa (Cambridge: Cambridge University Press, 2000), 245–58; Shai Lavi, "Crimes of Action, Crimes of Thought: Arendt on Reconciliation, Forgiveness, and Judgment," in *Thinking in Dark Times: Hannah Arendt on Ethics and Politics*, eds. Roger Berkowitz, Jeffrey Katz, and Thomas Keenan (New York: Fordham University Press, 2010), 229–34; David L. Marshall, "The Origin and Character of Hannah Arendt's Theory of Judgment," *Political Theory* 38, no. 3 (2010): 367–93; and Linda Zerilli, "We Feel Our Freedom': Imagination and Judgment in the Thought of Hannah Arendt," *Political Theory* 33, no. 2 (2005): 158–88.

59. Bonnie Honig, "Toward an Agonistic Feminism: Hannah Arendt and the Politics of Identity," in *Feminists Theorize the Political*, eds. Judith Butler and Joan W. Scott (New York: Routledge, 1992), 215–38.

60. See in particular the chapter "Work" in Arendt, *The Human Condition*, 136–74.

61. See the sections of *The Human Condition* in which Arendt discusses the violations of nature, entailed in work. Arendt, *The Human Condition*, 139.

62. Arendt, *The Human Condition*, 136–67.

63. Neil Roberts, *Freedom as Marronage* (Chicago: University of Chicago Press, 2015).

64. Guenther, *Solitary Confinement*.

65. The phrase "against a sharp white background" was originally written by Zora Neale Hurston in her 1928 essay, "How It Feels to Be Colored Me." Claudia Rankine later quoted it repeatedly in her lyric poem *Citizen*. See Zora Neale Hurston, "How It Feels to Be Colored Me," *The World Tomorrow* 11, no. 5 (1928): 1–4. See also Claudia Rankine, *Citizen: An American Lyric* (Minneapolis: Graywolf Press, 2014),

66. Sheldon Wolin, "Fugitive Democracy," in *Democracy and Difference: Contesting the Boundaries of the Political*, ed. Seyla Benhabib (Princeton: Princeton University Press, 1996), 31.

67. See Vesla Weaver and Amy Lerman's discussion of "custodial citizenship" in *Arresting Citizenship*.

68. See Sheldon Wolin, "What Revolutionary Action Means Today," in *Fugitive Democracy and Other Essays*, ed. Nicholas Xenos (Princeton: Princeton University Press, 2016), 369.

69. See the first chapter, "Domestic War Zones and the Extremities of Power," in Dylan Rodriguez's *Forced Passages*, 39–74.

70. Alex Zamalin, *The Struggle on Their Minds: The Political Thought of African American Resistance* (New York: Columbia University Press, 2019). Also see the following authors who attend to Black politics but leave aside captive resistance. Eddie Glaude Jr, *Democracy in Black: How Race Still Enslaves the American Soul* (New York: Broadway Books, 2017); Nikhil Pal Singh, *Black is a Country: Race and the Unfinished Struggle for Democracy* (Cambridge: Harvard University Press, 2005); and Nick Brommel, *The Time is Always Now: Black Thought and the Transformation of US Democracy* (New York: Oxford University Press, 2013).

71. See Jackson, *Soledad Brother*. Although I do not elaborate on Eldridge Cleaver's work, his book would fit well in the genre of Black carceral political thought. See Eldridge Cleaver, *Soul on Ice* (New York: Delta Books, 1999).

72. Berger, *Captive Nation*, 179.

73. Aside from a published, undergraduate thesis on the German Coast Slave Uprising, there is almost no published writing on it. See Daniel Rasmussen, *American Uprising: The Untold Story of America's Largest Slave Revolt* (New York: Harper Collins, 2011).

74. Chantal Mouffe, "Religion, Liberal Democracy, and Citizenship," in *Political Theologies: Public Religions in a Post-Secular World*, eds. Hent de Vries and Lawrence Sullivan (New York: Fordham University Press, 2006), 325.

75. Elisabeth Young-Bruehl's biography of Arendt is an extraordinarily helpful resource here. See Elisabeth Young-Bruehl, *Hannah Arendt: For Love of the World* (New Haven: Yale University Press, 1982).

76. Arendt's break with Heidegger should be understood in both personal and intellectual terms. After the termination of their love affair in 1928, they spoke sporadically over the next several years. Their friendship and romantic attachment, while painful, were highly productive for Arendt's scholarship. Once referring to Heidegger as "the last German romantic," his inclinations toward introspection, withdrawal into nature, and preferences for volk culture contributed to her early interest in German romanticism, which she began exploring around 1929, when the German political scene became increasingly ominous. Relatedly, his mounting antisemitism strained their relationship. He was rumored to exclude Jewish students from his seminars and rudely ignore his Jewish colleagues on campus. In October 1929, Heidegger wrote a letter to the Ministry of Education warning against "growing Judaisation." These disturbing prejudices culminated in 1933 when Heidegger became rector of Freiburg and joined the National Socialist Party weeks later. At this point, Arendt cut off all contact with him for the next decade. See Young-Bruehl, *Hannah Arendt*, 42–110.

77. On Heidegger's intellectual influences on Arendt, see Kurt H. Wolf, "On the Landscape of the Relation Between Hannah Arendt and Martin Heidegger," *The American Sociologist* 28, no. 1 (1997): 126–36; Dana Villa, "Arendt, Heidegger, and the Tradition," *Social Research* 74, no. 4 (2007): 983–1002; Daniel Maier-Katkin and Birgit Maier-Katkin, "Love and Reconciliation: The Case of Hannah Arendt and Martin Heidegger," *Harvard Review* 32 (2007): 34–48; Louis P. Hinchman and Sandra K. Hinchman, "In Heidegger's Shadow: Hannah Arendt's Phenomenological Humanism," *The Review of Politics* 46, no. 2 (1984): 183–211; Ronald Beiner, "The Presence of Art and the Absence of Heidegger," *Arendt Studies* 2 (2018): 9–16; and Richard Wolin, *Heidegger's Children: Hannah Arendt, Karl Löwith, Hans Jonas, and Herbert Marcuse* (Princeton: Princeton University Press, 2001), 30–69.

78. Commonality, one of the central features of a world, is the object of critique in Michaele Ferguson's *Sharing Democracy*, when she argues against orienting democratic commonality around an already existing object, like tables, political events, or laws. See chapters one and two of Michaele Ferguson, *Sharing Democracy* (New York: Oxford University Press, 2012). In her

book, *Worldly Ethics,* Ella Myers shows that world presents a fresh alternative to some of the tired ethical discourses of philosophy and political theory. See Ella Myers, *Worldly Ethics: Democratic Politics and Care for the World* (Durham: Duke University Press, 2013), 85–111.

79. Myers mobilizes world as an intervention into conventional ethical discourses of care for the self and other, arguing instead that democratic politics is better conceptualized as care for worldly things. Hers is an excellent book-length treatment of Arendt's concept of world, and other thinkers offer very fruitful engagements with it as well. See Roger Berkowitz, "Reconciling Oneself to the Impossibility of Reconciliation: Judgment and Worldliness in Hannah Arendt's Politics," in *Artifacts of Thinking: Reading Hannah Arendt's Denktagebuch,* eds. Roger Berkowitz and Ian Storey (New York: Fordham University Press, 2017); Lawrence J. Biskowski, "Practical Foundations for Political Judgment: Arendt on Action and World," *Journal of Politics* 55, no. 4 (1993): 867–87; Frederick Dolan, "Worldly Pleasure: Hannah Arendt, Friedrich Nietzsche, Wallace Stevens, and 'Political Consciousness,'" *Polity* 33, no. 3 (2001): 439–54; and John McGowan, "Ways of Worldmaking: Hannah Arendt and E.L. Doctorow Respond to Modernity," *College Literature* 38, no. 1 (2011): 150–75; Christopher Peys, *Reconsidering Cosmopolitanism and Forgiveness: Arendt, Derrida, and Care for the World* (New York: Rowman & Littlefield, 2022); and Emily Zakin, "Criss-Crossing Cosmopolitanism: State-Phobia, World-Alienation, and the Global Soul," *The Journal of Speculative Philosophy* 29, no. 1 (2015), 58–72.

80. See Lisa Guenther, "40 Years of Solitary Confinement: Resisting Social Death at Angola Prison, Louisiana," *New APPS: Art, Politics, Philosophy, Science,* April 17, 2012.

81. The most exhaustive, although highly contested account of the Attica prison uprising, is Heather Ann Thompson, *Blood in the Water* (New York: Vintage Books, 2017).

1. FROM PLANTATIONS TO PRISONS

1. Vijay Prashad, "From Plantation Slavery to Penal Slavery," *Economic and Political Weekly* 30, no. 36 (1995): 2239.

2. Howard Winant, *New Politics of Race: Globalism, Difference, Justice* (Minneapolis: University of Minnesota Press, 2004), 91.

3. Arthur Delaney, "The 'Modern Day Slavery' of Prison Labor Really Does Have a Link to Slavery," *Huffington Post,* August 8, 2018, https://www.huffpost.com/entry/prison-strike-modern-day-slavery_n_5b857777e4b0511db3d21da8.

4. Jaron Browne, "Rooted in Slavery: Prison Labor Exploitation," *Race, Poverty, and the Environment* 17, no. 1 (2010): 78–80.

5. Offering a conservative critique of prison slavery, Bozelko holds that incarcerated activists should focus their energies on converting prison labor into a legitimate system of paid employment. See Chandra Bozelko, "Give Working Prisoners Dignity—and Decent Wages," *National Review*, January 11, 2017, https://www.nationalreview.com/2017/01/prison-labor-laws-wages/.

6. Incarcerated Workers Organizing Committee, Prison Strike 2018, https://incarceratedworkers.org/campaigns/prison-strike-2018#:~:text=All%20persons%20imprisoned%20in%20any,or%20territory%20for%20their%20labor.&text=No%20imprisoned%20human%20shall%20be,label%20as%20a%20violent%20offender. Accessed August 15, 2019.

7. Kevin Rashid Johnson, "Prison Labor is Modern Slavery. I've Been Sent to Solitary for Speaking Out," *The Guardian*, August 23, 2019, https://www.theguardian.com/commentisfree/2018/aug/23/prisoner-speak-out-american-slave-labor-strike.

8. There is very little writing on the prison uprising at McAlester. See Burt Useem and Peter Kimball, *States of Siege: US Prison Riots 1971–1986* (New York: Oxford University Press, 1991), 31–34.

9. Anon, "Slave Labor in American Prisons," (Reprint from Winter Soldier), *NEPA News* 3, no. 2 (February 22, 1975), 778 Box 11, Folder 22. Tamiment Library and Robert F. Wagner Labor Archives at New York University, January 6, 2020.

10. Edward Baptist offers the most thorough economic history of slavery and its foundational role in the US economy. See Edward Baptist, *The Half Has Never Been Told* (New York: Basic Books, 2014), 412–13.

11. Joel Olson's concise account of the invention of race in the colonial period is part of his larger argument on the pervasive problem of white democracy. See Joel Olson, *The Abolition of White Democracy* (Minneapolis: University of Minnesota Press), 2004.

12. Olson, *The Abolition of White Democracy*.

13. A century after the construction of racial slavery in the colonies, its status as an institution became a lightning rod issue for the American founders. The questionable personhood of bondpeople was eventually reconciled in the infamous Three-Fifths Clause of the Constitution, also known as the Connecticut Compromise. For a discussion on how political compromise has been a key mode of the reproduction of white supremacy throughout US history, see Lena Zuckerwise, "'There Can be No Loser:' White Supremacy and the Cruelty of Compromise," *American Political Thought* 5, no. 3 (2016).

14. Political imagination is a common theme among abolitionist thinkers. See Angela Davis, *Are Prisons Obsolete?* (New York: Seven Stories Press, 2003), and *Abolition Democracy: Beyond Empire, Prisons, and Torture* (New York: Seven Stories Press, 2005). Also see Kim Gilmore, "Prison

Abolition—Understanding the Connections," *Social Justice* 27, no. 3 (2000): 195–205; Stephen Dillon, *Fugitive Life: The Queer Politics of the Prison State* (Durham: Duke University Press, 2018); and Allegra McLeod, "Prison Abolition and Grounded Justice," *UCLA Law Review* 62 (2015): 1156–1239.

15. Davis, *Are Prisons Obsolete*, 107.

16. Gilmore, "Prison Abolition—Understanding the Connections," 196.

17. CoreCivic and Geo Group are two major private-prison corporations. Most noteworthy in the rhetoric repeated throughout the companies' literature is the conspicuous absence of the term "prison." Geo Group, for example, calls itself a leader in "turnkey solutions." See CoreCivic, "Investor Relations," http://ir.corecivic.com/. Accessed July 25, 2020. Also see Geo Group, "Who We Are," https://www.geogroup.com/who_we_are. Accessed August 11, 2020.

18. Davis, *Abolition Democracy*, 108.

19. Undoubtedly, the 1980s and 1990s are crucially important to the history of mass incarceration. The discourse that "prison labor is slavery" largely emerged in the 1980s, due to the rise of neoliberalism and the accompanying move toward prison privatization in the Reagan era. This largely did away with bureaucratic limitations to the use of prison labor for private corporations, thus absorbing large percentages of the prison population into a system of virtually unpaid, penal servitude. The pervasive tendency to frame prison labor as "modern day slavery" arose from this context. The 1990s are no less significant: the vast expansions to the carceral state ushered in by President Clinton's Violent Crime Act of 1994 and the rollback of prisoners' rights under his 1996 Prison Litigation and Reform Act are centerpieces of mass incarceration in the present day. See Michael C. Campbell and Heather Schoenfeld, "The Transformation of America's Penal Order: A Historicized Sociology of Punishment," *American Journal of Sociology* 118, no. 5 (March 2013): 1375–1423; and Michelle Alexander, "The War on Drugs and the New Jim Crow," *Race, Poverty, and the Environment* 17, no. 1 (2010): 75–77. While these eras are pivotal years for the consolidation of mass incarceration, I suspect that disproportionate emphasis on these later years of carceral history has obscured the significance of prison resistance. Focusing on the earlier decades of growth in the prison system and especially on the resistance of incarcerated people in the 1960s and 1970s offers a fuller perspective on politics in captivity.

20. Carceral conditions shifted in the 1970s and 1980s to accommodate widespread political crackdowns on urban crime, particularly in the advent of the War on Drugs in 1971. The growth of private prisons in the 1980s saw a sea change in the scope and meaning of criminal punishment, permanently altering common views of how prisons should be funded, and, in conjunction with Reagan-era anti-drug policies, creating new openings for incarceration. Although privatization has always been part of the carceral landscape,

its meteoric rise in the 1980s should be understood as part of the broader story of the emergence of neoliberalism during the same period. Neoliberalism is an economic theory that freedom and better quality of life can best be advanced when liberating the entrepreneurial spirit of people, and that strong markets, not governments, are the best solutions to social and political problems. See David Harvey, *A Brief History of Neoliberalism* (New York: Oxford University Press, 2005), 39. Although its origins are contested, neoliberalism is generally associated with the 1970s stagflation crisis in the United States in which widespread unemployment was consistent with high inflation, and accompanying rollbacks of Johnson's Great Society programs during the Nixon administration. Fiscal crises in New York City and the state of California in the 1980s are both microcosmic and productive of neoliberalization and the accompanying turn to privatization. New York City saw a period of vast economic growth from 1965 to 1970 when Great Society programs gave substantial revenues to cities, vastly increasing the quantity and quality of public services. This sharply contrasted with the following decade in which Nixon-era tax cuts dramatically decreased federal tax funding for cities and replaced Great Society project-based grants with block grants for states. The city shifted from substantial public spending to austerity, cutting back on services, shutting down public programs, refinancing debt, and reducing the rolls of government employees. These measures were not limited to New York City, but other major urban centers as well. More and more, cities eliminated public programs, increased user fees for them, and transferred social services from the city to the state level. This was due in part to reduced revenues, but also concerted efforts of elite lawmakers and private citizens to lower taxes. Taxpayers in California in the late 1970s called on elected officials to control and limit the tax burden by decreasing property tax and curbing the numbers of government employees. Proposition 13 passed in 1978, a referendum that severely curtailed both taxes and government spending. Taken together, austerity in New York and reduced taxes in California, and similar moves in other American cities, the 1980s saw major declines in public services and historic booms in private sector jobs. By 1982, twenty states implemented state spending caps and President Reagan's administration established the Grace Commission, also called The President's Private Sector Survey on Cost Control. The principle recommendation of the commission was that the Reagan administration should form a new group within the Office of Federal Management to determine which public services would be well suited for privatization, further consolidating efforts to reduce government spending at the highest level of the federal government. Thus, the political and economic contexts for the privatization of formerly public services were established, setting the stage for increased interest in transforming the management and organizational structure of the prison system, on both federal and state levels. Reagan's tough-on-crime legislation is no less relevant to the expansion of private prisons than the rise of neoliberalism. The 1984 Sentencing Reform Act, which was folded into the larger Comprehensive Crime Control Act, claimed to hold judges accountable by requiring them to issue mandatory minimum sentences for even small-scale drug offenses. As Naomi Murakawa put it, "If the confluence of rights-exploiting criminals and liberal-elite judges bred lawlessness, then the remedy would discipline criminals and judges alike. This is precisely what the Sentencing Reform Act of 1984 accomplished." See Naomi Murakawa, *The First Civil Right, How Liberals Built Prison America* (New York: Oxford University Press, 2014), 91. Prior to its ratification, indeterminate sentencing was customary, meaning that an offender would often receive a range of years of possible prison time, not a precise figure. The ultimate duration of prison time was largely left to the discretion of prison and parole personnel, who would comprehensively assess the offender's progress and path toward rehabilitation. As a result of the Sentencing Reform Act, judges were required to explicitly name the exact number of years of required prison time, essentially doubling the average time served in federal prison, and decreasing by 50 percent the number of offenders punished with probation. Two years later, Congress passed the infamous Anti-Drug Abuse Act, which established sentencing disparities between crack cocaine, a drug closely associated with African American usage, and cocaine powder, most popular among middle-class and wealthy whites. See Peter C. Pihos, "The Local War on Drugs," in *The War on Drugs: A History*, ed. David Farber (New York: NYU Press, 2021), 131–59. Five-year sentences were issued automatically for offenders in possession of five grams of crack, whereas it took five hundred grams of cocaine powder to trigger the same sentence. Taken together, the Sentencing Reform and Anti-Drug Abuse Acts meant massive increases in the prison population, exacerbating logistical challenges, such as the shortage of cell space, overcrowding, and the high cost of operations. The increased demand for more prisons resulting from War on Drugs legislation, combined with the neoliberalization of public services, created an opening for the private sector to step in to take up the mantel of prison reconfiguration. In a context in which cost-efficiency and reductions in government spending had primacy, coupled with law-and-order policies that dramatically multiplied the prison population, privatization was a "rational" answer to the question of how to manage prisons efficiently.

21. The rise of privately owned and privately managed prisons was not merely a cost-saving solution to prison operations, but also introduced profit

motive into the domain of corrections: privatization removed bureaucratic barriers to both corporate investment in corrections and the use of prison labor by the private sector. Also taking place in this era was the consolidation of a new, extreme low-wage labor force of incarcerated workers. Because private prisons were not subject to the same bureaucratic apparatuses as public correctional facilities, they were able to more seamlessly subcontract with corporations to put prisoners to work. See Tara Herivel and Paul Wright, eds., *Prison Profiteers: Who Makes Money from Mass Incarceration?* (New York: New Press, 2007). The labor of prisoners subsidized the costs of their own incarceration and allowed businesses to profit off a captive workforce earning negligible cents per hour and enjoying none of the rights and protections of conventional workers. Although, as I addressed in the opening pages of this chapter, there has been no shortage of critiques of exploited prison labor, most departments of corrections, as well as the Federal Bureau of Prisons, have evaded accountability on this for a number of reasons. First, the fact that a long tradition of prison labor already existed and was largely perceived beneficial to the social order. Due to its alignment with ascetic, puritanical values of virtue and manual labor; the ease with which the values of prison labor can be translated into discourses of personal responsibility; and the narrative that "hard work" serves rehabilitative functions, redressing exploitation often takes a backseat to the so-called benefits of labor. Second, the two dominant political movements of the 1960s and 1970s (civil rights and second-wave feminism) generally did not include prisoners' rights on their agenda. Third, more so than many other public services, prison operations are cordoned off from public scrutiny and not often subjected to democratic deliberation. Especially at the state and local levels, carceral developments and reforms tend to escape public attention and accountability, for changes typically occur through the bureaucratic channels of administrative policy. Fourth, many criminologists and sociologists advocate for private carceral labor, thereby loaning it academic legitimacy. For example, Martin Sellers, commenting on the functional purposes of private prison labor states, "Prisoners are already producing products as diverse as prefab housing, data entry components, and photography materials. The expectation is that prisoners will not only be able to work to pay fines and restitution to victims, but also be able to contribute to the cost of their keep and prison operations." See Martin P. Sellers, *The History and Politics of Private Prisons: A Comparative Analysis* (Madison: Fairleigh Dickinson Press, 1993). This sanguine take on prison labor overlooks basic facts about its racial history, for it is premised on twin assumptions that the prison population is defined by criminal status, not race, and labor is rehabilitative, not exploitative. For a corrective to this, see Ruth Wilson Gilmore, *The Golden Gulag: Prisons,*

Surplus, Crisis, and Opposition in Globalizing California (Oakland: University of California Press, 2007), 30–128.

22. Dylan Rodriguez, "The Disorientation of the Teaching Act: Abolition as Pedagogical Position," *The Radical Teacher* 88 (2010): 7.

23. Michelle Alexander, *The New Jim Crow: Mass Incarceration in the Age of Colorblindness* (New York: New Press, 2012).

24. Ava Duvernay and Jason Moran. *13th*. Documentary film. USA, 2016.

25. Steve Fraser and Joshua Freeman, "In the Rearview Mirror: Barbarism and Progress: The Story of Convict Labor," *New Labor Forum* 21, no. 3 (2012): 95.

26. F. Emory Lyon, "Prison Labor and Social Justice," *The ANNALS of the American Academy of Political and Social Science* 46, no. 1 (1913): 147.

27. Howard P. Gill, "The Prison Labor Problem," *The ANNALS of the American Academy of Political and Social Science* 157 (1931): 100.

28. For a strong discussion of Southern strategies of debt peonage, see Pete R. Daniel, *The Shadow of Slavery: Peonage in the South 1901–1969* (Urbana: University of Illinois Press, 1990).

29. Sarah Haley, *No Mercy Here: Gender, Punishment, and the Making of Jim Crow Modernity* (Chapel Hill: University of North Carolina Press, 2016), 159.

30. James Manos, "From Commodity Fetishism to Prison Fetishism: Slavery, Convict-leasing, and the Ideological Productions of Incarceration," in *Death and Other Penalties: Philosophy in a Time of Mass Incarceration*, eds. Geoffrey Adelsberg, Lisa Guenther, and Scott Zeman (New York: Fordham University Press, 2015), 44.

31. David Oshinsky, *Worse Than Slavery: Parchman Farm and the Ordeal of Jim Crow Justice* (New York: Simon & Schuster, 1996).

32. Douglas Blackmon, *Slavery by Another Name: The Re-Enslavement of Black Americans from the Civil War to World War II* (New York: First Anchor Books, 2009).

33. W.E.B. Du Bois and Joseph Fracchia, "Die Negerfrage in den Vereinigten Staaten," *The New Centennial Review* 6, no. 3 (2005): 255.

34. Jill Locke offers an especially helpful discussion of the unique exploitations of chain gang labor. See Locke, "Work, Shame, and the Chain Gang: The New Civic Education," in *Vocations of Political Theory: Political Imagination in an Age of Uncertainty*, eds. Jason Frank and John Tambornino (Minneapolis: University of Minnesota Press, 2000), 284.

35. Joshua Price, *Prison and Social Death* (New Brunswick: Rutgers University Press, 2015), 86.

36. Price, *Prison and Social Death,* 84.

37. Saidiya Hartman, *Wayward Lives, Beautiful Experiments: Intimate Histories of Social Upheaval* (New York: W.W. Norton, 2019), 242.

38. Hartman, *Wayward Lives*, 243.
39. Hartman, *Wayward Lives*, 244.
40. Haley, *No Mercy Here*
41. C. Riley Snorton, *Black on Both Sides: A Racial History of Trans Identity* (Minneapolis: University of Minnesota Press, 2017), 55–98.
42. Haley, *No Mercy Here*, 160.
43. Haley, *No Mercy Here*, 160.
44. Haley, *No Mercy Here*, 159.
45. Haley, *No Mercy Here*.
46. Haley, *No Mercy Here*, 176–77.
47. Micol Seigel, "Critical Prison Studies: Review of a Field," *American Quarterly* 70, no. 1 (2018): 128.
48. Naomi Murakawa, *The First Civil Right*, 3.
49. Patrick A. Langan, John V. Fundis, Lawrence Greenfeld, and Victoria W. Schneider, "Historical Statistics on Prisoners in State and Federal Institutions, Yearend 1925–86," US Department of Justice, Bureau of Justice Statistics (1988): 1–16

2. BLACK CARCERAL POLITICAL THOUGHT

1. George Jackson, *Soledad Brother* (Chicago: Lawrence Hill Books, 1994), 26.
2. Robert Gooding-Williams, *In the Shadow of Du Bois: Afro-Modern Political Thought in America* (Cambridge: Harvard University Press, 2009).
3. See Kwame Ture and Charles V. Hamilton, *Black Power: The Politics of Liberation* (New York: Vintage Books, 1992).
4. There are a number of helpful sources on the subject of the politicization of Black prisoners, due to the strong presence of incarcerated members of the Black Power Movement, and in particular, the Black Panther Party. See Bobby Seale, *Seize the Time: The Story of the Black Panther Party and Huey Newton* (Baltimore: Black Classic Press, 1996); and Huey Newton, *Revolutionary Suicide* (New York: Penguin Books, 2009). Excellent secondary sources include Joshua Bloom and Waldo E. Martin Jr., *Black Against Empire: The History and Politics of the Black Panther Party* (Oakland: University of California Press, 2016); Robyn C. Spencer, *The Revolution Has Come: Black Power, Gender, and the Black Panther Party in Oakland* (Durham: Duke University Press, 2016); and Peniel E. Joseph, "Black Liberation Without Apology: Reconceptualizing the Black Power Movement," *The Black Scholar* 31, no. 3/4 (2001): 2–19.
5. Simon Rolston, "Prison Life Writing, African American Narrative Strategies and Bad: The Autobiography of James Carr," *MELUS Multi-Ethnic Literature of the US* 38, no. 4 (2013): 191–215.

6. H. Bruce Franklin, "The Inside Stories of the Global American Prison," *Texas Studies in Literature and Language* 50, no. 3 (2008): 235.

7. Angela Davis, *If They Come in the Morning: Voices of Resistance* (New York: Verso, 2016), 31.

8. Dan Berger, *Captive Nation: Black Prison Organizing in the Civil Rights Era* (Chapel Hill: University of North Carolina Press, 2014).

9. Berger, *Captive Nation*, 179.

10. Berger, *Captive Nation*, 179.

11. Berger, *Captive Nation*, 182.

12. Assata Shakur, *Assata: An Autobiography* (Chicago: Lawrence Hill Books, 2001), 175.

13. Shakur, *Assata*, 175.

14. Shakur, *Assata*, 262.

15. MP3 recording of "The Tradition" by Assata Shakur, n.d., Assata Shakur Collection, Freedom Archives, Oakland, California, https://search.freedomarchives.org/search.php?s=Assata+Shakur%2C+We+Carried+it+On. Accessed April 4, 2019.

16. Assata Shakur's importance to Black radical groups is well documented in the archives. After she gave birth to a daughter in October 1974, *The Friends of Assata Shakur and Sundiata Acoli* bulletin released the following statement: "We Celebrate this event and are deeply moved by the incredible resistance displayed by Assata, imprisoned by the state, but still able to create a new life." See press release of Assata Shakur Defense Committee, October 1974, Assata Shakur Collection, Freedom Archives, Oakland, California. Accessed April 20, 2019.

17. Jonathan Jackson freed McClain and other prisoners present in the room, William Christmas and Ruchell Magee. The group took several hostages, including the judge, Harold Haley, the deputy district attorney, and three jurors, and demanded the immediate release from prison of the Soledad Brothers: George Jackson, Fleeta Drumgo, and John Cluchette. The standoff ended in a shoot-out of which Magee was a survivor.

18. "A great deal has been said about the Black man and resistance, but very little about the unique relationship Black women bore to the resistance struggles during slavery. To understand the part she played in developing and sharpening the thrust toward freedom and broader meaning of slavery and of American slavery in particular must be explored." See Angela Davis, *The Black Woman's Role in the Community of Slaves* (Somerville: New England Free Press, 1972), 3.

19. Davis, *The Black Woman's Role in the Community of Slaves*, 4.

20. Angela Davis, "Exclusive: Angela Davis Answers 13 Questions: The People's Questions to Angela Davis," *Muhammed Speaks*. Date Unknown. Box PE 036, Folder 2. Tamiment Library and Robert F. Wagner Labor Archives at

New York University, New York University, New York, New York, January 7, 2020.

21. Angela Davis, *Abolition Democracy: Beyond Empire, Prisons, and Torture* (New York: Seven Stories Press, 2005), 34.

22. Davis, *Abolition Democracy*, 92.

23. See W.E.B. Du Bois, *Black Reconstruction in America: 1860–1880* (New York: The Free Press, 1998), 184. Also see Angela Y. Davis, Gina Dent, Erica R. Meiners, and Beth E. Richie, *Abolition. Feminism. Now.* (Chicago: Haymarket Books, 2022).

24. Angela Davis, *Women, Race, and Class* (New York: Random House, 1981).

25. Davis, interview in *Muhammed Speaks*.

26. Angela Davis, ed., *If They Come in the Morning: Voices of Resistance* (New York: Verso, 2016).

27. Davis and Jackson had an ambiguous love affair that endured via letters while he was incarcerated. She wrote about her admiration for him on multiple occasions, including after his death. See Angela Davis, "Angela Davis on George Jackson," *LA Free Press*, August 27, 1971.

28. Davis, *The Black Woman's Role in a Community of Slaves*, 1.

29. Angela Davis, "Angela on George Jackson," *Battle Acts* 1, no. 8 (Oct/Nov 1971): 13

30. Angela Davis, "A Statement on Our Fallen Comrade, George Jackson," *Black Panther*, Volume 1 (August 28, 1971): 19.

31. Erik Che Young, "George Jackson: A Study of the Life and Investigation into the Murder of Comrade George Lester Jackson 1941–1971," 527, Box 13. Tamiment Library and Robert F. Wagner Labor Archives at New York University, New York University, New York, New York, January 5, 2020.

32. Peter Haldane, "On George Jackson," 527, Box 13, Folder 2. Tamiment Library and Robert F. Wagner Labor Archives at New York University, January 7, 2020.

33. See Nick J. Sciullo, "George Jackson's December 1964 Letter to his Father: Agency from within the Prison Walls," *Journal for the Study of Radicalism* 11, no. 2 (2017): 161–82.

34. George Jackson, *Blood in My Eye* (Baltimore: Black Classic Press, 1996).

35. Jackson, *Blood in My Eye*, 10.

36. Jackson, *Soledad Brother*, 68.

37. Davis, *Abolition Democracy*, 12.

38. Jackson, *Soledad Brother*, 4.

39. Jackson, *Soledad Brother*, 4.

40. Jackson, *Soledad Brother*, 13.

41. Ruchell Magee, "Letters to Angela Y. Davis," in *If They Come in the Morning*, 180.

42. Writing on the death of Jonathan Jackson during the aforementioned standoff following Jackson's storming of the Marin County Courthouse, the civil rights activist Fania Davis Jordan, the sister of Angela Davis, peppers her description of the events with references to chattel slavery: "the leg-irons, manacles, and chains around the bodies of the six black and brown men, who sit in a courtroom authorities have transformed into a slave block, set the tone for the trial procedures." See Fania Davis Jordan, "The San Quentin Six: A Case of Vengeance," *Black Scholar* 5, no. 6 (1974): 45. Jordan uses the connections between enslavement and imprisonment as a rallying cry for action, arguing that the story of the San Quentin Six is part of a broader constellation of centuries of racial subjugation: "The historic struggle of black people in America has been to remove the chains of oppression. The chains that repress these six men are the very same chains that have bound us for centuries. We must come to the defense of these brothers. We must break the chains." See Jordan, "San Quentin Six," 50.

43. Ruchell "Cinque" Magee and Meharibi Muntu (Larry West), "The Barbarian Conspirators—Judges Contz, Christian, and Colvin," PE 036, Box 87. Tamiment Library and Robert F. Wagner Labor Archives at New York University, January 8, 2020.

44. Ruchell Magee, "Aint Nothing Changed," Eugene Coalition Liberation Support Movement, August 15, 1975, 42. Tamiment Library and Robert F. Wagner Labor Archives at New York University, January 8, 2020.

45. In an unprecedented move, the US Supreme Court case ruled in favor of the rebels and the safe return of Cinque to his home (what is now Sierra Leone). See Marcus Rediker, *The Amistad Rebellion: An Atlantic Odyssey of Slavery and Freedom* (New York: Penguin Books, 2013), 64–96.

46. Berger, *Captive Nation*, 182.

47. Cinque and Muntu, "The Barbarian Conspirators," 2.

48. Magee, "Letters to Angela Y. Davis," 183.

49. That so many Black radicals in the 1970s had roots in the South is likely one of the reasons that they drew on slavery to conceptualize racial captivity. Cleaver was originally from Little Rock; Huey Newton from Louisiana, the seventh child born to sharecropper parents; John Clutchette from Texas; Fleeta Drumgo from Louisiana; Johnny Sprain from Mississippi; Willie "Sundiata" Tate was born in Alabama and lived in Texas before moving to California; Ruchell Magee from Louisiana; and Angela Davis from Alabama. In Dan Berger's words, "they brought with them an understanding of slavery as the origin of the American state and its racial hierarchies." See Berger, *Captive Nation*, 183.

50. Michael Dawson, *Blacks in and Out of the Left* (Cambridge: Harvard University Press, 2013), 164.

51. See statements from the Revolutionary Action Movement: "RAM Believes US Owes Afro-Americans 880 Million Acres of Land," *Nite Life*, July 4, 1967.

52. Muhammed Ahmad, microfilm of writings, 1962–1991 "Selected Notes on Black Liberation," *Jihad One*, "Pan Africanism," 27. Black Power Movement: Papers of the Revolutionary Action Movement 1962–1996, Reel 2, Series 2, 0083.

53. Ahmad believes strongly in the capacities of students to provide the Black freedom struggle with leadership and backbone: "Black students, after developing a national organization, could be very helpful to the Black liberation struggle. For instance, if hospital workers in Charleston, S.C. should go on strike, Black students across America should strike in support of them and call on their mothers and fathers and Black workers at large to strike in support of them. In this way, Black students would be playing a direct role in the liberation struggle." See Muhammed Ahmad, "On the Black Student Movement, 1960–1970," Black Power Movement: Papers of the Revolutionary Action Movement 1962–1996, 17: 0242, 29.

54. Microfilm of Muhammed Ahmad, Writings, 1962–1991, "Selected Notes on Black Liberation," *Jihad One*.

55. Muhammed Ahmad, "We are all Prisoners of War," *The Black Scholar* 4, no. 2 (1972): 3

56. Ahmad, "We are all Prisoners of War," 2–5.

57. Ahmad, "We are all Prisoners of War," 4.

58. Ahmad, "We are all Prisoners of War," 4.

59. Anon, "Life in 4A—the Hole," *New England Prisoners' Association* 11, no. 8 (September 1974): 7. 778, Box 11. Tamiment Library and Robert F. Wagner Labor Archives at New York University, January 9, 2020.

60. Herbie Scott X and Deane Akil, "Take a Look Around," *New England Prisoners Association* 11, no. 8 (September 1974): 10. 778, Box 11. Tamiment Library and Robert F. Wagner Labor Archives at New York University, January 9, 2020.

61. Berger, *Captive Nation*, 183.

3. HISTORICAL AND THEORETICAL ERASURES OF SLAVE RESISTANCE

1. Edward Byron Reuter, *The American Race Problem* (New York: Thomas Y. Crowell, 1927), 7.

2. The author of this song, "The Hymn of Freedom," is unknown. It supposedly dates to a plot for rebellion in 1813. For a lengthy discussion of its

origins, see Mat Callahan, *Songs of Slavery and Emancipation* (Jackson: University Press of Mississippi, 2022), 25–82, 88–90.

3. Thomas Wentworth Higginson, *Black Rebellion: Five Slave Revolts* (Boston: De Capo Press, 1999), 79.

4. Douglas R. Egerton, *Gabriel's Rebellion: The Virginia Slave Conspiracies of 1800 and 1802* (Chapel Hill: University of North Carolina Press, 1993).

5. Arthur Scherr, "Governor James Monroe and the Southampton Slave Resistance of 1799," *The Historian* 61, No. 3 (1999), 557–78.

6. See Daniel Rasmussen, *American Uprising: The Untold Story of America's Largest Slave Revolt* (New York: Harper Collins, 2012); and a small collection of papers collected and edited by Albert Thrasher. See Albert Thrasher, *On to New Orleans* (Toronto: Cypress Press, 1966).

7. Political arrest within the Asante kingdom during this period has been well documented. Ivor Wilks, *Asante in the Nineteenth Century: The Structure and Evolution of a Political Order* (Cambridge: Cambridge University Press, 1989) offers a nuanced discussion of the politics of the region. Part IV of Molefi Kete Asante, *The History of Africa: The Quest for Eternal Harmony* (New York: Routledge, 2019) is another excellent resource on this subject.

8. Rasmussen, *American Uprising*. Also, on the transatlantic importation of Akan people to the Americas, see Kwasi Konadu, *The Akan Diaspora in the Americas* (New York: Oxford University Press, 2010); and A. Norman Klein, "Slavery and Akan Origins?" *Ethnohistory* 41, no. 4 (1994): 627–56.

9. Nathalie Dessens, *From Saint-Domingue to New Orleans: Migration and Influences* (Gainesville: University Press of Florida, 2010) is a wonderful source for this subject. For a very useful edited volume, see Carl A. Brasseaux and Glenn Conrad, eds., *The Road to Louisiana: The Saint-Domingue Refugees, 1792–1809*, trans. David Cheramie (Louisiana: University of Louisiana Press, 2016). For a discussion on the political influences of Haitians on African American history, see Gerald Horne, "The Haitian Revolution and the Central Question of African American History," *The Journal of African American History* 100, no. 1 (2015): 26–58.

10. See Paul F. Lachance, "The 1809 Immigration of Saint-Domingue Refugees to New Orleans: Reception, Integration and Impact," *Louisiana History: The Journal of the Louisiana Historical Association* 29, no. 2 (1988): 109–41; and James E. Wainwright, "William Claiborne and New Orleans's Battalion of Color, 1903–1915: Race and the Limits of Federal Power in the Early Republic," *Louisiana History: The Journal of the Louisiana Historical Association* 57, no. 1 (2016): 5–44. Both offer important perspectives on race, labor, and social relations in the Orleans territory during the time of the German Coast Slave Uprising.

11. C.L.R. James, *The Black Jacobins: Toussaint L'Ouverture and the San Domingo Revolution* (New York: Vintage Books, 1989), 261.

12. It is worth noting that there is some contestation in the historical literature about the scale, scope, and even existence of this plot. Some claim that, although thwarted, "the rising" could have been the largest and bloodiest slave revolt in American history. The historian Richard Wade claims that there is little solid evidence of this plot. He attributes the hysterical public response to Vesey to white fears of uprising, fueled by the skills and capabilities of the slave and free Black population in Charleston. "The Negroes in Charleston were not only numerous, but quite different from the imbruted field hands of the cane and cotton country. Many mastered skills, learned to read and write, joined churches, and in every way tried to comport themselves as free men. This was the source of fear. They seemed capable of both resenting their bondage and organizing an insurrection against it." See Richard C. Wade, "The Vesey Plot: A Reconsideration," *Journal of Southern History* 30, no 2 (1964): 143–61. See Robert Paquette and Douglas Egerton, "Of Facts and Fables: New Light on the Denmark Vesey Affair," *The South Carolina Historical Magazine* 105, no. 1 (2004): 8–48. Also see, James O'Neil Spady, "Power and Confession: On the Credibility of the Earliest Reports of the Denmark Vesey Slave Conspiracy," *The William and Mary Quarterly* 68, no. 2 (2011): 287–304.

13. Harvey Wish, "American Slave Insurrections Before 1861," *Journal of Negro History* 22, no. 3 (1937).

14. There is fairly vast literature on the Denmark Vesey plot. Two especially good sources are Jeremy Schipper, *Demark Vesey's Bible: The Thwarted Revolt that Put Slavery and Scripture on Trial* (Princeton: Princeton University Press, 2022); and Ethan J. Kytle and Blain Roberts, *Denmark Vesey's Garden: Slavery and Memory in the Cradle of the Confederacy* (New York: The New Press, 2018).

15. Nat Turner and Thomas R. Gray, *The Confessions of Nat Turner: An Authentic Account of the Whole Insurrection* (Scott's Valley: Createspace Independent Publishing Platform, 2015), 20.

16. Anthony E. Kaye, "Neighborhoods and Nat Turner: The Making of a Slave Rebel and the Unmaking of a Slave Rebellion," *Journal of the Early Republic* 27, No. 4 (Winter 2007): 705–20; Elizabeth Ann Beaulieu, "The Many Incarnations of Nat Turner," *The Southern Literary Journal, Volume 33*, no. 1 (Fall 2000): 150–153; Patrick H. Breen, *The Land Shall Be Deluged in Blood: A New History of the Nat Turner Revolt* (Oxford: Oxford University Press, 2016); and Stephen B. Oates, *The Fires of Jubilee: Nat Turner's Fierce Rebellion* (New York: Harper Perennial, 2016).

17. James C. Scott, *Weapons of the Weak: Everyday Forms of Peasant Resistance* (New Haven: Yale University Press, 1995), 29.

18. Lorenzo Ivy, "Lorenzo Ivy Life History (WPA, Virginia Writers' Project)," interviewed by Claude W. Anderson, *Online Exhibitions*, https://www.virginiamemory.com/online-exhibitions/items/show/169.

19. Stephanie Camp, *Closer to Freedom: Enslaved Women and Everyday Resistance in the Plantation South* (Chapel Hill: University of North Carolina Press, 2004), 45.

20. Camp, *Closer to Freedom*, 45.

21. Camp, *Closer to Freedom*, 80.

22. Raymond A. Bauer and Alice H. Bauer, "Day to Day Resistance to Slavery," *The Journal of Negro History* 27, no. 4 (1942): 388–419.

23. William Dusinberre, *Strategies for Survival: Recollections of Bondage in Antebellum Virginia* (Charlottesville: University of Virginia Press, 2009), 138.

24. Dusinberre, *Strategies for Survival*, 141.

25. Thomas R. Dew, *Review of the Debate in the Virginia Legislature of 1831 and 1832* (Richmond: T.W. White, 1832), 118.

26. James Henry Hammond, a white planter and South Carolina senator, testified in favor of slavery before the US senate on March 4, 1858. "The 'Mudsill' Theory," by James Henry Hammond, before the U.S. Senate: https://www.pbs.org/wgbh/aia/part4/4h3439t.html. Accessed February 15, 2019.

27. Stephen Howard Brown, "'This Unparalleled and Inhuman Massacre': The Gothic, the Sacred, and the Meaning of Nat Turner," *Rhetoric and Public Affairs* 3, no. 3 (2000): 315.

28. Stanley Elkins, *Slavery: A Problem of Institutional and Intellectual Life* (Chicago: University of Chicago Press, 1976).

29. Kenneth M. Stampp, *The Peculiar Institution* (New York: Vintage Books, 1989), 72.

30. Benjamin Botkin, the chief librarian for the Library of Congress, altered this generally unquestioned consensus in 1944, when he released the Federal Writers' Project slave narrative collection. This authorized public access to over 2,500 slave narratives, producing new legitimacy for and interest in them. While some scholars have taken issue with the legitimacy of the WPA interviews on the basis of racist suspicions about the trustworthiness of the testimony of former slaves, others have questioned the veracity of the interviews due to the racial biases of the interviewers. As Jermaine Archer says, "Given the contemporary racial climate, there was a tendency for southern white interviewers to omit responses of ex-slaves that ran counter to the paternalistic portrait they sought to paint." In Jermaine Archer, *Antebellum Slave Narratives: Cultural and Political Expressions of Africa* (New York: Routledge, 2009), 74.

31. See Ulrich Bonnell Philips, *American Negro Slavery: A Survey of the Supply, Employment, and Control of Negro Labor as Determined by the Plantation Regime* (Baton Rouge: Louisiana State University Press, 1969).

32. Thrasher, *On to New Orleans*, IX.

33. Much early- and mid-twentieth-century historical writing on slavery focused on slave conspiracies. See, for example, R. H. Taylor, "Slave Conspiracies of North Carolina," *The North Carolina Historical Review* 5, no. 1, (1928): 20–34; and Herbert Aptheker, "Notes on Slave Conspiracies in Confederate Mississippi," *Journal of Negro History* 29, no. 1 (1944): 75–79. More recently, see Jill Lepore, *New York Burning: Liberty, Slavery, and Conspiracy in Eighteenth-Century Manhattan* (New York: Vintage Books, 2006). Jason Sharples, writing on slave conspiracies in seventeenth-century Barbados, suggests in his fascinating analysis that the so-called discovery of a plot illuminates the fears and speculations of the planter class far more than the rebellious activities of enslaved people. See Sharples, "Discovering Slave Conspiracies: New Fears of Rebellion and Old Paradigms of Plotting in Seventeenth-Century Barbados," *American Historical Review* 120, no. 3 (2015): 811–43.

34. Eugene Genovese, *Roll, Jordan, Roll: The World the Slaves Made* (New York: Vintage Books, 1976).

35. "Galveston News," in *Clarksville Texas Standard*, January 17, 1857. Also reported in the same article, "The citizens of several of the eastern counties of the republic, have lately been thrown into some alarm on accounts of the suspicious movements of many of their slaves. In San Augustine, several slaves have run-away from their masters; and circumstances indicate that they have been decoyed away by some lurking scoundrels . . . either abolitionists or negro thieves. In Nacogdoches, the conduct of slaves has been such as to excite fears that an insurrection was contemplated by the slave population. Negroes might be seen at all hours of night, coming in and going out of town, and going from one plantation to another, on their master's saddle or perhaps plough horse, after his having been worked in the plough all day; negro dances were regular once and sometimes thrice a week. In order to put a stop to this evil, the citizens of Nacogdoches and the surrounding settlements held several meetings; and at a very large meeting held in that town, resolved themselves into patrol companies, their vigilance has been increasing, and it has had, so far, a most salutary effect."

36. Genovese, *Roll, Jordan, Roll*.

37. Herbert Aptheker, *American Negro Slave Revolts: On Nat Turner, Denmark Vesey, Gabriel, and Others* (New York: International Publishers, 2013).

38. Genovese, *Roll, Jordan, Roll*, 594.

39. Genovese, *Roll, Jordan, Roll*, 594.

40. See Stephanie Smallwood, *Saltwater Slavery: A Middle Passage from Africa to American Diaspora* (Cambridge: Harvard University Press, 2008); and Marcus Rediker, *The Slave Ship: A Human History* (New York: Viking, 2007). Also see Kevin Dawson, "Enslaved Ship Pilots in the Age of Revolutions:

Challenging Notions of Race and Slavery between the Boundaries of Land and Sea," *Journal of Social History* 47, no. 1 (Fall 2013): 71–100.

41. Harvey Wish, "American Slave Insurrections," 409.

42. See Anita Rupprecht, "Excessive Memories, Slavery, Insurance and Resistance," *History Workshop Journal* 64 (2007): 6–28.

43. John David Smith, "The Historiographic Rise and Fall and Resurrection of Ulrich Bonnell Phillips," *Georgia Historical Quarterly* 65, no. 2 (Summer 1981): 148.

44. Historians of the same period refuse to propagate what Genovese calls "the racist myth of black docility." Genovese, *Roll Jordan Roll,* 596. One such researcher is Aptheker, who argued that enslaved people founded a distinct revolutionary tradition. See Aptheker, *American Negro Slave Revolts,* 79–161.

45. Bauer and Bauer, "Day to Day Resistance to Slavery," 389.

46. Genovese, *Roll, Jordan Roll,* 595.

47. Genovese, *Roll, Jordan, Roll,* 598.

48. Camp, *Closer to Freedom.*

49. Camp, *Closer to Freedom.*

50. See Malick W. Ghachem, "Introduction: Slavery and Citizenship in the Age of Atlantic Revolutions," *Historical Reflections/Réflexions Historiques* 29, no. 1 (2003): 7–17; and Robert J. Reinstein, "Slavery, Executive Power, and International Law: The Haitian Revolution and American Constitutionalism," *The American Journal of Legal History* 53, no. 2 (2013): 141–237.

51. Examination of James, April 19, 1794, Granville County Miscellaneous Records, Insurrection Charges Made Against Slave Quillo, NCA. Accessed June 1, 2020.

52. Examination of James, 118.

53. John Herbert Roper and Lolita G. Brockington, "Slave Revolt, Slave Debate: A Comparison," *Phylon (1960–)* 45, no. 2 (1984): 98–110: 100.

54. See chapters 4 and 5 of Manisha Sinha, *The Slave's Cause: A History of Abolition* (New Haven: Yale University Press, 2017), 130–195.

55. Steven Hahn, *A Nation Under Our Feet: Black Political Struggles in the Rural South from Slavery to the Great Migration* (Cambridge: Harvard University Press, 2005), 15.

56. See the fourth chapter of *Black Reconstruction,* "The General Strike," in which Du Bois lays out, in detail, the organized efforts of enslaved Black workers. See W.E.B. Du Bois, *Black Reconstruction in America: 1860–1880* (New York: The Free Press, 1998), 55–83.

57. There is a good deal of literature on liberal racism, as well as the paradoxes of liberty, equality, and race. James Farr argues that there is no racist doctrine in Locke's writings, although the accusation that he is a racist is very founded. In short, his racist/colonialist actions are wholly separable from his

liberal philosophies. See James Farr, "'So Vile and Miserable an Estate': The Problem of Slavery in Locke's Political Thought," *Political Theory* 14, no. 2 (1986): 263–89. Other scholars, such as Barbara Arneil, disagree with that view, arguing that Locke's theory of property largely informs his support for British colonial policies. See Barbara Arneil, *John Locke and America: The Defence of English Colonialism* (New York: Oxford University Press, 1996). Also see Arenil, "Trade, Plantations, and Property: John Locke and the Economic Defense of Colonialism," *Journal of the History of Ideas* 55, no. 4 (1994): 591–609.

58. Many current theorists have been writing on race, slavery, and Black political thought for decades, long before the emergence of the Black Lives Matter movement. Only a few of many include: Robert Gooding-Williams, *In the Shadow of Du Bois: Afro-Modern Political Thought in America* (Cambridge: Harvard University Press 2009), *Look, A Negro!: Philosophical Essays on Race, Culture and Politics* (New York: Routledge, 2006), and *Reading Rodney King/Reading Urban Uprising* (New York: Routledge, 1993); see also Fred Moten, *In the Break: The Aesthetics of the Black Radical Tradition* (Minneapolis: University of Minnesota Press, 2003); Cedric Robinson, *Black Marxism: The Making of the Black Radical Tradition, Revised and Updated Third Edition* (Chapel Hill: University of North Carolina Press, 2020); Lawrie Balfour, *The Evidence of Things Not Said: James Baldwin and the Promise of American Democracy* (Ithaca: Cornell University Press, 2001), and *Democracy's Reconstruction: Thinking Politically with W.E.B. Du Bois* (New York: Oxford University Press, 2011); Saidiya Hartman, *Lose your Mother: A Journey Along the Atlantic Slave Route* (New York: Farrar, Straus & Giroux, 2007), and *Scenes of Subjection: Terror, Slavery, and Self-Making in Nineteenth-Century America* (New York: Oxford University Press, 1997); and Christina Sharpe, *Monstrous Intimacies: Making Post-Slavery Subjects* (Durham: Duke University Press, 2010). Since 2013, there has been an explosion of new works on anti-Black racism in political theory and other related disciplines. See Glenn Mackin, "Black Lives Matter and the Concept of the Counterworld," *Philosophy and Rhetoric* 49, no. 4 (2016): 459–81; Charmaine Chua, "Abolition is a Constant Struggle: Five Lessons from Minneapolis," *Theory and Event* 23, no. 4 (2020): 127–47; Jennifer Nash, "Black Maternal Aesthetics," *Theory and Event* 22, no. 3 (2019): 551–75; Juliet Hooker, "Black Lives Matter and the Paradoxes of U.S. Black Politics: From Democratic Sacrifice to Democratic Repair," *Political Theory* 44, no. 4 (2016): 448–69; and Alex Zamalin, "Dismantling Racial Progress for Black Liberation," *Political Theory* 46, no. 4 (2017): 650–658. This is by no means an exhaustive list.

59. While it is true that Alex Zamalin deals only peripherally with slave rebellion in *Struggle on Their Minds*, he is an important, prolific scholar of

Black political thought and his work has been central to the study of African American political resistance. See in particular chapters 5 and 8 of *Black Utopia: The History of an Idea from Black Nationalism to Afrofuturism* (New York: Columbia University Press, 2019). See also Zamalin's rich discussion of James Baldwin, Ralph Ellison, and Toni Morrison's intellectual and cultural contributions to resisting domination in *African American Political Thought and American Culture: The Nation's Struggle for Racial Justice* (New York: Palgrave Macmillan, 2015).

60. Alex Zamalin, *Struggle on Their Minds: The Political Thought of African American Resistance* (New York: Columbia University Press, 2019).

61. David Walker, *Appeal to the Coloured Citizens of the World* (Eastford: Martino Fine Books, 2015).

62. In addition to the WPA interviews, there is a good deal of published narratives offering firsthand accounts of lives in slavery. Some of these, by authors Harriet Jacobs and Solomon Northup, are well-known and widely read. Others like Lucy Delaney are far more obscure. See Harriet Jacobs, *Incidents in the Life of a Slave Girl* (Mineola: Dover Publications, 2001); Solomon Northup, *Twelve Years a Slave* (Boston: Squid Ink Classics, 2014); and Lucy Delaney, *From the Darkness Cometh the Light* (Saint Louis: J.T. Smith, 1891).

63. Nick Brommel, *The Time is Always Now: Black Thought and the Transformation of US Democracy* (New York: Oxford University Press, 2013).

64. Eddie Glaude Jr., *Democracy in Black: How Race Still Enslaves the American Soul* (New York: Broadway Books, 2017).

65. Nikhil Pal Singh, *Black is a Country: Race and the Unfinished Struggle for Democracy* (Cambridge: Harvard University Press, 2005).

66. Jack Turner, *Awakening to Race: Individualism and Social Consciousness in America* (Chicago: University of Chicago Press, 2012).

67. Isaiah Berlin, *Four Essays on Liberty*, ed. Henry Hardy (New York: Oxford University Press, 1990), 160.

68. Katherine McKittrick, *Demonic Grounds: Black Women and Cartographies of Struggle* (Minneapolis: University of Minnesota Press, 2006), 41.

69. McKittrick, *Demonic Grounds*, 40.

70. See Isaiah Berlin's discussion of "economic slavery" in "Two Concepts of Liberty," in *Four Essays on Liberty*, 166–218.

71. Jacobs, *Incidents in the Life of a Slave Girl*, 95–98.

72. Camp borrows "rival geography" from Said. Edward W. Said, *Orientalism* (New York: Pantheon, 1978).

73. Neil Roberts, *Freedom as Marronage* (Chicago: University of Chicago Press, 2015).

74. Camp, *Closer to Freedom*, 7.
75. Hartman, *Scenes of Subjection*, 69.
76. Hannah Arendt, *Between Past and Future* (New York: Penguin, 1993).
77. Hannah Arendt, *The Human Condition* (Chicago: University of Chicago Press, 1998), 215.
78. Shatema Threadcraft, *Intimate Justice: The Black Female Body and the Body Politic* (New York: Oxford, 2016).
79. Roberts, *Freedom as Marronage*, 4.

4. THE RACIAL LIMITS OF LIBERALISM

1. Charles Mills's concept of the "epistemology of ignorance," which describes the white inability to understand the very world they have constructed, is very relevant here. See Charles Mills, *The Racial Contract* (Ithaca: Cornell University Press, 1997), 93.
2. Duncan Bell, "What Is Liberalism?" *Political Theory* 42, no. 6 (2014): 682–715.
3. Judith Shklar, "The Liberalism of Fear," in *Liberalism and the Moral Life*, ed. Nancy Rosenblum (Cambridge: Harvard University Press, 2014), 21.
4. Carol Hay, "Consonances Between Liberalism and Pragmatism," *Transactions of the Charles S. Peirce Society: A Quarterly Journal in American Philosophy* 48, no. 2 (Spring 2012): 141–68: 143.
5. John Locke, *The Second Treatise on Civil Government* (Amherst: Prometheus Books, 1986).
6. For the best overall account of Keynes's economic theory, see John Maynard Keynes, *The General Theory of Employment, Interest, and Money* (New York: Harcourt Brace, 2016). Chapters five, six, and nine of Zachary D. Carter's recent book on Keynes helpfully explains his transformative effects on economic liberalism. See Zachary D. Carter, *The Price of Peace: Money, Democracy, and the Life of John Maynard Keynes* (New York: Random House, 2021).
7. See Fred Dallmayr, *Freedom and Solidarity: Toward New Beginnings* (Lexington: The University Press of Kentucky, 2016), 192.
8. Carol Hay, "Consonances between Liberalism and Pragmatism," 141–68.
9. Kenneth Minogue, *The Liberal Mind* (Carmel: Liberty Fund, 2001), 23.
10. Thomas Spragens, "Democratic Reasonableness," in *Reasonableness in Liberal Political Theory*, ed. Shaun Young (New York: Routledge, 2009). 89.
11. Nadia Urbinati, *Tyranny of the Moderns*, trans. Martin Thom (New Haven: Yale University Press, 2016), 46.
12. Naomi Murakawa, *The First Civil Right: How Liberals Built Prison America* (New York: Oxford University Press, 2014).
13. Mills, *Racial Contract*, 75.

14. Nadia Urbinati, *Tyranny of the Moderns*, 41–42.

15. Julie Novkov, "Mobilizing Liberalism in Defense of Racism," *The Good Society* 16, no. 1 (2007): 31.

16. There is no question that Rawls is one of the most renowned philosophers of the twentieth century. In the 1950s and 1960s, he published a series of articles that shifted the agenda of Anglo-American moral and political philosophy toward questions about what people should rightly do. *A Theory of Justice*, Rawls's most important book, reworked the social contract tradition for a more egalitarian theory of liberalism. See Martha Nussbaum's 2001 tribute to Rawls and a thorough discussion of his profound intellectual influence. Martha Nussbaum, "The Enduring Significance of John Rawls," *The Chronicle of Higher Education,* July 20, 2001.

17. Although there are far too many important Rawlsian philosophers and political thinkers to name here, *The Cambridge Companion to Rawls* is an excellent resource, including chapters by Burton Dreben, Samuel Freeman, Amy Gutman, Martha Nussbaum, and Samuel Scheffler (New York: Cambridge University Press, 2003). See also Joshua Cohen's essay, *The Natural Goodness of Humanity in Reclaiming the History of Ethics: Essays for John Rawls* (New York: Cambridge University Press, 1997), 102–139; and Amartya Sen, "What do We Want from A Theory of Justice?" *Journal of Philosophy* 103, no. 5 (2006): 215–38.

18. Urbinati, *Tyranny of the Moderns*, 165.

19. See Richard Rorty, *Consequences of Pragmatism and Contingency, Irony, and Solidarity* (New York: Cambridge University Press, 2009).

20. Michael Sandel, *Liberalism and the Limits of Justice* (New York: Cambridge University Press, 1998).

21. Thomas Pogge, *Realizing Rawls* (Ithaca: Cornell University Press, 1989).

22. It is worth noting that the membership of the Black Panther Party exceeded five thousand by 1971. The campaign to free Huey P. Newton culminated in his release from prison in 1970, one year before *Theories of Justice* was published. That same year saw the storming of the Marin County Courthouse and subsequent death of Jonathan Jackson and arrest of Angela Davis, launching the "Free Angela" campaign. This is to say that Black radicalism had exploded on the political scene during the time that Rawls was completing the book and thus, the absence of race and racism from the text is all the more conspicuous.

23. Charles W. Mills, "Rawls on Race / Race in Rawls," *The Southern Journal of Philosophy* 47, no. 1 (2009): 161.

24. John Rawls, "Interview with John Rawls," interviewed by Harvard University, *Harvard Review of Philosophy,* Spring 1991. http://www.hcs.harvard.edu/~hrp/issues/1991/Rawls.pdf.

25. Kenneth Minogue, *The Liberal Mind*.

26. Jeffrey Raiman, *As Free and as Just as Possible: The Theory of Marxian Liberalism* (Malden: Wiley Blackwell, 2012), 67.

27. David Conway, *Classical Liberalism: The Unvanquished Ideal* (New York, St. Martin's Press, 1995), 8.

28. Conway, *Classical Liberalism*, 135.

29. Barbara Arneil, *John Locke and America: The Defence of English Colonialism* (New York: Oxford University Press, 1996), 126.

30. John Locke, *Fundamental Constitution of the Carolinas* (1670), https://archive.org/details/collectionofseveoolock/page/n27/mode/2up?view=theater. Accessed August 8, 2020.

31. Arneil, *John Locke and America*, 127.

32. Mark Tunick argues against elitist interpretations of John Stuart Mill that suggest that he believed that certain populations are too unruly or uncivilized for civil government. Instead Tunick refers to Mill as a "tolerant imperialist," arguing that he supported colonial rule in India specifically to introduce the civilizing principles of liberalism to colonized people. See Mark Tunick, "Tolerant Imperialism: John Stuart Mill's Defense of British Rule in India," *Review of Politics* 68, no. 4 (2006): 586–611. Less sympathetically, Beate Jahn argues that Mill's view of international politics is largely informed by nineteenth-century imperialism. The failure of philosophers and political theorists to properly attend to this has resulted in widespread, uncritical acceptance of Mill's theories and rationalities of imperialism, at large.

33. John Stuart Mill, *Consideration on Representative Government* (Amherst: Prometheus, 1991), 203.

34. Charles Mills, *The Racial Contract*.

35. Bell, *What Is Liberalism?* 689.

36. Michaele Ferguson, "Choice Feminism's Honey Trap," *The Contemporary Condition*, March 19, 2014, http://contemporarycondition.blogspot.com/2014/03/choice-feminisms-honey-trap.html.

37. Chad Lavin, "Fear, Radical Democracy, Ontological Methadone," *Polity* 38, no. 2 (2006): 261.

38. Sheldon Wolin has written extensively on the distinction between common matters versus special interests, the distinction between which maps onto that of "the political" versus politics. See especially Sheldon Wolin, "Norm and Form: The Constitutionalizing of Democracy," in *Fugitive Democracy and Other Essays*, ed. Nicholas Xenos (Princeton: Princeton University Press, 2018), 77–99, and "Fugitive Democracy" in *Democracy and Difference: Contesting the Boundaries of the Political*, ed. Seyla Benhabib (Princeton: Princeton University Press, 1996), 31–46.

39. Barbara Cruikshank, *The Will to Empower: Democratic Citizens and Other Subjects* (Ithaca: Cornell University Press, 1999), 26.

40. Peeter Selg, "Justice and Liberal Strategy: Towards a Radical Democratic Reading of Rawls," *Social Theory and Practice* 38, no. 1 (2012): 84.

41. Sheldon Wolin, "What Revolutionary Action Means Today," in *Dimensions of Radical Democracy: Pluralism, Citizenship, Community*, ed. Chantal Mouffe (London: Verso, 1992), 245.

42. Sheldon Wolin, *Democracy Incorporated* (Princeton: Princeton University Press, 2008), 66.

43. See Mark Lilla's incendiary op-ed after the 2016 election of Donald Trump, "The End of Identity Liberalism," *New York Times,* November 18, 2016, https://www.nytimes.com/2016/11/20/opinion/sunday/the-end-of-identity-liberalism.html.

44. Jean-Jacques Rousseau, *Of the Social Contract and Other Political Writings* (New York: Penguin, 2012).

45. Lyle A. Downing and Robert B. Thigpen, "Virtue and the Common Good in Liberal Theory," *The Journal of Politics* 55, no. 4 (1993): 1051.

46. See Sheldon Wolin, *Tocqueville Between Two Worlds: The Making of a Political and Theoretical Life* (Princeton: Princeton University Press, 2003).

47. In contrast to my reading of Wolin, other political thinkers have mobilized his democratic theory for anti-racist purposes. For example, Romand Coles states the following: "Hence I am suggesting that Wolin's radical-democratic theory was engendered through his engagement with the receptive arts of political insurgency that had long been struggling to create some warmth and power in the 'iceberg' (as Moses called it) of American racism. It was precisely in resistance to racism—which from the beginning both inflected and undermined the deepest elements of 'democracy' in the U.S.—that radical democracy was brewing in theory and practice: liturgies of beloved community struggles fired the radical democratic political imagination of Wolin and many of those indebted to him. If we miss this fact, we miss the ways in which widespread democratic insurgency was born of this wound at the heart of U.S. democracy, and was itself an integral event giving birth to the 'lived experience'—the emotions, perceptions, imaginations, performances, tacit and explicit knowledges—through which Wolin's thinking was fashioned, inspired, and informed." See Stanley Hauerwas and Romand Coles, *Conversations Between a Radical Democrat and a Christian* (Cambridge: Lutterworth Press, 2008), 117.

48. Locke, *The Second Treatise on Civil Government*, 15–17.

49. Locke, *The Second Treatise on Civil Government*, 19–31.

50. Frederick Douglass, *What to the Slave is the Fourth of July?* (Berkeley: Mint Editions, 2021).

51. See the second chapter, "The Moral Government of the Universe: Natural Rights, Natural Law, and the Moral Demise of Slavery," in Peter C. Myers,

Race and the Rebirth of American Liberalism (Lawrence: University Press of Kansas, 2008), 47–83.

52. See the first chapter, "From Indignation to Dignity: What Anger Does for Democracy," in Nick Bromell, *The Time is Always Now: Black Thought and the Transformation of US Democracy* (New York: Oxford University Press, 2013), 13–36.

53. Olaudah Equiano, *The Life of Olaudah Equiano* (Mineola: Dover Publications, 1999).

54. Equiano, *The Life of Olaudah Equiano*, 131.

55. Elizabeth A. Bohls, *Slavery and the Politics of Place: Representing the Caribbean 1770–1833* (Cambridge: Cambridge University Press, 2017), 126.

56. Quobna Ottobah Cugoano, *Thoughts and Sentiments on the Evil of Slavery* (New York: Penguin, 1999), 86–87.

57. Adam Dahl, "Creolizing Natural Liberty: Transnational Obligation in the Thought of Ottobah Cugoano," *Journal of Politics* 82, no. 3 (2020): 909.

58. The influence of French revolutionary principles in Haiti is well documented. See the third chapter, "French Jacobins and Saint-Domingue Colonists," in Jeremy D. Popkin, *You are all Free: The Haitian Revolution and the Abolition of Slavery* (New York: Cambridge University Press, 2010), 85–121. See also the fourth chapter, "Who Belongs as Citizens: The Antinomies of Rights and Freedom," in Tessie P. Liu, *A Frail Liberty: Probationary Citizens in the French and Haitian Revolutions* (Lincoln: University of Nebraska Press, 2022), 125–57. See Suzanne Desan, "Internationalizing the French Revolution," *French Politics, Culture, and Society* 29, no. 2 (2011): 137–60; Adom Getachew, "Universalism After the Post-Colonial Turn: Interpreting the Haitian Revolution," *Political Theory* 44, no. 6 (2016): 821–45; and Alyssa Goldstein Sepinwall, "Beyond 'The Black Jacobins': Haitian Revolutionary Historiography Comes of Age," *Journal of Haitian Studies* 23, no. 1 (2017): 4–34.

59. Spragens, "Democratic Reasonableness."

60. Nat Turner and Thomas R. Gray, *The Confessions of Nat Turner: An Authentic Account of the Whole Insurrection* (Scott's Valley: Createspace Independent Publishing Platform, 2015), 20–21.

61. Turner and Gray, *Confessions of Nat Turner*, 31.

62. Turner and Gray, *Confessions of Nat Turner*, 14.

63. Robert L. Paquette, "The Rebellious Slave: Nat Turner in American Memory (Review)," *Journal of Social History* 38, no. 4 (2005): 1124–28: 1125.

64. Mary Kemp Davis, *Nat Turner Before the Bar of Judgment: Fictional Treatments of the Southampton Slave Insurrection* (Baton Rouge: Louisiana State University Press, 1999).

65. Joel Olson, "The Freshness of Fanaticism: The Abolitionist Defense of Zealotry," *Perspectives on Politics* 5, no. 4 (2007): 685–701.

66. Marcus Rediker has written extensively on shipboard slave insurrections, including the most thorough account and analysis of Cinque's rebellion aboard *La Amistad*. See Marcus Rediker, *The Amistad Rebellion: An Atlantic Odyssey of Slavery and Freedom* (New York: Penguin, 2013). Howard Jones's *Mutiny on the Amistad* offers an insightful view into its aftermath and effects on politics and society. See Jones, *Mutiny on the Amistad: The Saga of a Slave Revolt and its Impact on American Abolition, Law, and Diplomacy* (New York: Oxford University Press, 1987).

67. Thucydides said the following: "There is no exclusiveness in our public life, and in our private business we are not suspicious of one another, nor angry with our neighbor if he does what he likes; we do not put on sour looks at him which, though harmless, are not pleasant. While we are thus unconstrained in our private business, a spirit of reverence pervades our public acts." See "Pericles' Funeral Oration," *Thucydides' History of the Peloponnesian War, Book II*, xxxv–xlvi; and *History of the Peloponnesian War, Book II*, xxxv–xlvi, http://data.perseus.org/citations/urn:cts:greekLit:tlg0003.tlg001.perseus-end2:2. Accessed December 12, 2021.

68. Morton J. Horwitz, "History of the Public/Private Distinction," *University of Pennsylvania Law Review* 130, no. 6 (1982).

69. Many white second-wave feminists argue against the injustices of separate spheres. Betty Friedan's landmark text *The Feminine Mystique* details the myriad ways that women are relegated to the private, domestic sphere of the household while men enjoy the economic, political, and cultural benefits of public life. See Betty Friedan, *The Feminine Mystique* (New York: W.W. Norton, 2013). Carole Pateman's renowned argument that an original sexual contract underwrites the social contract in which the male parties to the social contract enjoy unfettered, conjugal access to women's bodies suggests that the public and private realms are both polar and interdependent. See Carole Pateman, *The Sexual Contract* (Stanford: Stanford University Press, 1990). Karen Engle believes that it is necessary to refrain from overstating the division between public and private, for this can undermine key aspects of women's lives in public. In addition, the dichotomy can be used to suggest that the private sphere is negative for women, although that is not always accurate. See Karen Engle, "After the Collapse of the Public/Private Distinction: Strategizing Women's Rights," in *Reconceiving Reality: Women and International Law*, ed. Dorinda Dallmeyer (Washington, D.C.: American Society of International Law, 1993), 143. Susan Moller Okin argues that the private realm is too often a site of subordination and terror, for it is cordoned off from the public where the just, liberal institutions and procedures can otherwise intervene. She posits liberalism in opposition to "culture" and maps this framework onto a public and private divide, meaning that liberal, political

values and practices (such as equality, liberty, representative government, voting, rule of law, choice) prevail in public, while violence and domination (in the forms of domestic abuse of women, polygamy, clitoridectomy, etc.) occur in private. See Susan Moller Okin, "Is Multiculturalism Bad for Women?" in *Is Multiculturalism Bad for Women?* ed. Susan Moller Okin (Princeton: Princeton University Press, 1999), 115–33. Other theorists argue that strict demarcations between public and private matters, or their conflation in the form of the social, leave intact structural forms of social power such as economic disparities, discriminatory practices against sexual and gender minorities, problematic divisions of labor within the family, and more. See Hanna Fenichel Pitkin, "Conformism, Housekeeping, and the Attack of the Blob: The Origins of Hannah Arendt's Concept of the Social," in *Feminist Interpretations of Hannah Arendt*, ed. Bonnie Honig (University Park: Pennsylvania State University Press, 1995), 78–79.

70. James Oakes, "The Political Significance of Slave Resistance," *History Workshop Journal* 22, no. 1 (1986): 91.

71. See Sylviane A. Diouf, *Slavery's Exiles: The Story of American Maroons* (New York: NYU Press, 2016); Daniel O. Sayers, *A Desolate Place for a Defiant People: The Archaeology of Maroons, Indigenous Americans, and Enslaved Laborers in the Great Dismal Swamp* (Gainesville: University Press of Florida, 2016); J. Brent Morris, *Dismal Freedom: A History of the Maroons of the Great Dismal Swamp* (Chapel Hill: University of North Carolina Press, 2022); and Tim Lockley and David Doddington, "Maroon and Slave Communities in South Carolina Before 1865," *The South Carolina Historical Magazine* 113, no. 2 (2012): 125–45.

72. Herbert Aptheker, *American Negro Slave Revolts: On Nat Turner, Denmark Vesey, Gabriel, and Others* (New York: International Publishers, 2013), 167.

73. Herbert Aptheker, "Maroons Within the Present Limits of the United States" *Journal of Negro History* 24, no. 2 (1939): 184.

74. There is a good deal of important scholarship on the effects of the Haitian Revolution on slavery in the United States. See in particular Julius S. Scott, *The Common Wind: Afro-American Currents in the Age of the Haitian Revolution* (New York: Verso, 2020), 159–202; Robin Blackburn, "Haiti, Slavery, and The Age of the Democratic Revolution," *William and Mary Quarterly* 63, no. 4 (2006): 643–74; Simon Newman, "American Political Culture and the French and Haitian Revolutions: Nathaniel Cutting and the Jeffersonian Republicans," in *The Impact of the Haitian Revolution in the Atlantic World*, ed. David P. Geggus (Columbia: University of South Carolina Press, 2001), 72–93; and also the older, but very useful, John E. Baur,

"International Repercussions of the Haitian Revolution," *The Americas* 26, no. 4 (1970): 394–418.

75. Daniel Rasmussen, *American Uprising: The Untold Story of America's Largest Slave Revolt* (New York: Harper Collins, 2011).

76. Rasmussen, *American Uprising*, 126.

77. William Dusinberre, *Strategies for Survival: Recollections of Bondage in Antebellum Virginia* (Charlottesville: University of Virginia Press, 2009), 101.

78. Dusinberre, *Strategies for Survival*, 100.

79. Saidiya Hartman, *Scenes of Subjection: Terror, Slavery, and Self-Making in Nineteenth-Century America* (New York: Oxford University Press, 1997), 69.

80. Sterling Lecater Bland Jr., *African American Slave Narratives, Volume 1* (Westport: Greenwood Press, 2001), 67.

81. John Blassingame, *Slave Testimony: Two Centuries of Letters, Speeches, Interviews, and Autobiographies* (Baton Rouge: Louisiana State University Press, 1977).

82. Stephanie Camp, *Closer to Freedom: Enslaved Women and Everyday Resistance in the Plantation South* (Chapel Hill: University of North Carolina Press, 2004).

83. This claim very much echoes Camp's argument. See Camp, *Closer to Freedom*, 78–87. Jayne Boisvert's discussion of enslaved Haitian women's resistance is also a great resource on this subject. See Jayne Boisvert, "Colonial Hell and Female Slave Resistance in Saint-Domingue," *Journal of Haitian Studies* 7, no. 1 (2001): 65.

84. C. Riley Snorton, *Black on Both Sides: A Racial History of Trans Identity* (Minneapolis: University of Minnesota Press, 2017); and Sarah Haley, *No Mercy Here: Gender, Punishment, and the Making of Jim Crow Modernity* (Chapel Hill: University of North Carolina Press, 2016).

5. THE CONCEPT OF WORLD

1. Hannah Arendt, *The Human Condition* (Chicago: University of Chicago Press, 1998), 7.

2. Hannah Arendt, letter to Donald Barclay (June 12, 1968), The Hannah Arendt Papers, General 1938–1976, n.d. "Bacc Barr" Miscellaneous, 1955–1971. Correspondence File, n.d. 004935. The Library of Congress, Washington, D.C., June 5, 2019.

3. Arendt penned this letter to Barclay only four years after James Chaney, Andrew Goodman, and Michael Schwerner were abducted and murdered during the Freedom Summer of 1964. For an excellent account of Freedom Summer, with detailed information about the murders of these activists, see

Stanley Nelson, dir, *Freedom Summer*. New York. Firelight Films, 2014. Also see Danielle McGuire, *At the Dark End of the Street: Black Women, Rape, Resistance—A New History of the Civil Rights Movement from Rosa Parks to the Rise of Black Power* (New York: Vintage, 2011), 212–46.

4. Michael Hanchard, "Contours of Black Political Thought: An Introduction and Perspective," *Political Theory* 38, no. 4 (2010): 519.

5. Robert Bernasconi, "The Double Face of the Political and the Social: Hannah Arendt and America's Racial Divisions," *Research in Phenomenology* 26 (1996): 3–24.

6. See Heather McGhee, *The Sum of Us: What Racism Costs Everyone and How We Can Prosper Together* (New York: One World, 2021), 17–41.

7. See Richard Rothstein, *The Color of Law: A Forgotten History of How Our Government Segregated America* (New York: W.W. Norton, 2017) for an excellent account of how housing discrimination was the result of deliberate, government-engineered policy, focusing, in particular, on redlining. Chapters 2 and 3 of Heather McGhee's *The Sum of Us* offers a rich discussion of this, as well.

8. McGee, *The Sum of Us*, 17.

9. Patchen Markell's discussion of the "territorial reading" of *The Human Condition* is very helpful here. In this essay, Markell argues against the common tendency of Arendt's readers to approach the tripartite terms labor, work, and action as if they are wholly separable and distinguishable concepts that can be used to neatly categorize different types of human activities. See Patchen Markell, "Arendt's Work: On the Architecture of the Human Condition," *College Literature* 38, no. 1 (2011): 15–44.

10. Markell, "Arendt's Work," 31.

11. In her biography of Rahel Varnhagen, Arendt conceptualizes world as a place which Varnhagen may, at times, be able to access, asking at one point how the world was going "to come to her?" This implies first, that humans can exist apart from the world, a possibility that anticipates the forced worldlessness of captivity, and second, that certain subjects, for example the parvenu, can be forcibly alienated from it. Here, Arendt positions Varnhagen in the orbit of the world, but not within it. The world appears in fixed terms, a feature of human life that asks nothing of its inhabitants. Her later writings on world and worldlessness would strongly deviate from this view. In the penultimate work of her career, *Life of the Mind: Thinking,* Arendt argues that retreating from the world (as Varnhagen did) would not pose any particular problem if humans were mere onlookers, as opposed to actors, in worldly affairs. Because they are not, but rather indispensable for the creation of and care for the world, a fully introspective life is lacking. Arendt takes note of this here: "The

primacy of appearance for all living creatures to whom the world appears in the mode of an it-seems-to-me is of great relevance to the topic we are going to deal with—those mental activities by which we distinguish ourselves from other animal species. For although there are great differences among these activities, they all have in common a withdrawal from the world as it appears and a bending back toward the self. This would cause no great problem if we were mere spectators, godlike creatures thrown into the world to look after it or enjoy it and be entertained by it, but still in possession of some other region as our natural habitat. However, we are of the world and not merely in it; we, too, are appearances by virtue of arriving and departing, of appearing and disappearing; and while we come from a nowhere, we arrive well equipped to deal with whatever appears to us and to take part of the play of the world." See Hannah Arendt, *Life of the Mind: Thinking* (New York: Harcourt Brace Jovanovich, 1978), 26.

12. Elisabeth Young-Bruehl offers the most detailed and comprehensive account of Arendt's life and work. See her biography of Arendt for a full discussion of Arendt's university years, which began in Berlin (1922) and eventually Marburg (1924). Young-Bruehl describes them as years of relative, though transitory, stability in Weimar Germany. Arendt was not particularly concerned with politics during this time. By contrast, she was immediately embroiled in an ongoing philosophical revolution, championed by leading phenomenologists at Marburg, Baden, and Freiburg, particularly Husserl and Heidegger. Weighty philosophical issues, including the ontological turn to things in themselves or their consciousness, as well as questions about philosophy's absolute value and essential properties, were subjects of debate and deliberation among phenomenologists and their students during this time. See Elisabeth Young-Bruehl, *Hannah Arendt: For Love of the World* (New Haven: Yale University Press, 1982), 5–262.

13. Arendt was part of a small cohort of students that worked closely with Heidegger, although her intellectual attachment to him was soon compounded by a romantic one, when the two undertook a torrid love affair. Ettinger says, "that Hannah Arendt was drawn to him is not surprising. Given the powerful influence he exerted on his students it was almost inevitable." Their relationship and the impossibility of its sustainability pushed the often-maudlin Arendt into depths of depression, which surfaces in her poetry during that period (see Young-Bruehl, *Hannah Arendt*, 54–58). Their relationship was one of reciprocal obsession and imbalanced power, for Heidegger sought to maintain his scholarly authority as master teacher in their relations and preserve her role as his intellectual apprentice. In personal and intellectual ways, her love affair with him was both a transformative and devastating experience

for her. Due to their romance, Arendt's time at Marburg was short-lived and she departed after just one year to study with Husserl at Freiburg. Heidegger arranged for her to complete her doctoral work in Heidelberg with his colleague and former thesis advisor, psychoanalyst-turned-philosopher Karl Jaspers. Although Jaspers would become a lifelong friend and mentor to Arendt, his early response to her work, particularly her dissertation, was quite critical. Arendt began her studies with him in 1926, withholding her address from Heidegger and refusing to contact him. He managed to find her through his student and Arendt's friend, Hans Jonas, and they reconvened their love affair for the next two years until Heidegger broke it off in 1928. Arendt completed her dissertation on the subject of love in the work of Saint Augustine under Jaspers's tutelage in 1929, while continuing to revise it for the next thirty years. Religion and philosophy were her primary areas of interest when she first entered Marburg, and her circle of friends and interlocutors at Heidelberg also engaged with these topics. Among them, for example, was Hans Jonas, whose book, *Augustine and the Pauline Problem of Freedom* was published in 1930. Arendt stated on multiple occasions that she was most interested in Augustine as a thinker rather than a bishop, a perspective also echoed in Jaspers's 1957 book, *Plato and Augustine*. See Hans Jonas, *Augustin und das Paulinische Freiheitsproblem* (Göttingen: Vandenhoeck & Ruprecht, 1930); and Karl Jaspers, *Plato and Augustine* (New York: Harvest Books, 1966).

14. Hannah Arendt, "Introduction into Politics," in *The Promise of Politics*, ed. Jerome Kohn (New York: Schocken Books, 2005), 206.

15. See Lena Zuckerwise, "Vita Mundi: Democratic Politics and the Concept of World," *Social Theory and Practice* 42, no. 3 (2016): 474–500.

16. Arendt, *The Human Condition*, 112.

17. In "Vita Mundi," I argue that the Arendtian world can "do" for democratic politics that which her theory of action cannot.

18. Because world is made by work, many view the world itself in the same instrumental terms applied to the activities of homo faber. This is a problem, for holding tenaciously to a merely instrumental conception of work and world conceals from view its political dimensions. Some hold that world is necessary for the emergence of politics. Canovan sees it as a vital safeguard against totalitarianism. See Margaret Canovan, *Hannah Arendt: A Reinterpretation of her Political Thought* (Cambridge: Cambridge University Press, 1994), 106. Calhoun argues that world is an antidote to the more alienating effects of the modern age. See Craig Calhoun, "Plurality, Promises, and Public Spaces," in *Hannah Arendt and the Meaning of Politics: Contradictions of Modernity*, ed. Craig Calhoun (Minneapolis: University of Minnesota Press, 1997), 232–59. Curtis claims it is the scene of any matter of appearance. None of these

interpretations are incorrect, for surely world performs all of the functions that Arendt's readers identify. At the same time, world is more than a gateway to a future political end. Rather, its creation and care are themselves political acts. See Kimberley Curtis, *Our Sense of the Real* (Ithaca: Cornell University Press, 1999), 97. Furthermore, the reduction of work and world to the rationality of means/ends is symptomatic of the tendency to ignore issues of race when formulating theoretical constructs of the political. The human activity of work is utterly central to the transatlantic slave trade and the institution of chattel slavery altogether, as well as, of course, rebellion against them.

19. See Ella Myers, *Worldly Ethics* (Durham: Duke University Press, 2013).

20. For an excellent discussion of Arendt on the Earth see Laura Ephraim, *Who Speaks for Nature? On the Politics of Science* (Philadelphia: University of Pennsylvania Press, 2018), 34–68.

21. Jerome Kohn, "Freedom and the Priority of the Political," in *Cambridge Companion to Hannah Arendt*, ed. Dana Villa (Cambridge: Cambridge University Press 2007), 115.

22. Arendt, *The Human Condition*, 57.

23. Zuckerwise, "Vita Mundi," 16–17.

24. Arendt, "Introduction into Politics," 128.

25. Arendt, "Introduction into Politics," 128.

26. Arendt, "Introduction into Politics," 128.

27. See Eve Kosofsky Sedgwick, *Epistemology of the Closet* (Oakland: University of California Press, 2008).

28. Sedgwick, *Epistemology of the Closet*, 137.

29. Curtis, *Our Sense of the Real*, 97.

30. Curtis, *Our Sense of the Real*, 98.

31. Canovan, *Hannah Arendt*, 106.

32. Lisa Jane Disch, *Hannah Arendt and the Limits of Philosophy* (Ithaca: Cornell University Press, 1994), 42.

33. Zuckerwise, "Vita Mundi," 489.

34. Linda Zerilli, "We Feel Our Freedom: Imagination and Judgment in the Thought of Hannah Arendt," *Political Theory* 33, no. 2 (2005): 158–88.

35. Hannah Arendt, "Action and the Pursuit of Happiness," (1960) Speeches and Writings File 1923–1975, American Political Science Association. New York, N.Y. Library of Congress: Washington, D.C., December 13, 2020.

36. Hannah Arendt, *Between Past and Future* (New York: Penguin, 2006), 95.

37. Hannah Arendt, "Breakdown of Authority," lecture, New York University. New York, New York 1953. Library of Congress.

38. Arendt, *Between Past and Future*, 93.

39. Arendt, *Between Past and Future*, 95.

40. Arendt, *The Human Condition*, 208.

41. Hannah Arendt, "Understanding and Politics," in *Essays in Understanding 1930–1964*, ed. Jerome Kohn (New York: Harcourt Brace, 1994), 318.

42. Hannah Arendt, *Origins of Totalitarianism* (New York: Harcourt Trade Publishers, 2001).

43. Arendt says in *Life of the Mind*, "For thinking, then, though not for philosophy, technically speaking, withdrawal from the world of appearances is the only essential precondition." See Arendt, *Life of the Mind: Thinking*, 78, 81.

44. Linda M.G. Zerilli, *Feminism and the Abyss of Freedom* (Chicago: University of Chicago Press, 2005), 127.

45. Disch, *Hannah Arendt and the Limits of Philosophy*, 176.

46. See Hannah Arendt, "Personal Responsibility Under Dictatorship," in *Responsibility and Judgment*, ed. Jerome Kohn (New York: Schocken Books, 2003), 17–49.

47. Hannah Arendt, "Lectures on Kant's Political Philosophy," in *Lectures on Kant's Political Philosophy*, ed. Ronald Beiner (Chicago: University of Chicago Press, 1992). Also, for a helpful account of Arendt on Kant's *Critique of Judgment*, see Elisabeth Young-Bruehl, *Why Arendt Matters* (New Haven: Yale University, Press, 2009), 170.

48. See Arendt, "Lectures on Kant's Political Philosophy"; and Arendt, *Life of the Mind: Thinking*.

49. Arendt, "Lectures on Kant's Political Philosophy," 49.

50. Arendt, *Life of the Mind: Thinking*, 192.

51. Hans Christian Andersen, "The Emperor's New Clothes," in *Hans Christian Andersen's Complete Fairy Tales* (San Diego: Canterbury Classics/Baker & Taylor, 2014), 55–58.

52. Sedgwick, *Epistemology of the Closet*.

53. Relatedly, Arendt observes in her essay "What is Authority?" that the surest way to undermine authority is laughter. See Arendt, "What is Authority?" in *Between Past and Future*, 45.

54. Although Arendt never completed the third volume of *Life of Mind*, on judgment, the subject has been taken up in Arendtian literature to very fruitful ends. See Roger Berkowitz, "Reconciling Oneself to the Impossibility of Reconciliation: Judgment and Worldliness in Hannah Arendt's Politics," in *Artifacts of Thinking: Reading Hannah Arendt's Denktagebuch*, eds. Roger Berkowitz and Ian Storey (New York: Fordham University Press, 2017), 9–36; Matthew C. Weidenfeld, "Visions of Judgment: Arendt, Kant, and the Misreading of Judgment," *Political Research Quarterly* 66, no. 2 (2013): 254–66; Andrew H. Tyner, "Action, Judgment, and Imagination in Hannah Arendt's

Thought," *Political Research Quarterly* 70, no. 3 (2017): 523–34; David L. Marshall, "The Origin and Character of Hannah Arendt's Theory of Judgment," *Political Theory* 38, no. 3 (2010): 367–93; and Steven DeCaroli, "A Capacity for Agreement: Hannah Arendt and the Critique of Judgment," *Social Theory and Practice* 33, no. 3 (2007): 361–86.

55. Lawrence Biskowski, "Practical Foundations for Political Judgment: Arendt on Action and World," *Journal of Politics* 55, no. 4 (1993): 875.

56. Zerilli, "We Feel Our Freedom," 179.

57. Hannah Arendt, "Labor, Work, Action: A Lecture" (1967), Speeches and Writings File 1923–1975, 023216. Library of Congress: Washington, D.C., April 18, 2019.

58. Arendt, *The Human Condition*, 137.

59. Arendt's criticisms of Marx are not only aimed at his elevation of labor, but also that he muddied the distinction between labor and work. See Hannah Arendt, "Karl Marx and the Tradition of Western Political Thought," *Social Research: An International Quarterly* 69, no. 2 (2002): 273–319.

60. Arendt, "Labor, Work, Action," 5.

61. While bondpeople labored daily in numerous settings, their efforts confound the distinction between labor and work. Like Arendt's concept of labor, their tasks were often cyclical, repetitive, and possessive of no clear beginning or end. On the other hand, it was through their labor that they literally built a world that would be inhabited and enjoyed by white Americans. In Aquia, Virginia at the government's quarry, enslaved people cut the rough stone that was later used to build the White House, the US Capitol, and other public buildings in the 1790s that would become the seats of power in the United States. It would be a little less than a century later that these institutions would hold any promise or possibility for the enslaved men that constructed them. See Garrett Peck, *The Smithsonian Castle and Seneca Quarry* (Cheltenham: The History Press, 2013), 30–42.

62. Arendt, *The Human Condition*, 137.

63. Arendt, "What is Freedom?"

64. Arendt, *The Human Condition*, 173.

65. It is unsurprising that Plato's hostility toward politics creates the philosophical conditions of world erosion. If a world without the freedom of political action need not exist at all, it naturally follows that its human inhabitants should turn their backs on it. Or to put it another way, contempt for politics might signal aversion to the world itself. These anti-political and anti-worldly inclinations that began with Plato paved the way for the consensus among early Christian thinkers that freedom resides in otherworldly domains and not the political sphere. Worse still, the rise of liberalism resulted in the

instrumentalization of politics for the sake of the private with the misguided notion that freedom entails the right to live one's private life as one chooses, rather than through action in public. The rise of "the social," a uniquely modern phenomenon that obscures the distinctions between labor, work, and action, as well as the boundaries between public and private, has had the effect of "conquering the public sphere" completely, making public life merely instrumental for private lifestyle. Freedom to express one's opinion, to do as one wishes as long as it does not harm another, and to exercise the right to personal choices are all examples of anti-political freedom in the modern age of which Arendt is critical. Subjects of this time not only misunderstand that freedom is political, says Arendt, but they have also lost their taste for greatness and immortality that are derived from action. See Arendt, *The Human Condition*, 175–243, for her analysis of this.

66. Arendt, *The Human Condition*, 95.
67. Canovan, *Hannah Arendt*, 129.
68. George Kateb, "Freedom and Worldliness in the Thought of Hannah Arendt," *Political Theory* 5, no. 2 (1977): 142.
69. Kateb, "Freedom and Worldliness," 148.
70. Arendt, *The Human Condition*, 173–74.
71. This passage and others like it provide justifications for action-centric readings of Arendt that view action as the highest form of human activity, the ultimate end of politics, and the dimension of the human condition of which the other two work in service.
72. Young-Bruehl, *Hannah Arendt*, 95.
73. Arendt, *The Human Condition*, 5.
74. Hannah Arendt, *Men in Dark Times* (Orlando: Harcourt Brace, 1995), 87.
75. See Arendt's critical discussion of progress in her essay, "On Violence," in *Crisis of the Republic* (New York: Harcourt Brace, 1972), 127–33.
76. Augustine, *The City of God*, ed. David Knowles, trans. Henry Bettenson (New York: Penguin Classics, 1972), 573.
77. Hannah Arendt, *Love and Saint Augustine*, eds. Joanna Vecchiarelli Scott and Judith Chelius Stark (Chicago: University of Chicago Press, 1996), 37.
78. Augustine, *The City of God*, 22–29.
79. Arendt, *Love and Saint Augustine*, 81.
80. Arendt, *The Human Condition*, 34.
81. Richard Wolin, *Heidegger's Children: Hannah Arendt, Karl Löwith, Hans Jonas, and Herbert Marcuse* (Princeton: Princeton University Press, 2001), 43.
82. Edmund Husserl, *The Crisis of the European Sciences and Transcendental Phenomenology: An Introduction to Phenomenological Philosophy* (Evanston: Northwestern University Press, 1970), 35.

83. Seyla Benhabib, *The Reluctant Modernism of Hannah Arendt* (New York: Rowman & Littlefield, 2003).

84. Fredrick Dolan, "Worldly Pleasure: Hannah Arendt, Friedrich Nietzsche, Wallace Stevens, and 'Political Consciousness,'" *Polity* 33, no. 3 (2001): 443.

85. Richard Bernstein, "Provocation and Appropriation: Hannah Arendt's Response to Martin Heidegger," *Constellations* 4, no. 2 (1997): 158–59.

86. Dana R. Villa, *Hannah Arendt and Martin Heidegger: The Fate of the Political* (Princeton: Princeton University Press, 2001), 113.

87. Arendt, *Between Past and Future*, 171.

88. Martin Heidegger, *Introduction to Metaphysics* (New Haven: Yale University Press, 2000), 181.

89. Heidegger, *Introduction to Metaphysics*, 18.

90. This view of Arendt's is likely attributable to her work on Augustine. See in particular Part II of "Creator and Creature: The Remembered Past," in Arendt, *Love and Saint Augustine*, 45–97.

91. Adom Getachew, *Worldmaking After Empire: The Rise and Fall of Self-Determination* (Princeton: Princeton University Press, 2019).

6. POLITICS IN CAPTIVITY

1. Much of Arendt's theory of totalitarianism, and the critique of nationalism and imperialism that underwrites it, is likely informed by her own experience in exile. Following the 1933 burning of the Reichstag and the ascension of Hitler, Arendt fled Germany for France where she worked for a variety of leftist, Zionist organizations. The conditions for Jews in Europe worsened throughout the 1930s and the city of Paris was certainly no exception. French citizens, particularly members of the Left, were embroiled in their own national struggles for social reform, most notably the 1936–1937 trade union movement, where the Leftist Popular Front won the general election and formed a coalition government that emboldened the working class to strike, en masse, across France. This brought about a series of short-lived social reforms that included wage increases, paid vacation, and a mandatory maximum work week of forty hours. Arendt claimed that this movement, and the radical instability that it produced, rendered the government unequipped to handle mass immigration, as well as the Jewish question. Refugees were left with few allies, while a proliferation of fascist groups gained power, such as Action Française, Propagande Nationale, Rassemblement Antijuif de France, and Mouvement Antijuif Continental. Arendt was forced to navigate this troubling political landscape during her time in France. She joined the League of International Antisemitism to offer legal assistance to David Frankfurter, a Jewish medical

student who murdered a Nazi party leader in Davos, Switzerland in 1936. In addition to her time with Artisant Agriculture and Youth Aliyah, she worked for an agency that assisted Austrian and Czech Jewish refugees in Paris. The situation in France worsened, culminating in the 1938 Anschluss, the German annexation of Austria, one of the early imperialist efforts by Hitler to recover territory lost to Germany after World War I. The months following the incorporation of Austria brought a rollout of antisemitic laws in France, including the restriction of Jews to certain trades, prohibition from owning their own businesses, and the requirement that they carry work permits. Naturally, hundreds of refugees were jailed when they failed to produce permits, creating a crisis of overpopulation in French jails. The disaster continued as Jewish communities became targets of physical attacks in France in response to the murder of the third secretary of the German Embassy at the hands of a Jewish attacker. Amazingly, the Fédération des Sociétés Juives de France issued a fearful call imploring Jews not to protest in Paris, most of whom complied with this order. Arendt was dismayed at the political quietude of Jewish organizations in France. Instead of taking to the streets, or even engaging in less risky political action, Jewish leaders issued resounding calls to return to Jewish values, and retreat into the shtetl. Time and again they displayed reluctance and even outright refusal to respond politically, instead assuming the approach of "pas de politique." See Elisabeth Young-Bruehl, *Hannah Arendt: For Love of the World* (New Haven: Yale University Press, 1982), 115–63.

2. Hannah Arendt, *Origins of Totalitarianism* (New York: Harcourt Trade Publishers, 2001), 137.

3. Hannah Arendt and Günter Gaus, "What Remains? The Language Remains: A Conversation with Günter Gaus," in *Essays in Understanding 1930–1954*, ed. Jerome Kohn (New York: Harcourt Brace, 1994), 17.

4. This is akin to Agamben's concept of bare life. See Giorgio Agamben, *Homo Sacer: Sovereign Power and Bare Life* (Stanford: Stanford University Press, 1998).

5. Seyla Benhabib, *The Reluctant Modernism of Hannah Arendt* (New York: Rowman & Littlefield, 2003), 66–67.

6. Arendt, *Origins of Totalitarianism*, 478.

7. Hannah Arendt, *Between Past and Future* (New York: Penguin, 2006).

8. Peter Baehr, *Hannah Arendt, Totalitarianism, and the Social Sciences* (Stanford: Stanford University Press, 2010).

9. Carl Friedrich, *Totalitarianism* (Cambridge: Harvard University Press, 1964).

10. Gresham Sykes, *Society of Captives: A Study of a Maximum Security Prison* (Princeton: Princeton University Press, 2007).

11. Sykes, *Society of Captives*, 74.

12. Erving Goffman, *Asylums* (New York: Knopf Doubleday, 1961).

13. Jeff Jurgens, "Are American Prisons Totalitarian," The Hannah Arendt Center for Politics and Humanities, https://hac.bard.edu/amor-mundi/are-american-prisons-totalitarian-2012-08-30. Accessed January 15, 2021.

14. See in particular the final chapter "Ideology and Terror," in Arendt, *Origins of Totalitarianism*, 460–479.

15. Angela Davis, "Lessons: From Attica to Soledad," in *If They Come in the Morning: Voices of Resistance*, ed. Angela Davis (New York: Verso, 2016), 45.

16. Davis, "Lessons," 44.

17. Arendt, *Origins of Totalitarianism*, 4.

18. Arendt, *Origins of Totalitarianism*, 437.

19. Joel Olson, *The Abolition of White Democracy* (Minnesota: University of Minnesota Press, 2004), 31–65.

20. Olson, *Abolition of White Democracy*, 32.

21. Thomas P. Stanford, "The Race Question in America," in *Six Women's Slave Narratives*, ed. William L. Andrews (New York: Oxford University Press, 1988), 36.

22. William Dusinberre, *Strategies for Survival: Recollections of Bondage in Antebellum Virginia* (Charlottesville: University of Virginia Press, 2009).

23. Stanford, "The Race Question in America," 64.

24. Orlando Patterson, *Slavery and Social Death: A Comparative Study* (Cambridge: Harvard University Press, 1982), 38.

25. Hannah Arendt, *The Human Condition* (Chicago: University of Chicago Press, 1998).

26. Ned Sublette and Constance Sublette, *The American Slave Coast* (Chicago: Chicago Review Press, 2015).

27. There is good deal of historical literature on the subject of bondpeople's leisure time. Enslaved people also offered firsthand accounts of gatherings and parties hosted by planters. See Solomon Northup, *Twelve Years a Slave* (Boston: Squid Ink Classics, 2014), 208–10. Also, for a strong discussion of the relations between planters and bondpeople, see the section "Masters" in Robert L. Paquette and Mark M. Smith, eds. *The Oxford Handbook of Slavery in the Americas* (New York: Oxford University Press, 2016), 534–55.

28. Dusinberre, *Strategies for Survival*.

29. Arendt, *The Human Condition*, 183–84.

30. Harriet Jacobs, *Incidents in the Life of a Slave Girl* (New York: Dover Publications, 2001), 16–17.

31. Although incarcerated people are disappeared from society, the image of the prison is a prominent feature of the American political and cultural

landscape. In the Bedford Stuyvesant neighborhood of Brooklyn, New York, a prison-themed playground is nestled among several buildings within a large public housing project: a heavy-handed homage to the school-to-prison pipeline. Prison looms large on popular television shows, like *Law and Order, NYPD Blue*, and *Blue Bloods*, and Hollywood feature films, from *Brute Force* (1947), *Cool Hand Luke* (1967), *Shawshank Redemption* (1994), to *I Love You, Philip Morris* (2009). Such cultural visibility does not challenge, but rather accentuates world loss. Because the prison is generally depicted in caricatured form, the reproduction of its image only widens the gulf between nonincarcerated citizens and carceral subjects, through the consumption of prison-centric pop culture.

32. Arendt, *Origins of Totalitarianism*, 438.

33. MCI Cedar Junction Procedure, Massachusetts Department of Correction. Massachusetts: Massachusetts Department of Correction, 2020. Procedure report, https://pigeonly.com/jail-prisons/massachusetts/massachusetts-correctional-institution-mci-cedar-junction-maximum-prison/visitation/.

34. Anon, "City as Prison," *NEPA News* 3, no. 2 (February 26, 1975), 10. Box 5, Folder 21. Tamiment Library and Robert F. Wagner Labor Archives at New York University. Accessed January 5, 2020.

35. Dusinberre, *Strategies for Survival*, 96–98

36. Arendt, *The Human Condition*, 137.

37. Arendt, *The Human Condition*, 137.

38. Lisa Guenther, *Solitary Confinement: Social Death and its Afterlives* (Minneapolis: University of Minnesota Press, 2013), 162; and Sharon Shalev, *Supermax: Controlling Risk Through Solitary Confinement* (London: William Publishing, 2009), 72.

39. Arendt, *The Human Condition*, 90–91.

40. See Tony G. Poveda, "Clinton, Crime, and the Justice Department," *Social Justice* 21, no. 2 (1994): 73–84; and Ronald Kramer and Raymond Michalowski, "The Iron Fist and the Velvet Tongue: Crime Control Policies in the Clinton Administration," *Social Justice* 22, no. 2 (1995): 87–100.

41. Kimberly Curtis, "Multicultural Education and Arendtian Conservatism: On Memory, Historical Injury, and Our Sense of the Common," in *Hannah Arendt and Education*, ed. Mordechai Gordon (New York: Routledge, 2001), 128; and Donna Murch, "The Clintons' War on Drugs: Why Black Lives Didn't Matter," in *Caging Borders and Carceral States: Incarcerations, Immigration Detentions, and Resistance*, ed. Robert T. Chase (Chapel Hill: University of North Carolina Press, 2019).

42. Arendt, *The Human Condition*, 120

43. Prisoners are able to vote in Maine and Vermont, although most do not avail themselves of this right. See "In Just Two States, All Prisoners Can Vote. Here's Why Few Do," *The Marshall Project*. June 11, 2019.

44. See Helga Ramsey-Kurz, *The Non-Literate Other* (Amsterdam: Rodopi, 2007), 317–29.

45. See prisoner writings that detail the immense control that is exercised over their movements and activities, preventing creativity and spontaneity, such as Bill Dunne, "Control Unit Prisons: Deceit and Folly in Modern Dungeons," in *The New Abolitionists: Neo-Slave Narratives and Contemporary Prison Writings*, ed. Joy James (Albany: SUNY Press, 2005), 39–44. Also see Adrian Switzer, "The Violence of the Supermax: Toward a Phenomenological Discussion of Prison Space," in *Death and Other Penalties: Philosophy in a Time of Mass Incarceration*, eds. Geoffrey Adelsberg, Lisa Guenther, and Scott Zemen (New York: Fordham University Press, 2015), 230–249.

46. Vesla Weaver and Amy Lerman, *Arresting Citizenship: Democratic Consequences of American Crime Control* (Chicago: University of Chicago Press, 2014), 157–98.

47. Arendt, "What is Freedom?" in *Between Past and Future*.

48. See especially the third chapter of Jordan T. Camp, *Incarcerating the Crisis: Freedom Struggles and the Rise of the Neoliberal State* (Oakland: University of California Press, 2016), 80, 86.

49. Arendt, *Origins of Totalitarianism*, 405

50. Guenther, *Solitary Confinement*, 34–35.

51. See Jackson's letters in *Soledad Brother* for lengthy discussions of how the prison system cannot tolerate relationships of love and camaraderie. George Jackson, *Soledad Brother* (Chicago: Lawrence Hill Books, 1994).

52. Weaver and Lerman, *Arresting Citizenship*, 114.

53. Weaver and Lerman, *Arresting Citizenship*, 117.

54. Jackson, *Soledad Brother*, 23.

55. Multiple Black carceral political thinkers have used this phrase (or very similar ones) in their work, although I cannot say with certainty who coined it. Huey Newton corrected one of his interviewers in 1970 who referred to the prison from where they were speaking as "minimum security." Newton responded that "the inmates and I are in a maximum security prison. You're in a minimum security prison—it's called America." In her autobiography, Assata Shakur stated that "the only difference between here [the Middlesex County workhouse] and the streets is that one is maximum security and the other is minimum security. The police patrol our communities just like the guards control here. I don't have the faintest idea what it feels like to be free . . . We

aren't free politically, economically, or socially. We have very little power over what happens in our lives." See "Huey Newton Speaks," interviewed by Mark Lane, Paredon P1004. July 4, 1970; and Assata Shakur, *Assata: An Autobiography* (Chicago: Lawrence Hill Books, 2001), 60.

56. Arendt, *The Human Condition*, 209.

57. See *The Black Codes in Georgia* for a primary example of the Black Codes. Dan Moore, Sr. and Michele Mitchell, *The Black Codes in Georgia* (Atlanta: The Apex Museum, 2006). Also see W.E.B. Du Bois's essay "Back Toward Slavery," in *Black Reconstruction, 1860–1880* (New York: The Free Press, 1998), 670–711. The secondary literature on this subject is vast. See Saidiya Hartman, *Wayward Lives, Beautiful Experiments: Intimate Histories of Riotous Black Girls, Troublesome Women, and Queer Radicals* (New York: W.W. Norton, 2019); Amy Louise Wood, *Lynching and Spectacle: Witnessing Racial Violence in America, 1890–1940* (Chapel Hill: University of North Carolina Press, 2009); and Elaine Frantz Parsons, *Ku-Klux: The Birth of the Klan During Reconstruction* (Chapel Hill: University of North Carolina Press, 2019).

58. Arendt, *The Human Condition*, 253.

59. Heather McGhee, *The Sum of Us: What Racism Costs Everyone and How We Can Prosper Together* (New York: One World, 2021), 17–41.

60. Richard Rothstein, *The Color of Law: A Forgotten History of How Our Government Segregated America* (New York: W.W. Norton, 2017).

61. Bruce Western and Becky Pettit, "Incarceration and Social Inequality," *Daedalus* 139, no. 3 (2010): 8–9.

62. Sarah Haley, *No Mercy Here: Gender, Punishment, and the Making of Jim Crow Modernity* (Chapel Hill: University of North Carolina Press, 2016), 212.

63. Frederick Law Olmsted, *Journey in the Seaboard States with Remarks on Their Economy* (London: Sampson Low, Son & Co., 1856).

64. See Haley's chapter "Sabotage and Black Feminist Refusal," in *No Mercy Here*, 195–248.

65. Haley, *No Mercy Here*, 201.

66. Haley, *No Mercy Here*, 161.

67. Haley, *No Mercy Here*, 199.

68. Edward Baptist, *The Half Has Never Been Told: Slavery and the Making of American Capitalism* (New York: Basic Books, 2014).

69. Haley, *No Mercy Here*, 199.

70. Haley, *No Mercy Here*, 200.

71. Arendt, *The Human Condition*, 203.

72. Haley, *No Mercy Here*, 199.

73. Walter Johnson, *Soul by Soul: Life Inside the Antebellum Slave Market* (Cambridge: Harvard University Press, 1999), 76–77.

74. See chapter 4 of Deborah Gray White, *A'r'nt I a Woman? Female Slaves in the Plantation South* (New York: W.W. Norton, 1999), 119–42. The chapter discusses unique forms of bonding and camaraderie among enslaved women.

75. Sergio Lussana, "'No Band of Brothers Could Be More Loving': Enslaved Male Homosociality, Friendship and Resistance in the Antebellum American South," *Journal of Social History* 46, no. 4 (Summer 2013): 872–95: 876.

76. Lussana, "No Band of Brothers," 874

77. Shobana Shankar, "Parchman Women Write the Blues? What Became of Black Women's Prison Music in Mississippi in the 1930s," *American Music* 31, no. 2 (Summer 2013): 184.

78. Haley, *No Mercy Here*, 16.

79. Mills describes colonial logic, "so the basic sequence ran something like this: there are no people there in the first place; in the second place, they're not improving the land; in the third place—oops!—they're all dead anyway (and, honestly, there weren't that many to begin with), so there are no people there, as we said in the first place." See Charles W. Mills, *The Racial Contract* (Ithaca: Cornell University Press, 1997), 50.

80. Ulrich Bonnell Phillips, referenced earlier, very much defined the field of pro-slavery American history in the twentieth century. In addition, see Herbert Gutman, *The Black Family in Slavery and Freedom* (New York: Vintage Books, 1977), in which he refutes the idea that Black families were destabilized by slavery. Also see Robert W. Fogel and Stanley L. Engerman, *Time on the Cross* (New York: W.W. Norton, 1989).

81. Thomas P. Barker, "Spatial Dialectics: Intimations of Freedom in Antebellum Slave Song," *Journal of Black Studies* 46, no. 4 (2015): 376.

82. Karen B. Bell, "Rice, Resistance, and Forced Transatlantic Communities: (Re)Envisioning the African Diaspora in Low Country Georgia, 1750–1800," *Journal of African American History* 95, no. 2 (2010): 157–82.

83. Two helpful, scholarly sources on this Black tradition include Yvonne P. Chireau, *Black Magic: Religion and the African American Conjuring Tradition* (Berkeley: University of California Press, 2003); and William C. Scuttles Jr., "African Religious Survivals as Factors in American Slave Revolts," *The Journal of Negro History* 56, no. 2 (1971): 97–104.

84. W.E.B. Du Bois, *The Souls of Black Folk* (New York: New American Library, 1982), 216.

85. Walter Rucker, "Conjure, Magic, and Power: The Influence of Afro-Atlantic Religious Practices on Slave Resistance and Rebellion," *Journal of Black Studies* 32, no. 1 (2001): 84–103.

86. Rucker, "Conjure, Magic, and Power," 85.

87. Herbert Aptheker, *American Negro Slave Revolts: On Nat Turner, Denmark Vesey, Gabriel, and Others* (New York: International Publishers, 2013), 173; and Joseph Cephas Carroll, *Slave Insurrections in the United States, 1800–1865* (New York: Negro Universities Press, 1938), 14–15.

88. Perry Kyles, "Resistance and Collaboration: Political Struggles Within the Afro-Carolinian Slave Community, 1700–1750," *Journal of African American History* 93, no. 4 (2008): 497–508.

89. See Daniel Rasmussen, *American Uprising: The Untold Story of America's Largest Slave Revolt* (New York: Harper Collins, 2011); John Herbert Roper and Lolita G. Brockington. "Slave Revolt, Slave Debate: A Comparison," *Phylon*. 45, no. 2 (1984): 98–110; and David Richardson, "Shipboard Revolts, African Authority, and the Atlantic Slave Trade," *The William and Mary Quarterly* 58, no. 1 (2001): 69–92.

90. Kyles, "Resistance and Collaboration," 500.

91. Kyles, "Resistance and Collaboration," 500.

92. Kyles, "Resistance and Collaboration," 502.

93. Historians often minimize the degree to which culture has informed strategies of the resistance of bondpeople. See Kyles, "Resistance and Collaboration," 497–508.

94. Arendt, "What Remains? The Language Remains," 20.

95. Hartman, *Wayward Lives*, 281.

96. Barker, "Spatial Dialectics," 376.

97. Angela Davis, "Lessons: From Attica to Soledad," 44.

7. BEYOND DEMOCRACY: THE ATTICA PRISON UPRISING

1. "Statement of Lewisburg Prisoners' Solidarity Committee," Prisoners' Solidarity Committee (September 30, 1971), 527. Box 15, Folder 33. Tamiment Library and Robert F. Wagner Labor Archives at New York University. Accessed January 5, 2020.

2. Heather Ann Thompson, *Blood in the Water: The Attica Prison Uprising of 1971 and its Legacy* (New York: Vintage Books, 2017).

3. Author unknown, "Massacre at Attica," *New York Times*, September 14, 1971.

4. LaShawn D. Harris, "New Perspectives on Criminal Justice and Incarceration," *Journal of African American History* 100, no. 3 (2015): 449.

5. Melinda Plastas and Eve Allegra Raimon, "Brutality and Brotherhood: James Baldwin and Prison Sexuality," *African American Review* 46, no. 4 (2013): 687–99.

6. Robert Weiss, "Attica: The 'Bitter Lessons' Forgotten?" *Social Justice* 18, no. 3 (1991): 4.

7. Anon, "McAlester Burns Twice," *New England Prisoners Association* 3, no. 1 (January 1975): 4. 778 Box 11. Tamiment Library and Robert F. Wagner Labor Archives at New York University. Accessed January 7, 2020.

8. Anon, *New England Prisoners Association* 3, no. 1 (January 1975). 778 Box 11. Tamiment Library and Robert F. Wagner Labor Archives at New York University. January 7, 2020.

9. Ruchell Magee Defense Committee News Release, 1973, press release, February 3, 1973. Box 87, Folder PE 036. Accessed January 6, 2020.

10. Vicky Munro-Bjorklund, "Popular Cultural Images of Criminals and Prisoners since Attica," *Social Justice* 18, no. 3 (1991): 55.

11. Ryan Chapman, *Riots I Have Known* (New York: Simon & Schuster, 2019).

12. Black Moon, "Powaful Impak!" 1992–1993, track 1 on *Enta Da Stage*, Nervous, 1993, compact disc.

13. Nas and Lauryn Hill, "If I Ruled the World," 1995, on *It Was Written*, Columbia Records, 1996, compact disc.

14. Ghostface Killah, "The Hilton," track 13 on *Bulletproof Wallets*, Epic and SME Records, 2001, compact disc.

15. Thompson opens *Blood in the Water* with an important discussion of why it is not in the interest of the state for citizens to know what really happened during the Attica uprising. See "Introduction: State Secrets," in *Blood in the Water*, xiii.

16. Sarah Haley, *No Mercy Here: Gender, Punishment, and the Making of Jim Crow Modernity* (Chapel Hill: University of North Carolina Press, 2016).

17. It is worth noting that Thompson's book has been criticized by prison abolitionists for making disproportionate use of state documents, rather than firsthand accounts of Attica prisoners. See Orisanmi Burton's "Diluting Radical History: Blood in the Water and the Politics of Erasure," *Abolition Journal* (January 26, 2017). Burton argues that Thompson offers up an ideological account of Attica that is cloaked in the false narrative of objectivity. The book not only relies disproportionately on official state documents, but also treats these records as if they speak the neutral truth. The prison historian Ashley Rubin argues that Thompson undermines the radicalism of the Attica prisoners, painting them instead as "moderate people forced into unjust and extreme circumstances." See Ashley Rubin's review of *Blood in the Water: The Attica*

Prison Uprising of 1971 and its Legacy by Heather Ann Thompson, *Punishment and Society* 21, no. 1 (2017): 132.

18. Thompson, *Blood in the Water*, 10.
19. Thompson, *Blood in the Water*, 11.
20. Thompson, *Blood in the Water*, 14.
21. Thompson, *Blood in the Water*, 29.
22. There is a rich literature on the efforts of COINTELPRO to sabotage the Black Panther Party and alienate it from moderate white and Black communities. See in particular Joshua Bloom and Waldo E. Martin Jr., *Black Against Empire: The History and Politics of the Black Panther Party* (Oakland: University of California Press, 2016). Also see Jeffrey Haas, *The Assassination of Fred Hampton: How the FBI and Chicago Police Murdered a Black Panther* (Chicago: Chicago Review Press, 2010). For an excellent discussion on the racial history of the FBI, see John Drabble, "To Ensure Domestic Tranquility: The FBI, COINTELPRO-WHITE HATE and Political Discourse, 1964–1971," *Journal of American Studies* 38, no. 2 (2004): 297–328.
23. Thompson, *Blood in the Water*, 34.
24. Thompson, *Blood in the Water*, 34.
25. Thompson, *Blood in the Water*, 14.
26. LeShawn Harris, "Attica: The Present and Recent Past," review of *Blood in the Water: The Attica Prison Uprising of 1971 and Its Legacy* by Heather Ann Thompson, *Journal of Civil and Human Rights* 3, no. 1 (2017): 101–105.
27. Thompson, *Blood in the Water*, 12.
28. Thompson, *Blood in the Water*, 17.
29. Thompson, *Blood in the Water*, 22.
30. Thompson, *Blood in the Water*, 23.
31. Ronald B. Herzman, who taught English courses at Attica in the 1980s, observed the following: "Dante's system of hell is not all that different from the way they were living from day to day inside the walls of Attica: hell and Attica are both systematic, hierarchical, and impersonal. And the endless rounds of locked gates in Attica are a reasonable substitute for Dante's circles." See Ronald B. Herzman "Attica Educations: Dante in Exile," *PMLA* 123, no. 3 (2008): 697–702.
32. Thompson, *Blood in the Water*, 24.
33. Mariam Kaba, *Attica Prison Uprising 101: A Short Primer* (Project NIA, 2011).
34. Burt Useem and Peter Kimball, *States of Siege: US Prison Riots 1971–1986* (New York: Oxford University Press, 1991), 31–34.
35. Thompson, *Blood in the Water*.

36. The seventh chapter of Danielle McGuire's *At the Dark End of the Street* includes an important discussion of racist narratives on bestial, violent, and voraciously sexual Black men and how these discourses were weaponized against them, at the same time as Black women were subjected to an epidemic of sexual assault perpetrated by white men. See Danielle McGuire, *At the Dark End of the Street: Black Women, Rape, Resistance—A New History of the Civil Rights Movement from Rosa Parks to the Rise of Black Power* (New York: Vintage, 2011), 54.

37. Robert T. Chase, "Rethinking the Rise of Carceral States," *Journal of American History* 102, no. 1 (2015): 74–75.

38. The works of many radical democratic thinkers could prove very fruitful for Black carceral resistance. See the first and third chapters of Romand Coles, *Visionary Pragmatism: Radical and Ecological Democracy in Neoliberal Times* (Durham: Duke University Press, 2016), 31–69, 115–59. Also see Keally McBride, "Emma Goldman and the Power of Revolutionary Love," in *How Not to Be Governed: Readings and Interpretations from a Critical Anarchist Left*, eds. Jimmy Casas Klausen and James Martel (Lanham: Lexington Books, 2011), 157–66; and Elena Loizidou, "This is What Democracy Looks Like," in *How Not to Be Governed*, 157–88.

39. Based on the contemporary democratic—theory literature, there is no question that the Attica protestors made use of democratic political strategies and practices during the uprising. From Tocqueville to Dahl, democratic theorists have detailed the importance of self-government to democracy. Tocqueville believed that these helped cultivate the habits of liberty in a country that could otherwise become overwhelmed by the value of equality. See Alexis de Tocqueville, *Democracy in America* (New York: Penguin, 2003), 67. Chapter five of Ian Shapiro's *The State of Democratic Theory* discusses the centrality of distribution to democracy. See Ian Shapiro, *The State of Democratic Theory* (Princeton: Princeton University Press, 2003), 104–46.

40. See Arjun Appadurai, "Deep Democracy: Urban Governmentality and the Horizon of Politics," *Environment and Urbanization* 13, no. 2 (October 2001): 23–43.

41. I selected Brown, Habermas, and Wolin because all of them have, in different ways, shaped the fields of contemporary political theory. Brown and Wolin are leading radical democratic theorists. Habermas is a (if not the) preeminent twentieth-century theorist of the public sphere.

42. See the sixth chapter, "Liberalism's Family Values," in Wendy Brown, *States of Injury* (Princeton: Princeton University Press, 1995), 135–165.

43. Brown, *States of Injury*, 135.

44. Wolin is consistent on this point, which is especially clear in his later work, *Democracy Incorporated*. See Sheldon Wolin, *Democracy Incorporated* (Princeton: Princeton University Press, 2008).

45. Brown's critique of the neoimperial project of post-9/11 democracy promotion appears here. See Wendy Brown, "We are all Democrats Now," *Theory and Event* 13, no. 2 (2010).

46. See Wendy Brown, "American Nightmare: Neoliberalism, Neoconservatism, and De-Democratization," *Political Theory* 34, no. 6 (2006): 690–714, *In the Ruins of Neoliberalism: The Rise of Antidemocratic Politics in the West* (New York: Columbia University Press, 2019), and "Neoliberalism and the End of Liberal Democracy," *Theory and Event* 7, no. 1 (2003).

47. Wendy Brown, "Democracy and Bad Dreams," *Theory & Event* 10, no. 1 (2007).

48. Plato, *The Republic*, trans. G.M.A Grube (Cambridge: Hackett Publishing, 1992), 186–212.

49. Andrew Dilts takes up the subject of felon disenfranchisement in *Punishment and Inclusion* to argue that the franchise is weaponized in the United States against disproportionately Black felons, and that the criminal punishment system works to regulate membership in the polity. This is only one of many examples of how "citizenship," a category casually deployed by democratic theorists, does not straightforwardly map onto the political lives of prisoners and ex-felons. See Andrew Dilts, *Punishment and Inclusion: Race, Membership, and the Limits of American Liberalism* (New York: Fordham University Press, 2014), 1–26.

50. Catherine Rottenberg, *The Rise of Neoliberal Feminism* (Oxford: Oxford University Press, 2018), 101.

51. Micol Seigel, "Critical Prison Studies: Review of the Field," *American Quarterly* 70, no. 1 (March 2018): 127.

52. Charles Mills holds in *The Racial Contract* that the nonliberal other has always been mobilized by liberals. He says, "The new secular category of *race*, by contrast, which gradually crystallized over a century or so, had the virtue of permanency over any given individual's lifetime. Drawing on the medieval legacy of the Wild Man, and giving this a color, the Racial Contract establishes a particular somatotype as the norm, deviation from which unfits one for full personhood and full membership in the polity." See Charles W. Mills, *The Racial Contract* (Ithaca: Cornell University Press, 1997), 54.

53. Wendy Brown, "At the Edge," *Political Theory* 30, no. 4 (2002): 561.

54. Bonnie Honig, "Toward an Agonistic Feminism: Hannah Arendt and the Politics of Identity," in *Feminists Theorize the Political*, eds. Judith Butler and Joan W. Scott (New York: Routledge, 1992), 225.

55. Habermas's oeuvre is far too vast to fully capture here, but for his seminal works on the public sphere, see Jürgen Habermas, *The Structural Transformation of the Public Sphere: An Inquiry into a Category of Bourgeois Society*. trans. Thomas Burger (Cambridge: MIT Press, 1991). He revises the category in Jürgen Habermas, *"Further Reflections on the Public Sphere,"* in *Habermas and the Public Sphere*, ed. Craig Calhoun (Cambridge: MIT Press, 1992), 421–61.

56. See Nancy Fraser's engagement with Habermas: Nancy Fraser, "Rethinking the Public Sphere: A Contribution to a Critique of Actually Existing Democracy," *Social Text* 25, no. 26 (1990): 56–80. Also see Seyla Benhabib, "Models of Public Space," in *Habermas and the Public Sphere*, ed. Craig Calhoun (Cambridge: MIT Press, 1992), 73–98.

57. Angela Davis discusses the strategic isolation of prisons from society. See Angela Davis, *Are Prisons Obsolete?* (New York: Seven Stories Press, 2003).

58. H. Bruce Franklin, "The Inside Stories of the Global American Prison," *Texas Studies in Literature and Language* 50, no. 3 (Fall 2008): 235–42.

59. The horrid conditions of prisons are a matter on which even the most moderate prison reformers and radical abolitionists tend to agree. See Ruth W. Gilmore, *Golden Gulag: Prisons, Surplus, Crisis, and Opposition in Globalizing California* (Chapel Hill: University of North Carolina Press, 2007); Mark Dow, *American Gulag: Inside U.S. Immigration Prisons* (Oakland, University of California Press, 2005); Erika Camplin, *Prison Food in America* (Lanham: Rowman & Littlefield, 2016); and Michelle Alexander, *The New Jim Crow: Mass Incarceration in the Age of Colorblindness* (New York: New Press, 2012). Beyond the academic scholarship, the most authoritative voices on this subject are actual prisoners. See the autobiography of Assata Shakur, *Assata: An Autobiography* (Chicago: Lawrence Hill Books, 2001); George Jackson, *Soledad Brother* (Chicago: Lawrence Hill Books, 1994); and Eric Stanley and Nat Smith, eds., *Captive Genders: Trans Embodiment and the Prison Industrial Complex* (Oakland: AK Press, 2015).

60. Many Arendt scholars, particularly feminists, take issue with the public/private distinction in Arendt's work. Most notably, Hanna Pitkin's *Attack of the Blob: Hannah Arendt's Concept of the Social* (Chicago: University of Chicago Press, 2000); Bonnie Honig, "Toward an Agonistic Feminism"; Joan W. Scott and Debra Keates, eds., *Going Public: Feminism and the Shifting Boundaries of the Private Sphere* (Champaign: University of Illinois Press, 2005); Joan B. Landes, ed., *Feminism, the Public, and the Private* (New York: Oxford University Press, 1998); Susan B. Boyd, *Challenging the Public/Private Divide: Feminism, Law, and Public Policy* (Toronto: University of Toronto Press, 1997); Mary Lyndon Shanley, "Privacy Publicity Power: Rethinking the

Feminist Public-Private Distinction," in *Resisting Citizenship: Feminist Essays on Politics, Community, and Democracy*, ed. Martha Ackelsberg (New York: Routledge, 2010).

61. "The Attica Liberation Faction Manifesto of Demands," *Race & Class* 53, no. 2 (October 2011): 28–35.

62. Hannah Arendt, *The Human Condition* (Chicago: University of Chicago Press, 1998), 107.

63. Arendt, *The Human Condition*, 69.

64. Arendt, *The Human Condition*, 167.

65. Arendt, *The Human Condition*, 88.

66. Arendt, *The Human Condition*, 137.

67. Thompson, *Blood in the Water*, 10.

EPILOGUE

1. Prisoners Solidarity Committee, "The Prisoners of Attica: Unity and Courage v. Rockefeller's Machine Guns," in *Prisoners Solidarity Committee, Special 8-Page Newsletter on Attica*, September 17, 1971. Freedom Archives (Oakland: Collection: Attica Prison Rebellion). Accessed September 1, 2021.

2. Judy's Man, "Freedom's Cry," *The Outlaw: Journal of the Prisoners Union* 1, no. 5 (1972): 9.

3. Anon, "City as Prison," *NEPA News* 3, no. 2 (February 26, 1975), 10. Box 5, Folder 21. Tamiment Library and Robert F. Wagner Labor Archives at New York University. Accessed January 5, 2020.

4. Anon, "City as Prison," 10.

Bibliography

Agamben, Giorgio. *Homo Sacer: Sovereign Power and Bare Life*. Stanford: Stanford University Press, 1998.
Ahmad, Muhammed. "On the Black Student Movement, 1960–1970." Black Power Movement: Papers of the Revolutionary Action Movement 1962–1996, 17: 0242, 29.
———. Microfilm of writings, 1962–1991. "Selected Notes on Black Liberation." *Jihad One*. Black Power Movement: Papers of the Revolutionary Action Movement 1962–1996, Reel 2, Series 2, 0083.
———. "We are all Prisoners of War." *The Black Scholar* 4, no. 2 (1972): 3–5.
Alexander, Michelle. *The New Jim Crow: Mass Incarceration in the Age of Colorblindness*. New York: New Press, 2012.
———. "The War on Drugs and the New Jim Crow." *Race, Poverty, and the Environment* 17, no. 1 (2010): 75–77.
Andersen, Hans Christian. *Hans Christian Andersen's Complete Fairy Tales*. San Diego: Canterbury Classics/Baker & Taylor, 2014.
Anon. "City as Prison." *NEPA News* 3, no. 2 (February 26, 1975), 10. Box 5, Folder 21. Tamiment Library and Robert F. Wagner Labor Archives at New York University. Accessed January 6, 2020.
———. "George Jackson." Reprinted from *Black Panther,* Volume 1. August 28, 1971.
———. "Life in 4A—the Hole." *New England Prisoners Association* 11, no. 7 (September 8, 1974). 778, Box 11. Tamiment Library and Robert F. Wagner Labor Archives at New York University. Accessed January 7, 2020.
———. "McAlester Burns Twice." *New England Prisoners Association* 3, no. 1 (January 1975), 4. 778 Box 11. Tamiment Library and Robert F. Wagner Labor Archives at New York University. Accessed January 7, 2020.

———. *New England Prisoners Association* 3, no. 1 (January 1975). 778 Box 11. Tamiment Library and Robert F. Wagner Labor Archives at New York University. Accessed January 7, 2020.

———. "Slave Labor in American Prisons," *(Reprint from Winter Soldier), NEPA News* 3, no. 2 (February 22, 1975), 778. Box 11, Folder 22. Tamiment Library and Robert F. Wagner Labor Archives at New York University. Accessed January 6, 2020.

Appadurai, Arjun. "Deep Democracy: Urban Governmentality and the Horizon of Politics." *Environment and Urbanization* 13, no. 2 (October 2001): 23–43.

Aptheker, Herbert. *American Negro Slave Revolts: On Nat Turner, Denmark Vesey, Gabriel, and Others.* New York: International Publishers, 2013.

———. "Maroons Within the Present Limits of the United States." *Journal of Negro History* 24, no. 2 (1939): 184.

———. "Notes on Slave Conspiracies in Confederate Mississippi." *Journal of Negro History* 29, no. 1 (1944): 75–79.

Archer, Jermaine. *Antebellum Slave Narratives: Cultural and Political Expressions of Africa.* New York: Routledge, 2009.

Arendt, Hannah. "Action and the Pursuit of Happiness" (1960). Speeches and Writings File 1923–1975. American Political Science Association. New York, N.Y. Library of Congress: Washington, D.C. Accessed December 13, 2020.

———. *Between Past and Future* (New York: Penguin, 2006).

———. "Breakdown of Authority." Lecture. New York University. New York, New York, 1953. Library of Congress: Washington, D.C. Accessed December 9, 2020.

———. *Crisis of the Republic.* New York: Harcourt Brace, 1972.

———. *The Human Condition.* Chicago: University of Chicago Press, 1998.

———. "Introduction into Politics." In *The Promise of Politics,* edited by Jerome Kohn, 93–200. New York: Schocken Books, 2005.

———. "Karl Marx and the Tradition of Western Political Thought." *Social Research: An International Quarterly* 69, no. 2 (2002): 273–319.

———. "Labor, Work, Action: A Lecture" (1967). *Speeches and Writings File* 1923–1975, 023216. Library of Congress: Washington, D.C. Accessed April 18, 2019.

———. "Lectures on Kant's Political Philosophy." In *Lectures on Kant's Political Philosophy,* edited by Ronald Beiner, 7–78. Chicago: University of Chicago Press, 1992.

———. Letter to Donald Barclay (June 12, 1968). *The Hannah Arendt Papers,* General 1938–1976, n.d. "Bacc Barr." Miscellaneous 1955–1971. Correspondence File, n.d. 004935. The Library of Congress: Washington, D.C. Accessed June 3, 2019.

———. *Life of the Mind: Thinking*. New York: Harcourt Brace Jovanovich, 1978.
———. *Love and Saint Augustine*. Edited by Joanna Vecchiarelli Scott and Judith Chelius Stark. Chicago: University of Chicago Press, 1996.
———. *Men in Dark Times*. Orlando: Harcourt Brace, 1995.
———. "The Nation." In *Essays in Understanding 1930–1954*, edited by Jerome Kohn, 206–11. New York: Schocken Books, 1994.
———. *The Origins of Totalitarianism*. New York: Harcourt Trade Publishers, 2001.
———. *On Revolution*. New York: Penguin, 1990.
———. *On Violence*. New York: Harvest Books, 1970.
———. "Personal Responsibility Under Dictatorship." In *Responsibility and Judgment*, edited by Jerome Kohn, 17–49. New York: Schocken Books, 2003.
———. "Race-Thinking Before Racism." *The Review of Politics* 6, no. 1 (1944): 36–73.
———. "Understanding and Politics." In *Essays in Understanding 1930–1964*, edited by Jerome Kohn, 307–27. New York: Harcourt Brace, 1994.
Arendt, Hannah, and Günter Gaus. "What Remains? The Language Remains." In *Essays in Understanding 1930–1954*, edited by Jerome Kohn, 1–23. New York: Harcourt Brace, 1994.
Arneil, Barbara. *John Locke and America: The Defence of English Colonialism*. New York: Oxford University Press, 1996.
———. "Trade, Plantations, and Property: John Locke and the Economic Defense of Colonialism." *Journal of the History of Ideas* 55, no. 4 (1994): 591–609.
Asante, Molefi Kete. *The History of Africa: The Quest for Eternal Harmony*. New York: Routledge, 2019.
Assata Shakur Defense Committee. October 1974, Assata Shakur Collection. Freedom Archives, Oakland, California. Accessed April 20, 2019.
"The Attica Liberation Faction Manifesto of Demands." *Race & Class* 53, no. 2 (October 2011): 28–35.
Augustine, *The City of God*. Edited by David Knowles. Translated by Henry Bettenson. New York: Penguin Classics, 1972.
Author unknown. "Massacre at Attica." *New York Times*, September 14, 1971.
Author and title unknown. "Galveston News." *Clarksville Texas Standard*, January 17, 1857.
Baehr, Peter. *Hannah Arendt, Totalitarianism, and the Social Sciences*. Stanford: Stanford University Press, 2010.
Balfour, Lawrie. *Democracy's Reconstruction: Thinking Politically with W.E.B. Du Bois*. New York: Oxford University Press, 2011.

———. *The Evidence of Things Not Said: James Baldwin and the Promise of American Democracy.* Ithaca: Cornell University Press, 2001.

Baptist, Edward. *The Half Has Never Been Told.* New York: Basic Books, 2014.

Barker, Thomas P. "Spatial Dialectics: Intimations of Freedom in Antebellum Slave Song." *Journal of Black Studies* 46, no. 4 (2015): 363–83.

Bauer, Raymond A., and Alice H. Bauer. "Day to Day Resistance to Slavery." *The Journal of Negro History* 27, no. 4 (1942): 388–419.

Baur, John E. "International Repercussions of the Haitian Revolution." *The Americas* 26, no. 4 (1970): 394–418.

Beate, Jahn. "Imperialism in the Philosophy of John Stuart Mill." *Review of International Studies* 31, no. 3 (2005): 599–618.

Beaulieu, Elizabeth Ann. "The Many Incarnations of Nat Turner." *The Southern Literary Journal* 33, no. 1 (Fall 2000): 150–53

Beiner, Ronald. "The Presence of Art and the Absence of Heidegger." *Arendt Studies* 2 (2018): 9–16

Bell, Duncan. "What Is Liberalism?" *Political Theory* 42, no. 6 (2014): 682–715.

Bell, Karen B. "Rice, Resistance, and Forced Transatlantic Communities: (Re)Envisioning the African Diaspora in Low Country Georgia, 1750–1800." *Journal of African American History* 95, no. 2 (2010): 157–182.

Benhabib, Seyla. "Models of Public Space." In *Habermas and the Public Sphere*, edited by Craig Calhoun, 73–98. Cambridge: MIT Press, 1992.

———. *The Reluctant Modernism of Hannah Arendt.* New York: Rowman & Littlefield, 2003.

Berger, Dan. *Captive Nation: Black Prison Organizing in the Civil Rights Era.* Chapel Hill: University of North Carolina Press, 2014.

Berkowitz, Roger. "Reconciling Oneself to the Impossibility of Reconciliation: Judgment and Worldliness in Hannah Arendt's Politics." In *Artifacts of Thinking: Reading Hannah Arendt's Denktagebuch*, edited by Roger Berkowitz and Ian Storey, 9–36. New York: Fordham University Press, 2017.

Berlin, Isaiah. "Two Concepts of Liberty." In *Four Essays on Liberty*, edited by Henry Hardy, 166–218. New York: Oxford University Press, 1990.

Bernasconi, Robert. "The Double Face of the Social and the Political: Hannah Arendt and America's Racial Divisions." *Research in Phenomenology* 26 (1996): 3–24.

Bernstein, Richard. "Provocation and Appropriation: Hannah Arendt's Response to Martin Heidegger." *Constellations* 4, no. 2 (1997): 158–59.

Biskowski, Lawrence. "Practical Foundations for Political Judgment: Arendt on Action and World." *Journal of Politics* 55, no. 4 (1993): 867–87.

Blackburn, Robin. "Haiti, Slavery, and The Age of the Democratic Revolution." *William and Mary Quarterly* 63, no. 4 (2006): 643–74.

Blackmon, Douglas. *Slavery by Another Name: The Re-Enslavement of Black Americans from the Civil War to World War II*. New York: First Anchor Books, 2009.
Black Moon. "Powaful Impak!" 1992–1993, track 1 on *Enta Da Stage*. Nervous 1993, compact disc.
Bland Jr., Sterling Lecater. *African American Slave Narratives, Volume 1*. Westport: Greenwood Press, 2001.
Blassingame, John. *Slave Community: Plantation Life in the Antebellum South*. New York: Oxford University Press, 1979.
———. *Slave Testimony: Two Centuries of Letters, Speeches, Interviews, and Autobiographies*. Baton Rouge: Louisiana State University Press, 1977.
Bloom, Joshua, and Waldo E. Martin Jr. *Black Against Empire: The History and Politics of the Black Panther Party*. Oakland: University of California Press, 2016.
Bohls, Elizabeth A. *Slavery and the Politics of Place: Representing the Caribbean 1770–1833*. New York: Cambridge University Press, 2017.
Boisvert, Jayne. "Colonial Hell and Female Slave Resistance in Saint-Domingue." *Journal of Haitian Studies* 7, no. 1 (2001): 61–76.
Boyd, Susan B. *Challenging the Public/Private Divide: Feminism, Law, and Public Policy*. Toronto: University of Toronto Press, 1997.
Bozelko, Chandra. "Give Working Prisoners Dignity—and Decent Wages." *National Review*, January 11, 2017. https://www.nationalreview.com/2017/01/prison-labor-laws-wages/.
Brasseaux, Carl A. and Glenn Conrad, eds. *The Road to Louisiana: The Saint-Domingue Refugees, 1792–1809*. Translated by David Cheramie. Louisiana: University of Louisiana Press, 2016.
Breen, Patrick H. *The Land Shall Be Deluged in Blood: A New History of the Nat Turner Revolt*. Oxford: Oxford University Press, 2016.
Brommel, Nick. *The Time is Always Now: Black Thought and the Transformation of US Democracy*. New York: Oxford University Press, 2013.
Brown, Stephen Howard. "'This Unparalleled and Inhuman Massacre': The Gothic, the Sacred, and the Meaning of Nat Turner." *Rhetoric and Public Affairs* 3, no. 3 (2000): 309–31.
Brown, Wendy. "American Nightmare: Neoliberalism, Neoconservatism, and De-Democratization." *Political Theory* 34, no. 6 (2006): 690–714.
———. "At the Edge." *Political Theory* 30, no. 4 (2002): 561.
———. "Democracy and Bad Dreams." *Theory & Event* 10, no. 1 (2007).
———. *In the Ruins of Neoliberalism: The Rise of Antidemocratic Politics in the West*. New York: Columbia University Press, 2019.
———. "Neoliberalism and the End of Liberal Democracy." *Theory & Event* 7, no. 1 (2003).

———. *States of Injury: Power and Freedom in Late Modernity.* Princeton: Princeton University Press, 1995.

———. "We are all Democrats Now." *Theory & Event* 13, no. 2 (2010).

Browne, Jaron. "Rooted in Slavery: Prison Labor Exploitation." *Race, Poverty, and the Environment* 17, no. 1 (2010): 78–80.

Burton, Orisanmi. "Diluting Radical History: Blood in the Water and the Politics of Erasure." *Abolition Journal* (January 26, 2017).

Calhoun, Craig. "Plurality, Promises, and Public Spaces." In *Hannah Arendt and the Meaning of Politics: Contradictions of Modernity,* edited by Craig Calhoun, 232–59. Minneapolis: University of Minnesota Press, 1997.

Callahan, Matt. *Songs of Slavery and Emancipation.* Jackson: University Press of Mississippi, 2022.

Camp, Jordan T. *Incarcerating the Crisis: Freedom Struggles and the Rise of the Neoliberal State.* Oakland: University of California Press, 2016.

Camp, Stephanie. *Closer to Freedom: Enslaved Women and Everyday Resistance in the Plantation South.* Chapel Hill: University of North Carolina Press, 2004.

Campbell, Micheal C., and Heather Schoenfeld. "The Transformation of America's Penal Order: A Historicized Sociology of Punishment." *American Journal of Sociology* 118, no. 5 (March 2013): 1375–1423.

Camplin, Erika. *Prison Food in America.* Lanham: Rowman & Littlefield, 2016.

Canovan, Margaret. *Hannah Arendt: A Reinterpretation of her Political Thought.* New York: Cambridge University Press, 1994.

Carroll, Joseph Cephas. *Slave Insurrections in the United States, 1800–1865.* New York: Negro Universities Press, 1938.

Carter, Zachary D. *The Price of Peace: Money, Democracy, and the Life of John Maynard Keynes.* New York: Random House, 2021.

Chapman, Ryan. *Riots I Have Known.* New York: Simon & Schuster, 2019.

Chase, Robert T. "Rethinking the Rise of Carceral States." *Journal of American History* 102, no. 1 (2015): 73–86.

Chireau, Yvonne P. *Black Magic: Religion and the African American Conjuring Tradition.* Oakland: University of California Press, 2003.

Chua, Charmaine. "Abolition is a Constant Struggle: Five Lessons from Minneapolis." *Theory & Event* 23, no. 4 (2020): 127–47.

Cleaver, Eldridge. *Soul on Ice.* New York: Delta Books, 1999.

Cobbett, William. *Essential Writings Volume 4.* Augsburg, Bavaria: Jazzybee Verlag, 2018.

Cohen, Joshua. *The Natural Goodness of Humanity in Reclaiming the History of Ethics: Essays for John Rawls.* New York: Cambridge University Press, 1997.

Coles, Romand. *Visionary Pragmatism: Radical and Ecological Democracy in Neoliberal Times*. Durham: Duke University Press, 2016.
Conway, David. *Classical Liberalism: The Unvanquished Ideal*. New York, St. Martin's Press, 1995.
CoreCivic. Investor Relations. http://ir.corecivic.com/. Accessed July 25, 2020.
Corrigan, Rose. "Making Meaning of Megan's Law." *Law and Social Inquiry* 31, no. 2 (2006): 267–312.
Cruikshank, Barbara. *The Will to Empower: Democratic Citizens and Other Subjects*. Ithaca: Cornell University Press, 1999.
Cugoano, Quobna Ottobah. *Thoughts and Sentiments on the Evil of Slavery*. New York: Penguin, 1999.
Curtis, Kimberly. "Multicultural Education and Arendtian Conservatism: On Memory, Historical Injury, and Our Sense of the Common." In *Hannah Arendt and Education*, edited by Mordechai Gordon, 127–52. New York: Routledge, 2001.
———. *Our Sense of the Real*. Ithaca: Cornell University Press, 1999.
d'Entreves, Maurizio Passerin. "Arendt's Theory of Judgment." In *Cambridge Companion to Hannah Arendt*, edited by Dana Villa, 245–58. New York: Cambridge University Press, 2000.
Dahl, Adam. "Creolizing Natural Liberty: Transnational Obligation in the Thought of Ottobah Cugoano." *Journal of Politics* 82, no. 3 (2020): 908–20.
Dallmayr, Fred. *Freedom and Solidarity: Toward New Beginnings*. Lexington: University Press of Kentucky, 2016.
Daniel, Pete R. *The Shadow of Slavery: Peonage in the South 1901–1969*. Urbana: University of Illinois Press, 1990.
Davis, Angela, ed. *If They Come in the Morning: Voices of Resistance*. New York: Verso, 2016.
Davis, Angela. *Abolition Democracy: Beyond Empire, Prisons, and Torture*. New York: Seven Stories Press, 2005.
———. "Angela on George Jackson," *Battle Acts* 1, no. 8 (Oct/Nov 1971): 13.
———. "Angela Davis on George Jackson." *LA Free Press*, August 27, 1971.
———. *Are Prisons Obsolete?* New York: Seven Stories Press, 2003.
———. "A Statement on Our Fallen Comrade, George Jackson," *Black Panther*, Volume 1 (August 28, 1971): 19.
———. "Exclusive: Angela Davis Answers 13 Questions: The People's Questions to Angela Davis." *Muhammed Speaks*. Date Unknown. Box PE 036, Folder 2. Tamiment Library and Robert F. Wagner Labor Archives at New York University, New York University, New York, New York. Accessed January 7, 2020.
———. "The Black Woman's Role in the Community of Slaves." Somerville: New England Free Press, 1972.

———. *Women, Race, and Class*. New York: Random House, 1981.
Davis, Angela, Gina Dent, Erica R. Meiners, and Beth E. Richie. *Abolition. Feminism. Now.* (Chicago: Haymarket Books, 2022).
Davis, Mary Kemp. *Nat Turner Before the Bar of Judgment: Fictional Treatments of the Southampton Slave Insurrection*. Baton Rouge: Louisiana State University Press, 1999.
Dawson, Kevin. "Enslaved Ship Pilots in the Age of Revolutions: Challenging Notions of Race and Slavery between the Boundaries of Land and Sea." *Journal of Social History* 47, no. 1 (Fall 2013): 71–100.
Dawson, Michael. *Blacks in and Out of the Left*. Cambridge: Harvard University Press, 2013.
de Tocqueville, Alexis. *Democracy in America*. New York: Penguin, 2003.
DeCaroli, Steven. "A Capacity for Agreement: Hannah Arendt and the Critique of Judgment." *Social Theory and Practice* 33, no. 3 (2007): 361–86.
Delaney, Arthur. "The 'Modern Day Slavery' of Prison Labor Really Does Have a Link to Slavery." *Huffington Post*. August 8, 2018. https://www.huffpost.com/entry/prison-strike-modern-day-slavery_n_5b857777e4b0511db3d21da8.
Delaney, Lucy. *From the Darkness Cometh the Light*. Saint Louis: Publishing House of J.T. Smith, 1891.
Desan, Suzanne. "Internationalizing the French Revolution." *French Politics, Culture, and Society* 29, no. 2 (2011): 137–60.
Dessens, Nathalie. *From Saint-Domingue to New Orleans: Migration and Influences*. Gainesville: University Press of Florida, 2010.
Dew, Thomas R. *Review of the Debate in the Virginia Legislature of 1831 and 1832*. Richmond: T.W. White, 1832.
Dillon, Stephen. *Fugitive Life: The Queer Politics of the Prison State*. Durham: Duke University Press, 2018.
Dilts, Andrew. *Punishment and Inclusion: Race, Membership, and the Limits of American Liberalism*. New York: Fordham University Press, 2014.
Diouf, Sylviane A. *Slavery's Exiles: The Story of American Maroons*. New York: NYU Press, 2016.
Disch, Lisa Jane. *Hannah Arendt and the Limits of Philosophy*. Ithaca: Cornell University Press, 1994.
Dolan, Frederick. "Worldly Pleasure: Hannah Arendt, Friedrich Nietzsche, Wallace Stevens, and 'Political Consciousness.'" *Polity* 33, no. 3 (2001): 439–54.
Douglass, Frederick. *What to the Slave is the Fourth of July?* Berkeley: Mint Editions, 2021.
Dow, Mark. *American Gulag: Inside U.S. Immigration Prisons*. Oakland, University of California Press, 2005.

Downing, Lyle A., and Robert B. Thigpen. "Virtue and the Common Good in Liberal Theory." *The Journal of Politics* 55, no. 4 (1993): 1046–59.
Drabble, John. "To Ensure Domestic Tranquility: The FBI, Cointelpro-White Hate and Political Discourse, 1964–1971." *Journal of American Studies* 38, no. 2 (2004): 297–328.
Du Bois, W.E.B. *Black Reconstruction in America: 1860–1880*. New York: The Free Press, 1998.
———. *The Souls of Black Folk*. New York: New American Library, 1982.
Du Bois, W.E.B., and Joseph Fracchia, *"Die Negerfrage in den Vereinigten Staaten." The New Centennial Review* 6, no. 3 (2005): 241–90.
Dunne, Bill. "Control Unit Prisons: Deceit and Folly in Modern Dungeons." In *The New Abolitionists: Neo-Slave Narratives and Contemporary Prison Writings*, edited by Joy James, 39–44. Albany: SUNY Press, 2005.
Dusinberre, William. *Strategies for Survival: Recollections of Bondage in Antebellum Virginia*. Charlottesville: University of Virginia Press, 2009.
Duvernay, Ava, and Jason Moran. *13th*. Documentary film. USA, 2016.
Egerton, Douglas R. *Gabriel's Rebellion: The Virginia Slave Conspiracies of 1800 and 1802*. Chapel Hill: University of North Carolina Press, 1993.
Elkins, Stanley. *Slavery: A Problem of Institutional and Intellectual Life*. Chicago: University of Chicago Press, 1976.
Engle, Karen. "After the Collapse of the Public/Private Distinction: Strategizing Women's Rights." In *Reconceiving Reality: Women and International Law*, edited by Dorinda Dallmeyer, 143–56. Washington, D.C.: American Society of International Law, 1993.
Ephraim, Laura. *Who Speaks for Nature? On the Politics of Science*. Philadelphia: University of Pennsylvania Press, 2018.
Equiano, Olaudah. *The Life of Olaudah Equiano*. Mineola: Dover Publications, 1999.
Examination of James. April 19, 1794. Granville County Miscellaneous Records. Insurrection Charges Made Against Slave Quillo. NCA. Accessed June 1, 2020.
Farr, James. "'So Vile and Miserable an Estate': The Problem of Slavery in Locke's Political Thought." *Political Theory* 14, no. 2 (1986): 263–89.
Ferguson, Michaele. "Choice Feminism's Honey Trap." *The Contemporary Condition*. March 19, 2014. http://contemporarycondition.blogspot.com/2014/03/choice-feminisms-honey-trap.html.
———. *Sharing Democracy*. New York: Oxford University Press, 2012.
Finkelman, Paul. *Rebellions, Resistance, and Runaways within the Slave South*. New York: Garland Publishing, 1989.
Finley, Alexandra J. *An Intimate Economy: Enslaved Women, Work, and America's Domestic Slave Trade*. Chapel Hill: University of North Carolina Press, 2020.

Fogel, Robert W., and Stanley L. Engerman. *Time on the Cross*. New York: W.W. Norton, 1989.
Foucault, Michel. *The Birth of Biopolitics: Lectures at the Collège de France 1977–1978*. New York: Picador, 2008.
———. *Security, Territory, and Population: Lectures at the Collège de France 1977–1978*. New York: Picador, 2007.
———. *Discipline & Punish: The Birth of the Prison*. New York: Vintage Books, 1995.
Franklin, H. Bruce. "The Inside Stories of the Global American Prison." *Texas Studies in Literature and Language* 50, no. 3 (2008): 235–42.
Fraser, Nancy. "Rethinking the Public Sphere: A Contribution to a Critique of Actually Existing Democracy." *Social Text* 25, no. 26 (1990): 56–80.
Fraser, Steve, and Joshua Freeman. "In the Rearview Mirror: Barbarism and Progress: The Story of Convict Labor." *New Labor Forum* 21, no. 3 (2012): 94–98.
Freeman, Samuel, ed. *The Cambridge Companion to Rawls*. New York: Cambridge University Press, 2003.
Friedan, Betty. *The Feminine Mystique*. New York: W.W. Norton, 2013.
Friedrich, Carl. *Totalitarianism*. Cambridge: Harvard University Press, 1964.
Genovese, Eugene. *Roll, Jordan, Roll: The World the Slaves Made*. New York: Vintage Books, 1976.
Genovese, Eugene D., and Douglas Ambrose. "Masters." In *The Oxford Handbook of Slavery in the Americas*, edited by Robert L. Paquette and Mark M. Smith, 534–55. New York: Oxford University Press, 2016.
GeoGroup. Who We Are. https://www.geogroup.com/who_we_are. Accessed August 11, 2020.
Getachew, Adom. *Worldmaking After Empire: The Rise and Fall of Self-Determination*. Princeton: Princeton University Press, 2019.
———. "Universalism After the Post-Colonial Turn: Interpreting the Haitian Revolution." *Political Theory* 44, no. 6 (2016): 821–45.
Ghachem, Malick W. "Introduction: Slavery and Citizenship in the Age of Atlantic Revolutions." *Historical Reflections/Réflexions Historiques* 29, no. 1 (2003): 7–17.
Ghostface Killah. "The Hilton." Track 13 on *Bulletproof Wallets*, Epic and SME Records 2001, compact disc.
Gill, Howard P. "The Prison Labor Problem." *The ANNALS of the American Academy of Political and Social Science* 157 (1931): 83–101.
Gilmore, Kim. "Prison Abolition—Understanding the Connections." *Social Justice* 27, no. 3 (2000): 195–205
Gilmore, Ruth Wilson. *The Golden Gulag: Prisons, Surplus, Crisis, and Opposition in Globalizing California*. Oakland: University of California Press, 2007.

Gines, Kathryn. *Hannah Arendt and the Negro Question*. Bloomington: Indiana University Press, 2014.
Glaude Jr, Eddie. *Democracy in Black: How Race Still Enslaves the American Soul*. New York: Broadway Books, 2017.
Goffman, Erving. *Asylums*. New York: Knopf Doubleday, 1961.
Gooding-Williams, Robert. *In the Shadow of Du Bois: Afro-Modern Political Thought in America*. Cambridge: Harvard University Press 2009.
———. *Look, A Negro!: Philosophical Essays on Race, Culture, and Politics*. New York: Routledge, 2006.
———. *Reading Rodney King/Reading Urban Uprising*. New York: Routledge, 1993.
Guenther, Lisa. *Solitary Confinement: Social Death and Its Afterlives*. Minneapolis: University of Minnesota Press, 2013.
———. "40 Years of Solitary Confinement: Resisting Social Death at Angola Prison, Louisiana." *New APPS: Art, Politics, Philosophy, Science*. April 17, 2012.
Gutman, Herbert. *The Black Family in Slavery and Freedom*. New York: Vintage Books, 1977.
Haas, Jeffrey. *The Assassination of Fred Hampton: How the FBI and Chicago Police Murdered a Black Panther*. Chicago: Chicago Review Press, 2010.
Habermas, Jürgen. "Further Reflections on the Public Sphere." In *Habermas and the Public Sphere*, edited by Craig Calhoun, 421–61. Cambridge: MIT Press, 1992.
———. *The Structural Transformation of the Public Sphere: An Inquiry into a Category of Bourgeois Society*. Translated by Thomas Burger. Cambridge: MIT Press, 1991.
Hahn, Stephen. *A Nation Under Our Feet: Black Political Struggles in the Rural South from Slavery to the Great Migration*. Cambridge: Harvard University Press, 2005.
Haldane, Peter. "On George Jackson." 527 Box 13, Folder 2. The Tamiment Library and Robert F. Wagner Labor Archives at New York University, New York University, New York, New York. Accessed January 6, 2020.
Haley, Sarah. *No Mercy Here: Gender, Punishment, and the Making of Jim Crow Modernity*. Chapel Hill: University of North Carolina Press, 2016.
Hammond, James Henry. "The 'Mudsill' Theory.'" U.S. Senate. https://www.pbs.org/wgbh/aia/part4/4h3439t.html. Accessed February 15, 2019.
Hanchard, Michael. "Contours of Black Political Thought: An Introduction and Perspective." *Political Theory* 38, no. 4 (2010): 519.
Harris, LaShawn. "Attica: The Present and Recent Past." Review of *Blood in the Water: The Attica Prison Uprising of 1971 and Its Legacy*, by Heather Ann Thompson. *Journal of Civil and Human Rights* 3, no. 1 (2017): 101–105.

———. "New Perspectives on Criminal Justice and Incarceration." *Journal of African American History* 100, no. 3 (2015): 448–60.
Hartman, Saidiya. *Wayward Lives, Beautiful Experiments: Intimate Histories of Riotous Black Girls, Troublesome Women, and Queer Radicals*. New York: W.W. Norton, 2019.
———. *Lose Your Mother: A Journey Along the Atlantic Slave Route*. New York City: Farrar, Straus & Giroux, 2007.
———. *Scenes of Subjection: Terror, Slavery, and Self-Making in Nineteenth-Century America*. New York: Oxford University Press, 1997.
Harvey, David. *A Brief History of Neoliberalism*. New York: Oxford University Press, 2005.
Hauerwas, Stanley, and Romand Coles. *Conversations Between a Radical Democrat and a Christian*. Cambridge: Lutterworth Press, 2008.
Hay, Carol. "Consonances Between Liberalism and Pragmatism." *Transactions of the Charles S. Peirce Society: A Quarterly Journal in American Philosophy* 48, no. 2 (Spring 2012): 141–68.
Heidegger, Martin. *Introduction to Metaphysics*. New Haven: Yale University Press, 2000.
Herivel, Tara, and Paul Wright, eds. *Prison Profiteers: Who Makes Money from Mass Incarceration?* New York: New Press, 2007.
Herzman, Ronald B. "Attica Educations: Dante in Exile." *PMLA* 123, no. 3 (2008): 697–702.
Higginson, Thomas Wentworth. *Black Rebellion: Five Slave Revolts*. Boston: De Capo Press 1999.
Hinchman, Louis P., and Sandra K. Hinchman. "In Heidegger's Shadow: Hannah Arendt's Phenomenological Humanism." *The Review of Politics* 46, no. 2 (1984): 183–211.
Honig, Bonnie. "Toward an Agonistic Feminism: Hannah Arendt and the Politics of Identity." In *Feminists Theorize the Political*, edited by Judith Butler and Joan W. Scott, 215–38. New York: Routledge, 1992.
Hooker, Juliet. "Black Lives Matter and the Paradoxes of US Black Politics: From Democratic Sacrifice to Democratic Repair." *Political Theory* 44, no. 4 (2016): 448–69.
Horne, Gerald. "The Haitian Revolution and the Central Question of African American History." *The Journal of African American History* 100, no. 1 (2015): 26–58.
Horwitz, Morton J. "History of the Public/Private Distinction." *University of Pennsylvania Law Review* 130, no. 6 (1982):1423–28.
Hurston, Zora Neale. "How It Feels to Be Colored Me." *The World Tomorrow* 11, no. 5 (1928): 1–4.

Husserl, Edmund. *Crisis of the European Sciences and Transcendental Phenomenology: An Introduction to Phenomenological Philosophy*. Evanston: Northwestern University Press, 1970.
"In Just Two States, All Prisoners Can Vote. Here's Why Few Do," *The Marshall Project*. June 11, 2019.
Incarcerated Workers Organizing Committee. Prison Strike 2018. https://incarceratedworkers.org/campaigns/prison-strike2018#:~:text=All%20persons%20imprisoned%20in%20any,or%20territory%20for%20their%20labor.&text=No%20imprisoned%20human%20shall%20be,label%20as%20a%20violent%20offender. Accessed August 15, 2019.
Isaac, Jeffrey. *Arendt, Camus, and Modern Rebellion*. New Haven: Yale University Press, 1992.
Ivy, Lorenzo. "Lorenzo Ivy Life History." *WPA, Virginia Writers' Project*. Interviewed by Claude W. Anderson. *Online Exhibitions*. https://www.virginiamemory.com/online-exhibitions/items/show/169.
Jackson, George. *Blood in My Eye*. Baltimore: Black Classic Press, 1990.
———. *Soledad Brother*. Chicago: Lawrence Hill Books, 1994.
Jacobs, Harriet. *Incidents in the Life of a Slave Girl*. New York: Dover Publications, 2001.
James, C.L.R., *The Black Jacobins: Toussaint L'Ouverture and the San Domingo Revolution*. New York: Vintage Books, 1989.
Jaspers, Karl. *Plato and Augustine*. New York: Harvest Books, 1966.
Johnson, Kevin Rashid. "Prison Labor is Modern Slavery. I've Been Sent to Solitary for Speaking Out." *The Guardian*. August 23, 2019. https://www.theguardian.com/commentisfree/2018/aug/23/prisoner-speak-out-american-slave-labor-strike.
Johnson, Walter. *Soul by Soul: Life Inside the Antebellum Slave Market*. Cambridge: Harvard University Press, 1999.
Jonas, Hans. *Augustin und das Paulinische Freiheitsproblem*. Göttingen: Vandenhoeck & Ruprecht, 1930.
Jones, Howard. *Mutiny on the Amistad: The Saga of a Slave Revolt and its Impact on American Abolition, Law, and Diplomacy*. New York: Oxford University Press, 1987.
Jones-Rogers, Stephanie E. *They Were Her Property: White Women as Slave Owners in the American South*. New Haven: Yale University Press, 2020.
Jordan, Fania Davis. "The San Quentin Six: A Case of Vengeance." *Black Scholar* 5, no. 6 (1974): 44–50.
Joseph, Peniel E. "Black Liberation Without Apology: Reconceptualizing the Black Power Movement." *The Black Scholar* 31, no. 3/4 (2001): 2–19.
Judy's Man, "Freedom's Cry." *The Outlaw: Journal of the Prisoners Union* 1, no. 5 (1972): 9.

Jurgens, Jeff. "Are American Prisons Totalitarian?" *Reading Hannah Arendt*. The Hannah Arendt Center for Politics and Humanities. https://hac.bard.edu/amor-mundi/are-american-prisons-totalitarian-2012-08-30. January 15, 2021.

Kaba, Mariam. *Attica Prison Uprising 101: A Short Primer*. Project NIA, 2011.

Kateb, George. "Freedom and Worldliness in the Thought of Hannah Arendt." *Political Theory* 5, no. 2 (1977): 141–82.

Kautzer, Chad. "Political Violence and Race: A Critique of Hannah Arendt." *Comparative Literature and Culture* 21, no. 3 (2019): 1–12.

Kaye, Anthony E. "Neighborhoods and Nat Turner: The Making of a Slave Rebel and the Unmaking of a Slave Rebellion." *Journal of the Early Republic* 27, no. 4 (Winter 2007): 705–20.

Keynes, John Maynard. *The General Theory of Employment, Interest, and Money*. New York: Harcourt Brace, 2016.

Klausen, Jimmy Casas. "Hannah Arendt's Antiprimitivism." *Political Theory* 38, no. 3 (2010): 394–423.

Klein, A Norman. "Slavery and Akan Origins?" *Ethnohistory* 41, no. 4 (1994): 627–56.

Kleis, Kathryn M. "Facilitating Failure: Parole, Re-Entry, and Obstacles to Success." *Dialectical Anthropology* 34, no. 4 (2010): 525–31.

Kohn, Jerome. "Freedom and the Priority of the Political." In *Cambridge Companion to Hannah Arendt*, edited by Dana Villa, 113–29. New York: Cambridge University Press 2007.

Konadu, Kwasi. *The Akan Diaspora in the Americas*. New York: Oxford University Press, 2010.

Kramer, Ronald, and Raymond Michalowski. "The Iron Fist and the Velvet Tongue: Crime Control Policies in the Clinton Administration." *Social Justice* 22, no. 2 (1995): 87–100.

Kyles, Perry. "Resistance and Collaboration: Political Struggles Within the Afro-Carolinian Slave Community, 1700–1750." *Journal of African American History* 93, no. 4 (2008): 497–508.

Kytle, Ethan J., and Blain Roberts. *Denmark Vesey's Garden: Slavery and Memory in the Cradle of the Confederacy*. New York: The New Press, 2018.

Lachance, Paul F. "The 1809 Immigration of Saint-Domingue Refugees to New Orleans: Reception, Integration and Impact." *Louisiana History: The Journal of the Louisiana Historical Association* 29, no. 2 (1988): 109–41.

Landes, Joan B., ed. *Feminism, the Public, and the Private*. New York: Oxford University Press, 1998.

Langan, Patrick A., John V. Fundis, Lawrence Greenfeld, and Victoria W. Schneider. "Historical Statistics of Prisoners in State and Federal Institutions Yearend 1925–1986." US Department of Justice, Bureau of Justice Statistics (1988): 1–16.

Lavi, Shai. "Crimes of Action, Crimes of Thought: Arendt on Reconciliation, Forgiveness, and Judgment." In *Thinking in Dark Times: Hannah Arendt on Ethics and Politics*, edited by Roger Berkowitz, Jeffrey Katz, and Thomas Keenan, 229–34. New York: Fordham University Press, 2010.

Lavin, Chad. "Fear, Radical Democracy, Ontological Methadone." *Polity* 38, no. 2 (2006): 254–75.

Lepore, Jill. *New York Burning: Liberty, Slavery, and Conspiracy in Eighteenth-Century Manhattan*. New York: Vintage Books, 2006.

Library of Congress. "Limitations of the Slave Narrative Collection: Problems of Memory." Washington, D.C.: Library of Congress. Accessed January 10, 2021.

Lilla, Mark. "The End of Identity Liberalism." *New York Times.* November 18, 2016. https://www.nytimes.com/2016/11/20/opinion/sunday/the-end-of-identity-liberalism.html.

Liu, Tessie P. *A Frail Liberty: Probationary Citizens in the French and Haitian Revolutions*. Lincoln: University of Nebraska Press, 2022.

Locke, Jill. "Little Rock's Social Question: Reading Arendt on School Desegregation and Social Climbing." *Political Theory* 41, no. 4 (2013): 533–61.

———. "Work, Shame, and the Chain Gang: The New Civic Education." In *Vocations of Political Theory: Political Imagination in an Age of Uncertainty*, edited by Jason Frank and John Tambornino, 284–304. Minneapolis: University of Minnesota Press, 2000.

Locke, John. *Fundamental Constitution of the Carolinas* (1670): https://archive.org/details/collectionofseveoolock/page/n27/mode/2up?view=theater. Accessed August 8, 2020.

———. *The Second Treatise on Civil Government*. Amherst: Prometheus Books, 1986.

Lockley, Tim, and David Doddington. "Maroon and Slave Communities in South Carolina Before 1865." *The South Carolina Historical Magazine* 113, no. 2 (2012): 125–45.

Loizidou, Elena. "This is What Democracy Looks Like." In *How Not to be Governed: Readings and Interpretations from a Critical Anarchist Left*. Lanham: Lexington Books, 2011.

Lussana, Sergio. "'No Band of Brothers Could Be More Loving': Enslaved Male Homosociality, Friendship and Resistance in the Antebellum American South." *Journal of Social History* 46, no. 4 (Summer 2013): 872–95.

Lyon, F. Emory. "Prison Labor and Social Justice." *The ANNALS of the American Academy of Political and Social Science* 46, no. 1 (1913): 147–53.

Mackin, Glenn. "Black Lives Matter and the Concept of the Counterworld." *Philosophy and Rhetoric* 49, no. 4 (2016): 459–81.

Magee, Ruchell. "Letters to Angela Y. Davis." In *If They Come in the Morning: Voices of Resistance,* edited by Angela Y. Davis, 175–80. New York: Verso, 2016.

———. "'Aint Nothing Changed.'" Eugene Coalition Liberation Support Movement. August 15, 1975, 42. Tamiment Library and Robert F. Wagner Labor Archives at New York University, New York University, New York, New York. Accessed January 8, 2020.

Ruchell Magee Defense Committee News Release, 1973. Press Release. February 3, 1973. Box 87, Folder PE 036. Accessed January 6, 2020.

Magee, Ruchell "Cinque," and Meharibi Muntu (Larry West). "The Barbarian Conspirators—Judges Contz, Christian, and Colvin." PE 036, Box 87. Tamiment Library and Robert F. Wagner Labor Archives at New York University, New York University, New York, New York. Accessed January 6, 2020.

Maier-Katkin, Daniel, and Birgit Maier-Katkin. "Love and Reconciliation: The Case of Hannah Arendt and Martin Heidegger." *Harvard Review* 32, (2007): 34–48.

Manos, James. "From Commodity Fetishism to Prison Fetishism: Slavery, Convict-leasing, and the Ideological Productions of Incarceration." In *Death and Other Penalties: Philosophy in a Time of Mass Incarceration,* edited by Geoffrey Adelsberg, Lisa Guenther, and Scott Zeman, 43–59. New York: Fordham University Press, 2015.

Markell, Patchen. "Arendt's Work: On the Architecture of the Human Condition." *College Literature* 38, no. 1 (2011): 15–44.

Markovits, Elizabeth. "Birthrights: Freedom, Responsibility, and Democratic Comportment in Aeschylus' 'Oresteia.'" *The American Political Science Review* 103, no. 3 (2009): 421–44.

Marshall, David L. "The Origin and Character of Hannah Arendt's Theory of Judgment." *Political Theory* 38, no. 3 (2010): 367–93.

MCI-Cedar Junction Procedure. Massachusetts Department of Correction. Massachusetts: Massachusetts Department of Correction, 2020. Procedure report. https://pigeonly.com/jail-prisons/massachusetts/massachusetts-correctional-institution-mci-cedar-junction-maximum-prison/visitation/. May 21, 2021.

McBride, Keally. "Emma Goldman and the Power of Revolutionary Love." In *How Not to be Governed: Readings and Interpretations from a Critical Anarchist Left,* edited by Jimmy Casas Klausen and James Martel, 157–66. Lanham: Lexington Books, 2011.

McGhee, Heather. *The Sum of Us: What Racism Costs Everyone and How We Can Prosper Together.* New York: One World, 2021.

McGowan, John. "Ways of Worldmaking: Hannah Arendt and E. L. Doctorow Respond to Modernity." *College Literature* 38, no. 1 (2011): 150–75.

McGuire, Danielle. *At the Dark End of the Street: Black Women, Rape, Resistance—A New History of the Civil Rights Movement from Rosa Parks to the Rise of Black Power.* New York: Vintage, 2011.

McKittrick, Katherine. *Demonic Grounds: Black Women and Cartographies of Struggle*. Minneapolis: University of Minnesota Press, 2006.
McLeod, Allegra. "Prison Abolition and Grounded Justice." *UCLA Law Review* 62 (2015): 1156–1239.
Mill, John Stuart. *Considerations on Representative Government*. Amherst: Prometheus Books, 1991.
Mills, Charles W. "Rawls on Race/Race in Rawls." *The Southern Journal of Philosophy* 47, no. 1 (2009): 161–84.
———. *The Racial Contract*. Ithaca: Cornell University Press, 1997.
Minogue, Kenneth. *The Liberal Mind*. Carmel: Liberty Fund, 2001.
Moore, Sr., Dan, and Michele Mitchell. *The Black Codes in Georgia*. Atlanta: The Apex Museum, 2006.
Morris, Brent. *Dismal Freedom: A History of the Maroons of the Great Dismal Swamp*. Chapel Hill: University of North Carolina Press, 2022.
Moten, Fred. *In the Break: The Aesthetics of the Black Radical Tradition*. Minneapolis: University of Minnesota Press, 2003.
Mouffe, Chantal. "Religion, Liberal Democracy, and Citizenship." In *Political Theologies: Public Religions in a Post-Secular World*, edited by Hent de Vries and Lawrence Sullivan, 318–26. New York: Fordham University Press, 2006.
Munro-Bjorklund, Vicky. "Popular Cultural Images of Criminals and Prisoners since Attica." *Social Justice* 18, no. 3 (1991): 48–70.
Murakawa, Naomi. *The First Civil Right: How Liberals Built Prison America*. New York: Oxford University Press, 2014.
Murch, Donna. "The Clintons' War on Drugs: Why Black Lives Didn't Matter." In *Caging Borders and Carceral States: Incarcerations, Immigration Detentions, and Resistance*, edited by Robert T. Chase, 341–52. Chapel Hill: University of North Carolina Press, 2019.
Mustakeem, Sowande M. *Slavery at Sea: Terror, Sex, and Sickness in the Middle Passage*. Champaign: University of Illinois Press, 2016.
Myers, Ella. *Worldly Ethics: Democratic Politics and Care for the World*. Durham: Duke University Press, 2013.
Myers, Peter C. *Race and the Rebirth of American Liberalism*. Lawrence: University Press of Kansas, 2008.
Nas and Lauryn Hill. "If I Ruled the World." *It Was Written*, Columbia Records. 1996, compact disc.
Nash, Jennifer. "Black Maternal Aesthetics." *Theory & Event* 22, no. 3 (2019): 551–75.
Nelson, Stanley, dir. *Freedom Summer*. New York: Firelight Films, 2014.
Newman, Simon. "American Political Culture and the French and Haitian Revolutions: Nathaniel Cutting and the Jeffersonian Republicans." In *The*

Impact of the Haitian Revolution in the Atlantic World, edited by David P. Geggus, 72–93. Columbia: University of South Carolina Press, 2001.

Newton, Huey. *Revolutionary Suicide*. New York: Penguin, 2009.

———. "Huey Newton Speaks." Interviewed by Mark Lane. Paredon P1004. July 4, 1970.

Northup, Solomon. *Twelve Years a Slave*. Boston: Squid Ink Classics, 2014.

Norton, Anne. "Heart of Darkness: Africa and African Americans in the Writings of Hannah Arendt." In *Feminist Interpretations of Hannah Arendt*, edited by Bonnie Honig, 247–61. University Park: Penn State University Press, 1995.

Novkov, Julie. "Mobilizing Liberalism in Defense of Racism." *The Good Society* 16, no. 1 (2007): 30–39.

Nussbaum, Martha. "The Enduring Significance of John Rawls." *The Chronicle of Higher Education*, July 20, 2001.

Oakes, James. "The Political Significance of Slave Resistance." *History Workshop Journal* 22, no. 1 (1986): 89–107.

Oates, Stephen B. *The Fires of Jubilee: Nat Turner's Fierce Rebellion*. New York: Harper Perennial, 2016.

Okin, Susan Moller. "Is Multiculturalism Bad for Women?" In *Is Multiculturalism Bad for Women?* edited by Susan Moller Okin, 115–33. Princeton: Princeton University Press, 1999.

Olmsted, Frederick Law. *Journey in the Seaboard States with Remarks on Their Economy*. London: Sampson Low, Son & Co., 1856.

Olson, Joel. "The Freshness of Fanaticism: The Abolitionist Defense of Zealotry." *Perspectives on Politics* 5, no. 4 (2007): 685–701.

———. *The Abolition of White Democracy*. Minneapolis: University of Minnesota Press, 2004.

Oshinsky, David. *Worse Than Slavery: Parchman Farm and the Ordeal of Jim Crow Justice*. New York: Simon & Schuster, 1996.

Paquette, Robert L. "The Rebellious Slave: Nat Turner in American Memory (Review)." *Journal of Social History* 38, no. 4 (2005): 1124–28.

Paquette, Robert L., and Douglas Egerton. "Of Facts and Fables: New Light on the Denmark Vesey Affair," *The South Carolina Historical Magazine* 105, no. 1 (2004): 8–48.

Paquette, Robert L., and Mark M. Smith, ed., "Masters," in *The Oxford Handbook of Slavery in the Americas* (New York: Oxford University Press, 2016).

Parsons, Elaine Frantz. *Ku-Klux: The Birth of the Klan During Reconstruction*. Chapel Hill: University of North Carolina Press, 2019.

Pateman, Carole. *The Sexual Contract*. Stanford: Stanford University Press, 1990.

Patterson, Orlando. *Slavery and Social Death: A Comparative Study*. Cambridge: Harvard University Press, 1982.

Peck, Garrett. *The Smithsonian Castle and Seneca Quarry*. Cheltenham: The History Press, 2013.

Penningroth, Dylan C. *The Claims of Kinfolk: African American Property and Community in the Nineteenth Century South* (Chapel Hill: University of North Carolina Press, 2003).

Peys, Christopher. *Reconsidering Cosmopolitanism and Forgiveness: Arendt, Derrida, and Care for the World* (New York: Rowman & Littlefield, 2022).

Philips, Ulrich Bonnell. *American Negro Slavery: A Survey of the Supply, Employment and Control of Negro Labor as Determined by the Plantation Regime*. Baton Rouge: Louisiana State University Press, 1969.

Pihos, Peter C. "The Local War on Drugs." In *The War on Drugs: A History*, edited by David Farber, 131–59. New York: NYU Press, 2021.

Pitkin, Hanna. *Attack of the Blob: Hannah Arendt's Concept of the Social*. Chicago: University of Chicago Press, 2000.

———. "Conformism, Housekeeping, and the Attack of the Blob: The Origins of Hannah Arendt's Concept of the Social." In *Feminist Interpretations of Hannah Arendt,* edited by Bonnie Honig, 51–81. University Park: Pennsylvania State University Press, 1995.

———. "Justice: On Relating Private and Public." *Political Theory* 9, no. 3 (1981): 327–52.

Plastas, Melinda, and Eve Allegra Raimon. "Brutality and Brotherhood: James Baldwin and Prison Sexuality." *African American Review* 46, no. 4 (2013): 687–99.

Plato. *The Republic*. Translated by G.M.A Grube. Cambridge: Hackett Publishing, 1992.

Pogge, Thomas. *Realizing Rawls*. Ithaca: Cornell University Press, 1989.

Popkin, Jeremy D. *You are all Free: The Haitian Revolution and the Abolition of Slavery*. New York: Cambridge University Press, 2010.

Poveda, Tony G. "Clinton, Crime, and the Justice Department." *Social Justice* 21, no. 2 (1994): 73–84.

Prashad, Vijay. "From Plantation Slavery to Penal Slavery." *Economic and Political Weekly* 30, no. 36 (1995): 2237–41.

Price, Joshua. *Prison and Social Death*. New Brunswick: Rutgers University Press, 2015.

Prisoners Solidarity Committee. "The Prisoners of Attica: Unity and Courage v. Rockefeller's Machine Guns." In *Prisoners Solidarity Committee, Special 8-Page Newsletter on Attica*. September 17, 1971. Freedom Archives, Oakland, CA. Collection: Attica Prison Rebellion. Accessed September 1, 2021.

Raiman, Jeffrey. *As Free and as Just as Possible: The Theory of Marxian Liberalism*. Malden: Wiley-Blackwell, 2012.

Ramsey-Kurz, Helga. *The Non-Literate Other*. Amsterdam: Rodopi, 2007.

Rankine, Claudia. *Citizen: An American Lyric*. Minneapolis: Graywolf Press, 2014.

Rasmussen, Daniel. *American Uprising: The Untold Story of America's Largest Slave Revolt*. New York: Harper Collins, 2011.

Rawls, John. "Interview with John Rawls." Interviewed by Harvard University. *Harvard Review of Philosophy*, Spring 1991. https://www.pdcnet.org/collection/fshow?id=harvardreview_1991_0001_0001_0038_0047&pdfname=harvardreview_1991_0001_0001_0038_0047.pdf&file_type=pdf.

———. *A Theory of Justice*. Cambridge: The Belknap Press of Harvard University Press, 1971.

Rediker, Marcus. *The Amistad Rebellion: An Atlantic Odyssey of Slavery and Freedom*. New York: Penguin, 2013.

———. *The Slave Ship: A Human History*. New York: Viking, 2007.

Reinstein, Robert J. "Slavery, Executive Power, and International Law: The Haitian Revolution and American Constitutionalism." *The American Journal of Legal History* 53, no. 2 (2013): 141–237.

Reuter, Edward Byron. *The American Race Problem*. New York: Thomas Y Crowell Company, 1927.

Revolutionary Action Movement. "RAM Believes US Owes Afro-Americans 880 Million Acres of Land." *Nite Life*, July 4, 1967.

Richardson, David. "Shipboard Revolts, African Authority, and the Atlantic Slave Trade." *The William and Mary Quarterly* 58, no. 1 (2001): 69–92.

Roberts, Neil. *Freedom as Marronage*. Chicago: University of Chicago Press, 2015.

Robinson, Cedric. *Black Marxism: The Making of the Black Radical Tradition, Revised and Updated Third Edition*. Chapel Hill: University of North Carolina Press, 2020.

Rodriguez, Dylan. "The Disorientation of the Teaching Act: Abolition as Pedagogical Position." *The Radical Teacher* 88 (2010): 7–19.

———. *Forced Passages: Imprisoned Racial Intellectuals and the US Prison Regime*. Minneapolis: University of Minnesota Press, 2006.

Rolston, Simon. "Prison Life Writing, African American Narrative Strategies and Bad: The Autobiography of James Carr." *Multi-Ethnic Literature of the US* 38, no. 4 (2013): 191–215.

Roper, John Herbert, and Lolita G. Brockington. "Slave Revolt, Slave Debate: A Comparison." *Phylon*. 45, no. 2 (1984): 98–110.

Rorty, Richard. *Consequences of Pragmatism and Contingency, Irony, and Solidarity*. New York: Cambridge University Press, 2009.

Rothstein, Richard. *The Color of Law: A Forgotten History of how our Government Segregated America*. New York: W.W. Norton, 2017.

Rottenberg, Catherine. *The Rise of Neoliberal Feminism*. Oxford: Oxford University Press, 2018.

Rousseau, Jean-Jacques. *Of the Social Contract and Other Political Writings*. New York: Penguin, 2012.
Rubin, Ashley. Review of *Blood in the Water: The Attica Prison Uprising of 1971 and its Legacy*, by Heather Ann Thompson. *Punishment and Society* 21, no. 1 (2017): 131–37.
Rucker, Walter. "Conjure, Magic, and Power: The Influence of Afro-Atlantic Religious Practices on Slave Resistance and Rebellion." *Journal of Black Studies* 32, no. 1 (2001): 84–103.
Rupprecht, Anita. "Excessive Memories, Slavery, Insurance and Resistance." *History Workshop Journal* 64 (2007): 6–28.
Said, Edward W. *Orientalism*. New York: Pantheon, 1978.
Salah-El, Tiyo Attalah. "A Call for the Abolition of Prisons." In *The New Abolitionists: (Neo)Slave Narratives and Contemporary Prison Writings*, edited by Joy James, 69–74. Albany: SUNY Press, 2005.
Sandel, Michael. *Liberalism and the Limits of Justice*. New York: Cambridge University Press, 1998.
Sayers, Daniel O. *A Desolate Place for a Defiant People: The Archaeology of Maroons, Indigenous Americans and Enslaved Laborers in the Great Dismal Swamp*. Gainesville: University Press of Florida, 2016.
Scherr, Arthur. "Governor James Monroe and the Southampton Slave Resistance of 1799." *The Historian* 61, No. 3 (1999): 557–78.
Schipper, Jeremy. *Demark Vesey's Bible: The Thwarted Revolt That Put Slavery and Scripture on Trial*. Princeton: Princeton University Press, 2022.
Sciullo, Nick J. "George Jackson's December 1964 Letter to His Father: Agency from within the Prison Walls." *Journal for the Study of Radicalism* 11, no. 2 (2017): 161–82.
Scott, James C. *Weapons of the Weak: Everyday Forms of Peasant Resistance*. New Haven: Yale University Press, 1995.
Scott, Joan W., and Debra Keates, eds. *Going Public: Feminism and the Shifting Boundaries of the Private Sphere*. Champaign: University of Illinois Press, 2005.
Scott, Julius S. *The Common Wind: Afro-American Currents in the Age of the Haitian Revolution*. New York: Verso, 2020.
Scuttles Jr., William C. "African Religious Survivals as Factors in American Slave Revolts." *The Journal of Negro History* 56, no. 2 (1971): 97–104.
Seale, Bobby. *Seize the Time: The Story of the Black Panther Party and Huey Newton*. Baltimore: Black Classic Press, 1996.
Sedgwick, Eve Kosofsky. *Epistemology of the Closet*. Oakland: University of California Press, 2008.
Seigel, Micol. "Critical Prison Studies: Review of a Field." *American Quarterly* 70, no. 1 (2018): 123–37.

Seim, Josh, and David J. Harding. "Parolefare: Post-Prison Supervision and Low-Wage Work." *The Russel Sage Foundation Journal of the Social Sciences* 6, no. 1 (2020): 173–95.

Selg, Peeter. "Justice and Liberal Strategy: Towards a Radical Democratic Reading of Rawls." *Social Theory and Practice* 38, no. 1 (2012): 83–114.

Sellers, Martin P. *The History and Politics of Private Prisons: A Comparative Analysis.* Madison: Farleigh Dickinson Press, 1993.

Sepinwall, Alyssa Goldstein. "Beyond 'The Black Jacobins': Haitian Revolutionary Historiography Comes of Age." *Journal of Haitian Studies* 23, no. 1 (2017): 4–34.

Sen, Amartya. "What Do We Want from a Theory of Justice?" *Journal of Philosophy* 103, no. 5 (2006): 215–38.

Shakur, Assata. *Assata: An Autobiography.* Chicago: Lawrence Hill Books, 2001.

———. "The Tradition," MP3 recording of "The Tradition" by Assata Shakur. n.d. Assata Shakur Collection. Freedom Archives, Oakland, California. https://search.freedomarchives.org/search.php?s=Assata+Shakur%2C+We+Carried+it+On. Accessed April 4, 2019.

Shalev, Sharon. *Supermax: Controlling Risk Through Solitary Confinement.* London: William Publishing, 2009.

Shankar, Shobana. "Parchman Women Write the Blues? What Became of Black Women's Prison Music in Mississippi in the 1930s." *American Music* 31, no. 2 (Summer 2013): 183–202.

Shanley, Mary Lyndon. "Privacy Publicity Power: Rethinking the Feminist Public-Private Distinction." In *Resisting Citizenship: Feminist Essays on Politics, Community, and Democracy,* edited by Martha A. Ackelsberg, 70–84. New York: Routledge, 2010.

Shapiro, Ian. *The State of Democratic Theory.* Princeton: Princeton University Press, 2003.

Sharpe, Christina. *Monstrous Intimacies: Making Post-Slavery Subjects.* Durham: Duke University Press, 2010.

Sharples, Jason. "Discovering Slave Conspiracies: New Fears of Rebellion and Old Paradigms of Plotting in Seventeenth-Century Barbados." *American Historical Review* 120, no. 3 (2015): 811–43.

Shklar, Judith. "The Liberalism of Fear." In *Liberalism and the Moral Life,* edited by Nancy Rosenblum, 21–38. Cambridge: Harvard University Press, 2014.

Singh, Nikhil Pal. *Black is a Country: Race and the Unfinished Struggle for Democracy.* Cambridge: Harvard University Press, 2005.

Sinha, Manisha. *The Slave's Cause: A History of Abolition*. New Haven: Yale University Press, 2017.
Smallwood, Stephanie E. *Saltwater Slavery: A Middle Passage from Africa to American Diaspora*. Cambridge: Harvard University Press, 2007.
Smith, John David. "The Historiographic Rise and Fall and Resurrection of Ulrich Bonnell Phillips." *Georgia Historical Quarterly* 65, no. 2 (Summer 1981): 138–53.
Snorton, C. Riley. *Black on Both Sides: A Racial History of Trans Identity*. Minneapolis: University of Minnesota Press, 2017.
Spady, James O'Neil. "Power and Confession: On the Credibility of the Earliest Reports of the Denmark Vesey Slave Conspiracy." *The William and Mary Quarterly* 68, no. 2 (2011): 287–304.
Spencer, Robyn C. *The Revolution Has Come: Black Power, Gender, and the Black Panther Party in Oakland*. Durham: Duke University Press, 2016.
Spragens, Thomas A. "Democratic Reasonableness." *Critical Review of International Social and Political Philosophy* 11, no. 2 (2008): 193–214
Stampp, Kenneth M. *The Peculiar Institution*. New York: Vintage Books, 1989.
Stanford, Thomas P. "The Race Question in America." In *Six Women's Slave Narratives*. Edited by William L. Andrews. New York: Oxford 1988.
Stanley, Eric A., and Nat Smith, eds. *Captive Genders: Trans Embodiment and the Prison Industrial Complex*. Oakland: AK Press, 2015.
"Statement of Lewisburg Prisoners' Solidarity Committee." Prisoners' Solidarity Committee (September 30, 1971), 527. Box 15, Folder 33. Tamiment Library and Robert F. Wagner Labor Archives at New York. Accessed January 5, 2020.
Sublette, Ned, and Constance Sublette. *The American Slave Coast: A History of the Slave-Breeding Industry*. Chicago: Lawrence Hill Books, 2016.
Switzer, Adrian. "The Violence of the Supermax: Toward a Phenomenological Discussion of Prison Space." In *Death and Other Penalties: Philosophy in a Time of Mass Incarceration*, edited by Geoffrey Adelsberg, Lisa Guenther, and Scott Zemen, 230–49. New York: Fordham University Press, 2015.
Sykes, Gresham. *Society of Captives: A Study of a Maximum Security Prison*. Princeton: Princeton University Press, 2007.
Taylor, R.H. "Slave Conspiracies of North Carolina." *The North Carolina Historical Review* 5, no. 1 (1928): 20–34.
Thompson, Heather Ann. *Blood in the Water: The Attica Prison Uprising of 1971 and its Legacy*. New York: Vintage Books, 2017.
Thrasher, Albert. *On to New Orleans*. Toronto: Cypress Press, 1966.
Threadcraft, Shatema. *Intimate Justice: The Black Female Body and the Body Politic*. New York: Oxford University Press, 2016.

Thucydides. *History of the Peloponnesian War, Book II, xxxv–xlvi.* http://data.perseus.org/citations/urn:cts:greekLit:tlg0003.tlg001.perseus-end2:2.

Tunick, Mark. "Tolerant Imperialism: John Stuart Mill's Defense of British Rule in India." *Review of Politics* 68, no. 4 (2006): 586–611.

Ture, Kwame, and Charles V. Hamilton. *Black Power: The Politics of Liberation.* New York: Vintage Books, 1992.

Turner, Jack. *Awakening to Race: Individualism and Social Consciousness in America.* Chicago: University of Chicago Press, 2012.

Turner, Nat, and Thomas R. Gray. *The Confessions of Nat Turner: An Authentic Account of the Whole Insurrection.* Scott's Valley: Createspace. Independent Publishing Platform, 2015.

Tyner, Andrew H. "Action, Judgment, and Imagination in Hannah Arendt's Thought." *Political Research Quarterly* 70, no. 3 (2017): 523–34.

Urbinati, Nadia. *Tyranny of the Moderns.* Translated by Martin Thom. New Haven: Yale University Press. 2016.

Useem, Burt, and Peter Kimball. *States of Siege: US Prison Riots 1971–1986.* New York: Oxford University Press, 1991.

Villa, Dana. *Public Freedom.* Princeton: Princeton University Press, 2008.

———. "Arendt, Heidegger, and the Tradition." *Social Research* 74, no. 4 (2007): 983–1002.

———. *Hannah Arendt and Martin Heidegger: The Fate of the Political.* Princeton: Princeton University Press, 2001.

Wade, Richard C. "The Vesey Plot: A Reconsideration," *Journal of Southern History* 30, no. 2 (1964): 143–61.

Wainwright, James E. "William Claiborne and New Orleans's Battalion of Color, 1903–1915: Race and the Limits of Federal Power in the Early Republic." *Louisiana History: The Journal of the Louisiana Historical Association* 57, no. 1 (2016): 5–44.

Walker, David. *Appeal to the Coloured Citizens of the World.* Eastford: Martino Fine Books, 2015.

Weaver, Vesla, and Amy Lerman. *Arresting Citizenship: Democratic Consequences of American Crime Control.* Chicago: University of Chicago Press, 2014.

Weidenfeld, Matthew C. "Visions of Judgment: Arendt, Kant, and the Misreading of Judgment." *Political Research Quarterly* 66, no. 2 (2013): 254–66.

Weiss, Robert. "Attica: The 'Bitter Lessons' Forgotten?" *Social Justice* 18, no. 3 (1991): 4.

Western, Bruce, and Becky Pettit. "Incarceration and Social Inequality." *Daedalus* 139, no. 3 (2010): 8–19.

White, Deborah Gray. *A'r'nt I a Woman? Female Slaves in the Plantation South.* New York: W.W. Norton, 1999.

Wilks, Ivor. *Asante in the Nineteenth Century: The Structure and Evolution of a Political Order*. New York: Cambridge University Press, 1989.

Winant, Howard. *New Politics of Race: Globalism, Difference, Justice*. Minneapolis: University of Minnesota Press, 2004.

Wish, Harvey. "American Slave Insurrections Before 1861." *Journal of Negro History* 22, no. 3 (1937): 299–320.

Wolf, Kurt H. "On the Landscape of the Relation Between Hannah Arendt and Martin Heidegger." *The American Sociologist* 28, no. 1 (1997): 126–36.

Wolin, Richard. *Heidegger's Children: Hannah Arendt, Karl Löwith, Hans Jonas, and Herbert Marcuse*. Princeton: Princeton University Press, 2001.

Wolin, Sheldon. "Norm and Form: The Constitutionalizing of Democracy." In *Fugitive Democracy and Other Essays,* edited by Nicholas Xenos, 77–99. Princeton: Princeton University Press, 2018.

———. *Democracy Incorporated*. Princeton: Princeton University Press, 2008.

———. *Tocqueville Between Two Worlds: The Making of a Political and Theoretical Life*. Princeton: Princeton University Press, 2003.

———. "Fugitive Democracy." In *Democracy and Difference: Contesting the Boundaries of the Political*, edited by Seyla Benhabib, 31–45. Princeton: Princeton University Press, 1996.

———. "What Revolutionary Action Means Today." In *Dimensions of Radical Democracy: Pluralism, Citizenship, Community,* edited by Chantal Mouffe, 240–53. London: Verso, 1992.

Wood, Amy Louise. *Lynching and Spectacle: Witnessing Racial Violence in America, 1890–1940*. Chapel Hill: University of North Carolina Press, 2009.

X, Herbie Scott, and Deane Akil. "Take a Look Around." *New England Prisoners Association* 11, no. 8 (September 1974): 10. 778, Box 11. Tamiment Library and Robert F. Wagner Labor Archives at New York University. Accessed January 5, 2020.

Young-Bruehl, Elisabeth. *Why Arendt Matters*. New Haven: Yale University Press, 2009.

———. *Hannah Arendt: For Love of the World*. New Haven: Yale University Press, 1982.

Young, Erik Che. "George Jackson: A Study of the Life and Investigation into the Murder of Comrade George Lester Jackson 1941–1971." 527, Box 13. Tamiment Library and Robert F. Wagner Labor Archives at New York University. Accessed January 7, 2020.

Zakin, Emily. "Criss-Crossing Cosmopolitanism: State-Phobia, World-Alienation, and the Global Soul." *The Journal of Speculative Philosophy* 29, no. 1 (2015): 58–72.

Zamalin, Alex. *African American Political Thought and American Culture: The Nation's Struggle for Racial Justice*. New York: Palgrave Macmillan, 2015.

———. *Black Utopia: The History of an Idea from Black Nationalism to Afrofuturism.* New York: Columbia University Press, 2019.

———. "Dismantling Racial Progress for Black Liberation." *Political Theory* 46, no. 4 (2017): 650–58.

———. *The Struggle on Their Minds: The Political Thought of African American Resistance.* New York: Columbia University Press, 2019.

Zerilli, Linda M.G. *Feminism and the Abyss of Freedom.* Chicago: University of Chicago Press, 2005.

———. "'We Feel Our Freedom': Imagination and Judgment in the Thought of Hannah Arendt." *Political Theory* 33, 2 (2005): 158–88.

Zuckerwise, Lena. "'There Can be No Loser': White Supremacy and the Cruelty of Compromise." *American Political Thought* 5, no. 3 (2016): 467–93.

———. "Vita Mundi: Democratic Politics and the Concept of World." *Social Theory and Practice* 42, no. 3 (2016): 474–500.

Index

abolition, 6, 14–15, 22, 25, 31–32, 36, 38, 46, 67, 70–71, 73, 76–77, 100; liberalism and, 96–99; prison, 32, 52, 53, 58, 165, 195n1, 204n13
Abolition. Feminism. Now. (Davis, A.), 53
"abroad" marriages, 141
abuse, 31, 36, 37, 39
accommodation, 73
accomodationism, 106
action: Arendt's concept of, 8, 12–13, 80, 82, 106, 110, 113, 122–24, 126, 119, 130, 132, 146–48, 162–63, 203n79, 236n65, 238n1; centric readings of Arendt, 15, 22, 200n58, 232n17; work and labor and, 113, 124–28; and totalitarianism, 138
Action Française, 237n1
African Americans. *See* Black Americans
African People's Congress, 60
African People's Party, 61
Africans, 5, 9–10, 14, 29, 34, 48, 58, 60, 61–62, 65–67, 71, 75–76, 91, 109, 139, 158–62
"afterlives": of slavery, 59
Agamben, Giorgio, 136
agency: political, 19, 46, 78, 80–81, 147, 162; slave, 76, 78, 109
Ahmad, Muhammad (Maxwell Stanford), 20, 27, 42, 44–45, 47, 60–62
Akil, Deane, 63
Alabama, 37, 104
Alcatraz, 165
Alexander, Michelle, 34
alienation, 136, 139, 148–51, 203n79
"Allegory of the Cave" (Plato), 178

American Political Science Association, 119
American Political Science Review, The, 168
American Revolution, 11, 65, 75
Amistad, La (ship), 58, 101
"Anarchy of Colored Girls Assembled in a Riotous Manner" (Hartman), 196n10
Angola, 159
animal laborans (laboring animal), 6
anti-Blackness, xi, 8–9, 31, 34, 41–42, 49, 59, 61, 77, 88–90, 112, 176, 220n58; Arendt's own, 111–13, 197, 199n39; and exclusion, 151
Anti-Drug Abuse Acts, 205n20
antiprimitivism, 10
antisemitism, 135, 202n76; European, 8
anti-white sentiment, 66
Appadurai, Arjun, 177
Appeal (Walker), 77
Aptheker, Herbert, 72, 76, 104
Archer, Jermaine, 217n30
Arendt, Hannah, 22, 23, 80, 102, 110; action-centric readings of, 200n38; on the categories of the human condition, 125–28; concept of freedom in the work of, 80; concept of world, 13–23, 82, 113–19, 130, 135, 138, 141, 146–47, 151–53, 157, 162–63, 203n79, 232n18; distinction between the social and political in the writings of, 111–13, 236n65; Heidegger and, 202n76, 231n13; on judgment, 235n54; race and Blackness in the work of, 6–13, 197n19, 199n39; separation between the public and private in the work of, 102, 113, 182–84; thinking in the

Arendt, Hannah (*continued*)
   work of, 145, 230n11; totalitarianism in the work of, 135–38, 143, 148, 150, 237n1; university years of, 231n12; Varnhagen and, on the web of human relationships, 142. *See also* world; worldlessness; *specific topics; specific works*
Are Prisons Obsolete? (Davis, A.), 53
Aristotle, 95
Arneil, Barbara, 91
Artisant Agriculture and Youth Aliyah, 237n1
Asante Kingdom, 65
assimilation, 133, 159
Athens, Greece, 102
Atlantic slavery, 8–9, 29, 60, 86, 154, 160, 215n8, 233n18
At the Dark End of the Street (McGuire), 230n3, 247n36
"Attica Liberation Faction Manifesto of Demands and Anti-Depression Platform," 182
Attica prison uprising (1971), 18, 23–26, 163–68, 175, 186, 245n17; in context, 169–74; limits of democracy and, 176–82; world-building beyond democracy, 182–84
Attica Riots, The, (band), 167
"Attica State" (Lennon), 167
Auburn Correctional Facility, 165, 168, 172, 173
Augustine (Saint), 113, 128–30, 232n13
"Aunt" Adelaide (bondwoman), 68
authority, world and, 113, 119–22, 124, 137, 148, 199
Awakening to Race (Turner, J.), 77

"badman," 45–46
Baehr, Peter, 137
Bahama Adventurers, 91
Baldwin, James, 55
Baptist, Edward, 28, 204n10
Baraka, Imamu Amiri, 60
Barbados, 218n33
"Barbarian Conspirators-Judges Contz, Christian, and Colvin, The" (Muntu), 59
Barclay, Donald, 110, 112, 230n3
bare life, 136
Barker, Thomas, 158
Bastille Day, 66
Bauer, Alice, 68, 73
Bauer, Raymond, 68, 73

Bedford Hills, 196n10
Being and Time (Heidegger), 131
Bell, Duncan, 84, 92
Bell, Karen, 158–59
Benhabib, Seyla, 131, 136
Berger, Dan, 3, 19, 44, 46–47, 63, 213n49
Berkowitz, Roger, 22
Berlin, Isaiah, 78–80
Bernasconi, Robert, 11, 112, 198n20
Bernstein, Richard, 132
Berry, Fannie, 106–7
Bettelheim, Bruno, 137
Between Past and Future (Arendt), 22, 131
Bibb, Henry, 68
Bight of Benin, 161
Bight of Biafra, 161
bio-power, 2, 195n3
Biskowski, Lawrence, 22, 124
Black Americans, xii, 10, 12, 30–31, 39, 46, 56, 67, 76–77, 91, 103, 155, 247n36; Ahmad on, 27, 60–62, 214n53; Arendt on, 10–12, 111–12, 197n19, 199n39; citizenship of, 17, 149–51; custodial enslaved, 29, 56, 62, 67, 75, 96, 103, 159–60, 162, 200n54, 216n12, 220n58, 244n43; exclusion of, 52; individualism of, 87; liberal values and, 87; liberation of, 30, 37–39, 76; in Middle Passage, 14; political tradition of, 33; property and, 151; in prison, 24, 27, 34, 41, 55–56, 60, 62, 138, 171, 196n11, 210n4; race liberals on, 41; resistance of, xii, 6–7, 17–20, 23, 27, 33, 44–67, 71–81, 96, 105–11, 133–34, 152–63, 166–71, 96, 200n56, 201n70, 247n38; Shakur on, 49; Slave Codes and, 37; vagrancy statutes and, 38; worldlessness and, 139. *See also* Black carceral political thought
Black captivity: in connection with prison labor, 25, 27, 29, 38, 40, 45–49, 51–52, 54; George Jackson on, 55–57; Muhammed Ahmad on, 62–63; politics in, 6–7, 16, 17, 19, 22, 23, 33, 82–83, 102, 106, 113, 133–35, 177, 179, 205n19; Ruchell Magee on, 58–59, 163; in slavery, 63, 66, 68, 70, 75 75, 79–83, 101, 104, 197n12; theories of, xii–xiii, 5–7, 21, 33, 92, 148, 150, 176, 180, 182, 213n49, 230n11; and totalitarianism 9, 23, 138–40; world-building in 13–19, 145, 152–56, 163, 169
Black carceral political thought, 20, 34, 44, 138, 166, 201n71; conclusions, 62–63; emergence of, 45–48; on slavery, 48–62

Black Codes, 37, 38, 150
Black feminism, 79, 102 196n10, 197n11, 242n64
Black Guerilla Party, 3, 55
Black Is a Country (Singh), 77
Black Jacobins, The (James), 66
Black liberation, 21, 48, 51, 66, 69, 80, 167, 185, 210n4, 214n53, 221n58
Black Liberation Army (BLA), 42, 45, 49, 61
Black Liberation Party, 3
#BlackLivesMatter, 77
Black men, 103, 175, 247n36; in the carceral sphere, 30, 39, 54, 57–58, 173; enslaved, 65–66, 75, 77, 105, 144, 156–57, 160, 175
Blackmon, Douglas, 36
Black Moon, 167
Black Muslims, 173
Black nationalism, 60
Blackness, 19, 39, 47, 91, 111, 197; anti-Blackness, 8, 9; in Arendt works, 7–12; world and, 110–13. *See also* anti-Blackness; Black resistance
Black Panther Intercommunal News Service, 55
Black Panther Party, 3, 20, 49, 60, 173, 223n22, 246n22
Black Power Movement, 20, 33, 42, 44–45, 47, 56, 61, 88
Black rebellion. *See* Black resistance
Black Reconstruction (Du Bois), 53, 76
Black resistance, 4–6, 19, 50, 32–33, 200n57; Assata Shakur on, 48–51; cultural production and, 157–62; culturalist interpretations of, 159–62; erasure of, 69–72; 92, 95–96, 134, 176–77, 179, 200n56, 201n70, 205n19, 221n59; everyday, 15–16, 20–21, 23, 68–69, 73, 82, 95, 106–9, 152, 154–56, 184, 197n13; as extraordinary and armed, 5, 15–16, 18, 20–21, 48, 63, 65–67, 69, 71, 75, 99–101, 105, 160, 163; friendship as, 155–57; limited views of, 72–78; Muhammed Ahmad on, 61–62; as politics in captivity, 33, 44–53; preemption of 27; in prison 4–7, 15, 63, 166–69, 171, 196n13, 197n13; as response to forced worldlessness in slavery, 57–58, 65–82, 97, 99; 106–7; terminology, xi–xii; of women and girls, 109, 155–56; as world-building, 15–23, 111, 133, 148, 152–55, 163, 136, 144, 152–53; weapons of, 155–57
Black Scholar, The (journal), 27

Black Solidarity Day, 173
"Black Woman's Role in the Community of Slaves, The" (Davis, A.), 51
Black women: blues music of, 157; in the carceral sphere, 36, 39–41, 153, 198n37; experiences in slavery, 51, 53, 74, 81
Blood in My Eye (Jackson, G.), 56
Blood in the Water (Thompson), 23, 169
Blue Bloods (TV show), 240n31
blues music, 157–58
Boers, 9
Bohls, Elizabeth, 97
Botkin, Benjamin, 217n30
Bozelko, Chandra, 26, 204n5
"Breakdown of Authority, The" (Arendt), 120
Brent, Linda (pseudonym of Jacobs), 78–79
Britain, 97
British Empire, 161
Brockington, Lolita G., 75
Bromell, Nick, 77, 97
Brown, Duncan, 84
Brown, James, 105
Brown, John, 46
Brown, Rap, 60
Brown, Wendy, 177–80
Browne, Jaron, 26
Browne, Stephen Howard, 70, 100
Brute Force (film), 240n31
"Bulletproof Wallets," 168

California Institute for Women, 185
California Penal Code, 51
Cambridge Companion to Rawls, The, 223n17
Camp, Stephanie, 80, 104, 197n13, 200n54, 222n72
Canovan, Margaret, 117, 126
capitalism, 28, 45–46, 55, 84, 92, 97, 115; racial, 56, 145
Capitol, US, 118
Captive Nation (Berger), 3
captive rebellion. *See* Black resistance
Carmichael, Stokely. *See* Ture, Kwame
Carver, George Washington, 48
Center for Law and Social Policy, 26
chain gangs, 39–40
Chaney, James, 230n3
Chapman, Ryan, 167
Chase, Robert T., 176
chattel slavery, xi, 5–7, 14–15, 18, 27–28, 30–36, 38, 40, 46–49, 52, 56–59, 62, 91, 82, 98, 102, 139, 154–56, 160, 197n13, 213n42, 233n18. *See also* slavery

children, 108; enslaved, 106–7
Christmas, William, 211n17
citizenship, 41, 60, 62, 75, 93, 106, 151, 169, 178–80; custodial, 17, 149, 196n11
"City as Prison" (Arendt), 144
City of God (Augustine), 128
Civil Rights Act, 42, 45, 112
civil rights movement, 41, 45, 95, 208n21
Civil War, US, 30, 36–37, 71, 76, 104, 150
Cleaver, Eldridge, 46, 47, 213n49
Clinton, Bill, 146, 205n19
Clinton Correctional Facility for Women, 49
Cluchette, John, 51, 213n49
CO. *See* corrections officer
Cohn, David, 157
COINTELPRO. *See* Counterintelligence Program
Cold War, 42, 85
Coles, Romand, 225n47
colonialism, 92, 115, 133
colorblindness, 87
Color of Law, The (Rothstein), 151
"Coming Home / Attica" (Rzewski), 167
commonality, 138, 140–44, 202n78; plurality and, 116–18
common good, 95
common sense, 136; world and, 119–22
Communist Party, 53
Comprehensive Crime Control Act, 205n20
concentration camps, 9, 136, 138–39
Confederacy, 103, 161
Confederate monuments: removal of, 16
Confessions (Augustine), 130
Confessions of Nat Turner, The (Browne, S.), 100
confinement: freedom versus, 4; solitary, 62–63, 148
Congress of the Republic of Texas, 72
conjuration, 159–62
Connecticut Compromise, 204n13
Constitution: US, 204n13
constitutional liberalism, 94
convict leasing, 34, 35–36, 39–40
convict rehabilitation schemes, 25–26
Conway, David, 90
Cool Hand Luke (film), 240n31
CoreCivic, 205n17
corrections officers (CO), 2, 55, 60, 164, 172–73
Counterintelligence Program (COINTELPRO), 42, 60, 170, 246n22
Covey, Edward, 77
Creole traditions, 159

creolization of natural liberty, 98
crime against humanity: slavery as, 8
Crisis of European Sciences and Transcendental Phenomenology, The (Husserl), 130
Critical Resistance, 53
crown lands, 102
Cruikshank, Barbara, 93
Cuba, 49
Cugoano, Quobna Ottobah, 22, 98–99
cultural production, 71, 146, 157–59
Curtis, Kimberley, 116, 117
custodial citizenship. *See* citizenship

Dahl, Adam, 98
daily resistance. *See* Black resistance
"Dark Continent, The" (Arendt), 9
Davis, Angela, 20, 31, 44, 47, 165, 213nn42,49; on Attica prison uprising, 138, 163; Critical Resistance and, 53; "Free Angela" campaign, 223n22; Jackson, G., and, 48, 53–54, 56; prison industrial complex and, 32; slave fugitivity and, 51
Davis, Mary Kemp, 101
debt patronage, 30, 35–36, 151, 209n28
Delaney, Lucy, 77
democracy, 33, 52, 61, 74–75, 85, 168, 179; "deep democracy," 177; fugitive, 17, 19; liberal, 76–78, 162; limits of, 176–82; radical, 33, 94; self-government and, 247n39; theories of, 17, 19, 82, 92–95, 168–69, 175–83, 201n70, 204n11, 225n38, 247n39; world-building beyond, 182–84
"Democracy and Bad Dreams" (Brown, W.), 177
"democracy from below," 177
Democracy in Black (Glaude), 77
Democracy Incorporated (Wolin, S.), 177
democracy promotion, 177
democratic republics, 137
democratic theory. *See* democracy
Department of Corrections, 174
Deslondes, Charles, 18, 65, 105
Dew, Thomas R., 69
Dewey, John, 85
"Difficulties in Understanding, The" (Arendt), 121
Dilts, Andrew, 248n49
Disch, Lisa Jane, 116, 122
disenfranchisement: felon, 248n49
diversity: human, 115
Dolan, Frederick, 22, 131

domination, 4, 6, 10, 23, 82, 92; aspiration of total, 14, 18, 21, 69, 89, 148, 186; white, xii, 37, 41, 59, 69, 72, 78, 80–81, 90, 111, 153, 162
Douglass, Frederick, 22, 77–78, 96–97, 99
Drumgo, Fleeta, 51, 213n49
Du Bois, W.E.B., 36, 53, 76, 159
durability, 12–14, 116, 118–21, 124, 136, 140, 144–46, 153
Dusinberre, William, 69, 106, 140
Duvernay, Ava, 34
D Yard, at Attica, 174–75, 183, 186
dysaesthesia aethiopica, 69

Earth, 114–15, 129
East India Company, 91
economy: US, 28, 30, 32; waste, 133
Elkins, Stanley, 70
Emancipation, 29, 32, 34, 36–38, 40, 60
Emancipation Proclamation, 56, 62
"Emperor's New Clothes, The" (fable), 123–24
Encyclopedia of Political Thought, 168
Engels, Friedrich, 55
England: riots in, 3–4
Engle, Karen, 227n69
Enlightenment, 179
enslaved children, 106–7
enslaved women, 5, 15, 68, 74, 79, 80, 109, 156, 197n13, 200n54, 243n74. *See also* women
"Enta Da Stage," 167
epistemology of ignorance, 222n1
Equiano, Olaudah, 22, 97–98, 99
essential identity, 116
Eurocentrism, 158, 160
European antisemitism, 8
Eve, Arthur O., 175
everyday resistance. *See* Black resistance
extraordinary rebellion. *See* Black resistance

factual reality, 148
fairness: justice as, 87
fanaticism, 101
Fanon, Frantz, 56
Farr, James, 220n57
fascism, 115, 121
Federal Bureau of Investigation (FBI), 42, 60
Federal Bureau of Prisons, 208n21
Federal Prison Industries. *See* UNICOR
Federal Writers' Project, 217n30

Fédération des Sociétés Juives de France, 237–38n1
Feminine Mystique, The (Friedan), 227n69
feminism, 79, 102, 179–80, 182, 196n10, 249n60; neoliberal, 92; second-wave, 208n21, 227n69; white, 53, 227n69. *See also* Black feminism
Ferguson, Michaele, 92, 202n78
Ferguson, Missouri, 77
Finkelman, Paul, 200n56
First Civil Right, The (Murakawa), 41
flight, 6, 17, 44, 81; Angela Davis's 51–52; from the political realm, 128; from slavery 57, 74, 78, 80–81, 108; temporary, 163; from the Third Reich, 113
Florida, 104
Floyd, George, 30
Foerster, Werner, 49
folk magic. *See* Hudu
Folsom State Prison, 44, 63, 171, 182
Forced Passage (Rodriguez), 3
forced worldlessness. *See* worldlessness
Foucault, Michel, 4, 177, 195n3
France, 237n1
Frank, Jason, 94
Frankfurter, David, 237n1
Franklin, H. Bruce, 46, 181
"Free Angela" campaign, 223n22
freedom, 17, 32, 73, 148; Arendt's concept of, 8, 12–13, 15, 22, 113, 115, 125–26, 128, 132–34, 147–48; captivity versus, 4, 38, 65, 72, 96, 108; as immortality, 126; for Locke, 96; and prison, 41, 46; theories of, 17, 33, 48, 60–62, 69, 77–82, 84, 85, 87, 92–93, 98
Freedom as Marronage (Roberts), 17, 80
Freedom Summer (1964), 230n3
French Revolution, 66, 99
French, Scott, 67, 101
Friedan, Betty, 227n69
Friedrich, Carl, 137
friendships, 141, 155–57
Friends of Assata Shakur and Sundiata Acoli, The (bulletin), 211n16
fugitive democracy, 17
Fugitive Slave Law (1850), 103
fugitivity, 5, 44, 51, 71, 74, 80, 104, 107–8, 140, 152, 155

Gabriel's rebellion, 65, 101, 144
Galveston News (newspaper), 72
Gaus, Günter, 12, 162
gendered continuities, 36

gender fungibility, 40, 109
general good, 97
genocide, 115
Genovese, Eugene, 72–76, 106, 159, 219n44
Geo Group, 205n17
Georgia, 30, 104
Georgia General Assembly, 40
Georgia Lowcountry, 158–59
German Coast Slave Uprising (1811), 18, 20–21, 65–66, 71, 75, 101–6, 109, 154, 201n73, 215n10
Germany, 140, 237n1
Getachew, Adom, 133
Ghana. *See* Gold Coast
Ghostface Killah, 168
Gill, Howard P., 35
Gilmore, Kim, 31
Gines, Kathryn, 11, 197n19, 199n39
Glaude, Eddie S., Jr., 77
God, 64, 99, 128–30, 140
Goffman, Erving, 137
Gold Coast, 65, 66, 159
Golden Drums (Black student organization), 48
Gooch, John, 107
Gooding-Williams, Robert, 44
Goodman, Andrew, 230n3
Grace Commission, 205n20
Gray, Jesse, 60
Great Depression, 85
Great Society, 20, 45, 170, 205n20
Greece, 7; Athens, 102
Guardian, The (newspaper), 26
Guenther, Lisa, 17, 23, 148

Habermas, Jürgen, 133, 180
Hahn, Steven, 76
Haitian Revolution, 8, 65–67, 75, 99, 105, 215n9, 219n50, 226n58, 229n74
Haley, Harold, 211n17
Haley, Sarah, 36, 39–40, 109, 153–55, 157, 169, 196n10, 197n13, 198n37
Hammond, James Henry, 70, 217n26
Hanchard, Michael, 112
Hanks, Angela, 26
Hannah Arendt and the Negro Question (Gines), 11
Hannah Arendt, Totalitarianism, and the Social Sciences (Baehr), 137
Harris, LeShawn, 171
Hartman, Saidiya, 38, 39, 59, 80, 107, 196n10, 199n51, 220n58, 242n57

Hathim, Malik Zir, 166
Hay, Carol, 84
"Heart of Darkness" (Norton), 10
Heidegger, Martin, 22, 113, 130–32, 202n76, 231n13
Hill, Lauryn, 167
homo faber (working man), 12–13, 114, 124, 153, 232n18
honey trap, 92–93
Honig, Bonnie, 93, 180
Horowitz, Morton, 102
House of Commons, 3, 73
house slaves, 109
Housing Act (1949), 11
"How It Feels to Be Colored Me" (Hurston), 201n65
Hudu (folk magic), 159
Huggins, Ericka, 47
Human Condition, The (Arendt), 12, 13, 16, 22, 113, 116, 123–24, 127–28, 131, 134, 141, 151, 184, 199n42, 201n60, 230n9, 236n65; *animal laborans* and, 6; slave rebellion in, 80
human diversity, 115
Hurston, Zora Neale, 201n65
Husserl, Edmund, 22, 130, 131, 133
"Hymn of Freedom, The" (unknown), 64
hypervisibility: of prisons, 143

identity, 115–16, 124, 136, 145; essential, 116; gender 15, 40, 109, 200n54
"If I Ruled the World," 167
If They Come in the Morning (Davis, A.), 53
illegal slavery, 58
illiteracy, 147
I Love You, Philip Morris (film), 240n31
immortality, 125
imperialism, 10, 56, 135, 166, 224n32, 237n1
Incarcerated Workers' Organizing Committee, 26
Incidents in the Life of a Slave Girl (Jacobs), 142–43
independent individuals, 89
India, 91
individualism, 22, 76, 78, 81, 84–87, 89, 92–93, 95, 99, 106–8, 147
Industrial Revolution, 97
Injustice, 26, 35, 88, 90, 102, 151, 172, 186, 227n16
insubordination, 39
interest groups, 94
intersectionality, 53
Intimate Justice (Threadcraft), 81

Index   283

"Introduction Into Politics" (Arendt), 113
inverted totalitarianism, 95, 177
invisibility: of prisons, 143
isolation: worldlessness as, 149–50
Ivy, Lorenzo, 68

Jackson, George, 3, 20, 44, 46–47, 51, 63, 150, 165; Davis, A., and, 48, 53–54, 56; death of, 55; *Soledad Brother,* 53, 56–57
Jackson, Jonathan, 51, 211n17, 213n42, 223n22
Jacobs, Harriet, 77–79, 96, 142–43, 221n62
Jahn, Beate, 224n32
Jailhouse Lawyers Speak, 26
Jamaica, 160
James, C.L.R., 66
Jarvis, Harry, 108
Jaspers, Karl, 127
Jefferson, Thomas, 119
Jewish people, 199n39, 202n76, 237n1
Jim Crow segregation laws, 11, 34, 39–41, 52, 111, 154
Johnson, Kevin Rashid, 26
Johnson, Lyndon B., 42, 45, 170, 205n20
Johnson, Walter, 156
Jordan, Fania Davis, 213n42
Journal of Politics, The, 168
Journey in the Seaboard Slave States, A (Olmsted), 154
Judging (Arendt). *See* judgment
judgment, 16, 22, 98, 118–19, 122–24, 136, 138, 148, 200n58, 203n79, 235n54
justice, 15, 30–31, 47, 52, 59, 75, 77, 96, 98; as fairness, 87–88; social, 35, 85, 88–89, 176, 223n16

Kant, Immanuel, 122–23
Kateb, George, 126
Kenner, Harry, 105
Keynes, John Maynard, 85
King, Martin Luther, Jr., 42
kinships, 141, 156
Klausen, Jimmy Casas, 10
Knight, Etheridge, 47
Knowles, John, 160–61
Kohn, Jerome, 115
Kook, 18, 65, 66, 105
Kunstler, William, 175
Kyles, Perry, 160–62

laboring animal. *See animal laborans*
laboring classes, 6
Labranche, Alexandre, 105

Law and Order (TV show), 240n31
Law Enforcement Assistance Administration (LEAA), 42
League of International Antisemitism, 237n1
League of Revolutionary Black Workers, 60
Lectures on Kant's Political Philosophy (Arendt), 22
leisure time, 15, 105, 140–41, 157, 254n27
Lenin, Vladimir, 55
Lennon, John, 167
Lerman, Amy, 17, 149, 196n11, 201n67, 241n46
Lessing Prize, 127
"Lessons" (Davis, A.), 163
Levin, Chad, 93
Lewis, George "Big Jake," 3
liberal democracy, 162. *See also* democracy
liberal fundamentalism, 21
liberalism, 19, 21–22, 82, 128, 177–80, 236n65; abolitionism and, 96–99; brief excursus on, 84–92; classical, 83, 84; constitutional, 94; daily resistance and, 106–9; neoliberalism, 205nn19–20; public/private distinction of, 101–6; self-interest and, 106–9; Southampton Insurrection and, 99–101
Liberalism and the Limits of Justice (Sandel), 88
liberal myopia, 82–83; of democratic theory, 92–95
liberal racism, 220n57
liberty, 8, 66, 75–76, 78, 81, 84–85, 87, 89–93, 96, 98–99, 102, 178, 180, 220n57
Library of Congress, 217n30
"Life in 4A—The Hole" (anonymous), 62
Life of the Mind (Arendt), 122–23, 231n11, 234n43, 235n54
lifeworld, 128–34
literacy, 80, 147
Locke, John, 84, 91, 92, 96, 220n57
Lost Cause, 21
Louisiana, 70; New Orleans, 18, 20, 65–66, 105, 144
love: of the world, 129
low-wage work, 25, 39, 112, 151, 155, 208n21
Lussana, Sergio, 156–57
Lyon, F. Emory, 35

Magee, Ruchell, 20, 44, 47, 53, 58–60, 166–67, 211n17, 213n49
magic, 159–60, 244n83
Malcolm X, 46, 52, 60

Mancusi, Vincent, 172, 174
Manhattan Community College, 48
Manos, James, 36
Mao Zedong, 55
Mariah (bondwoman), 68
Marin County Courthouse, 51–53, 167, 213n42, 223n22
Markell, Patchen, 12, 113, 199n42, 230n9
maroons, 101–6
marriages: "abroad," 141
Marx, Karl, 55, 124
Marxism-Leninism, 60
Massachusetts Review (publication), 51
"Massacre at Attica," 165
mass incarceration, 34, 42, 205n19
maximum security prisons, 18, 143–44, 150, 165, 181, 183, 242n55
McAlester State Penitentiary, 26, 165–66
McCall, A.R., 68
McGhee, Heather, 151
McGowan, John, 22
McGuire, Danielle, 247n36
MCI-Cedar Junction, 143–44
McKittrick, Katherine, 79
medium security men's prison, 1
Megan's Law, 152
Melville, Herman, 118
men, Black, 30, 39, 57–58, 77, 175, 247n36
Meuillion Plantation, 163
Middle Passage, 5, 14, 61, 65, 72, 97, 141, 161, 199n51, 219n40
Mill, John Stuart, 87, 91–92, 224n32
Milledgeville Georgia State Farm Prison, 40
Mills, Charles, 87, 158, 178, 222n1, 243n79, 248n52
Mingus, Charles, 167
"minimum security" of the street, 150
Minogue, Kenneth, 85, 89
miscegenation, 37
Mississippi, 36–37, 104
Missouri, 77
Moby Dick (Melville), 118
Montgomery Bus Boycott (1956), 42
morality, 84, 123
Mouffe, Chantal, 21
Mouvement Antijuif Continental, 237n1
"movement break," 2
Movement for Black Lives, 19, 30
Muhammed Speaks (publication), 52, 53
multiculturalism, 93
Muntu, Meharibi, 59
Murakawa, Naomi, 41, 205n20
music, 167–68; blues, 157–58

Myers, Ella, 22, 202n78, 203n79, 233n19
Myers, Peter C., 96, 97
mysticism, 159

nationalism, 10, 237n1
National Review (magazine), 26
Native Americans, 91
Nat Turner Before the Bar of Judgment (Davis, M.), 101
Nat Turner's Rebellion. *See* Southampton Insurrection
natural rights, 62, 65, 76, 92, 96
Nazism, 115
"Negerfrage in den Vereinigten Staaten, Die" (Du Bois), 36–37
neoliberal feminism, 92
neoliberalism, 205nn19,20
neoslavery, 36
NEPA News, 186
New Jersey, 49
New Jim Crow, The (Alexander), 34
New Orleans, Louisiana, 18, 20, 65–66, 105, 144
Newton, Huey P., 47, 213n49, 223n22, 242n55
New York City, 160
New York Times (newspaper), 165, 175
New York University (NYU), 120
Nigeria, 97, 159
Nixon, Richard, 42–43, 57, 205n20
Nolen, W.L., 3, 55
No Mercy Here (Haley, S.), 36, 39–40, 109, 153–55, 157, 169, 196n10, 197n13, 198n37
North Carolina, 42, 75, 104
Northup, Solomon, 77, 221n62
Norton, Anne, 10
Novkov, Julie, 87
NYPD Blue (TV show), 240n31
NYU. *See* New York University

Oakes, James, 73, 103
Obeah, 160
objectivity, 13–14, 138, 141, 246n17; of world, 115–17, 124, 128, 130–31, 138, 145, 184
Office of Federal Management, 205n20
Okin, Susan Moller, 227n69
Old South Confederacy, 70
Olmsted, Frederick Law, 154
Olson, Joel, 29, 204n11
Omnibus Crime Control and Safe Streets Act (1968), 42, 170
On Revolution (Arendt), 8
"On Violence" (Arendt), 11, 111, 137

organized loneliness, 136, 148–49, 181
Origins of Totalitarianism (Arendt), 111–12, 121, 124, 133, 135, 138, 148, 198n20; slavery as crime against humanity in, 8; worldlessness in, 22–23
Oshinsky, David, 36
Oswald, Russell, 174
Outlaw, The (periodical), 185–86

Paik, Naomi, 179
Palestine, 53
Pan-Africanism, 61
Parchman Penitentiary, 157
Pateman, Carole, 227n69
Patterson, Orlando, 54, 140
Peculiar Institution, The (Stampp), 70
pejorative tradition, 101
Pell Grants, 146, 170
Perspectives on Politics, 168
"Peter the Doctor," 160
Pettit, Becky, 151
Peys, Christopher, 22
Phillips, Ulrich Bonnell, 71, 73, 76, 243n80
plantations, 5–7, 9, 14–15, 19–23, 34, 66, 68–69, 74, 78–80, 103–7, 109, 138–39, 141, 154, 156–57, 161; connections with prisons, 34, 36, 44–47, 52, 57, 63, 133–34, 152, 179, 182, 186; Meuillion, 163; rice-growing, 161
Plato, 7, 119, 132, 178, 236n65
plurality, 13, 128, 146–48; commonality and, 116–18; worldlessness and property, 150–52; worldlessness as isolation, 149–50
Pogge, Thomas, 88
police, 39, 42, 49, 149, 242n55; at Attica, 175; brutality, 55, 77, 87; enforcement of vagrancy statutes, 39; George Floyd and, 30; militarization of, 42; slave-catching origins of, 31
political movement, 4, 5
political sphere, 11
Political Theory (journal), 168
Political Theory and the Displacement of Politics (Honig), 93
Polyani, Karl, 85
power, xii, 28, 37, 61, 76, 85, 92, 96, 162–63, 180, 186, 227n69; in Arendt's work, 7, 13–14, 114, 120, 128, 135–37; bio-, 2, 195n3; carceral 4, 26, 34, 176, 196n9; corporate 94–95, 177; exercised by prisoners, 23, 54, 183; of God, 130, 195n3; police, 42; political, 43, 88, 111–12, 183, 235n61; slave resistance, 17, 21, 70, 74, 80, 140, 147;

state, 84, 87, 89, 91, 178–79; supernatural, 159; white, 69, 78
POWER (group), 26
pragmatism, 85
Prashad, Vijay, 25–26
President's Private Sector Survey on Cost Control, The, 205n20
prison abolition, 32, 52–53, 196n11, 249n59
prisoner rehabilitation, 146
Prisoners Solidarity Committee, 185
prison industrial complex, 32, 52–53.
prison labor: as not slavery, 27–30; as slavery, 25–27, 205n19
"Prison Labor and Social Justice" (Lyon), 35
Prison Litigation and Reform Act, 205n19
prison privatization, 205n19
prison reform, 165
prison regime, 4, 18, 33–34
privately owned prisons, 208n21
private property, 85, 86, 92, 102, 105
private sphere, 7, 12, 101–6, 180–81, 227n69
progress, 38
Progressive Era, 33, 40
propaganda, 14, 121, 136, 138
Propagande Nationale, 237n1
Property, 37–38, 199n52; for Arendt, 115; destruction of, 3–5, 16, 18, 26, 66, 100, 106–7, 153–54; in liberalism, 84–86, 96, 220n57; private, 14, 85, 86, 92, 102, 105, 155; rights, 29, 92, 98, 179; worldlessness and, 150–52
Proposition 13, 205n20
Prosser, Gabriel, 65
public/private distinction, 12, 22, 99, 101–6, 112–13, 123, 149, 152, 169, 179–80, 182, 227n69, 249n60
public sphere, 12, 101–6, 125–26, 130, 143, 150, 180–81, 236n65, 247n41, 249n55
Puerto Ricans, 172
Punishment, 3, 5, 26–27, 31, 34–36, 46, 52, 55, 62, 82, 107–8, 140, 145, 147–49, 154, 157, 171–78, 181, 248n49; industry, 32, 37–43; retributive, 3
Punishment and Inclusion (Dilts), 248n49

Quamana (bondman), 18, 65, 66, 105
Quillo (bondman), 75

"race question," 41
racial capitalism, 56, 145
Racial Contract, The (Mills), 87, 158, 178, 248n52
racial criminality, 149

racial domination, 32, 47, 77, 82, 92. *See also* domination: white
racial equality, 34, 41, 90, 96, 103, 151, 172
racial history, 29, 208n21, 246n22
racial labor, 25–27, 32, 91, 97–98, 155
racism, 10, 56, 63; anti-Black, xi, 39, 46, 49, 51, 55, 58–59, 61, 77, 81–82, 112; Arendt on, 10, 111–12, 197n19, 199n39; liberal, 220n57. *See also* anti-Blackness
radical democracy, 17, 33, 167; theories of, 94, 176–78, 220n58, 225nn38,47, 247nn38,39,41
Raiman, Jeffrey, 89, 90
RAM. *See* Revolutionary Action Movement
rascality, 69
Rasmussen, Daniel, 105
Rassemblement Antijuif de France, 237n1
rationalism, 99
Rawls, John, 86–89, 94, 223n16
Reagan, Ronald, 205nn19,20
reality: factual, 148; realization of, 119–22
Realizing Rawls (Pogge), 88
reason, 86; limits of, 99–101
Reasonableness and Liberal Political Theory (Spragens), 99
rebellions. *See* Black resistance
Rebellions, Resistance, and Runaways (Finkelman), 200n56
Rebellious Slave, The (French), 101
receiving area ("the trap"), 2
Reconsidering Cosmopolitanism and Forgiveness (Peys), 22
Reconstruction period, 35
Rediker, Marcus, 72, 227n66
redlining, 112
"Reflections on Little Rock" (Arendt), 111–12, 197n19
rehabilitation: prisoner, 146
"Remember Rockefeller at Attica" (Mingus), 167
Representative Government (Mill), 92
Republic, The, 119
retributive punishment, 3
Reuter, Edward Byron, 64
revolt contagion, 67
Revolutionary Action Movement (RAM), 42, 45, 60
rice-growing plantations, 161
rights, 17, 29, 37, 58, 83, 169, 172–73, 178, 183, 205n19; civil, 41–43, 45, 95, 110, 112, 208n21; in liberalism, 84–86, 88, 91, 93, 179; natural, 62, 65, 76, 92, 96, 99; prisoners without,15; 208n21; property, 98, 154; and slavery, 8–9, 59, 82, 100; women's rights movements, 53
riots, 111; in England, 3–4
Riots I Have Known (Chapman), 167
"Rising, The" (slave rebellion), 66, 101
rival geography, 80, 104
Roberts, Neil, 17, 80–81
"Rock, the" (solitary confinement unit), 26
Rockefeller, Nelson, 164, 175
Rodriguez, Dylan, 3, 33
Rolston, Simon, 45
Roman republic, 120–21
Roper, John Herbert, 75
Roper, Moses, 107–8
Rorty, Robert, 88
Rothstein, Richard, 151
Rottenberg, Catherine, 179
Rousseau, Jean-Jacques, 95
Royal Africa Company, 91
Rubin, Ashley, 245n17
Rucker, Walter, 159
Russia, 140
Rzewski, Frederic, 167

sabotage, 68, 153–55, 157, 169, 196n10
Said, Edward, 80
Saint-Domingue, 66
Salah-El, Tiyo Attalah, 1
Sale Day, 142
Sandel, Michael, 88
San Quentin Prison, 55
Schwerner, Michael, 230n3
scientific developments, 127
Scott, James C., 68
Seale, Bobby, 175, 210n4
Second Treatise on Civil Government, The (Locke), 84, 91, 96
second-wave feminism, 208n21, 227n69
Sedgwick, Eve, 116, 123
segregated housing units (SHU), 173
Seigel, Micol, 41
self-determination, 61, 133
self-government, 247n39
self-interest, 35, 86, 137, 141; captive resistance as, 15, 18, 46, 95, 101, 109; versus solidarity 22, 94, 99; 106–9
Sellers, Martin, 208n21
Senegambia, 159
Sentencing Reform Act, 205n20
sex crimes, 152
sexual contract, 227n69
Shakur, Assata, 20, 42, 44–45, 47–51, 61, 211n16

sharecropping, 34, 35, 155
Sharing Democracy (Ferguson), 202n78
Sharples, Jason, 218n33
Shawshank Redemption (film), 240n31
Shklar, Judith, 84, 93
SHU. *See* segregated housing units
Singh, Nikhil Pal, 77
Sinha, Manisha, 76
Slave Codes, 37
slave fugitivity, 51
slave labor, 25
"Slave Labor in American Prisons" (anonymous), 27
"Slave Narrative Collection," 195n1
slave patrols, 103, 105, 218n36
slave quarters, 68, 105, 147
slave rebellions, xi, xii, 14–15, 17–18, 20–21, 23, 33, 156; as action in public, 106; in Black carceral political thought, 48, 50–51, 58, 63, 65–82, 103, 142; as conjuration, 159–62; as cultural production, 157–59; fear of, 37, 142; Gabriel's 144; German Coast, 101–6; Nat Turner's, 99–101; political theories that do not account for, 76–82, 95, 152. *See also* Black resistance
slave resistance. *See* Black resistance
slavery, 5–7, 14, 18, 32, 46–47, 58, 68–82, 79, 86–87, 89, 95, 97, 102–3, 105–7, 138–47, 154, 213n42; "afterlives" of, 59; Arendt and, 8, 9, 11, 112, 140–41; Atlantic, 8–9; Black carceral political theorists on, 45–46, 48–63; cultural practices of, 158–63; durability and, 144–46; economic, 79; erasure of, 17, 21, 65–67; gendered continuities and, 36, 109; legacies of, 20, 150–57; leisure time and, 141; liberalism and 22, 89–92, 95–99; linguistic categories of, 79; maroons, 101–6; moral questions of, 101; neoslavery, 36–37; politics, 83, 134; plurality and, 146–52; prison labor and, 19, 25–35; 205n19; terminology, xi, xii; totalitarianism and, 9, 139; transatlantic slave trade, 14–15, 60; vagrancy perpetuating, 38–40; wage, 35
Slavery (Elkins), 70
Slavery by Another Name (Blackmon), 36
Smallwood, Stephanie, 72
Smith, Frank "Big Black," 167, 169
Smith, John David, 73
SNCC. *See* Student Nonviolent Coordinating Committee
Snorton, C. Riley, 40, 109

social contract, 227n69
Social Contract, The (Rousseau), 95
social death, 54, 140, 196n10, 203n80
social justice, 35, 85, 88–89, 176, 223n16. *See also* justice
social/political distinction, 11–12, 102–3, 110–13, 136
social sphere, 11–12, 111–12, 198n20, 228n69
Society of Captives (Sykes), 137
Soledad Brother (Jackson, G.), 53, 56–57
Soledad Brothers, 51, 55, 211n17
Soledad State Prison, 3, 55
solidarity, 29, 63, 107, 108, 154, 176; Black Solidarity Day, 173; in opposition to self-interest, 22, 99, 106–8
solitary confinement, 3–5, 14, 17–18, 23, 26, 49, 55, 62–63, 148, 172–74, 196n10
Solitary Confinement (Guenther), 17
South Africa, 9
Southampton Insurrection (Nat Turner's Rebellion), 21, 67, 77, 99–101, 109
South Carolina, 42, 67, 70, 104, 161
Southern Christian Leadership Conference, 42
"southern strategy," 43
Spragens, Thomas A., 86, 99
Sprain, Johnny, 213n49
Sputnik, 127
Stalinism, 115
Stampp, Kenneth, 70
Stanford, Maxwell. *See* Ahmad, Muhammad
Stanford, P. Thomas, 138–39
"Statement of the Lewisburg Prisoners' Solidarity Committee," 164
state power. *See* power
State Prison Colony, 35
status criminality, 39
status quo, 18, 29, 42, 88
Struggle on Their Minds, The (Zamalin), 19, 77, 221n59
Student Nonviolent Coordinating Committee (SNCC), 42
student/teacher relation, 120
subjecthood, 69, 96, 162, 179
Sublette, Constance, 197n12
Sublette, Ned, 197n12
subordination, 23, 89, 227n69
Sum of Us, The (McGhee), 151
supernatural powers, 159
Supreme Court, US, 57
Sykes, Gresham, 137

"Take a Look Around" (X, H. S., and Akil), 63
technology, 127
temporary suspension, 18
tenant farming, 34, 35, 155
territorial reading: of *The Human Condition*, 12, 113, 230n9
Territory of Orleans, 20
Theory of Communicative Action (Habermas), 133
Theory of Justice, A (Rawls), 88
Third Reich, 113
Third World internationalism, 60
13th (documentary), 34
13th Amendment, 34–35
Thompson, Heather Ann, 23, 169, 171–72, 183, 245n17
Thrasher, Albert, 71
Threadcraft, Shatema, 81
Three-Fifths Clause, 204n13
Thucydides, 227n67
Tocqueville, Alexis de, 247n39
Tocqueville Between Two Worlds (Wolin), 95
total institutions, 137
totalitarianism, 9, 13, 23, 121–22, 233n18, 237n1; inverted, 95, 177; worldlessness and, 135–40. See also *Origins of Totalitarianism*
Totalitarianism (Friedrich), 137
"tough on crime" ideology, 146
"Toward an Agonistic Feminism" (Honig), 180
"Tradition" (Shakur), 49–50
transatlantic slave trade, 29, 60, 86, 91, 154, 199n51, 213n45, 215n8, 227n66, 232n18
"trap, the" (receiving area), 2
Travis, Joseph, 67
Trepagnier, Francois, 105
Trial and Death of Socrates, The, 1
tribalism, 10
Trotsky, Leon, 55
truancy, 79–80
Trump, Donald, 118–19
Tubman, Harriet, 48
Tunick, Mark, 224n32
Ture, Kwame (Stokely Carmichael), 45, 60
Turner, Jack, 77–78, 94
Turner, Nat, 18, 46, 48; Southampton Insurrection, 21, 67, 77, 99–101, 109

Underground Railroad, 48
UNICOR (Federal Prison Industries), 28

United States (US), 31, 99, 179; American Revolution, 11, 65, 75; anti-Black racism in, 61, 77; capitalism, 28; Capitol, 118; Civil War, 30, 36–37, 71, 76, 104, 150; Constitution, 204n13; economy of, 28, 30, 32; maroon communities in, 104; racial politics in, 7; Supreme Court, 57. See also specific states
universal theories, 76, 81, 87, 96, 99, 116, 177
uprisings. See Black resistance
Urbinati, Nadia, 86, 88
US. See United States

vagrancy, 38–40, 59, 112
Varnhagen, Rahel, 230n11
Vesey, Denmark, 19, 66–67, 77, 101
Vietnam War, 46
Villa, Dana, 132
Violent Crime Act, 146, 205n19
Virginia, 42, 65, 68, 70, 100, 104, 154; 235n61; General Assembly 29, 67, 100
Voting Rights Act, 42, 45

Wade, Richard, 216n12
wage-slavery, 35
Walker, David, 77
War on Drugs, 34, 205n20
waste economy, 133
Wayward Lives, Beautiful Experiments (Hartman), 196n10
Wealth building, 151–52; enslaved people prohibited from, 139; plantation, 105–6, 155;
"We Are All Prisoners of War" (Ahmad), 62
Weaver, Vesla, 17, 149
Weimar Republic, 113
West Africa, 58, 65–66, 109, 159, 162
Western, Bruce, 151
"What Is Authority?" (Arendt), 137
"What Is Freedom?" (Arendt), 80, 125, 132, 147
white 40–41, 103, 109, 180, 198n37. See also Black women; white women
White, Deborah G., 156
white feminism, 53
white supremacy, xii, 20, 30, 34–35, 38, 59, 154, 156, 160, 162–63, 204n13
white women, 40–41, 103, 109, 180, 198n37
Williams, Nancy, 68
Williams, Robert, 60
Winant, Howard, 26

Wolin, Richard, 130
Wolin, Sheldon, 17–18, 93–95, 177, 225n38
women: Black incarcerated, 36, 39–41, 153, 198n37; blues music of, 157; enslaved, 15, 51, 53, 74, 81; friendships between, 156
Women, Race, and Class (Davis, A.), 53
women's rights movements, 53
Woodson, Carter G., 73
work: Arendtian, 12, 16, 113–15, 118, 124–28, 130, 146, 163; labor and action and, 124–28; low-wage, 39, 155, 208n21; strike 168, 172, 214n53
working man. See *homo faber*
world (concept), 6, 7, 10, 12–13, 19, 22–24, 82, 110–17; authority and, 119–22; common sense and, 13–14, 118–22, 124, 136, 148; durability of, 12–14, 110, 116–21, 124, 136, 140, 144–46; Earth and, 129–30; Heidegger's theory of, 132–33; Husserl on, 131–32; judgment and, 122–24; labor, work, and action, 12–13, 113, 124–28, 130–31, 32; lifeworld and, 128, 133; plurality and commonality, 13, 114–18, 123–24, 130, 136, 138–41, 143, 202n78; and reality, 10, 13, 114–15, 118–22, 124, 126, 129, 132, 136, 139, 146, 148, 162, 186; social/political distinction and, 110–13; things of the, 125–26, 183–84, 186–87

world-building, 15, 16, 82, 163, 187; beyond democracy, 182–84; as resistance in captivity, 111, 152–55, 187
worldlessness (concept), 6, 7, 9, 13–19, 22–23, 82; forced, 135–36, 138–14, 148–69, 181–82; as isolation, 149–50; property and, 150–52; totalitarianism and, 135–38. *See also* world
Worldly Ethics (Myers, E.), 22
Worldmaking After Empire (Getachew), 133
World War I, 237n1
Worse Than Slavery (Oshinsky), 36
WPA, 70
Wretched of the Earth (Fanon), 56
Wu Tang Clan, 168

X, Herbie Scott, 63
X, Malcolm, 46, 52, 60

Young, Erik Che, 55
Young-Bruehl, Elisabeth, 231n12

Zakin, Emily, 22
Zamalin, Alex, 19, 77, 221n59
zealotry, 101
Zerilli, Linda, 122, 124

Lena Zuckerwise is Associate Professor of Political Science at Simmons University.

just ideas

Roger Berkowitz, *The Gift of Science: Leibniz and the Modern Legal Tradition*

Jean-Luc Nancy, translated by Pascale-Anne Brault and Michael Naas, *The Truth of Democracy*

Drucilla Cornell and Kenneth Michael Panfilio, *Symbolic Forms for a New Humanity: Cultural and Racial Reconfigurations of Critical Theory*

Karl Shoemaker, *Sanctuary and Crime in the Middle Ages, 400–1500*

Michael J. Monahan, *The Creolizing Subject: Race, Reason, and the Politics of Purity*

Drucilla Cornell and Nyoko Muvangua (eds.), *uBuntu and the Law: African Ideals and Postapartheid Jurisprudence*

Drucilla Cornell, Stu Woolman, Sam Fuller, Jason Brickhill, Michael Bishop, and Diana Dunbar (eds.), *The Dignity Jurisprudence of the Constitutional Court of South Africa: Cases and Materials, Volumes I & II*

Nicholas Tampio, *Kantian Courage: Advancing the Enlightenment in Contemporary Political Theory*

Carrol Clarkson, *Drawing the Line: Toward an Aesthetics of Transitional Justice*

Jane Anna Gordon, *Creolizing Political Theory: Reading Rousseau through Fanon*

Jimmy Casas Klausen, *Fugitive Rousseau: Slavery, Primitivism, and Political Freedom*

Drucilla Cornell, *Law and Revolution in South Africa: uBuntu, Dignity, and the Struggle for Constitutional Transformation*

Abraham Acosta, *Thresholds of Illiteracy: Theory, Latin America, and the Crisis of Resistance*

Andrew Dilts, *Punishment and Inclusion: Race, Membership, and the Limits of American Liberalism*

Lewis R. Gordon, *What Fanon Said: A Philosophical Introduction to His Life and Thought.* Foreword by Sonia Dayan-Herzbrun, Afterword by Drucilla Cornell

Gaymon Bennett, *Technicians of Human Dignity: On the Politics of Intrinsic Worth*

Drucilla Cornell and Nick Friedman, *The Mandate of Dignity: Ronald Dworkin, Revolutionary Constitutionalism, and the Claims of Justice*

Richard A. Lynch, *Foucault's Critical Ethics*

Peter Banki, *The Forgiveness to Come: The Holocaust and the Hyper-Ethical*

Peter Goodrich and Michel Rosenfeld (eds.), *Administering Interpretation: Derrida, Agamben, and the Political Theology of Law*

Thomas Claviez and Viola Marchi (eds.), *Throwing Moral Dice: Ethics and the Problem of Contingency*

www.ingramcontent.com/pod-product-compliance
Lightning Source LLC
Chambersburg PA
CBHW020355080526
44584CB00014B/1034